# ESSENTIALS OF ACCOUNTING FOR GOVERNMENTAL AND NOT-FOR-PROFIT ORGANIZATIONS

# ESSENTIALS OF ACCOUNTING FOR GOVERNMENTAL AND NOT-FOR-PROFIT ORGANIZATIONS

Leon E. Hay, Ph.D., CPA
*Ralph McQueen Distinguished Professor
of Accounting
University of Arkansas–Fayetteville*

John H. Engstrom, D.B.A., CPA
*Professor of Accountancy
Northern Illinois University*

Second Edition     1990

**IRWIN**
Homewood, IL 60430
Boston, MA 02116

Sponsoring editor: Ron M. Regis
Project editor: Karen Smith
Production manager: Irene H. Sotiroff
Compositor: Weimer Typesetting Company, Inc.
Typeface: 10/12 Times Roman
Printer: R. R. Donnelley & Sons Company

**Library of Congress Cataloging-in-Publication Data**

Hay, Leon Edwards, 1923-
    Essentials of accounting for governmental and not-for-profit
organization / Leon E. Hay, John H. Engstrom.—2nd ed.
        p.   cm.
    Includes index.
    ISBN 0-256-06943-3
    1. Finance, Public—United States—Accounting.   2. Administrative
agencies—United States—Accounting.   3. Corporations, Nonprofit-
United States—Accounting.   I. Engstrom, John H.   II. Title.
HJ9801.H39   1990
657'.98—dc20                                                89–15361
                                                              CIP

*Printed in the United States of America*
1 2 3 4 5 6 7 8 9 DO 6 5 4 3 2 1 0 9

# PREFACE

The preface to the first edition of this text noted that the text was intended to provide a much more comprehensive coverage of accounting and financial reporting standards for governmental and not-for-profit organizations than is available in Advanced Accounting texts, but that would be brief enough to allow coverage of the material in less than a three semester-hour or four quarter-hour course. The first edition was well received by instructors whose objective is to teach public administration majors and others who need to be able to use financial reports of governments and not-for-profit organizations, as well as by instructors whose objective is to stress preparation for the Uniform CPA Examination. This edition of the text and the accompanying *Instructor's Guide* and the *Suggested Quiz and Examination Questions and Problems* booklet have been revised in accord with suggestions of users of the first edition as well as to incorporate changes in standards issued by the Governmental Accounting Standards Board, the Financial Accounting Standards Board, the United States General Accounting Office, and the American Institute of Certified Public Accountants.

The authors are indebted to the members of the Governmental Accounting Standards Board, and to the GASB's research staff, for access to their thinking, as well as permission to quote the GASB publications. The authors also wish to express their appreciation to the American Institute of Certified Public Accountants, which allowed use of questions and problems for Uniform CPA Examinations and permitted quotations from its publications, particularly in the audit guide series.

The authors would appreciate suggestions from users of this text for improvement of the presentation of material in the chapters, and suggestions for additional or improved questions and exercises.

Leon E. Hay
John H. Engstrom

# CONTENTS IN BRIEF

1   The Framework for Accounting and Financial Reporting
for Governmental and Not-for-Profit Organizations     1

2   General Funds and Special Revenue Funds—
Budgetary Accounting     20

3   General Funds and Special Revenue Funds—
Illustrative Transactions and Financial Statements     48

4   Capital Projects Funds     75

5   General Fixed Assets Account Group     94

6   Debt Service Funds     109

7   General Long-Term Debt Account Group     126

8   Proprietary Funds     142

9   Fiduciary Funds     171

10   Interfund Transactions; Financial Reporting for State and
Local Governmental Units; Auditing     200

11   College and University Accounting     234

12   Accounting for Hospitals and Other Health Care Providers        271

13   Accounting for Voluntary Health and
     Welfare Organizations                                          297

14   Accounting for Other Nonprofit Organizations                   324

Index                                                               341

# CONTENTS

1   **The Framework for Accounting and Financial Reporting
    for Governmental and Not-for-Profit Organizations**                    1

Objectives of Accounting and Financial Reporting: *Objectives of
Financial Reporting by Not-for-Profit Entities. Objectives of
Accounting and Financial Reporting for Governmental Units.*
Principles of Accounting and Financial Reporting for States and Local
Governments: *Governmental Funds. Proprietary Funds. Fiduciary
Funds. Number of Funds Required. Budgetary Accounting.*
Governmental Financial Reporting: *Comprehensive Annual Financial
Report. The Governmental Reporting Entity.* Accounting and
Financial Reporting for Not-for-Profit Organizations Other Than State
and Local Governments: *Federal Government Agencies. Public
Schools. Not-for-Profit Organizations.*


2   **General Funds and Special Revenue Funds—
    Budgetary Accounting**                                                 20

Budgets as Legal Documents. Balance Sheet and Operating
Statement Accounts. Budgets and Budgetary Accounts. Recording the
Budget. Accounting for Revenues. Accounting for Encumbrances and
Expenditures. *Reconciliation of Amounts Reported in Illustration 2–1
with Amounts Reported in Illustration 2–2.* Classification of Estimated
Revenues and Revenues. Ad Valorem Taxes. Classification of
Appropriations and Expenditures. Interfund Transactions, Transfers,
and Proceeds of Debt Issues.


3   **General Funds and Special Revenue Funds—
    Illustrative Transactions and Financial Statements**                   48

Illustrative Case—General Fund: *Recording the Budget. Tax
Anticipation Notes Payable. Payment of Liabilities as Recorded.*

*Encumbrances of Prior Year. Encumbrance Entry. Recording Property Tax Levy. Collection of Delinquent Taxes. Revenue Recognized on Cash Basis. Collection of Current Taxes. Repayment of Tax Anticipation Notes. Recognition of Expenditures for Encumbered Items. Payrolls and Payroll Taxes. Payment of Vouchers and Other Items. Correction of Errors. Revision of the Budget. Interfund Transactions. Write-off of Uncollectible Delinquent Taxes. Reclassification of Current Taxes. Accrual of Interest and Penalties. Pre-Closing Trial Balance. Closing Entries. Year-End Financial Statements. Procedures for Recognition of Inventories in Governmental Funds. Special Revenue Funds.*

**4   Capital Projects Funds                                              75**

Illustrative Case: *Transactions and Events in 19x6. Transactions and Events in 19x7.* Acquisition of General Fixed Assets by Lease Agreements. *Construction of General Fixed Assets Financed by Special Assessment Debt.*

**5   General Fixed Assets Account Group                             94**

General Fixed Assets. Illustrative Entries: *Fixed Assets Acquired by Proprietary Fund. Disposal of General Fixed Assets. Detailed Property Records. Statements of General Fixed Assets.*

**6   Debt Service Funds                                              109**

*The Accrual Basis—Meaning for Debt Service. Additional Uses of Debt Service Funds. Debt Service Accounting for Regular Serial Bonds. Debt Service Accounting for Deferred Serial Bonds. Debt Service Accounting for Term Bonds. Debt Service Accounting for Capital Lease Payments.* Combining Statements for Debt Service Funds.

**7   General Long-Term Debt Account Group                          126**

Illustrative Case: *General Long-Term Debt Arising from Capital Lease Agreements. Claims, Judgments, Compensated Absences, and Other Long-Term Debt Not Evidenced by Bonds or Notes. Changes in Long-Term Debt. Principal and Interest Payable in Future Years. Debt Limit and Debt Margin. Direct and Overlapping Debt.*

**8   Proprietary Funds                                             142**

Internal Service Funds: *Establishment and Operation of Internal Service Funds. Illustrative Case—Supplies Fund. Illustrative Financial*

*Statements—Supplies Fund.* Enterprise Funds: *Illustrative Case—
Water Utility Fund. Illustrative Financial Statements—Water Utility
Fund. Accounting for Nonutility Enterprises. Required Segment
Information.*

### 9 Fiduciary Funds                                                                171

Agency Funds: *Tax Agency Funds. Accounting for Tax Agency Funds.
Financial Reporting for Agency Funds. Trust Funds: Illustrative Case—
Nonexpendable Trust Funds and Expendable Trust Funds. Illustrative
Entries—Nonexpendable Trust Fund. Illustrative Financial
Statements—Nonexpendable Trust Fund. Illustrative Entries—
Expendable Trust Fund. Illustrative Financial Statements—Expendable
Trust Fund.* Public Employee Retirement Systems (Pension Trust
Funds): *Objectives of PERS and Government Employer Financial
Reporting. Required Balance Sheet Disclosure—Retirement Plans.
Additional Financial Statements and Note Disclosures Required for
PERS. PERS—Illustrative Case. Summary of Requirements for
Government Employers' Financial Reporting.*

### 10 Interfund Transactions; Financial Reporting for State and Local Governmental Units; Auditing                 200

Summary of Interfund Transactions: *Interfund Loans and Advances.
Quasi-External Transactions. Reimbursements. Operating Transfers.
Equity Transfers. Events Requiring Recognition in More than One
Accounting Entity.* The Governmental Reporting Entity. Financial
Reporting: *Interim Financial Reports. Comprehensive Annual
Financial Report. General Purpose Financial Statements. Combining
Statements. Individual Fund and Account Groups Statements.
Statistical Tables.* Audits of State and Local Governments: *Auditor's
Reports.*

### 11 College and University Accounting                                              234

*Summary—College and University Accounting. The Fund Structure
for Colleges and Universities.* Illustrative Transactions: *Current
Funds—Unrestricted. Current Funds—Restricted. Loan Funds.
Endowment and Similar Funds. Annuity and Life Income Funds. Plant
Funds. Agency Funds.* Illustrative Financial Statements.

### 12 Accounting for Hospitals and Other Health Care Providers        271

*Summary—Accounting for Health Care Providers. The Fund Structure
for Health Care Providers. General Funds. Restricted Funds.*
Illustrative Transactions: *General Funds. Restricted Funds. Specific*

*Purpose Funds. Plant Replacement and Expansion Funds. Endowment Funds.* Illustrative Financial Statements for Hospitals: *Balance Sheet. Statement of Revenues and Expenses. Statement of Changes in Fund Balances. Statement of Changes in Financial Position of General Funds.*

**13  Accounting for Voluntary Health and
      Welfare Organizations                                                297**

Summary—Voluntary Health and Welfare Organization Accounting. Public Support and Revenue. Program Services and Supporting Services Expenses. Asset Valuation. Liabilities. Fund Balances. Illustrative Transactions—Voluntary Health and Welfare Organizations: Current Fund—Unrestricted. Current Funds—Restricted. Land, Building, and Equipment Fund. Endowment Funds. Financial Statements for Voluntary Health and Welfare Organizations.

**14  Accounting for Other Nonprofit Organizations                       324**

*Accounting and Financial Reporting Standards.* Illustrative Transactions—Other Nonprofit Organizations: *Unrestricted Funds. Endowment Funds. Plant Funds. Financial Statements.*

**Index                                                                   341**

# ESSENTIALS OF ACCOUNTING FOR GOVERNMENTAL AND NOT-FOR-PROFIT ORGANIZATIONS

# Chapter 1

# THE FRAMEWORK FOR ACCOUNTING AND FINANCIAL REPORTING FOR GOVERNMENTAL AND NOT-FOR-PROFIT ORGANIZATIONS

**M**any persons who practice accounting and many who teach accounting maintain that there is only one "body of generally accepted accounting principles" (GAAP) which applies to accounting and financial reporting by all entities. Although a number of attempts have been made, no one has ever succeeded in producing a definitive description of universal GAAP. In place of a concise statement of GAAP, a series of statements of accounting and financial reporting standards have been issued by organizations whose pronouncements are accepted as authoritative. One such organization in the United States is the Financial Accounting Standards Board (FASB). The FASB sets standards for financial reports published by profit-seeking businesses for distribution to stockholders and creditors, and others not actively involved in the management of the business.

A second organization, the Governmental Accounting Standards Board (GASB), sets accounting and financial reporting standards for state and local governments in the United States. A separate standards-setting organization was considered necessary because governments have no stockholders or other owners, they render services with no expectation of earning net income, and have the power to require taxpayers to support financial operations whether or not they receive benefits in proportion to taxes paid. Further, the form of government in the United States requires interrelationships between a state government and local governments established in conformity with state law, and interrelationships within any one government between the executive and legislative branches, that have no parallel in business organizations. Thus, it is to be expected that GASB standards, discussed in the chapters of this book devoted to accounting for state and local governments, differ in many respects from FASB standards discussed in books concerned with financial accounting for businesses.

Commonly, colleges and universities, voluntary health and welfare organizations, libraries, museums, churches, and so on are similar to governments in that they exist to render services to constituents with no expectation of earning net income from those services, have no owners, and seek financial resources from persons who do not expect either repayment or economic benefits proportionate to the resources provided. At the present time, however, the FASB has the authority to establish accounting and financial reporting standards for nongovernmental not-for-profit entities, while the GASB has the authority to establish standards for not-for-profit entities whose financial data may be included in the financial statements of a governmental reporting entity.[1] Neither the FASB nor the GASB has issued statements explicitly intended to establish a comprehensive set of accounting and financial reporting standards for not-for-profit entities. The FASB has established standards for recognition of depreciation and has proposed standards for recognition of revenue from contributions, which supersede certain portions of AICPA audit guides and Statements of Position issued prior to 1982. Accordingly the chapters of this book concerned with colleges and universities, hospitals, voluntary health and welfare organizations, and other not-for-profit entities are based on pronouncements of the American Institute of Certified Public Accountants (AICPA) and other bodies whose pronouncements are considered as authoritative, as amended by FASB statements applicable to nongovernmental entities. Illustration 1–1 lists the major sources of GAAP for governments and not-for-profit entities.

## OBJECTIVES OF ACCOUNTING AND FINANCIAL REPORTING

Both the Financial Accounting Standards Board and the Governmental Accounting Standards Board have taken the position that the establishment of accounting and financial reporting standards should be guided by conceptual considerations in order that the body of standards be internally consistent and that the standards address broad issues expected to be of importance for a significant period of time. The corner-

---

[1]According to a proposal approved for exposure by the Financial Accounting Foundation, each governmentally owned college, university, health care institution, and gas or electric utility is to be required to follow FASB financial reporting standards unless its governing board makes an irrevocable election to follow GASB standards.

**ILLUSTRATION 1–1    Major Sources of Accounting and Financial Reporting Standards for Governmental and Not-for-Profit Organizations**

| Organization | Major Sources of Standards |
| --- | --- |
| Federal government agencies | U.S. General Accounting Office, *GAO Policy and Procedures Manual for Guidance of Federal Agencies, Title 2— Accounting.* |
| | U.S. Office of Management and Budget, *U.S. Government Standard General Ledger.* |
| | U.S. Department of the Treasury, *Treasury Financial Manual.* |
| State and local governments | Governmental Accounting Standards Board, *Statements, Interpretations,* and *Technical Bulletins.* |
| Public schools | National Center for Education Statistics, *Financial Accounting for Local and State School Systems.* |
| Colleges and universities* | American Institute of Certified Public Accountants (AICPA), *Audits of Colleges and Universities.* |
| | National Association of College and University Business Officers, *College and University Business Administration.* |
| Health care providers* | AICPA, Audit and Accounting Guide, *Audits of Health Care Providers* |
| Voluntary health and welfare organizations* | AICPA, *Audits of Voluntary Health and Welfare Organizations.* |
| Other not-for-profit organizations* | AICPA, *Audits of Certain Nonprofit Organizations.* |

*The FASB has the responsibility for issuing financial reporting standards for nongovernmental, not-for-profit organizations. The GASB has jurisdiction over financial reporting of governmentally related not-for-profit organizations. Also see footnote 1 on p. 2.

stone of a conceptual framework is said to be a statement of the objectives of financial reporting.

## Objectives of Financial Reporting by Not-for-Profit Entities

In its *Statement of Financial Accounting Concepts No. 6,* the FASB emphasized that its concern is with financial reporting to users who lack the authority to prescribe the information they want and who must rely on the information management communicates to them. Further, the FASB believes that such persons use financial information for only economic decisions. Therefore, the FASB stresses that the objective of financial reporting by not-for-profit organizations is to provide information to "present and potential resource providers and others in making rational decisions about allocating resources to not-for-profit organizations."[2]

---

[2]Financial Accounting Standards Board, *Statement of Financial Accounting Concepts No. 6* (Norwalk, Conn., 1985), par. 9.

**Objectives of Accounting and Financial Reporting for Governmental Units**

The Governmental Accounting Standards Board was established in 1984 as the successor to the National Council on Governmental Accounting (NCGA). In 1987 the GASB issued its *Concepts Statement No. 1, Objectives of Financial Reporting* for state and local governments. In that statement the Board noted:

> The Board believes that financial reporting plays a major role in fulfilling government's duty to be publicly accountable in a democratic society. Public accountability is based on the belief that the taxpayer has a "right to know," a right to receive openly declared facts that may lead to public debate by the citizens and their elected representatives. Use of financial reporting by citizens and legislative and oversight officials is pervasive. . . .[3]

Financial reports of state and local governments, according to the Governmental Accounting Standards Board, are used primarily: (1) to compare actual financial results with the legally adopted budget; (2) to assess financial condition and results of operations; (3) to assist in determining compliance with finance-related laws, rules, and regulations; and (4) to assist in evaluating efficiency and effectiveness.

## PRINCIPLES OF ACCOUNTING AND FINANCIAL REPORTING FOR STATES AND LOCAL GOVERNMENTS

The objectives of accounting and financial reporting for states and local governments are reflected in 12 principles which are set forth and explained in the GASB *Codification of Governmental Accounting and Financial Reporting Standards*. Those principles which are most important for the purposes of this chapter are reproduced below. Chapters 2 through 10 of this book present more detailed explanations of the principles and illustrate their application to accounting and financial reporting of governmental units. The first principle states:

> A governmental accounting system must make it possible both: *(a)* to present fairly and with full disclosure the financial position and results of financial operations of the funds and account groups of the governmental unit in conformity with generally accepted accounting principles; and *(b)* to determine and demonstrate compliance with finance-related legal and contractual provisions.

The American Institute of Certified Public Accountants (AICPA) accepts the GASB as being vested with the responsibility for the issuance

---

[3]Governmental Accounting Standards Board, *Concepts Statement No. 1, Objectives of Financial Reporting* (Norwalk, Conn., 1987), p. ii.

of pronouncements on governmental accounting standards. Auditors of state and local governmental entities should look to GASB pronouncements as the primary source of generally accepted accounting principles.[4] However, some state laws require governmental units to follow practices (such as cash basis accounting) which are not consistent with generally accepted accounting principles. In those cases, financial statements and reports prepared in compliance with state law are considered to be "special reports" or "supplemental schedules" and are **not** the basic general purpose financial statements discussed in the section "Governmental Financial Reporting."

The financial managers of governmental units are called upon to demonstrate compliance with numerous legal and contractual requirements. Accordingly, fund accounting is required. Fund accounting, and the term **fund,** are defined by the GASB as:

> Governmental accounting systems should be organized and operated on a fund basis. A fund is defined as a **fiscal and accounting entity** with a self-balancing set of accounts recording cash and other financial resources, together with all related liabilities and residual equities or balances, and changes therein, which are segregated for the purpose of carrying on specific activities or attaining certain objectives in accordance with special regulations, restrictions, or limitations.[5] (Emphasis added.)

Note that the definition of the word **fund** given above requires that two conditions must be met for a fund, in a technical sense, to exist: (1) there must be a **fiscal entity**—assets set aside for specific purposes, and (2) there must be a double entry **accounting entity** created to account for the fiscal entity.

States and local governments use seven types of funds to achieve the objectives outlined above. The seven funds are organized into three categories:

## Governmental Funds

Four fund types are classified as **governmental** funds. These are:

1. The **general fund,** which accounts for most of the basic services provided by the governmental unit. Technically, this fund accounts for all resources other than those required to be accounted for in another fund.

---

[4]American Institute of Certified Public Accountants, *Statement on Auditing Standards No. 52, The Meaning of "Present Fairly in Conformity with Generally Accepted Accounting Principles" in the Independent Auditor's Report* (New York, 1988), par. 1.

[5]Governmental Accounting Standards Board, *Codification of Governmental and Financial Reporting Standards,* 2nd ed. (Norwalk, Conn., 1987), par. 1100.102.

2. **Special revenue funds,** which account for resources that are legally restricted, other than for debt service, major capital projects, and trust and agency relationships. Accounting for general funds and special revenue funds is discussed in Chapters 2 and 3 of this text.
3. **Capital projects funds,** which account for major capital projects other than those financed by proprietary or trust funds. Capital projects fund accounting is illustrated in Chapter 4.
4. **Debt service funds** (discussed in Chapter 6), which account for the payment of principal and interest on general long-term debt.

**Measurement focus**  The GASB states that the four types of funds listed above are segregations of the financial resources and related liabilities of governmental-type activities; that is, activities undertaken in response to the needs of the public. Governmental-type activities are financed by taxes and other involuntary contributions from persons (and organizations) who do not receive services in any way related to the contributions they make. GASB standards provide that accounting systems of governmental funds are designed to measure *(a)* the extent to which financial resources obtained during a period are sufficient to cover claims incurred during that period against financial resources and *(b)* the net financial resources available for future periods. Thus, governmental funds are said to have a **flow of financial resources measurement focus,** as distinguished from business organizations which have an income determination measurement focus. Note that measurement focus refers to **what** is being expressed in reporting an entity's financial performance and position. Since all resources of governmental funds are raised in order to be expended, these funds are called **expendable** funds. Generally, governmental funds account only for assets held in the form of cash or which are expected to be turned into cash during the normal operations of the fund. If prepaid expenses and/or supplies inventories of a governmental fund are material in amount, and are expected to be consumed in the year following balance sheet date, they should be reported as current assets of the fund. Governmental funds do not account for fixed assets used in fund operations; fixed assets of this nature are called **general fixed assets,** and are placed under accounting control by recording them in the **General Fixed Assets Account Group (GFAAG).** The GFAAG is only an accounting entity, not a fiscal entity; therefore, not a fund. Chapter 5 discusses accounting and reporting standards for the GFAAG.

Each governmental fund accounts for current liabilities which are to be paid from assets of that fund. Liabilities to be paid in the future (such as claims and judgments, compensated absences, and pension contributions) and long-term debt related to the acquisition of general fixed assets is recorded in the **General Long-Term Debt Account Group**

**(GLTDAG).**[6] As is true of the GFAAG, the GLTDAG is only an accounting entity, not a fiscal entity; therefore, not a fund. Chapter 7 discusses accounting and reporting standards for the GLTDAG.

**Basis of accounting** The flow of financial resources measurement focus is accomplished by using an **accrual basis of accounting** to recognize the increases and decreases in net financial resources. Basis of accounting refers to **when** the effects of transitions or events should be recognized for financial reporting purposes. Until recently the basis of accounting for governmental funds was described as the "modified accrual" basis. From a practical viewpoint, the accrual basis now specified in GASB standards and the modified accrual basis formerly required both mean that accrual accounting, as it is understood in accounting for business organizations, is used in accounting for governmental funds to the extent that it is reasonable to do so. No transaction or event can be recorded in accounts unless the effects of the transaction or event can be expressed in terms of a monetary unit. Thus, it is said the effects must be **measurable.** An amount need not be known exactly to be measurable; it is considered measurable if a reasonable estimate can be made. In business accounting financial resource inflows must not only be measurable to be recognized as revenues of period, they must also be earned. In the case of governmental funds, the concept of earning is not always as clear-cut as it is in businesses. Under the modified accrual basis of accounting formerly required for governmental funds the criteria for recognition of revenues were **measurable** and **available** to finance expenditures of the fiscal period. Although the term "available" was dropped along with the term "modified accrual," the concept still exists in that GASB standards provide that property tax collections received before the period for which the taxes were levied should be reported as deferred revenues, a liability, rather than as revenues.

Under the accrual basis of accounting for governmental funds the rule is that expenditures are recognized when goods or services are received; thus, generally, in the case of expenditures, the accrual basis for governmental funds is the same as the accrual basis for business organizations. In the case of interest on general long-term debt, expenditure recognition under the governmental fund accrual basis does diverge from the business accrual basis, as explained in Chapter 6.

---

[6]In 1987 the GASB proposed that all liabilities to be paid in the future, except long-term debt related to the acquisition of general fixed assets, be reported by the fund incurring the debt. As of mid-1989, the 1987 proposal has not been adopted; all general long-term debt is reported in the GLTDAG.

## Proprietary Funds

Two types of funds used by state and local governments are classified as **proprietary** funds. The term indicates that the funds are used to account for a government's ongoing organizations and activities that are similar to those often found in the private sector. Proprietary funds are discussed in Chapter 8. The two types of proprietary funds are:

1. **Enterprise funds,** which are used when resources are provided primarily through the use of service charges to those receiving the benefit, or where it is deemed best to display a matching of revenues and expenses in the manner used by business enterprises. Examples of enterprise funds would be water and other utilities, airports, swimming pools, and transit systems.
2. **Internal service funds,** which account for services provided by one department or government, such as a print shop or motor pool, to another on a cost reimbursement basis.

Proprietary funds are considered to be "nonexpendable," in that the revenues are generated through user charges intended to cover operating costs and expenses. Proprietary funds use accrual accounting, in the same manner as business enterprises.

## Fiduciary Funds

The third general category of funds used by state and local governments is called **fiduciary.** These are:

**Trust and agency funds,** which account for resources for which the governmental unit is acting as a trustee or as a collecting/disbursing agent. The type of accounting used by trust and agency funds depends upon the nature and purpose of the fund. **Agency funds** and **expendable trust funds** are accounted for in a manner similar to governmental funds. **Nonexpendable trust funds** and **pension trust funds** are accounted for in a manner similar to proprietary funds. Fiduciary funds are discussed in Chapter 9.

Transactions and events which require recognition in two or more fund types and/or account groups are discussed in Chapter 10.

## Number of Funds Required

In the GASB Summary Statement of Principles, the principle which follows the definition of fund types and account groups is often overlooked. This principle states that *governmental units should establish and maintain those funds required by law and sound financial administration.* It means exactly what it says: If in a specific governmental unit state law and/or agreements with creditors do not require that the receipt of revenues which are raised specifically and solely for a payment of interest on general obligation debt (for example), and the payment of such interest, be accounted for by a debt service fund, *and* if administrators do not feel that use of a debt service fund is needed in order for them to be able to demonstrate that revenues which were raised solely for debt service were expended for that purpose and not for any other purpose, it is in conformity with GAAP (GASB standards) for the debt service activity to be accounted for by the General Fund. Similarly, if neither laws nor agreements with creditors or grantors financing the construction require that the construction of general fixed assets be accounted for by a capital projects fund, and if administrators do not feel that use of a capital projects fund is needed for sound financial administration, revenues and expenditures related to the construction project may be accounted for by the General Fund. In the large majority of cases, however, governmental units use debt service funds and capital projects funds as provided in GASB standards.

## Budgetary Accounting

GASB standards recognize that state laws generally require administrators of state agencies and of local governmental units to obtain formal approval of the appropriate legislative body of all plans to raise revenues and formal approval of all proposed expenditures. Additionally, it is common for state agencies to be given the responsibility for monitoring the financial plans and financial operations of local governmental units within the state. Therefore, GASB standards contain the following budgetary principle:

*a.* An annual budget(s) should be adopted by every governmental unit.
*b.* The accounting system should provide the basis for appropriate budgetary control.
*c.* Budgetary comparisons should be included in the appropriate financial statements and schedules for governmental funds for which an annual budget has been adopted.

Part *a* of the "principle" is not an accounting or financial reporting principle, but it is a necessary precondition to parts *b* and *c*. A budget, when adopted according to procedures specified in state laws, is binding upon the administrators of a governmental unit. Accordingly, a distinctive characteristic of governmental accounting resulting from the need to demonstrate compliance with laws governing the sources of revenues available to governmental units, and laws governing the utilization of those revenues, is the formal recording of the legally approved budget in the accounts of funds operated on an annual basis. The nature and operation of budgetary accounts are explained in appropriate detail in Chapter 2.

## GOVERNMENTAL FINANCIAL REPORTING

The discussion of the objectives of accounting and financial reporting for governmental units in the early pages of this chapter stresses that organizations which set accounting and reporting standards for state and local governmental units traditionally are concerned with the financial information needs of many diverse groups: citizen groups, legislative and oversight officials, and investors and creditors. It is also made clear that reporting standards for governments recognize that decisions made by these groups involve political and social decisions as well as economic decisions. Accordingly governmental financial reporting standards are much more inclusive than FASB standards which consider the needs of only investors and creditors concerned with economic decisions. GASB standards relating to the Comprehensive Annual Financial Report of a government are summarized below.

### Comprehensive Annual Financial Report

The discussion of financial reporting in the GASB Codification Sec. 2200 sets standards for the content of the comprehensive annual financial report of a state or local governmental reporting entity. A comprehensive annual financial report (called CAFR for short) is the governmental reporting entity's official annual report prepared and published as a matter of public record. In addition to the general purpose financial statements (GPFS in GASB nomenclature), and other financial statements, the CAFR should contain introductory material, schedules necessary to demonstrate legal compliance, and statistical tables.

**Introductory section**  Introductory material should include a title page and contents page, a letter of transmittal, and other material deemed appropriate by management. The "letter of transmittal" may be literally that—a letter from the chief finance officer addressed to the chief executive and governing body of the governmental unit—or it may be a narrative over the signature of the chief executive. The letter should cite legal and policy requirements for the report and discuss briefly the important aspects of the financial condition and financial operations of the reporting entity as a whole and of the entity's funds and account groups. Significant changes since the prior annual report and changes expected during the coming year should be brought to the attention of the reader of the report.

**Financial section**  The financial section of a comprehensive annual financial report should include (1) an auditor's report, (2) general purpose financial statements, and (3) combining and individual fund and account group statements and schedules.

Laws relating to the audit of governmental units vary markedly from state to state. In some, all state agencies and all governmental units created pursuant to the state law are required to be audited by an audit agency of the state government. In others, local governmental units are audited by independent certified public accountants.

The financial section should contain sufficient information to disclose fully and present fairly the financial position and results of financial operations during the fiscal year. The GASB Codification Sec. 2200.105 states that the basic general purpose financial statements (GPFS) of a government are required for conformity with generally accepted accounting principles; the AICPA states that the independent auditor's report covers the GPFS.[7] The GPFS consist of the following combined statements.

1. Combined Balance Sheet—All Fund Types and Account Groups.
2. Combined Statement of Revenues, Expenditures, and Changes in Fund Balances—All Governmental Fund Types.
3. Combined Statement of Revenues, Expenditures, and Changes in Fund Balances—Budget and Actual—General and Special Revenue Fund Types.
4. Combined Statement of Revenues, Expenses, and Changes in Retained Earnings (or Equity)—All Proprietary Fund Types.
5. Combined Statement of Changes in Financial Position—All Proprietary Fund Types.[8]

"Notes to the Financial Statements" is sometimes listed as No. 6 in the above list because the Notes are considered to be an integral part of the GPFS and should be read in conjunction with the five combined statements. Entities with pension activities also are required by GASB standards to present specified trend information and other data in a section called **Required Supplementary Information,** generally following the Notes to the Financial Statements.

The general purpose financial statements (GPFS) are a necessary part of an official CAFR, but the GASB Codification Sec. 2200.102 specifically provides that the GPFS may also be issued separately for widespread distribution to users requiring less detailed information than is contained in the complete CAFR.

The combined financial statements are illustrated in Chapter 10 of this book, and the reader may wish to refer to them at this time. The statements are called "combined" statements because a separate column is used in the statement to report on each of the **fund types** and **account groups** of the governmental unit preparing the financial statements. Interfund transactions are not eliminated, therefore the statements are **not consolidated.**

---

[7]American Institute of Certified Public Accountants, *Audits of State and Local Governmental Units,* rev. ed. (New York, 1986).

[8]For years beginning after December 15, 1989, this statement will be replaced by a Combined Statement of Cash Flows.

**Statistical tables**  Statistical tables present social and economic data, financial trends, and the fiscal capacity of the government in detail needed by readers who are more than casually interested in the activities of the governmental unit. The GASB Codification Sec. 2800 suggests the content of tables usually considered necessary in a CAFR. Statistical tables are discussed at greater length in Chapter 10.

## The Governmental Reporting Entity

The GASB Codification Sec. 2100 requires that activities which are under the direct economic control of a given governmental entity must be included in the annual financial report of that entity, even if a separate legal organization exists. The GASB Codification Sec. 2600 requires that activities included in annual financial reports of governmental units be defined as "component units," and that separately issued financial reports of the component units be called "Component Unit Financial Reports" (CUFR). Examples of such component units are public universities in state reports, housing authorities, retirement systems, and arts organizations, which are under the economic control of the governmental units in which they are located and serve.

## ACCOUNTING AND FINANCIAL REPORTING FOR NOT-FOR-PROFIT ORGANIZATIONS OTHER THAN STATE AND LOCAL GOVERNMENTS

### Federal Government Agencies

Illustration 1–1 lists the major sources of information about accounting and financial reporting standards for governments and not-for-profit organizations. The Comptroller General of the United States has the statutory responsibility for establishing accounting and financial reporting standards for agencies of the U.S. government. The Comptroller General was instrumental in encouraging the formation of the Governmental Accounting Standards Board, and has announced that standards set for federal agencies will be consistent to the maximum extent possible with standards set by the GASB for state and local governments. A detailed presentation of federal government agency accounting and reporting standards is beyond the scope of this text.

### Public Schools

**Public schools** are, by definition, governmental units. In two thirds of the states all public schools are operated by public school **districts,** which are independent of other governmental units. In five states public schools are operated by a general governmental unit (such as the state itself, a county, a city, and so on). The remaining states have some independent school districts and other school systems operated by a general governmental unit. Whether public schools are independent or dependent their accounting and general purpose financial reporting should conform to the standards set forth in the National Center for Education Statistics (NCES) publication listed in Illustration 1–1. The standards set forth in that NCES publication are consistent with the standards developed by the National Council on Governmental Accounting, now incorporated in the GASB *Codification of Governmental Accounting and Financial Reporting Standards* discussed briefly in preceding sections of this chapter, and presented in some detail in Chapters 2 through 10 of this text. (Schools not governmental in nature are **private schools;** private schools which are not operated for profit are included in Illustration 1–1, and in Chapter 14 of this text.)

## Not-for-Profit Organizations

As noted in the first section of this chapter, jurisdiction over setting accounting and financial reporting standards for colleges and universities, hospitals, voluntary health and welfare, and other not-for-profit organizations is split between the FASB and the GASB. Neither the FASB nor the GASB has yet issued any comprehensive set of authoritative pronouncements intended to supersede standards set forth in the publications listed in Illustration 1–1.

Standards for accounting and financial reporting for **colleges** and **universities** are similar in many respects to those developed for state and local governments, whether the colleges or universities are related to a governmental unit or whether they are church related, or operated by a nonprofit corporation.[9] This is discussed in Chapter 11.

**Hospitals,** once largely owned and operated by a government, a nonprofit corporation, or a religious group, have undergone significant changes. Recent statistics indicate that over one eighth of the hospitals in the United States are now members of investor-owned chains of hospitals; within another 10 years it is expected that investor-owned chains will operate one fourth of the hospitals. Whether hospitals are investor owned, owned by nonprofit corporations, or government owned, they all are, at the present time, expected to adhere to the same accounting and financial reporting standards, which are generally consistent with those of business organizations.[10] Accounting and reporting for hospitals and other providers of health care services is discussed in Chapter 12.

Chapter 13 presents accounting and financial reporting standards applicable to voluntary health and welfare organizations—not-for-profit organizations that derive their support primarily from contributions from the general public to be used for health, welfare, or community service activities. Chapter 14 discusses accounting and financial reporting standards established for the guidance of auditors of **not-for-profit organizations not subject to any other AICPA audit guide.** Cemetery

---

[9]See footnote 1.
[10]See footnote 1.

organizations, civic organizations, fraternal organizations, labor unions, libraries, museums, other cultural and performing arts organizations, political parties, private schools, and religious organizations, are among the entities which should follow the standards discussed in Chapter 14.

## SELECTED REFERENCES

American Institute of Certified Public Accountants.

_____. *Audits of Certain Nonprofit Organizations.* New York, 1981.

_____. *Audits of Colleges and Universities.* 2nd ed. New York, 1975.

_____. *Audits of Health Care Providers.* New York, 1989.

_____. *Audits of State and Local Governmental Units.* Rev. ed. New York, 1986.

_____. *Audits of Voluntary Health and Welfare Organizations.* New York, 1974.

Financial Accounting Standards Board. *Statement of Financial Accounting Concepts No. 4: Objectives of Financial Reporting by Nonbusiness Organizations.* Norwalk, Conn., 1980.

_____. *Statement of Financial Accounting Concepts No. 6: Elements of Financial Statements.* Norwalk, Conn., 1985.

_____. *Statement of Financial Accounting Standards No. 32: Specialized Accounting and Reporting Principles and Practices in AICPA Statements of Position and Guides on Accounting and Auditing Matters.* Norwalk, Conn., 1979.

Governmental Accounting Standards Board. *Codification of Governmental Accounting and Financial Reporting Standards.* 2nd ed. Norwalk, Conn., 1987.

_____. *Statement No. 8: Applicability of FASB Statement No. 93, Recognition of Depreciation by Not-for-Profit Organizations, to Certain State and Local Governmental Entities.* Norwalk, Conn., 1988.

National Association of College and University Business Officers. *College and University Business Administration: Administrative Service.* Washington, D.C. In looseleaf form with periodic changes and supplements.

National Center for Education Statistics. *Financial Accounting for Local and State School Systems.* State Educational Records and Reports Series: Handbook II. 2nd rev. ed. Washington, D.C.: U.S. Government Printing Office, 1980.

U.S. General Accounting Office. *Accounting Principles and Standards for Federal Agencies.* Washington, D.C., 1984.

## QUESTIONS AND EXERCISES

**1–1.**  Obtain a copy of a recent Comprehensive Annual Financial Report. These may be obtained by writing the Director of Finance in a city or county of your choice. Your instructor may have these available for you. You will have questions related to the annual report in each of Chapters 1 through 10. Answer the following questions related to the CAFR.

    *a.* What are the inclusive dates of the fiscal year?

    *b.* Write the name and address of the independent auditor. Is the auditor's opinion unqualified? If not, describe the qualification. Is the report modified to provide information about uncertainties of any nature?

    *c.* Does the report contain an organization chart? A table of contents? A list of principal officials? A letter of transmittal? Is the letter of transmittal dated and signed by the chief financial officer?

    *d.* Read the letter of transmittal. Does the letter of transmittal include a discussion of: (1) the accounting entity, (2) the fund structure, (3) the accounting methods employed for the various funds, (4) general government revenues and expenditures, (5) internal accounting controls, (6) the independent audit, (7) prospects for the future, and (8) acknowledgments? What other major topics are included?

    *e.* Look at the Combined Balance Sheet in the front of the Financial Section. Does the report include all of the seven fund types and two account groups described in this chapter? Are the funds grouped into the three categories?

    *f.* Become familiar with the content of the Notes to the Financial Statements. In the Summary of Significant Accounting Policies (usually the first note) read the information about the bases of accounting used by the reporting entity. Are the bases used for the governmental fund types and for the proprietary fund types the same as described in this chapter?

**1–2.** Write the numbers 1 through 10 on a sheet of paper. Beside each number write the letter corresponding to the best answer to each of the following questions:

    1. Which of the following funds of a governmental unit uses the same basis of accounting as an enterprise fund?

      *a.* Special revenue.

      *b.* Expendable trust.

      *c.* Capital projects.

      *d.* Internal service.

    2. The comprehensive annual financial report (CAFR) of a governmental unit should contain a combined statement of revenue, expenditures, and changes in fund balances for

| | Account Groups | Proprietary Funds |
|---|---|---|
| *a.* | Yes | No |
| *b.* | Yes | Yes |
| *c.* | No | Yes |
| *d.* | No | No |

    3. A local governmental unit could use which of the following types of funds?

| | Fiduciary | Proprietary |
|---|---|---|
| *a.* | Yes | No |
| *b.* | Yes | Yes |
| *c.* | No | Yes |
| *d.* | No | No |

    4. Which of the following funds of a governmental unit uses the same basis of accounting as the special revenue fund?

      *a.* Internal service.

      *b.* Expendable trust.

     *c.* Nonexpendable trust.

     *d.* Enterprise.

5. A debt service fund of a local government is an example of which of the following types of fund?

     *a.* Fiduciary.

     *b.* Governmental.

     *c.* Proprietary.

     *d.* Internal service.

6. One of the differences between accounting for a governmental (not-for-profit) unit and a commercial (for-profit) enterprise is that a governmental (not-for-profit) unit should:

     *a.* Not record depreciation expense in any of its funds.

     *b.* Always establish and maintain complete self-balancing accounts for each fund.

     *c.* Use only the cash basis of accounting.

     *d.* Use only the full accrual basis of accounting.

7. If a governmental unit established a data processing center to service all agencies within the unit, the data processing center should be accounted for as a(an):

     *a.* Capital projects fund.

     *b.* Internal service fund.

     *c.* Agency fund.

     *d.* Trust fund.

8. Recreational facilities run by a governmental unit and financed on a user-charge basis would be accounted for in which fund?

     *a.* General.

     *b.* Trust.

     *c.* Enterprise.

     *d.* Capital projects.

9. Fixed assets should be accounted for in the General Fixed Assets Account Group for:

| | *Governmental Funds* | *Proprietary Funds* |
|---|---|---|
| *a.* | No | Yes |
| *b.* | No | No |
| *c.* | Yes | No |
| *d.* | Yes | Yes |

10. Revenues of a special revenue fund of a governmental unit should be recognized in the period in which the:

     *a.* Budget is recorded.

     *b.* Revenues become measurable.

     *c.* Revenues are billed.

     *d.* Cash is received.

(AICPA, adapted)

**1–3.**    *a.* Distinguish between the terms *measurement focus* and *basis of accounting*.

       *b.* In accounting for state and local governments, what is the measurement focus of the types of funds classified as governmental funds? Of proprietary funds?

      *c*. In accounting for state and local governments, what basis of accounting should be used for governmental funds? For proprietary funds?

**1–4.**    *a*. Explain the significance to financial statement preparers, and to independent auditors, of the term *general purpose financial statements*.

      *b*. List the financial statements which are considered to be the General Purpose Financial Statements (GPFS) of a state or local governmental unit.

      *c*. In addition to the GPFS, what information is required to be presented in a Comprehensive Annual Financial Report (CAFR) of a state or local government?

      *d*. List the categories of users the GASB believes to be the primary external users of state and local government financial reports.

**1–5.**    Chapter 1 lists and discusses the seven fund types and two account groups presented in GASB accounting and financial reporting standards.

      *a*. Discuss some inherent differences between business organizations and government that make standards setting boards specify fund accounting for governments but not for business organizations.

      *b*. Discuss the principal differences between the governmental funds (general, special revenue, debt service, capital projects) and the proprietary funds (enterprise, internal service) that result in the measurement focus and the basis of accounting prescribed for governmental funds differing from the measurement focus and basis of accounting prescribed for proprietary funds.

## CONTINUOUS PROBLEM

**Note:** The assignments in the Continuous Problem printed at the ends of Chapters 2 through 10 of this text are intended to be solved manually. Instructors may prefer to use the microcomputer to maintain accounting records and prepare financial statements. In that event the instructor may use the *revised edition* of the City of Bingham Continuous Problem Adapted for Microcomputer Solution; instruction booklets and diskettes for use with IBM personal computers or closely compatible personal computers are available from the publisher of this text. Be sure to specify the 1989 edition, not the 1987 edition.

**1–C.**    Chapters 2 through 10 deal with specific knowledge needed to understand the accounting for the fund types provided for use by state and local governmental units. In order to help the student keep the entire accounting area in perspective, a continuous problem is presented. The problem covers all of the funds and account groups of the City of Everlasting Sunshine. At the end of each chapter, the problems are designated 2–C, 3–C, 4–C, and so forth. At appropriate stages, preparation of the five combined statements as well as combining statements for the two debt service funds is required. The following funds and account groups are included in this series of problems.

> General Fund
> Special Revenue—Street and Highway Fund
> Capital Projects—City Hall Annex Construction Fund
> Debt Service—City Hall Annex Debt Service Fund
>         —City Hall Debt Service Fund
> Internal Service—Stores and Services Fund

Enterprise—Water and Sewer Fund
Agency—Tax Collection Fund
Expendable Trust—Library Endowment Revenues Fund
Nonexpendable Trust—Library Endowment Principal Fund
Pension Trust—Fire and Police Retirement Fund
General Fixed Assets Account Group
General Long-Term Debt Account Group

**Required:**

*a.* Open a general journal for the General Fund. Allow seven pages of 8½ by 11-inch looseleaf journal paper, or its equivalent. (Do not open general journals for other funds until instructed to do so in subsequent "C" problems.) Use the form specified by the instructor or the following:

| Date | Accounts and Explanation | Ref. | Debit | Credit |
| --- | --- | --- | --- | --- |

*b.* Open a general ledger for the General Fund. Use the form specified by your instructor or the following three-column form:

| Date | Explanation | Ref. | Debit | Credit | Balance |
| --- | --- | --- | --- | --- | --- |

Allow five pages of 8½ by 11-inch looseleaf ledger paper, or its equivalent. On each page allow six lines for each of the following accounts:

Cash
Taxes Receivable—Current
Estimated Uncollectible Current Taxes
Taxes Receivable—Delinquent
Estimated Uncollectible Delinquent Taxes
Interest and Penalties Receivable on Taxes
Estimated Uncollectible Interest and Penalties
Due from Other Funds
Due from State Government
Inventory of Supplies
Estimated Revenues
Estimated Other Financing Sources
Revenues
Other Financing Sources—Operating Transfers In
Vouchers Payable
Tax Anticipation Notes Payable
Due to Other Funds
Due to Federal Government
Due to State Government
Deferred Revenues
Appropriations
Estimated Other Financing Uses
Expenditures—19y1
Expenditures—19y0
Other Financing Uses—Operating Transfers Out—19y1
Encumbrances—19y1
Reserve for Encumbrances—19y1
Reserve for Encumbrances—19y0
Reserve for Inventory of Supplies
Fund Balance

*c.* The Balance Sheet of the General Fund of the City of Everlasting Sunshine as of December 31, 19y0 is shown below. Enter the balance sheet amounts directly in the proper general ledger accounts; date each "1/1/y1."

## CITY OF EVERLASTING SUNSHINE
### General Fund Balance Sheet
### As of December 31, 19y0

**Assets**

| | | |
|---|---:|---:|
| Cash . . . . . . . . . . . . . . . . . . . . . . . | | $ 75,500 |
| Taxes receivable—delinquent . . . . . . . . . . . . . | $215,855 | |
| Less: Estimated uncollectible delinquent taxes . . . . . | 37,333 | 178,522 |
| Interest and penalties receivable on taxes . . . . . . . | 21,211 | |
| Less: Estimated uncollectible interest and penalties . . . | 4,155 | 17,056 |
| Due from state government . . . . . . . . . . . . . . | | 330,000 |
| Inventory of supplies . . . . . . . . . . . . . . . . | | 77,500 |
| Total Assets . . . . . . . . . . . . . . . . . . . . | | $678,578 |

**Liabilities and Fund Equity**

| | | |
|---|---:|---:|
| Liabilities: | | |
| Vouchers payable . . . . . . . . . . . . . . . . | | $150,750 |
| Due to other funds . . . . . . . . . . . . . . . . | | 35,250 |
| Deferred revenues . . . . . . . . . . . . . . . . | | 20,000 |
| Total Liabilities . . . . . . . . . . . . . . . . | | 206,000 |
| Fund Equity: | | |
| Reserve for encumbrances—19y0 . . . . . . . . . . | $ 29,000 | |
| Reserve for inventory of supplies . . . . . . . . . | 77,500 | |
| Fund balance . . . . . . . . . . . . . . . . . . | 366,078 | |
| Total Fund Equity . . . . . . . . . . . . . . . . | | 472,578 |
| Total Liabilities and Fund Equity . . . . . . . . . . . | | $678,578 |

Chapter **2**

# GENERAL FUNDS AND SPECIAL REVENUE FUNDS—BUDGETARY ACCOUNTING

The General Fund of a state or local governmental unit is the entity which accounts for all the assets and resources used for financing the general administration of the unit and the traditional services provided to the people. GASB standards require that each governmental reporting entity display only one general fund in its general purpose financial statements.

A typical governmental unit now engages in many activities which for legal and historical reasons are financed by sources other than those available to the general fund. Whenever a tax or other revenue source is authorized by a legislative body to be used for a specified purpose only, a governmental unit availing itself of that source may create a special revenue fund in order to be able to demonstrate that all revenue from that source was used for the specified purpose. A common example of a special revenue fund is one used to account for state gasoline tax receipts distributed to a local government; in many states the use of this money is restricted to the construction and maintenance of streets, highways, and bridges. Special revenue funds are commonly used, also, to account for federal and state grants, and for libraries and other activities supported by special taxes. Accounting and financial reporting standards applicable to special revenue funds are identical with those applicable to general funds.

## BUDGETS AS LEGAL DOCUMENTS

The General Fund, special revenue funds, and all other fund types classified as governmental funds, are created in accord with legal requirements. A governmental unit may raise revenues only from sources allowed by law. Laws commonly set a maximum amount that may be raised from each source, or set a maximum rate that may be applied to the base used in computation of revenue from a given source. Revenues to be raised pursuant to law during a budget period are set forth in an **Estimated Revenues** budget. Revenues are raised to finance governmental activities, but revenues may be expended only for purposes and in amounts approved by the legislative branch in compliance with laws of competent jurisdictions—this is known as the **appropriations process.** An **Appropriations** budget when enacted into law, is *the legal authorization for the administrators of the governmental unit to incur liabilities during the budget period for purposes specified in the appropriations statute or ordinance and not to exceed the amount specified for each purpose.* When a liability is incurred as authorized by an appropriation, the appropriation is said to be **expended.** At the end of the budget period unencumbered, unexpended appropriations lapse; that is, administrators no longer have the authority to incur liabilities under the lapsed appropriation. However, in most jurisdictions administrators continue to have the authority to disburse cash in payment of liabilities legally incurred in a prior period.

## BALANCE SHEET AND OPERATING STATEMENT ACCOUNTS

The General Fund, special revenue funds, and all other fund types classified as governmental funds account for only cash and those other assets which may be expected to be converted into cash in the normal operations of the governmental unit. Assets such as land, buildings, and equipment utilized in fund operations are recorded in the General Fixed Assets Account Group (GFAAG) rather than in the General Fund or in special revenue funds because they are not normally converted into cash. Similarly, a general fund or special revenue fund accounts for only those liabilities which will be liquidated by use of fund assets; liabilities to be paid in future years are accounted for in the General Long-Term Debt Account Group (GLTDAG).[1]

---

[1]The GASB's proposed *Statement on Measurement Focus and Basis of Accounting—Governmental Funds* proposes that the GLTDAG be used only to record long-term debt incurred for the acquisition of general fixed assets. Other long-term debt such as the noncurrent portion of claims and judgments payable, compensated absences, and pension obligations would be reported by the governmental funds incurring such debt. Whenever GASB standards are changed the publishers will distribute to persons who have adopted this text a bulletin detailing the effects of the new standards on explanations and illustrations in each chapter of this text.

The arithmetic difference between total fund assets and total fund liabilities is the Fund Equity. Residents of the governmental unit have no legal claim on any excess of fund assets over fund liabilities; therefore, the Fund Equity is not analogous to the capital of an investor-owned entity. In order to disclose to readers of the financial statements that a portion of the Fund Equity as of balance sheet date is, for reasons to be explained later, not available for appropriation, **reserve** accounts are established; the portion of equity which is available for appropriation is disclosed in an account called **Fund Balance.**

In addition to the Balance Sheet accounts described above, the General Fund and special revenue funds account for financial activities during a fiscal year in accounts classified as Revenues, Other Financing Sources, Expenditures, and Other Financing Uses. **Revenue** is defined as increases in fund financial resources other than from interfund transfers and debt issue proceeds. Operating transfers to a fund and debt issue proceeds received by a fund are classified as **Other Financing Sources** of the fund. Accounting standards specify that the revenues of all fund types classified as **governmental funds** (the General Fund, special revenue funds, capital projects funds, and debt service funds) be recognized on an accrual basis, formerly designated in the GASB standards as the modified accrual basis. Because the operations of governmental funds are subject to rather detailed legal restrictions governmental fund revenues should be recognized in the fiscal year in which they are available for expenditure. (In a few jurisdictions taxes must be collected in the year before the year in which they are available for expenditure. In such jurisdictions, tax collections should be credited to Deferred Revenues when cash is debited; in the following year Deferred Revenues should be debited and Revenues should be credited.)

**Expenditure** is a term which replaces both the terms **costs** and **expenses** used in accounting for profit-seeking entities. Expenditures are defined as decreases in fund financial resources other than through interfund transfers. Operating transfers out of a fund are classified as **Other Financing Uses.** Under the modified accrual basis an expenditure is recognized when a liability to be met from fund assets is incurred; thus, in this respect, it may be said that expenditures are recognized on the accrual basis. It is important to note that an appropriation is considered to be expended in the amount of a liability incurred whether the liability is for salaries (an expense), for supplies (a current asset), or for a long-lived capital asset, such as land, buildings, or equipment.

An example of the use of transfer accounts occurs in those jurisdictions where a portion of the taxes recognized as revenue by the general fund of a unit is transferred to a debt service fund which will record expenditures for payment of interest and principal of general obligation debt. The General Fund would record the amounts transferred as Operating Transfers Out; the debt service fund would record the amount received as Operating Transfers In. Thus, use of the transfer accounts achieves the desired objective that revenues be recognized in the fund which levied the taxes and expenditures be recognized in the fund which expends the revenue. Other Financing Sources accounts and Other Financing Uses accounts are closed to Fund Balance in a manner identical with the closing of Revenues and Expenditures but are disclosed separately in the Statement of Revenues, Expenditures, and Changes in Fund Balances, as shown in Illustration 2–1.

## BUDGETS AND BUDGETARY ACCOUNTS

The fact that budgets are legally binding upon administrators has led to the incorporation of budgetary accounts in the General Fund and in special revenue funds and in all other funds required by state laws to adopt a budget. GASB standards require that, in addition to the statement shown as Illustration 2–1, a Combined Statement of Revenues, Expenditures, and Changes in Fund Balances—Budget and Actual be presented as one of the five combined statements required for conformity with generally accepted accounting principles. The budgetary comparison statement, shown as Illustration 2–2, must include the General Fund, special revenue funds, and all other governmental fund types for which annual budgets have been legally adopted. In this example, it is assumed that legal budgets are required for only the General Fund and all special revenue funds. The amounts in the "Actual" column are to be reported on the basis required by law for budget preparation, even if that basis differs from the basis provided in GASB standards. For example, in some states revenues must be budgeted on the cash basis. If the "Budget" and "Actual" columns of the Combined Statement differ from GASB standards, the heading of the statement should so indicate. Budgetary practices of a government may differ from GAAP accounting practices in respects other than basis. GASB standards identify **timing, entity,** and **perspective** differences. Discussion of these differences is beyond the scope of this text; it is sufficient to emphasize that GASB standards require that the amounts shown in the "Actual" column of the Budget versus Actual statement conform in all respects with practices used to develop the amounts shown in the "Budget" column of the statement, so there is a true comparison. Standards further require that either on the face of the Budget versus Actual statement, or in the notes to the financial statements the amounts in the "Actual" column of the Budget versus Actual statement (Illustration 2–2) must be reconciled with the amounts shown in the Combined Statement of Revenues, Expenditures, and Changes in Fund Balances (Illustration 2–1) prepared in

**ILLUSTRATION 2–1**

## NAME OF GOVERNMENTAL UNIT
### Combined Statement of Revenues, Expenditures, and Changes in Fund Balances—
### All Governmental Fund Types and Expendable Trust Funds
### For the Fiscal Year Ended December 31, 19x2

| | Governmental Fund Types | | | | Fiduciary Fund Type | Totals (Memorandum Only) Year Ended | |
| | General | Special Revenue | Debt Service | Capital Projects | Expendable Trust | December 31, 19x2 | December 31, 19x1 |
|---|---|---|---|---|---|---|---|
| Revenues: | | | | | | | |
| Taxes . . . . . . . | $ 881,300 | $ 189,300 | $ 79,177 | $ — | $ — | $1,149,777 | $1,137,900 |
| Special assessments . . | — | — | 55,500 | — | — | 55,500 | 250,400 |
| Licenses and permits . . | 103,000 | — | — | — | — | 103,000 | 96,500 |
| Intergovernmental revenues . | 186,500 | 831,100 | 41,500 | 1,250,000 | — | 2,309,100 | 2,058,800 |
| Charges for services . . | 91,000 | 79,100 | — | — | — | 170,100 | 160,400 |
| Fines and forfeits . . . | 33,200 | — | — | — | — | 33,200 | 26,300 |
| Miscellaneous revenues . . | 19,500 | 71,625 | 36,235 | 3,750 | 200 | 131,310 | 111,500 |
| Total Revenues . . . | 1,314,500 | 1,171,125 | 212,412 | 1,253,750 | 200 | 3,951,987 | 3,841,800 |
| Expenditures: | | | | | | | |
| Current operating: | | | | | | | |
| General government . . | 253,610 | — | — | — | — | 253,610 | 248,200 |
| Public safety . . . . | 534,200 | 480,000 | — | — | — | 1,014,200 | 964,400 |
| Highways and streets . . | — | 502,400 | — | — | — | 502,400 | 490,600 |
| Health and welfare . . | 226,100 | — | — | — | 2,420 | 228,520 | 229,650 |
| Culture and recreation . . | 170,800 | 171,050 | — | — | — | 341,850 | 335,850 |

24

| | | | | | | | |
|---|---|---|---|---|---|---|---|
| Total Current Operating Expenditures | 1,184,710 | 1,153,450 | — | — | 2,420 | 2,340,580 | 2,268,700 |
| Capital outlay | — | — | — | 1,939,100 | — | 1,939,100 | 1,603,000 |
| Debt service: | | | | | | | |
|   Principal repaid | — | — | 115,500 | — | — | 115,500 | 52,100 |
|   Interest paid | — | — | 68,420 | — | — | 68,420 | 50,000 |
| Chargeable to prior year's appropriations: | | | | | | | |
|   Public safety | 24,000 | 33,050 | — | — | — | 57,050 | 46,000 |
| Total Expenditures | 1,208,710 | 1,186,500 | 183,920 | 1,939,100 | 2,420 | 4,520,650 | 4,019,800 |
| Excess of Revenues over (under) Expenditures | 105,790 | (15,375) | 28,492 | (685,350) | (2,220) | (568,663) | (178,000) |
| Other Financing Sources (Uses): | | | | | | | |
|   Operating transfers in (out) | (74,500) | — | — | 74,500 | 2,530 | 2,530 | 2,120 |
|   Proceeds of long-term debt | — | — | — | 1,090,500 | — | 1,090,500 | — |
| Total Other Financing Sources (Uses) | (74,500) | — | — | 1,165,000 | 2,530 | 1,093,030 | 2,120 |
| Excess of Revenues and Other Sources over (under) Expenditures and Other Uses | 31,290 | (15,375) | 28,492 | 479,650 | 310 | 524,367 | (175,880) |
| Fund Balances—January 1 | 202,500 | 151,035 | 227,788 | 605,450 | 26,555 | 1,213,328 | 1,449,208 |
| Equity Transfers In (Out) | (15,000) | — | — | — | — | (15,000) | — |
| (Increase) Decrease in Reserve for Encumbrances | (14,000) | (13,450) | — | — | — | (27,450) | (60,000) |
| Fund Balance—December 31 | $204,790 | $122,210 | $256,280 | $1,085,100 | $26,865 | $1,695,245 | $1,213,328 |

Adapted from GASB Codification Sec. 2200.604.

# ILLUSTRATION 2-2

## NAME OF GOVERNMENTAL UNIT
### Combined Statement of Revenues, Expenditures, and Changes in Fund Balances—Budget and Actual—General and Special Revenue Fund Types
#### Non-GAAP Presentation
#### For the Fiscal Year Ended December 31, 19x2

| | General Fund | | | Special Revenue Funds | | | Totals (memorandum only) | | |
|---|---|---|---|---|---|---|---|---|---|
| | Budget | Actual | Actual Over (Under) Budget | Budget | Actual | Actual Over (Under) Budget | Budget | Actual | Actual Over (Under) Budget |
| **Revenues:** | | | | | | | | | |
| Taxes | $ 882,500 | $ 881,300 | $ (1,200) | $ 189,500 | $ 189,300 | $ (200) | $1,072,000 | $1,070,600 | $ (1,400) |
| Licenses and permits | 125,500 | 103,000 | (22,500) | — | — | — | 125,500 | 103,000 | (22,500) |
| Intergovernmental revenues | 200,000 | 186,500 | (13,500) | 837,600 | 831,100 | (6,500) | 1,037,600 | 1,017,600 | (20,000) |
| Charges for services | 90,000 | 91,000 | 1,000 | 78,000 | 79,100 | 1,100 | 168,000 | 170,100 | 2,100 |
| Fines and forfeits | 32,500 | 33,200 | 700 | — | — | — | 32,500 | 33,200 | 700 |
| Miscellaneous revenues | 19,500 | 19,500 | — | 81,475 | 71,625 | (9,850) | 100,975 | 91,125 | (9,850) |
| Total Revenues | 1,350,000 | 1,314,500 | (35,500) | 1,186,575 | 1,171,125 | (15,450) | 2,536,575 | 2,485,625 | (50,950) |
| **Expenditures and Encumbrances:** | | | | | | | | | |
| General government | 258,000 | 257,610 | (390) | — | — | — | 258,000 | 257,610 | (390) |
| Public safety | 554,600 | 554,200 | (400) | 494,500 | 494,000 | (500) | 1,049,100 | 1,048,200 | (900) |
| Highways and streets | — | — | — | 520,500 | 520,400 | (100) | 520,500 | 520,400 | (100) |
| Health and welfare | 228,400 | 227,600 | (800) | — | — | — | 228,400 | 227,600 | (800) |
| Culture and recreation | 184,500 | 183,300 | (1,200) | 187,500 | 185,550 | (1,950) | 372,000 | 368,850 | (3,150) |
| Total Expenditures and Encumbrances | 1,225,500 | 1,222,710 | (2,790) | 1,202,500 | 1,199,950 | (2,550) | 2,428,000 | 2,422,660 | (5,340) |
| Excess of Revenues over Expenditures and Encumbrances | 124,500 | 91,790 | (32,710) | (15,925) | (28,825) | (12,900) | 108,575 | 62,965 | (45,610) |
| | (74,500) | (74,500) | — | — | — | — | (74,500) | (74,500) | — |
| Excess of Revenues over Expenditures, Encumbrances, and Other Uses | 50,000 | 17,290 | (32,710) | (15,925) | (28,825) | (12,900) | 34,075 | (11,535) | (45,610) |
| Fund Balances—January 1 | 202,500 | 202,500 | — | 151,035 | 151,035 | — | 353,535 | 353,535 | — |
| Equity Transfers In (Out) | (15,000) | (15,000) | — | — | — | — | (15,000) | (15,000) | — |
| Fund Balances—December 31 | $ 237,500 | $ 204,790 | $(32,710) | $ 135,110 | $ 122,210 | $(12,900) | $ 372,610 | $ 327,000 | $(45,610) |

Adapted from GASB Codification Sec. 2200.605.

conformity with GAAP. Reconciliation of the amounts shown in the two statements is discussed and illustrated in a later section of this chapter.

In order to facilitate preparation of budgets and preparation of the Combined Statement of Revenues, Expenditures, and Changes in Fund Balances—Budget and Actual required for GAAP conformity, accounting systems of funds for which budgets are required by law should incorporate **budgetary accounts.** Only three general ledger control accounts are needed to provide appropriate budgetary control: **Estimated Revenues, Appropriations,** and **Encumbrances.** Budgeted interfund transfers and debt proceeds may be recorded in **Estimated Other Financing Sources** and **Estimated Other Financing Uses** control accounts supported by subsidiary accounts as needed.

At the beginning of the budget period, the Estimated Revenues control account is debited for the total amount of revenues expected to be recognized, as provided in the Revenues budget. The amount of revenue expected from each source specified in the Revenues budget is recorded in a subsidiary ledger account, so that the total of subsidiary ledger detail agrees with the debit to the control account, and both agree with the adopted budget. If a separate entry is to be made to record the Revenues budget, the general ledger debit to the Estimated Revenues control account is offset by a credit to Fund Balance. Recall that the Fund Balance account, before the budget is recorded, would normally have a credit balance representing the excess of fund assets over the total of liabilities and reserved Fund Equity. (If fund liabilities and reserved Fund Equity exceed fund assets, the Fund Balance account would have a debit balance—referred to as a **deficit.**) After the Revenues budget is recorded, Fund Balance represents the excess of fund assets *plus* the estimated revenues for the budget period over liabilities and reserves. The credit balance of the Fund Balance account, therefore, is the total amount available to finance appropriations. Consequently, the accounting entry to record the legally approved appropriations budget is a debit to Fund Balance and a credit to Appropriations for the total amount appropriated for the activities accounted for by the fund. The Appropriations control account is supported by a subsidiary ledger kept in the same detail as provided in the appropriations ordinance, so that the total of the subsidiary ledger detail agrees with the credit to the Appropriations control account, and both agree with the adopted budget. The use of the Encumbrances account is explained in a following section of this chapter.

## RECORDING THE BUDGET

In order to illustrate entries in journal form to record a budget, assume that the amounts in the first money column of Illustration 2–2 are the amounts which have been legally approved as the budget for the

General Fund of a certain governmental unit for the fiscal year ending December 31, 19x2. As of January 1, 19x2, the first day of the fiscal year, the total Estimated Revenues should be recorded in the General Fund general ledger accounts, and the amounts which are expected to be recognized during 19x2 from each revenue source specified in the budget should be recorded in the subsidiary ledger accounts. If the budget provided for other financing sources such as operating transfers in, Entry 1 would indicate a debit to Estimated Other Financing Sources. An appropriate entry would be:

|  | General Ledger | | Subsidiary Ledger | |
|---|---|---|---|---|
|  | Debits | Credits | Debits | Credits |
| 1. Estimated Revenues . . . . . . . | 1,350,000 |  |  |  |
|    Fund Balance . . . . . . . . . |  | 1,350,000 |  |  |
|  |  |  |  |  |
| *Revenues ledger:* |  |  |  |  |
| Taxes  . . . . . . . . . . . . . |  |  | 882,500 |  |
| Licenses and Permits   . . . . . . |  |  | 125,500 |  |
| Intergovernmental Revenues  . . . |  |  | 200,000 |  |
| Charges for Services . . . . . . . |  |  | 90,000 |  |
| Fines and Forfeits . . . . . . . . |  |  | 32,500 |  |
| Miscellaneous Revenues . . . . . |  |  | 19,500 |  |

The total Appropriations legally approved for 19x2 for the General Fund of the same governmental unit should also be recorded in the General Fund general ledger accounts, and the amounts which are appropriated for each function itemized in the budget should be recorded in subsidiary ledger accounts. An appropriate entry would be:

|  | General Ledger | | Subsidiary Ledger | |
|---|---|---|---|---|
|  | Debits | Credits | Debits | Credits |
| 2. Fund Balance . . . . . . . . . | 1,300,000 |  |  |  |
|    Appropriations   . . . . . . . |  | 1,225,500 |  |  |
|    Estimated Other Financing |  |  |  |  |
|      Uses . . . . . . . . . . . . |  | 74,500 |  |  |
|  |  |  |  |  |
| *Appropriations ledger:* |  |  |  |  |
| General Government   . . . . . |  |  |  | 258,000 |
| Public Safety . . . . . . . . . |  |  |  | 554,600 |
| Health and Welfare . . . . . . |  |  |  | 228,400 |
| Culture and Recreation  . . . . |  |  |  | 184,500 |
|  |  |  |  |  |
| *Other Financing Uses ledger:* |  |  |  |  |
| Operating Transfers Out  . . . . |  |  |  | 74,500 |

It would, of course, be acceptable to combine the two entries illustrated above and make one General Fund entry to record Estimated Revenues and Appropriations; in this case there would be a credit to

Fund Balance for $50,000 (the amount by which Estimated Revenues exceed Appropriations and Estimated Other Financing Uses).

## ACCOUNTING FOR REVENUES

During a fiscal year, actual revenues should be recognized in the general ledger accounts of governmental funds by credits to the Revenues account (offset by debits to receivable accounts for those classes of revenues susceptible to accrual or by debits to Cash for the classes of revenues which are recognized on the cash basis). The general ledger Revenues account is a control account which is supported by Revenues subsidiary ledger accounts kept in exactly the same detail as kept for the Estimated Revenues subsidiary ledger accounts. For example, assume that the General Fund of the governmental unit for which budgetary entries are illustrated in the preceding section collected revenues in cash during the month of January from the following sources in the following amounts: Licenses and Permits, $13,200; Intergovernmental Revenues, $50,000; Charges for Services, $7,800; Fines and Forfeits, $2,600; and Miscellaneous Revenues, $1,500. The following entry illustrates the effect on the General Fund accounts of collections during the month of January:

|  | General Ledger | | Subsidiary Ledger | |
| --- | --- | --- | --- | --- |
|  | Debits | Credits | Debits | Credits |
| 3. Cash . . . . . . . . . . . . . . | 75,100 | | | |
| Revenues . . . . . . . . . . . | | 75,100 | | |
| | | | | |
| *Revenues ledger:* | | | | |
| Licenses and Permits . . . . . | | | | 13,200 |
| Intergovernmental Revenues . . | | | | 50,000 |
| Charges for Services . . . . . . | | | | 7,800 |
| Fines and Forfeits . . . . . . . | | | | 2,600 |
| Miscellaneous Revenues . . . . | | | | 1,500 |

Comparability between Estimated Revenues subsidiary accounts and Revenues subsidiary accounts is necessary so that periodically throughout the fiscal year actual revenues from each source can be compared with estimated revenues from that source. Illustration 2–3 shows a form of Revenues subsidiary ledger in which the debit column is subsidiary to the Estimated Revenues general ledger control account and the credit column is subsidiary to the Revenues general ledger control account. Normally, during a fiscal year the amount of revenue budgeted from each source will exceed the amount of revenue from that source realized to date, consequently the Balance column will have a debit balance and

**ILLUSTRATION 2–3**

Revenues Ledger
NAME OF GOVERNMENTAL UNIT
General Fund

Class: Licenses and Permits                                    Number: 351.1
Subclass:                                                      Title:

| Date | Item | Reference | Estimated Revenues DR. | Revenues CR. | Balance DR. (CR.) |
|------|------|-----------|------------------------|--------------|-------------------|
| 19x2 | | | | | |
| January   1 | Budget estimate | J 1 | $125,500 | | $125,500 |
| 31 | Collections | CR 6 | | $13,200 | 112,300 |

may be headed "Estimated Revenues Not Yet Realized." This amount
is a **resource** of the governmental unit—legally and realistically budgeted
revenues which will be recognized as assets before the end of the
fiscal year.

## ACCOUNTING FOR ENCUMBRANCES AND EXPENDITURES

An appropriation, when enacted into law, is an authorization for ad-
ministrations to incur on behalf of the governmental unit liabilities in
the amounts specified in the appropriation ordinance or statute, for the
purposes set forth in that ordinance or statute, during the period of time
specified. An appropriation is considered to be **expended** when the authorized liabilities have been incurred. Because penalties are imposed
by law on an administrator who incurs liabilities for any amount in excess of that appropriated, or for any purpose not covered by an appropriation, or who incurs liabilities after the authority to do so has
expired, prudence dictates that each purchase order and each contract
be reviewed before it is signed to determine that a valid and sufficient
appropriation exists to which the expenditure can be charged when
goods or services are received. Purchase orders and contracts will result
in liabilities when the purchase orders are filled and the contracts exe-
cuted. Such expected liabilities are called **encumbrances.** In order to
keep track of purchase orders and contracts outstanding it is recommended that the Encumbrance control account (and the subsidiary account for the specific appropriation encumbered) be debited, and the
Reserve for Encumbrances account credited, for the amount of each
purchase order or contract issued. When goods or services are received,
two entries are necessary: (1) Reserve for Encumbrances is debited and

Encumbrances (and the proper subsidiary account) is credited for the amount entered in these accounts when the encumbrance documents were issued; and (2) Expenditures (and the proper subsidiary account) is debited and a liability account is credited for the amount to be paid to the creditor. In order to accomplish the necessary matching of Appropriations, Encumbrances, and Expenditures it is necessary that subsidiary ledger classifications of all three correspond exactly. Note that no subsidiary accounts need be kept for Reserve for Encumbrances because the Reserve account is reported in total as a reservation of Fund Equity. At year-end, budgetary authority expires, therefore the balances of the Appropriations, Expenditures, and Encumbrances accounts are closed to Fund Balance. In many jurisdictions, however, the government continues to have authority to receive and pay for in subsequent years goods and services ordered under purchase orders and contracts outstanding at year-end.

The following entries illustrate accounting for Encumbrances and Expenditures for the General Fund of the governmental unit for which entries are illustrated in previous sections of this chapter. Entry 4 is made on the assumption that early in January purchase orders are issued pursuant to the authority contained in the General Fund appropriations; assumed amounts chargeable to each function for which purchase orders are issued on this date are shown in the debits to the Encumbrances subsidiary accounts.

|  | General Ledger | | Subsidiary Ledger | |
| --- | --- | --- | --- | --- |
|  | Debits | Credits | Debits | Credits |
| 4. Encumbrances—19x2 . . . . . . | 29,600 | | | |
| Reserve for Encumbrances—19x2 | | 29,600 | | |
| | | | | |
| *Encumbrances ledger:* | | | | |
| General Government . . . . . . | | | 4,000 | |
| Public Safety . . . . . . . . . . | | | 9,300 | |
| Health and Welfare . . . . . . . | | | 3,700 | |
| Culture and Recreation . . . . . | | | 12,600 | |

Entries 5a and 5b illustrate entries required to record the receipt of some of the items for which purchase orders were recorded in Entry 4. Note that Entry 4 is made for the amounts estimated at the time purchase orders or other commitment documents are issued. When the purchase orders are filled, the actual amount approved by the governmental unit for payment to the supplier often differs from the estimated amount recorded in the Encumbrances account (and subsidiary ledger accounts) because the quantity of goods actually received differs from the quantity ordered, prices of items have changed, and so on. Since the Encumbrances account was debited in Entry 4 for the estimated amount, the Encumbrances account must be credited for the same estimate to the extent that purchase orders are filled (or canceled). The balance remaining in Encumbrances, therefore, is the estimated dollar amount of purchase orders outstanding. Entry 5a shows the entry necessary on the assumption that certain purchase orders recorded in Entry 4 have now been filled. Expenditures, however, should be recorded at the actual amount the governmental unit agrees to pay the vendors who have filled the purchase orders. Entry 5b shows the entry necessary to record the liability for invoices approved for payment. The fact that estimated and actual amounts differ causes no accounting difficulties as long as goods or services are received in the same fiscal period as ordered. The accounting treatment required when encumbrances outstanding at year-end are filled, or canceled, in a following year is illustrated in Chapter 3.

|  | General Ledger | | Subsidiary Ledger | |
| --- | --- | --- | --- | --- |
|  | Debits | Credits | Debits | Credits |
| 5a. Reserve for Encumbrances—19x2 | 26,000 |  |  |  |
| Encumbrances—19x2 . . . . . |  | 26,000 |  |  |
|  |  |  |  |  |
| Encumbrances ledger: |  |  |  |  |
| General Government . . . . . |  |  |  | 3,000 |
| Public Safety . . . . . . . |  |  |  | 9,300 |
| Health and Welfare . . . . . . |  |  |  | 3,700 |
| Culture and Recreation . . . . |  |  |  | 10,000 |

|  | General Ledger | | Subsidiary Ledger | |
| --- | --- | --- | --- | --- |
|  | Debits | Credits | Debits | Credits |
| 5b. Expenditures—19x2 . . . . . . | 26,400 |  |  |  |
| Vouchers Payable . . . . . . |  | 26,400 |  |  |
|  |  |  |  |  |
| Expenditures ledger: |  |  |  |  |
| General Government . . . . . . |  |  | 3,100 |  |
| Public Safety . . . . . . . . |  |  | 9,380 |  |
| Health and Welfare . . . . . . . |  |  | 3,720 |  |
| Culture and Recreation . . . . . |  |  | 10,200 |  |

The encumbrance procedure is not always needed to make sure that appropriations are not overexpended. For example, although salaries and wages of governmental employees must be chargeable against valid and sufficient appropriations in order to give rise to legal expenditures, many governmental units do not find it necessary to encumber the departmental personal services appropriations for estimated payrolls of recurring, relatively constant amounts. Departments having payrolls that fluctuate greatly from one season to another may follow the encumbrance procedure to make sure that the personal service appropriation is not overexpended. Entry 6 shows the recording of expenditures of appropriations for salaries and wages not previously encumbered, assuming that gross pay is vouchered.

|  | | General Ledger | | Subsidiary Ledger | |
|---|---|---|---|---|---|
|  | | Debits | Credits | Debits | Credits |
| 6. | Expenditures—19x2 . . . . . . . | 75,300 | | | |
|  | Vouchers Payable . . . . . . . | | 75,300 | | |
|  | | | | | |
|  | *Expenditures ledger:* | | | | |
|  | General Government . . . . . . | | | 14,000 | |
|  | Public Safety . . . . . . . . . | | | 32,000 | |
|  | Health and Welfare . . . . . . | | | 15,300 | |
|  | Culture and Recreation . . . . | | | 14,000 | |

Illustration 2–4 shows a form of subsidiary ledger which supports all three general ledger control accounts: Appropriations, Expenditures, and Encumbrances.

**ILLUSTRATION 2–4**

### NAME OF GOVERNMENT UNIT
**Appropriations, Expenditures, and Encumbrances Ledger**

Code No.: 0607–03
Fund: General

Year: 19x2

Function: General Government

| Month and Day | Reference | Encumbrances | | | Expenditures | | Appropriations | |
|---|---|---|---|---|---|---|---|---|
|  |  | Debit | Credit | Open | Debit | Cumulative Total | Credit | Available Balance |
| Jan. 2 | Budget (Entry 2) | | | | | | $258,000 | $258,000 |
| 3 | Purchase orders issued (Entry 4) | $4,000 | | $4,000 | | | | 254,000 |
| 17 | Invoices approved for payment (Entries 5a, 5b) | | $3,000 | 1,000 | $ 3,100 | $ 3,100 | | 253,900 |
| 31 | Payrolls (Entry 6) | | | | 14,000 | 17,100 | | 239,900 |

### Reconciliation of Amounts Reported in Illustration 2–1 with Amounts Reported in Illustration 2–2

As noted in a previous section of this chapter, GASB standards require that differences between amounts reported in the GAAP basis operating statement (Illustration 2–1) and those reported in conformity with budgetary practices (Illustration 2–2) be reconciled either on the face of the statements or in the notes to the financial statements. Readers will note that the amounts in the Revenues section of the Actual column of Illustration 2–2 are the same as the Revenues reported in

Illustration 2–2 because in this example the budget for revenues is prepared on the same basis as is used in the accounts. The amounts in the Expenditures section of the Actual column of Illustration 2–2 differ from the Expenditures reported in Illustration 2–1, however, because the latter, in conformity with GASB standards, reports Expenditures chargeable to the prior year's appropriations as well as Expenditures chargeable to 19x2 appropriations and does not report Encumbrances as Expenditures. In contrast, Encumbrances outstanding at the end of fiscal year 19x2 are added to 19x2 Expenditures in Illustration 2–2 because both are uses of the 19x2 appropriation authority (reported in the Budget column). Expenditures chargeable to the prior year's appropriation are excluded from Illustration 2–2 because it relates only to the 19x2 Budget and Actual. Consequently, the notes to the financial statements should include a reconciliation of the General Fund and Special Revenue Funds Expenditures reported in the two statements illustrated. One form of reconciliation appears below (the year-end Reserve for Encumbrances in each fund is taken from the illustrative combined balance sheet in the GASB Codification Sec. 2200.603):

|  | General Fund | Special Revenue Funds |
|---|---|---|
| Expenditures of 19x2 appropriations, budgetary basis (Illustration 2–2) . . . . . . . . . . | $1,222,710 | $1,199,950 |
| Less: Reserve for Encumbrances, December 31, 19x2  . . . . . . . . . . . . . | 38,000 | 46,500 |
| Expenditures for 19x2, GAAP basis (Illustration 2–1) . . . . . . . . . . . . . . . . | $1,184,710 | $1,153,450 |

A second form of reconciliation sometimes found in practice is:

|  | General Fund | Special Revenue Funds |
|---|---|---|
| Excess of revenues over (under) expenditures and other uses, budgetary basis (Illustration 2–2) . . . . . . . . . | $17,290 | $(28,825) |
| Increase in Reserve for Encumbrances (Illustration 2–1) . . . . . . . . . . . . . . | 14,000 | 13,450 |
| Excess of revenues over (under) expenditures and other uses, GAAP basis (Illustration 2–1)  . . . . . . . . . . | $31,290 | $(15,375) |

## CLASSIFICATION OF ESTIMATED REVENUES AND REVENUES

In order for administrators to determine that proposed expenditures can be financed by resources available to the budgeting jurisdiction, a revenue budget should be prepared. The budget should include all sources, including interfund transfers and bond issue proceeds as well as taxes, licenses and permits, fees, forfeits, and other revenue sources. It should be emphasized that a governmental unit may raise revenues only from sources which are available to it by law.

The primary classification of governmental revenue is by **fund.** Within each fund the major classification is by **source.** Within each major source class it is desirable to have as many secondary classes as are needed to facilitate revenue budgeting and accounting. Major revenue source classes commonly used are those used in Entry 1 of this chapter:

| | |
|---|---|
| Taxes | Charges for services |
| Licenses and permits | Fines and forfeits |
| Intergovernmental revenues | Miscellaneous revenues |

In addition to the revenue source classes listed above, Illustration 2–1 shows that an additional revenue source, special assessments, is utilized in this example by the Debt Service Fund type. In some jurisdictions services normally financed by the General Fund, or by a special revenue fund, may be extended to property owners outside the normal service area of the government, or may be provided at a higher level or at more frequent intervals than for the general public to property owners who pay additional fees ("special assessments"). In such cases the Special Assessments revenue source class would be utilized by the General Fund or by a special revenue fund, as appropriate.

In order to determine during a fiscal year that revenues are being realized from each budgeted source in amounts consistent with the budget, actual revenues should be accounted for on the same classification system as used in the Estimated Revenues budget. The control account "Estimated Revenues" may include interfund transfers and bond issue proceeds, or a separate control account such as "Estimated Other Financing Sources" may be used as illustrated in this book.

## AD VALOREM TAXES

Ad valorem (based on value) property taxes are a major source of revenue for many local units of government. Property taxes may be levied against real or personal property. "When a property tax levy is made it is to finance the budget of a particular period. Property (or ad valorem) tax revenues should be recognized in the period **for which** they are levied, regardless of when cash is received. Property taxes received before the period for which levied should be reported as deferred revenues."[2]

The amount of a property tax levy depends on two factors: (1) the assessed valuation of the property being taxed, and (2) the tax rate. The

---

[2] Proposed Statement of the Governmental Accounting Standards Board, *Measurement Focus and Basis of Accounting—Governmental Funds,* par. 51.

valuation of each parcel of taxable real property, and of the taxable property owned by each taxpayer, is assigned by a legal process known as **property assessment.** The assessment process differs state by state, and, in some states, by jurisdictions within the state. The tax rate is set by one of two widely different procedures: (1) the governmental body simply multiplies the assessed valuation of property in its jurisdiction by a flat rate—either the maximum rate allowable under state law or a rate determined by policy—or (2) the property tax is treated as a residual source of revenue. In the latter event, revenues to be recognized from all sources other than property taxes must be budgeted; the total of those sources must be compared with the total appropriations in order to determine the amount to be raised from property taxes. Illustration 2–5 shows the computation of the total amount of revenues to be raised from property taxes under the assumption that property taxes are a residual source of revenues.

The computation of the amount of revenue to be raised from property taxes is one step in determining the tax levy for the year. A second step is the determination from historical data and economic forecasts of the percentage of the tax levy which is expected to be collectible. (Even though property taxes are a lien against the property, personal property may be removed from the taxing jurisdiction and some parcels of real property may not be salable for enough for the taxing jurisdiction to recover accumulated taxes against the property.) Therefore, the levy must be large enough to allow for estimated uncollectible taxes. For example, assume that the City of Janesville can reasonably expect to collect only 97 percent of the 19x7 levy. Thus if tax revenue is to be

**ILLUSTRATION 2–5**

**CITY OF JANESVILLE**
**Statement of Amount to Be Raised by Property Taxes for 19x7**
**July 31, 19x6**

| | | |
|---|---:|---:|
| Requirements: | | |
| Estimated expenditures, August 1–December 31, 19x6 | | $ 3,500,000 |
| Proposed appropriations for 19x7 | | 8,000,000 |
| Estimated working balance required for beginning of 19x8 | | 600,000 |
| Estimated total requirements | | $12,100,000 |
| Resources other than tax levy for 19x7: | | |
| Actual balance, July 31, 19x6 | $ 750,000 | |
| Amount to be received from second installment of 19x6 taxes | 2,000,000 | |
| Miscellaneous receipts expected during balance of 19x6 | 1,600,000 | |
| Revenue expected from sources other than property taxes during 19x7 | 4,300,000 | |
| Estimated total resources other than property tax levy | | 8,650,000 |
| Amount required from property taxes in 19x7 | | $ 3,450,000 |

$3,450,000 (per Illustration 2–5) the gross levy must be $3,450,000 ÷ .97 or $3,556,701.

When the gross levy is known the tax rate may be computed on the basis of the assessed valuation of taxable property lying within the taxing jurisdiction. The term **taxable property** is used in the preceding sentence in recognition of the fact that property owned by governmental units, and property used by religious and charitable organizations, is often not taxable by the local government. Additionally, senior citizens, war veterans, and others may have statutory exemption from taxation for a limited portion of the assessed valuation of property. Continuing the City of Janesville example, assume that the net assessed valuation of property taxable by that city is $205,500,000. In that case the gross property tax levy ($3,556,701) is divided by the net assessed valuation ($205,500,000) to determine the property tax rate. The rate would be expressed as "$1.73 per $100 assessed valuation," or "$17.31 per $1,000 assessed valuation"—rounding up the actual decimal fraction (.017307) to two places to the right of the decimal, as is customary.

## CLASSIFICATION OF APPROPRIATIONS AND EXPENDITURES

Recall that an appropriation, when enacted into law, is an authorization to incur on behalf of the governmental unit liabilities for goods, services, and facilities to be used for purposes specified in the appropriation ordinance, or statute, in amounts not in excess of those specified for each purpose. When liabilities authorized by an appropriation have been incurred, the appropriation is said to be expended. Classification by fund is, of course, essential. Within each fund one or more of the following classification schemes are used to meet the needs of financial statement users: (1) function or program, (2) organization unit, (3) activity, (4) character, and (5) object. Common terminology and classifications should be used consistently throughout the budget, the accounts, and the financial reports of each fund.

Examples of classifications by **function** shown in Illustration 2–2 are general government, public safety, highways and streets, and so on. While most governmental units would report by function, others report by **program,** such as protection of persons and property and environmental protection. Programs are often performed by more than one department; consequently, program expenditures often cross departmental lines. Examples of classification by **department,** which is useful for budgetary control, are the Mayor's Office, the Police Department, and so on. **Activities** are specific and distinguishable lines of work performed by organizational units. Examples of activities would be solid waste collection and solid waste disposal, both in the Public Works Department. Classification by **character** deals with the time period involved and

includes current expenditures, capital outlays, and debt service. Classification by **object** reports the inputs, or the item or service received,
such as personal services, supplies, other services and charges, capital
outlays, and debt service. Generally, more detailed object classes are
used for each of the major categories.

## INTERFUND TRANSACTIONS, TRANSFERS, AND PROCEEDS OF DEBT ISSUES

**Quasi-external transactions**   Interfund transactions which would result
in the recognition of revenues, expenditures, or expenses if the transactions involved organizations external to the governmental unit should be
accounted for as revenues, expenditures, or expenses of the funds involved. For example, it is common for enterprise funds to remit to the
General Fund a payment in lieu of taxes. If the enterprise had been
investor owned it would have paid taxes to the General Fund. Since
taxes are an item of General Fund revenue, the payment in lieu of taxes
is also considered to be General Fund revenue even though from the
viewpoint of the governmental unit as a whole there is no increase in
net assets because the enterprise fund records an expense equal in
amount to the General Fund revenue.

Internal service fund billings to other funds, routine employer contributions from a General Fund to an employees' retirement fund, and routine service charges for services provided by a department financed by
one fund to a department financed by another fund are additional examples of "quasi-external" interfund transactions that properly result in
the recognition of fund revenue, expenditures, or expenses, even though
from the viewpoint of the governmental unit as a whole there is no net
effect.

**Reimbursements**   In certain instances, one fund may record as an expenditure an item that should have been recorded as an expenditure by
another fund. When the second fund reimburses the first fund, the first
fund should recognize the reimbursement as a reduction of its Expenditures account, not as an item of revenue.

**Operating transfers**   In essence, all routine, recurring transfers of resources from one fund to another are operating transfers. For example,
state laws may require that taxes be levied by a General Fund or a special revenue fund to finance an expenditure to be made from another
fund (such as a debt service fund). Since the general rule is that revenues should be recorded as such only once, the transfer of tax revenue
to the expending fund is recorded by the transferor as "Operating Transfers Out" and by the transferee as "Operating Transfers In." In Illustra-

tions 2–1 and 2–2 operating transfers are reported in the "Other Financing Sources (Uses)" section of the statement. An alternative presentation is illustrated in Chapter 4 (see Illustration 4–3).

**Equity transfers**  In contrast with operating transfers which are recurring and routine, governments may create a new fund by transfer of assets from an existing fund, or may transfer residual balances from an inactive fund to another fund of the same type (or to whatever fund the law allows). In either case the transfer is a transfer of equity, and does not result in the recognition of Revenues or an "Other Financing Source" by the receiving fund, nor an Expenditure or an "Other Financing Use" by the fund giving up the assets. Consequently, equity transfers should be reported in the "Changes in Fund Balances" section of the Statement of Revenues, Expenditures, and Changes in Fund Balances.

**Proceeds of debt issues; capital leases**  General Funds, special revenue funds, capital projects funds, and debt service funds report only liabilities to be paid from fund assets.[3] General obligation debt which is not reportable as a liability of these four fund types is reported in the General Long-Term Debt Account Group. Accordingly, when a fund in any of these four fund types receives the proceeds of noncurrent debt it has an increase in assets not offset by an increase in liabilities, therefore the Fund Equity is increased. Increases in Fund Equity arising from the receipt of proceeds of noncurrent debt is considered as an "Other Financing Source" and reported under that caption in the Statement of Revenues, Expenditures, and Changes in Fund Balances for the fund. Debt issue proceeds are reported in this manner, rather than as revenue because the debt is a liability of the governmental unit even though not a liability of the fund.

General fixed assets acquired under capital lease agreements are reported in the General Fixed Assets Account Group; the offsetting liability under the lease is reported in the General Long-Term Debt Account Group. Additionally, acquisition of a general fixed asset under a capital lease should be reflected as an expenditure and as an "Other Financing Source" of a governmental fund, just as if the general fixed asset had been constructed or acquired from debt issue proceeds.

## SELECTED REFERENCES

American Institute of Certified Public Accountants. *Audits of State and Local Governmental Units.* Rev. ed. New York, 1986.

Governmental Accounting Standards Board. *Codification of Governmental Accounting and Financial Reporting Standards.* 2nd ed. Norwalk, Conn., 1987.

---

[3]See footnote 1.

## QUESTIONS AND EXERCISES

**2–1.**   Using the annual financial report obtained for Exercise 1–1, answer the following questions.

   *a.* Look at the Statement of Revenues, Expenditures, and Changes in Fund Balances—All Governmental Fund Types and Expendable Trust Funds. List the revenue source classes. Do they agree with those discussed in this chapter? List the functional classifications for expenditures. Do they agree with those discussed in the chapter? Are expenditures reported by character? Are Other Financing Sources (Uses) reported separately from Revenues and Expenditures?

   *b.* Look at the Statement of Revenues, Expenditures, and Changes in Fund Balances—Budget and Actual—General and Special Revenue Fund Types. Which funds are included? (In addition to the general and special revenue funds, other governmental funds which adopt annual budgets should be included.) Do revenues exceed estimates in all cases? List exceptions. Are expenditures less than appropriations in all cases? List exceptions.

   *c.* Look at the note that describes the basis of budgeting (usually in the "Summary of Significant Accounting Policies"). Is the budget prepared on the modified accrual basis, or is another basis used? If another basis, is a reconciliation prepared either in the notes or in the Statement of Revenues, Expenditures, and Changes in Fund Balances—Budget and Actual?

   *d.* Look at the Combining Statements for the Special Revenue Funds. List the names of the funds. Does the divider page preceding the statements describe the nature and purpose of each fund? Do any of the funds have negative fund balances? Did any of the funds have an excess of expenditures over revenues during the fiscal year? Did any of the funds have expenditures and encumbrances in excess of appropriations for the fiscal year?

   *e.* Are individual reports presented for the general and/or special revenue funds? If so, are revenues and expenditures reported in greater detail than in the combined statements? Are comparisons of total revenues and expenditures reported with the preceding fiscal year? Are expenditures reported by object classification? By any other means?

**2–2.**   Write the numbers 1 through 10 on a sheet of paper. Beside each number write the letter corresponding to the best answer to each of the following questions:

   1. The estimated revenues control account of a governmental unit is debited when
      *a.* The budget is closed at the end of the year.
      *b.* The budget is recorded.
      *c.* Actual revenues are recorded.
      *d.* Actual revenues are collected.

   2. The revenues control account of a governmental unit is increased when
      *a.* The budget is recorded.
      *b.* Property taxes are recorded.
      *c.* Appropriations are recorded.
      *d.* The budgetary accounts are closed.

   3. The fund balance reserved for encumbrances account of a governmental unit is decreased when

a. Supplies previously ordered are received.
b. A purchase order is approved.
c. The vouchers are paid.
d. Appropriations are recorded.

4. Which of the following accounts of a governmental unit is debited when a purchase order is approved?
a. Appropriations control.
b. Vouchers payable.
c. Fund balance reserved for encumbrances.
d. Encumbrances control.

5. The following proceeds were received by Kew City from specific revenue sources that are legally restricted to expenditure for specified purposes:

Gasoline taxes to finance road repairs . . . . . . . . . . . . . . . . $400,000
Special fees charged to property owners who desire a higher
   level of service from the Sanitation Department than is
   routinely provided . . . . . . . . . . . . . . . . . . . . . . . . 300,000

The amount that should be accounted for in Kew's special revenue funds is
a. $0.
b. $300,000.
c. $400,000.
d. $700,000.

6. The following balances are included in the subsidiary records of Burwood Village's Parks and Recreation Department at March 31, 19x2:

Appropriations—supplies . . . . . . . . . . . . . . . . . . . . . . . $7,500
Expenditures—supplies . . . . . . . . . . . . . . . . . . . . . . . . 4,500
Encumbrances—supply orders . . . . . . . . . . . . . . . . . . . . 750

How much does the Department have available for additional purchases of supplies?
a. $0.
b. $2,250.
c. $3,000.
d. $6,750.

7. Which of the following funds of a governmental unit integrates budgetary accounts into the accounting system?
a. Enterprise.
b. Special revenue.
c. Internal service.
d. Nonexpendable trust.

8. Kingsford City incurred $100,000 of salaries and wages for the month ended March 31, 19x2. How should this be recorded at that date?

|  | Dr. | Cr. |
|---|---|---|
| a. Expenditures—Salaries and Wages . . . . . . . . . . | 100,000 | |
|    Vouchers Payable . . . . . . . . . . . . . . . . . | | 100,000 |
| b. Salaries and Wages Expense . . . . . . . . . . . . | 100,000 | |
|    Vouchers Payable . . . . . . . . . . . . . . . . . | | 100,000 |

|                                                    | Dr.     | Cr.     |
|----------------------------------------------------|---------|---------|
| c. Encumbrances—Salaries and Wages .........        | 100,000 |         |
|     Vouchers Payable .................              |         | 100,000 |
| d. Fund Balance .....................               | 100,000 |         |
|     Vouchers Payable .................              |         | 100,000 |

9. What type of account is used to earmark the fund balance in the amount of contingent obligations of goods ordered but not yet received?
   a. Appropriations.
   b. Encumbrances.
   c. Obligations.
   d. Reserve for encumbrances.
10. Property tax revenue should be recognized in the period:
   a. For which the taxes are levied.
   b. In which the tax bills are mailed.
   c. In which the assessed valuation of the property is determined.
   d. In which the taxes are collected.

(Items 1 through 9, AICPA, adapted)

2–3.    Explain in your own words the meaning of each of the following governmental accounting terms. Your explanation of each term should be brief but complete.
   a. Appropriations.
   b. Encumbrances.
   c. Equity Transfers.
   d. Estimated Revenues.
   e. Expenditures.
   f. Fund Balance.
   g. Operating Transfers.
   h. Other Financing Sources (Uses).
   i. Reserve for Encumbrances.
   j. Revenues.

2–4.    Indicate for each of the following whether the transaction should be recorded as an increase or decrease in one of the following General Fund accounts: Revenues, Expenditures, Encumbrances, Operating Transfers In, Operating Transfers Out, Equity Transfers In, or Equity Transfers Out. If a transaction affects none of the accounts listed, state how the transaction should be reported.
   a. Issuance of a purchase order in the amount of $10,000 for supplies.
   b. The receipt of the supplies issued in (a) and recognition of the liability in the amount of $10,200.
   c. Payment, at a later date, for the supplies mentioned in (a) and (b).
   d. A nonrecurring transfer of $500,000 cash to establish a Motor Pool (internal service) Fund.
   e. A transfer of $100,000 cash to a debt service fund for the payment of principal and interest on general obligation long-term debt. A transfer of this nature is made annually.
   f. Payment of $50,000 to the Water Utility Fund for water supplied during the year to departments accounted for by the General Fund.
   g. Payment of $30,000 to the Motor Pool Fund for use of vehicles during the year by departments accounted for by the General Fund.

      *h.* A transfer of $500 cash from a special revenue fund for the special revenue fund's share of supplies previously received (and recorded as an expenditure) by the General Fund.

      *i.* Receipt of $20,000 cash from the Water Utility Fund as a contribution in lieu of taxes.

      *j.* Payment of $100,000 to the Pension Trust Fund by the General Fund as the employer's contribution for benefits earned by employees during the year.

**2–5.** The City of Garfield passed an appropriations ordinance for the General Fund for a certain fiscal year in the amount of $30 million. Revenues were anticipated from sources other than the property tax in the amount of $8 million. The total market value of property in the City amounts to $2 billion, but $500 million is exempt from taxation for religious and other reasons. The assessment ratio (assessment percentage of market value) for all cities in the state is 33⅓ percent. Owners of property have filed for and received household, old age, and other exemptions in the amount of $80 million. It is anticipated that 2 percent of the assessed taxes will not be collected.

*Required:*

   *a.* Compute the amount to be raised from property taxes.

   *b.* Compute the gross levy required to raise revenue in the amount you computed for requirement (*a*). Round computation to nearest dollar.

   *c.* Compute the property tax rate per $100 net assessed valuation.

   *d.* Compute the property tax rate per $1,000 NAV (this rate is often called the "millage"). Round fractional cents to the next higher whole cent.

   *e.* You own a home with a market value of $120,000. Compute the gross assessed valuation. You are eligible for a homestead exemption of $2,000; deduct this amount from the gross assessed valuation to determine the net assessed valuation of your house. Multiply the NAV by the property tax rate computed in part (*c*) of this problem to determine the property tax payable on your house.

**2–6.** Presented below are several transactions and events of the General Fund of the Town of Sellars. All transactions and events relate to calendar year 19x0.

   1. Estimated revenues from the following sources were legally budgeted for 19x0:

| | |
|---|---:|
| Sales taxes | $3,500,000 |
| Fines and forfeits | 2,000,000 |
| Licenses and permits | 1,750,000 |
| Intergovernmental revenues | 350,000 |
| Total | $7,600,000 |

   2. Appropriations for the following functions were legally budgeted for 19x0:

| | |
|---|---:|
| General government | $1,400,000 |
| Public safety | 3,900,000 |
| Culture and recreation | 280,000 |
| Health and welfare | 2,000,000 |
| Total | $7,580,000 |

   3. During the year revenues were received in cash from the following sources:

| | |
|---|---|
| Sales taxes . . . . . . . . . . . . . . . . . . . . . | $3,530,000 |
| Fines and forfeits . . . . . . . . . . . . . . . . . | 1,890,000 |
| Licenses and permits . . . . . . . . . . . . . . | 1,740,000 |
| Intergovernmental revenues . . . . . . . . . . . | 385,000 |
| Total . . . . . . . . . . . . . . . . . . . . | $7,545,000 |

4. During the year, contracts and purchase orders were issued as follows:

| | |
|---|---|
| General government . . . . . . . . . . . . . . . | $300,000 |
| Public safety . . . . . . . . . . . . . . . . . . . | 800,000 |
| Culture and recreation . . . . . . . . . . . . . | 80,000 |
| Health and welfare . . . . . . . . . . . . . . . | 250,000 |
| Total . . . . . . . . . . . . . . . . . . . . | $1,430,000 |

5. Goods and services (ordered in transaction 4) were received, as follows:

| | Estimated | Actual |
|---|---|---|
| General government . . . . . . . . . . . . . . . | $300,000 | $305,000 |
| Public safety . . . . . . . . . . . . . . . . . . . | 500,000 | 510,000 |
| Culture and recreation . . . . . . . . . . . . . | 75,000 | 74,000 |
| Health and welfare . . . . . . . . . . . . . . . | 250,000 | 260,000 |
| Total . . . . . . . . . . . . . . . . . . . . | $1,125,000 | $1,149,000 |

6. Vouchers were issued for items not previously encumbered, primarily personal services, in the following amounts:

| | |
|---|---|
| General government . . . . . . . . . . . . . . . | $1,092,000 |
| Public safety . . . . . . . . . . . . . . . . . . . | 3,088,000 |
| Culture and recreation . . . . . . . . . . . . . | 200,000 |
| Health and welfare . . . . . . . . . . . . . . . | 1,740,000 |
| Total . . . . . . . . . . . . . . . . . . . . | $6,120,000 |

*Required:*
a. Record the above transactions in general journal form. Include subsidiary accounts as illustrated in this chapter.
b. Open general ledger accounts and post the above transactions.
c. Open Revenue and Appropriations, Expenditures, and Encumbrances subsidiary ledgers. Post the transactions. Prove that the control account balances agree with the related subsidiary ledger accounts.
d. Prepare a Statement of Revenues, Expenditures, and Changes in Fund Balances—Budget and Actual for the General Fund. Assume a beginning Fund Balance of $103,500.
e. Assuming that encumbered appropriations do *not* lapse at the end of the budget year, how much of the 19x0 appropriations, by function, did lapse at the end of 19x0? Show computations in good form.

2–7. The Village of Genoa's records reflected the following budget and actual data for the General Fund for the fiscal year ended April 30, 19y1. Both budget data and actual data are on the accrual basis required by GASB standards for governmental funds, and no timing, entity, or perspective differences exist.
1. Estimated Revenues:

| | |
|---|---|
| Taxes . . . . . . . . . . . . . . . . . . . . . . | $1,500,000 |
| Licenses and permits . . . . . . . . . . . . . . | 800,000 |
| Intergovernmental revenues . . . . . . . . . . . | 400,000 |
| Miscellaneous revenues . . . . . . . . . . . . . | 200,000 |

2. Revenues:

| | |
|---|---|
| Taxes | $1,498,650 |
| Licenses and permits | 801,320 |
| Intergovernmental revenues | 387,000 |
| Miscellaneous revenues | 198,000 |

3. Appropriations:

| | |
|---|---|
| General government | 700,000 |
| Public safety | 1,250,000 |
| Health | 350,000 |
| Welfare | 400,000 |

4. Expenditures of 19y1 Appropriations:

| | |
|---|---|
| General government | 680,600 |
| Public safety | 1,199,500 |
| Health | 348,000 |
| Welfare | 397,000 |

5. Encumbrances of 19y1 Appropriations, outstanding as of April 30, 19y1:

| | |
|---|---|
| General government | 18,000 |
| Public safety | 50,000 |

6. Expenditures during 19y1 of 19y0 Appropriations:

| | |
|---|---|
| Public safety | 57,000 |

7. Operating Transfer to Debt Service Fund:

| | |
|---|---|
| Budget | 200,000 |
| Actual | 200,000 |

8. Nonrecurring transfer to Water Utility Fund:

| | |
|---|---|
| Budget | 500,000 |
| Actual | 500,000 |

9. Reserve for Encumbrances—19y0 . . . . . . . . 57,000

10. Fund Balance, May 1, 19y0 . . . . . . . . . . 1,038,000

*Required:*

*a.* Prepare a Statement of Revenues, Expenditures, and Changes in Fund Balance—Budget and Actual for the General Fund for the Year Ended April 30, 19y1. In your statement show Other Financing Sources (Uses) in a section following the "Excess of Revenues over Expenditures" line; show any equity transfers in the Changes in Fund Balance section.

*b.* Prepare a Statement of Revenues, Expenditures, and Changes in Fund Balances for the General Fund for the year ended April 30, 19y1, using the format as specified in part (*a*) of this problem.

*c.* Prepare a reconciliation of the "Actual" Total Expenditures presented in part (*a*) with the Total Expenditures reported in part (*b*) of this problem.

## CONTINUOUS PROBLEM

2–C.    This portion of the continuous problem continues the General Fund example
        by requiring the recording and posting of the budgetary entry. In addition, a
        special revenue fund, the Street and Highway Fund, is to be created and the
        budget of that fund recorded. Problem 3–C completes the General and Special
        Revenue Funds transactions. In order to reduce clerical effort required for
        the solution subsidiary accounts are not required in the continuous problem.
        However, the student should keep in mind the fact that subsidiary revenue
        and appropriations expenditure ledgers should be maintained for all govern-
        mental funds, in the manner illustrated in this chapter and in Exercise 2–6,
        in an actual governmental unit.

        *Part 1.* As of January 1, 19y1, the City Council approved and the mayor
        signed a budget calling for $10,200,000 in property tax and other revenue,
        $500,000 to be transferred in from the Street and Highway Fund, $9,300,000
        in appropriations for expenditures, and $1,280,000 to be transferred to two
        debt service funds for the payment of principal and interest. Record the
        budget in the general journal for the General Fund and post to the ledger.

        *Part 2.* The City of Everlasting Sunshine also maintained accounts for the
        Street and Highway Fund, a special revenue fund.

        *a.* Open a general journal for the Street and Highway Fund. Allow two pages
            of 8½ by 11-inch looseleaf journal paper.

        *b.* Open a general ledger for the Street and Highway Fund. Allow two pages
            of 8½ by 11-inch looseleaf ledger paper, or its equivalent. On each page
            allow six lines for each account below. Enter the balance sheet amounts
            directly in the general ledger accounts; date each "1/1/y1."

                        Cash
                        Investments
                        Due from Other Governmental Units
                        Estimated Revenues
                        Revenues
                        Vouchers Payable
                        Appropriations
                        Estimated Other Financing Uses
                        Expenditures—19y1
                        Other Financing Uses—Operating Transfers Out—19y1
                        Encumbrances—19y1
                        Reserve for Encumbrances—19y1
                        Fund Balance

**CITY OF EVERLASTING SUNSHINE**
**Street and Highway Fund Balance Sheet**
**As of December 31, 19y0**

**Assets**

| | |
|---|---|
| Cash . . . . . . . . . . . . . . . . . . . . . . . . . . . . . . . . . . . | $ 1,500 |
| Investments . . . . . . . . . . . . . . . . . . . . . . . . . . . . . . . | 55,000 |
| Due from other governmental units . . . . . . . . . . . . . . . . . | 200,000 |
| Total Assets . . . . . . . . . . . . . . . . . . . . . . . . . . . . . . | $256,500 |

**Liabilities and Fund Equity**

| | |
|---|---|
| Liabilities: | |
|   Vouchers payable . . . . . . . . . . . . . . . . . . . . . . . . . . | $ 1,300 |
| Fund Equity: | |
|   Fund balance . . . . . . . . . . . . . . . . . . . . . . . . . . . . . | 255,200 |
| Total Liabilities and Fund Equity . . . . . . . . . . . . . . . . . . . | $256,500 |

*c.* The City Council approved and the Mayor signed a budget for the Street and Highway Fund that provided for estimated revenues from the state government in the amount of $950,000, appropriations of $420,000, and an anticipated transfer to the General Fund in the amount of $500,000. Record the budget in the general journal and post to the ledger.

# Chapter 3

# GENERAL FUNDS AND SPECIAL REVENUE FUNDS— ILLUSTRATIVE TRANSACTIONS AND FINANCIAL STATEMENTS

In Chapter 2, the use of budgetary accounts (Estimated Revenues, Estimated Other Financing Sources, Appropriations, Estimated Other Financing Uses, and Encumbrances) and related proprietary accounts (Revenues, Other Financing Sources, Expenditures, Other Financing Uses) is discussed and illustrated. The necessity for subsidiary ledgers supporting the budgetary accounts and related operating statement accounts is also discussed in Chapter 2. In this chapter, common transactions and events in the operation of the General Fund of a hypothetical local governmental unit, the Village of Elizabeth, are discussed, and appropriate accounting entries and financial statements are illustrated. In addition, a few unique entries are presented for special revenue funds. In this chapter, subsidiary ledgers are not illustrated for the budgetary and operating statement accounts. However, the reader should keep in mind that subsidiary accounts, as described in Chapter 2, would be required in actual situations.

## ILLUSTRATIVE CASE—GENERAL FUND

Assume that at the end of a fiscal year, 19x5, the Village of Elizabeth's General Fund had the following balances in its accounts:

|                                              | Debit      | Credit     |
|----------------------------------------------|------------|------------|
| Cash                                         | $ 70,000   |            |
| Taxes receivable—delinquent                  | 250,000    |            |
| Estimated uncollectible delinquent taxes     |            | $ 20,000   |
| Interest and penalties receivable on taxes   | 2,500      |            |
| Estimated uncollectible interest and penalties |          | 200        |
| Vouchers payable                             |            | 90,000     |
| Due to federal government                    |            | 30,000     |
| Reserve for encumbrances—19x5                |            | 15,500     |
| Fund balance                                 |            | 166,800    |
| Totals                                       | $322,500   | $322,500   |

## Recording the Budget

At the beginning of the following fiscal year, 19x6, it is necessary to record the budget (assuming that all legal requirements have been complied with). If the total estimated revenue budget for 19x6 is $3,900,000, the total appropriations are $3,300,000, the total planned transfer to debt service funds is $400,000, and a planned contribution to establish an internal service fund is $100,000, the necessary entry to record the budget would be as shown below (keeping in mind that appropriate subsidiary ledger detail would be required in actual situations). The budgetary account, Estimated Equity Transfers, provides authorization for the permanent transfer in the same manner as Estimated Other Financing Uses provides authorization for the operating transfer to debt service funds. Alternatively, the account, Appropriations, could control the entire $3,800,000.

|                                         | Debit     | Credit    |
|-----------------------------------------|-----------|-----------|
| 1. Estimated Revenues                   | 3,900,000 |           |
|    Appropriations                       |           | 3,300,000 |
|    Estimated Other Financing Uses       |           | 400,000   |
|    Estimated Equity Transfers           |           | 100,000   |
|    Fund Balance                         |           | 100,000   |

## Tax Anticipation Notes Payable

In the trial balance of the General Fund of the Village of Elizabeth, liabilities (Vouchers Payable and Due to Federal Government) total $120,000. Cash of the General Fund on the date of the trial balance amounts to $70,000. Although some collections of delinquent taxes receivable are expected early in the year, payrolls and other liabilities will be incurred and must be paid before substantial amounts of cash will be collected; accordingly it is desirable to arrange a short-term loan. The taxing power of the Village is ample security for a short-term debt; local banks customarily meet the working capital needs of governmental units by accepting a "tax anticipation note" from the government officials. If the amount of $200,000 is borrowed at this time the necessary entry is:

|   |   | Debit | Credit |
|---|---|-------|--------|
| 2. Cash . . . . . . . . . . . . . . . . . . . . . . |   | 200,000 |   |
|      Tax Anticipation Notes Payable . . . . . . . . |   |   | 200,000 |

## Payment of Liabilities as Recorded

Checks were drawn to pay the vouchers payable and the amount due to the federal government as of the end of 19x5 was:

|   | Debit | Credit |
|---|-------|--------|
| 3. Vouchers Payable . . . . . . . . . . . . . . . | 90,000 |   |
|     Due to Federal Government . . . . . . . . . . | 30,000 |   |
|     Cash . . . . . . . . . . . . . . . . . . . . . |   | 120,000 |

Entry 3 illustrates the difference between an expenditure and a disbursement. An expenditure is the use of appropriation authority, whereas a disbursement is the use of cash. Appropriations were expended in 19x5 when goods and services were received; the liability accounts shown in the trial balance as of the end of 19x5 were credited at the time the Expenditures—19x5 account was debited. Consequently, in 19x6 when the liabilities are paid, it is necessary only to record the disbursement of cash.

## Encumbrances of Prior Year

In the trial balance as of the end of 19x5 the item Reserve for Encumbrances—19x5 indicates that purchase orders or contracts issued in 19x5 were open at the end of the year—that is, the goods or services had not yet been received. At the end of 19x5 the Encumbrance account, as well as the Appropriations and Expenditures accounts for 19x5 were closed, effectively charging the estimated cost of goods and services on order at the end of 19x5 against the appropriations for that year. When the goods or services are received their actual cost may not be the same as the estimate. If the actual cost is greater, the excess must be treated as an expenditure of the current year. In the Village of Elizabeth example the estimated cost was $15,500. Assuming that the items were received at an invoice amount of $15,700 which was approved for payment, an appropriate entry would be:

|   | Debit | Credit |
|---|-------|--------|
| 4. Expenditures—19x5 . . . . . . . . . . . . . . . | 15,500 |   |
|     Expenditures—19x6 . . . . . . . . . . . . . . | 200 |   |
|     Vouchers Payable . . . . . . . . . . . . . . |   | 15,700 |

The Expenditures—19x5 account will be closed at year-end to the Reserve for Encumbrances—19x5 account (see Entry 26).

The procedures described above are common. In some jurisdictions however, encumbrances as well as unexpended appropriations lapse at year-end, and the estimated cost of goods and services on order at year-end must be included in the appropriations for the following year. In such jurisdictions the Reserve for Encumbrances account would be closed at year-end, and an entry made at the beginning of the following year debiting Encumbrances and crediting Reserve for Encumbrances in the estimated amount. When the goods are received, and the invoice approved for payment, the encumbrance entry would be reversed and the expenditure recorded as shown in Chapter 2 and, also, in Entry 11 of this chapter.

## Encumbrance Entry

Purchase orders for materials and supplies are issued in the total amount of $500,000. The general ledger entry to record the encumbrances for the purchase orders is (subsidiary ledger detail is omitted from this example, but should be recorded by an actual governmental unit):

|  | Debit | Credit |
|---|---|---|
| 5. Encumbrances—19x6 | 500,000 | |
| Reserve for Encumbrances—19x6 | | 500,000 |

## Recording Property Tax Levy

Assume that the budgeted revenue from property taxes, included in the total Estimated Revenues recorded in Entry 1 of this chapter, was $2,000,000. Assume further that 5 percent of these taxes are estimated to be uncollectible due to tax collection policy and local economic conditions. In order to generate revenues of $2,000,000 the gross levy must be in the amount of $2,105,263 ($2,000,000 ÷ .95). Therefore, at the time property tax bills are prepared, the following entry should be made:

|  | Debit | Credit |
|---|---|---|
| 6. Taxes Receivable—Current | 2,105,263 | |
| Estimated Uncollectible Current Taxes | | 105,263 |
| Revenues | | 2,000,000 |

Keep in mind that the account "Revenues" is a control account in the General Fund general ledger. It is supported by a subsidiary ledger in the manner illustrated in Chapter 2. "Taxes Receivable—Current" is also a control account and is supported by a subsidiary ledger organized by parcels of property according to their legal descriptions. In many cases this subsidiary ledger is maintained by the county officer responsible for collecting property taxes as agent for all funds and governmental units within the county.

## Collection of Delinquent Taxes

Delinquent taxes are subject to interest and penalties which must be paid at the time the tax bill is paid. It is possible for a government to record the amount of the penalties at the time that the taxes become delinquent. Interest may be computed and recorded at year-end so that financial statements report the account on the accrual basis. Interest must also be computed and recorded for the period from the date of last recording to the date when a taxpayer pays the delinquent taxes. Assume that the taxpayers of the Village of Elizabeth have paid delinquent taxes in the amount of $230,000, on which interest and penalties of $2,300 had been recorded as receivable at the end of 19x5; further assume that $500 additional interest was paid for the period from the first day of 19x6 to the dates on which the delinquent taxes were paid.

|  |  | Debit | Credit |
|---|---|---|---|
| 7a. | Interest and Penalties Receivable on Taxes . . . . . | 500 | |
|  | Revenues   . . . . . . . . . . . . . . . . . . | | 500 |
| 7b. | Cash   . . . . . . . . . . . . . . . . . . . . | 232,800 | |
|  | Taxes Receivable—Delinquent . . . . . . . . | | 230,000 |
|  | Interest and Penalties Receivable on Taxes . . . | | 2,800 |

## Revenue Recognized on Cash Basis

Revenue from licenses and permits, fines and forfeits, and other sources not susceptible to accrual is recognized on the cash basis. Collections during the year 19x6 are assumed to be $1,800,000.

|  |  | Debit | Credit |
|---|---|---|---|
| 8. | Cash . . . . . . . . . . . . . . . . . . . . . . | 1,800,000 | |
|  | Revenues . . . . . . . . . . . . . . . . . . | | 1,800,000 |

## Collection of Current Taxes

Collections during 19x6 of property taxes levied for 19x6 are assumed to be $1,700,000. Since the revenue was recognized at the time the receivable was recorded (see Entry 6), the following entry would be made:

|  |  | Debit | Credit |
|---|---|---|---|
| 9. | Cash . . . . . . . . . . . . . . . . . . . . . | 1,700,000 | |
|  | Taxes Receivable—Current . . . . . . . . . . | | 1,700,000 |

## Repayment of Tax Anticipation Notes

As tax collections begin to exceed current disbursements it becomes possible for the Village of Elizabeth to repay the local bank for the money borrowed in tax anticipation notes (transaction 2). Just as borrowing money did not involve the recognition of revenue, the repayment of the principal is merely the extinguishment of debt of the General Fund and not an expenditure. Payment of interest, however, must be recognized as the expenditure of an appropriation. Assuming the interest is $5,000, the entry is:

|  | Debit | Credit |
|---|---|---|
| 10. Tax Anticipation Notes Payable . . . . . . . . . | 200,000 | |
| Expenditures—19x6 . . . . . . . . . . . . . . . | 5,000 | |
| Cash . . . . . . . . . . . . . . . . . . . . | | 205,000 |

## Recognition of Expenditures for Encumbered Items

Some of the materials and supplies ordered (see Entry 5) were received. Invoices for the items received totaled $470,000; related purchase orders totaled $465,000. After inspection of the goods and supplies and preaudit of the invoices, they were approved for payment and vouchers were issued. Since the purchase orders had been recorded as encumbrances against the appropriations it is necessary to reverse the encumbered amount and record the expenditure in the amount of the actual liability:

|  | Debit | Credit |
|---|---|---|
| 11. Reserve for Encumbrances—19x6 . . . . . . . . | 465,000 | |
| Expenditures—19x6 . . . . . . . . . . . . . . | 470,000 | |
| Encumbrances—19x6 . . . . . . . . . . . . . | | 465,000 |
| Vouchers Payable . . . . . . . . . . . . . . | | 470,000 |

The net effect of Entry 11 on the departmental appropriations accounts is a $5,000 reduction in total available balances.

## Payrolls and Payroll Taxes

The gross pay of employees of general fund departments amounted to $2,123,000. The Village of Elizabeth does not use the encumbrance procedure for payrolls. Deductions from gross pay for the period amount to $167,500 for employees' share of FICA tax; $275,000 for employees' federal withholding tax; and $25,000 for employees' state withholding tax. The first two will, of course, have to be remitted by the Village to the federal government, and the last item will have to be remitted to the state government. The gross pay is chargeable to the appropriations of the individual departments. Assuming the liability for net pay is vouchered, the entry is:

|  | Debit | Credit |
|---|---|---|
| 12a. Expenditures—19x6 . . . . . . . . . . . . . . | 2,123,000 | |
| Due to Federal Government . . . . . . . . | | 442,500 |
| Due to State Government . . . . . . . . . . | | 25,000 |
| Vouchers Payable . . . . . . . . . . . . . | | 1,655,500 |

Payment of the vouchers for the net pay results in the following entry:

|  | Debit | Credit |
|---|---|---|
| 12b. Vouchers Payable . . . . . . . . . . . . . . | 1,655,500 | |
| Cash . . . . . . . . . . . . . . . . . . . . | | 1,655,500 |

Inasmuch as the Village is liable for the employer's share of FICA taxes ($167,500) and for contributions to additional retirement funds established by state law, assumed to amount to $125,000 for the year, it is necessary that the Village's liabilities for its contributions be recorded:

|  | Debit | Credit |
|---|---|---|
| 13. Expenditures—19x6 . . . . . . . . . . . . . . . | 292,500 | |
| Due to Federal Government . . . . . . . . . | | 167,500 |
| Due to State Government . . . . . . . . . . | | 125,000 |

## Payment of Vouchers and Other Items

Assume now that payment is made on $315,000 of the outstanding vouchers and that the amounts due the state and federal governments are paid in full:

|  | Debit | Credit |
|---|---|---|
| 14. Vouchers Payable . . . . . . . . . . . . . . . . | 315,000 | |
| Due to Federal Government . . . . . . . . . . | 610,000 | |
| Due to State Government . . . . . . . . . . . | 150,000 | |
| Cash . . . . . . . . . . . . . . . . . . . | | 1,075,000 |

## Correction of Errors

No problems arise in the collection of current taxes if they are collected as billed; the collections are debited to Cash and credited to Taxes Receivable—Current. Sometimes, even in a well-designed and well-operated system, errors occur and must be corrected. If, for example, duplicate tax bills totaling $1,200 were sent out for the same piece of property, the following entry would be required. (The error also caused a slight overstatement of the credit to Estimated Uncollectible Current Taxes in Entry 6, but the error in that account is not considered material enough to correct.)

|  | Debit | Credit |
|---|---|---|
| 15. Revenues . . . . . . . . . . . . . . . . . . . | 1,200 | |
| Taxes Receivable—Current . . . . . . . . . . | | 1,200 |

Postaudit may disclose errors in the recording of expenditures during the current year, or during a prior year. If the error occurred during the current year, the Expenditures control account and the proper subsidiary ledger account can be debited or credited as needed to correct it. If the error occurred in a prior year, however, the Expenditures account in error has been closed to Fund Balance, so theoretically the correcting entry should be made to the Fund Balance account. As a practical matter, immaterial changes resulting from corrections of prior period errors in expenditures may be recorded in the Revenues or Expenditures accounts.

## Revision of the Budget

Comparisons of budgeted and actual revenues by sources, and comparisons of departmental or program appropriations with expenditures and encumbrances, as well as interpretation of information which was not available at the time the budgets were originally adopted, may indicate the desirability or necessity of legally amending the budget during the fiscal year. For example, assume that the revenues budget was increased by $50,000 in the Charges for Services source category and that the appropriation for the Public Works Department was increased by $100,000. The amendments to the budget would be recorded when they are legally approved, as shown in Entry 16.

|  |  | Debit | Credit |
|---|---|---|---|
| 16. | Estimated Revenues . . . . . . . . . . . . . . . . | 50,000 | |
| | Fund Balance . . . . . . . . . . . . . . . . . | 50,000 | |
| | Appropriations . . . . . . . . . . . . . . . . | | 100,000 |

Corresponding changes would be made in the subsidiary ledger accounts as illustrated in Chapter 2.

## Interfund Transactions

**Quasi-external transactions**   Quasi-external transactions are recognized as revenues or expenditures (or expenses in the case of proprietary funds) of the funds involved because they would be recognized as revenues and expenditures (or expenses) if the transactions involved organizations external to the governmental unit.

Water utilities ordinarily provide a city with fire hydrants and water service for fire protection at a flat annual charge. A governmentally owned water utility expected to support the cost of its operations by user charges should be accounted for as an enterprise fund. Fire protection is logically budgeted as an activity of the Fire Department, a General Fund department. Assuming that the amount charged by the water utility to the General Fund for hydrants and water service is $40,000, the General Fund entry would be:

|  |  | Debit | Credit |
|---|---|---|---|
| 17. | Expenditures—19x6 . . . . . . . . . . . . . . . | 40,000 | |
| | Due to Water Utility Fund . . . . . . . . . . | | 40,000 |

Governmentally owned utility property is not assessed for property tax purposes, but a number of government utilities make an annual contribution to the General Fund of the governmental unit in recognition of the fact that the utility does receive police and fire protection, and other services. If the water utility of the Village of Elizabeth agrees to contribute $30,000 to the General Fund in lieu of taxes, the General Fund entry is:

|                                                             | Debit   | Credit  |
|-------------------------------------------------------------|---------|---------|
| 18. Due from Water Utility Fund . . . . . . . . . . .        | 30,000  |         |
|     Revenues  . . . . . . . . . . . . . . . . . . . |         | 30,000  |

Another common quasi-external transaction for the General Fund is the receipt of supplies or services from an internal service fund. Assume that the General Fund received $377,000 in supplies from the Supplies Fund and later made a partial payment of $322,000 in cash. The entries would be:

|                                                             | Debit    | Credit   |
|-------------------------------------------------------------|----------|----------|
| 19a. Expenditures—19x6  . . . . . . . . . . . . . .          | 377,000  |          |
|     Due to Supplies Fund  . . . . . . . . . . .  |          | 377,000  |
| 19b. Due to Supplies Fund  . . . . . . . . . . . .           | 322,000  |          |
|     Cash . . . . . . . . . . . . . . . . . .     |          | 322,000  |

**Operating transfers**   In order to avoid reporting revenues and expenditures more than once in the governmental unit, operating transfers are used. Assuming that the General Fund makes an operating transfer to a Debt Service Fund for the payment of debt service, the General Fund entry would be:

|                                                             | Debit    | Credit   |
|-------------------------------------------------------------|----------|----------|
| 20a. Other Financing Uses—Operating Transfers               |          |          |
|       Out—19x6  . . . . . . . . . . . . . . . . . | 400,000  |          |
|       Due to Debt Service Fund  . . . . . . . . . |          | 400,000  |

When the cash is transferred, the entry would be:

|                                                             | Debit    | Credit   |
|-------------------------------------------------------------|----------|----------|
| 20b. Due to Debt Service Fund  . . . . . . . . . . .         | 400,000  |          |
|     Cash . . . . . . . . . . . . . . . . . .     |          | 400,000  |

**Equity transfers**   Equity transfers are nonroutine transactions, often made to establish or liquidate a fund. Assume that the General Fund made a permanent transfer of $100,000 to establish an internal service fund. The General Fund entry would be:

|                                                             | Debit    | Credit   |
|-------------------------------------------------------------|----------|----------|
| 21. Equity Transfers Out—19x6  . . . . . . . . . . .         | 100,000  |          |
|     Cash  . . . . . . . . . . . . . . . . . .    |          | 100,000  |

The account "Equity Transfers Out" is essentially an adjustment of the beginning Fund Balance and is displayed in operating statements in the Changes in Fund Balance section.

## Write-Off of Uncollectible Delinquent Taxes

Just as officers of profit-seeking entities should review aged trial balances of receivables periodically in order to determine the adequacy of allowance accounts, and authorize the write-offs of items judged to be uncollectible, so should officers of a governmental unit review aged trial balances of taxes receivable, and other receivables. Although the levy of property taxes creates a lien against the underlying property in the amount of the tax, accumulated taxes may exceed the market value of the property, or, in the case of personal property, the property may have been removed from the jurisdiction of the governmental unit. When delinquent taxes are deemed to be uncollectible, the related interest and penalties must also be written off. If the Treasurer of the Village of Elizabeth receives approval to write off delinquent taxes totaling $15,000, and related interest and penalties of $150, the entry would be:

|  | Debit | Credit |
|---|---|---|
| 22. Estimated Uncollectible Delinquent Taxes . . . . . | 15,000 | |
| Estimated Uncollectible Interest and Penalties . . . | 150 | |
| Taxes Receivable—Delinquent . . . . . . . . | | 15,000 |
| Interest and Penalties Receivable on Taxes . . . | | 150 |

When delinquent taxes are written off, the tax bills are retained in the files, although no longer subject to general ledger control, because changes in conditions may make it possible to collect the amounts in the future. If collections of written-off taxes are made it is highly desirable to return the tax bills to general ledger control by making an entry which is the reverse of the write-off entry, so that the procedures described in Entries 7a and 7b may be followed.

### Reclassification of Current Taxes

Assuming that all property taxes levied by the Village of Elizabeth in 19x6 were to have been paid by property owners before the end of the year, any balance of taxes receivable at year-end is properly classified as "delinquent," rather than "current." The related allowance for estimated uncollectible taxes should also be transferred to the "delinquent" classification. A review should be made at this time to ensure that the estimated uncollectible amount is reasonable in relation to the delinquent taxes. Assuming the estimate is reasonable, the entry would be:

|  | Debit | Credit |
|---|---|---|
| 23. Taxes Receivable—Delinquent . . . . . . . . . . | 404,063 | |
| Estimated Uncollectible Current Taxes . . . . . . | 105,263 | |
| Taxes Receivable—Current . . . . . . . . . . | | 404,063 |
| Estimated Uncollectible Delinquent Taxes . . . | | 105,263 |

### Accrual of Interest and Penalties

Delinquent taxes are subject to interest and penalties, as discussed previously. If the amount of interest and penalties earned in 19x6 by the General Fund of the Village of Elizabeth and not yet recognized is $4,041, but it is expected that only $2,990 of that can be collected, the following entry is necessary:

|                                                              | Debit | Credit |
|--------------------------------------------------------------|-------|--------|
| 24. Interest and Penalties Receivable on Taxes . . . . .     | 4,041 |        |
|     Estimated Uncollectible Interest and Penalties . |       | 1,051  |
|     Revenues   . . . . . . . . . . . . . . . . . .   |       | 2,990  |

## Pre-Closing Trial Balance

Assuming that the illustrated entries for the transactions and events pertaining to the year 19x6 for the Village of Elizabeth have been made and posted, the trial balance below shows the General Fund general ledger accounts before closing entries:

**VILLAGE OF ELIZABETH**
**General Fund**
**Trial Balance Pre-Closing**
**As of December 31, 19x6**

|                                                              | Debit       | Credit      |
|--------------------------------------------------------------|-------------|-------------|
| Cash  . . . . . . . . . . . . . . . . . . . . . . . .        | $ 125,300   |             |
| Taxes Receivable—Delinquent . . . . . . . . . . . . .        | 409,063     |             |
| Estimated Uncollectible Delinquent Taxes . . . . . . . . .   |             | $ 110,263   |
| Interest and Penalties Receivable on Taxes  . . . . . . . .  | 4,091       |             |
| Estimated Uncollectible Interest and Penalties . . . . . . . |             | 1,101       |
| Due from Water Utility Fund  . . . . . . . . . . . . .       | 30,000      |             |
| Vouchers Payable  . . . . . . . . . . . . . . . . .          |             | 170,700     |
| Due to Water Utility Fund . . . . . . . . . . . . . . .      |             | 40,000      |
| Due to Supplies Fund . . . . . . . . . . . . . . . . .       |             | 55,000      |
| Reserve for Encumbrances—19x6 . . . . . . . . . . . .        |             | 35,000      |
| Reserve for Encumbrances—19x5  . . . . . . . . . . .         |             | 15,500      |
| Fund Balance  . . . . . . . . . . . . . . . . . . .          |             | 216,800     |
| Estimated Revenues  . . . . . . . . . . . . . . . . .        | 3,950,000   |             |
| Revenues  . . . . . . . . . . . . . . . . . . . . .          |             | 3,832,290   |
| Appropriations . . . . . . . . . . . . . . . . . . .         |             | 3,400,000   |
| Estimated Other Financing Uses . . . . . . . . . . . .       |             | 400,000     |
| Estimated Equity Transfers . . . . . . . . . . . . . .       |             | 100,000     |
| Expenditures—19x6  . . . . . . . . . . . . . . . . .         | 3,307,700   |             |
| Expenditures—19x5  . . . . . . . . . . . . . . . . .         | 15,500      |             |
| Encumbrances—19x6 . . . . . . . . . . . . . . . . .          | 35,000      |             |
| Other Financing Uses—Operating Transfers Out—19x6 . . .      | 400,000     |             |
| Equity Transfers Out—19x6  . . . . . . . . . . . . . .       | 100,000     |             |
| Totals  . . . . . . . . . . . . . . . . . . . . . .          | $8,376,654  | $8,376,654  |

## Closing Entries

The essence of the closing process for the General Fund or special revenue funds of a state or local governmental unit is the transfer of the balances of the operating statement accounts and the balances of the budgetary accounts for the year to the Fund Balance account. Note that the closing entry has the effect of reversing the entry to record the budget (Entry 1) and the entry to amend the budget (Entry 16). After the closing entry is posted the Fund Balance account represents the net amount of liquid assets available for appropriation.

|  | Debit | Credit |
|---|---|---|
| 25. Revenues | 3,832,290 | |
| Appropriations | 3,400,000 | |
| Estimated Other Financing Uses | 400,000 | |
| Estimated Equity Transfers | 100,000 | |
| Fund Balance | 60,410 | |
| Expenditures—19x6 | | 3,307,700 |
| Estimated Revenues | | 3,950,000 |
| Other Financing Uses—Operating Transfers Out—19x6 | | 400,000 |
| Equity Transfers Out—19x6 | | 100,000 |
| Encumbrances—19x6 | | 35,000 |

It is also necessary to close the Expenditures—19x5 account and the Reserve for Encumbrances—19x5 account.

|  | Debit | Credit |
|---|---|---|
| 26. Reserve for Encumbrances—19x5 | 15,500 | |
| Expenditures—19x5 | | 15,500 |

## Year-End Financial Statements

The Balance Sheet for the General Fund of the Village of Elizabeth as of the end of 19x6 is shown as Illustration 3–1. Note that the amount due *from* the Water Utility Fund has been offset against the amount due *to* the Water Utility Fund. (It should be emphasized, however, that it is not acceptable to offset a receivable from one fund against a payable to a different fund.)

A second financial statement that should be presented in the year-end comprehensive annual financial report is a Statement of Revenues,

**ILLUSTRATION 3–1**

**VILLAGE OF ELIZABETH**
**General Fund Balance Sheet**
**As of December 31, 19x6**

**Assets**

| | | |
|---|---|---|
| Cash | | $125,300 |
| Taxes receivable—delinquent | $409,063 | |
| Less: Estimated uncollectible | 110,263 | 298,800 |
| Interest and penalties receivables on taxes | 4,091 | |
| Less: Estimated uncollectible | 1,101 | 2,990 |
| Total Assets | | $427,090 |

**Liabilities and Fund Equity**

| | | |
|---|---|---|
| Liabilities: | | |
| Vouchers payable | $170,700 | |
| Due to water utility fund | 10,000 | |
| Due to supplies fund | 55,000 | |
| Total Liabilities | | $235,700 |
| Fund Equity: | | |
| Reserve for encumbrances—19x6 | 35,000 | |
| Fund balance | 156,390 | 191,390 |
| Total Liabilities and Fund Equity | | $427,090 |

**ILLUSTRATION 3–2**

**VILLAGE OF ELIZABETH**
**General Fund**
**Statement of Revenues, Expenditures, and**
**Changes in Fund Balance**
**For the Year Ended December 31, 19x6**

Revenues (amounts assumed):
| | | |
|---|---|---|
| Property taxes | $2,098,800 | |
| Interest and penalties on delinquent taxes | 3,490 | |
| Sales taxes | 615,000 | |
| Licenses and permits | 240,000 | |
| Fines and forfeits | 330,000 | |
| Intergovernmental revenue | 450,000 | |
| Charges for services | 70,000 | |
| Miscellaneous revenues | 25,000 | |
| Total Revenues | | $3,832,290 |

Expenditures (amounts assumed):
Authorized by 19x6 appropriations:
| | | |
|---|---|---|
| General government | 405,000 | |
| Public safety | 1,394,500 | |
| Public works | 630,000 | |
| Health and welfare | 515,600 | |
| Parks and recreation | 227,400 | |
| Contribution to retirement funds | 125,000 | |
| Miscellaneous expenditures | 10,200 | |
| Total expenditures of 19x6 appropriations | 3,307,700 | |

Authorized by 19x5 appropriations:
| | | |
|---|---|---|
| Public safety | 15,500 | |
| Total Expenditures | | 3,323,200 |
| Excess of Revenues over Expenditures | | 509,090 |

Other Financing Uses:
| | | |
|---|---|---|
| Operating Transfers Out | | 400,000 |
| Excess of Revenues over Expenditures and Other Financing Uses | | 109,090 |
| Fund Balance, January 1, 19x6 | | 166,800 |
| Equity Transfer to Internal Service Fund | | (100,000) |
| (Increase) in Reserve for Encumbrances | | (19,500) |
| Fund Balance, December 31, 19x6 | | $  156,390 |

Expenditures, and Changes in Fund Balance (see Illustration 3–2). Illustration 3–2 presents the actual revenues and actual expenditures that resulted from transactions illustrated in this chapter. Note also that the expenditures include the prior year expenditures of $15,500 (see Entry 4) but do not include the current encumbrances of $35,000, because GASB standards specify that encumbrances are not to be reported as expenditures (except in statements prepared in conformity with budgetary practices instead of GAAP).

Information shown here as Illustration 3–2 would be presented in columnar form in the Combined Statement of Revenues, Expenditures, and Changes in Fund Balances—All Governmental Fund Types and Expendable Trust Funds, one of the five combined statements required for GAAP (Illustration 2–1).

A third statement that should be prepared at year-end is the Statement of Revenues, Expenditures, and Changes in Fund Balance—Budget and Actual (Illustration 3–3). This statement should also be in columnar form in the Combined Statement of Revenues, Expenditures, and Changes in Fund Balances—Budget and Actual, another of the five combined statements (Illustration 2–2).

Illustration 3–3 has been compiled under the assumption that the budget was prepared on the basis required by GASB standards for governmental funds. Expenditures, however, include the $35,000 in En-

**ILLUSTRATION 3–3**

**VILLAGE OF ELIZABETH**
**General Fund**
**Statement of Revenues, Expenditures, and**
**Changes in Fund Balance—Budget and Actual**
**Non-GAAP Presentation**
**For the Year Ended December 31, 19x6**

| | Budget | Actual | Actual Over (Under) Budget |
|---|---|---|---|
| Revenues (amounts assumed): | | | |
| Taxes: | | | |
| Property taxes | $2,100,000 | $2,098,800 | $ (1,200) |
| Interest and penalties on taxes | 3,500 | 3,490 | (10) |
| Sales taxes | 660,000 | 615,000 | (45,000) |
| Total Taxes | 2,763,500 | 2,717,290 | (46,210) |
| Licenses and permits | 235,000 | 240,000 | 5,000 |
| Fines and forfeits | 345,000 | 330,000 | (15,000) |
| Intergovernmental revenue | 500,000 | 450,000 | (50,000) |
| Charges for services | 76,500 | 70,000 | (6,500) |
| Miscellaneous revenues | 30,000 | 25,000 | (5,000) |
| Total Revenues | 3,950,000 | 3,832,290 | (117,710) |
| Expenditures and Encumbrances (amounts assumed):* | | | |
| General government | 410,000 | 408,500 | 1,500 |
| Public safety | 1,420,000 | 1,412,500 | 7,500 |
| Public works | 640,000 | 633,000 | 7,000 |
| Health and welfare | 520,000 | 515,600 | 4,400 |
| Parks and recreation | 230,000 | 228,000 | 2,000 |
| Contribution to retirement fund | 125,000 | 125,000 | — |
| Miscellaneous expenditures | 55,000 | 20,100 | 34,900 |
| Total Expenditures and Encumbrances | 3,400,000 | 3,342,700 | 57,300 |
| Excess of Revenues over Expenditures and Encumbrances | 550,000 | 489,590 | (60,410) |
| Other Financing Uses: | | | |
| Operating transfers out | 400,000 | 400,000 | — |
| Change in Fund Balance for Year | 150,000 | 89,590 | (60,410) |
| Fund Balance, January 1, 19x6 | 166,800 | 166,800 | — |
| Equity transfers out | (100,000) | (100,000) | — |
| Fund Balance, December 31, 19x6 | $ 216,800 | $ 156,390 | $ (60,410) |

*"Actual" expenditures for this budget comparison statement include the item shown as Expenditures of 19x6 appropriations in Illustration 3–2 ($3,307,700) plus outstanding encumbrances authorized by the 19x6 appropriations budget ($35,000); a total of $3,342,700 as reported in this illustration.

cumbrances charged against the departmental budgets because the total use of appropriation authority for 19x6 is the sum of Expenditures—19x6 and Encumbrances—19x6. Similarly, the Budget and Actual statement does not include the $15,500 expenditures authorized by the 19x5 appropriations which is reported in Illustration 3–2, prepared in conformity with GAAP, since Illustration 3–3 is prepared in conformity with budgetary practices. Remember that the Statement of Revenues, Expenditures, and Changes in Fund Balance (Illustration 3–2) is to be prepared on the GAAP basis, so that **all** expenditures for the current year are to be included. The "budget-actual" statement (Illustration 3–3) is to be prepared in conformity with budgetary practices; the only difference assumed here is that current-year encumbrances are reported as expenditures as they are charged against the budget. It is possible that the budget might be prepared on the cash or other basis. If this is the case, the heading of the "budget-actual" statement should indicate that the data are not in conformity with GAAP and should provide a reconciliation, either on the statement or in the notes, of the ending Fund Balance with the Fund Balance in the Statement of Revenues, Expenditures, and Changes in Fund Balance.

### Procedures for Recognition of Inventories in Governmental Funds

If a governmental unit is large enough to have sizable inventories of supplies used by a number of departments and funds, the purchasing function is usually centralized and the supply activity is accounted for by an internal service fund. Internal service funds normally use the perpetual inventory method, as illustrated in Chapter 8. Many smaller governmental units account for inventories in the General Fund, and use a physical inventory method. In such cases, materials and supplies may be charged to Expenditures when they are purchased *or* when they are used. The former is called the **purchases method;** the latter, the **consumption method.** Both methods are acceptable under current GASB standards as long as significant amounts of inventory are reported on the balance sheet. Since the inventory will not be converted into cash in the normal operations of a governmental fund, it is not a liquid asset. Accordingly, the Inventory account should be offset by a Reserve for Inventory account reported in a balance sheet as a segregation of Fund Equity, in the same manner as Reserve for Encumbrances.

If a governmental unit has a significant investment in inventory to be reported as an asset of a governmental fund an acceptable entry to record the inventory and the related reserve would be (assuming the **purchases method** and assuming the amount to be $35,000):

|  | Debit | Credit |
|---|---|---|
| Inventory of Supplies | 35,000 | |
| Reserve for Inventory of Supplies | | 35,000 |

If the **consumption method** were used, the following entries would be required:

|  | Debit | Credit |
|---|---|---|
| Inventory of Supplies . . . . . . . . . . . . . . . . . . | 35,000 |  |
| Expenditures . . . . . . . . . . . . . . . . . . . . |  | 35,000 |
| Fund Balance . . . . . . . . . . . . . . . . . . . . . | 35,000 |  |
| Reserve for Inventory of Supplies . . . . . . . . . . . |  | 35,000 |

Whenever financial statements are to be prepared, the balance in the Inventory and Reserve accounts should be adjusted to the actual physical inventory, using either method.

## SPECIAL REVENUE FUNDS

As indicated in Chapter 2, special revenue funds are needed when legal or policy considerations require that separate funds be created for current purposes other than those served by proprietary or fiduciary funds. Examples of special revenue funds include State Motor Fuel Tax, CETA, and Library Operating. The first two are created for legal reasons; the Library Operating Fund might be created due to a special tax levy or simply the desire of the governing board to have a separate fund to account for an activity which differs from other governmental activities. Governmental units should attempt to keep the number of special revenue and other funds to a minimum; often, a functional classification in the General Fund will provide as much information as is needed.

**Grant accounting**  As has been seen, special revenue funds are often created to account for state and federal grants. If a grant is restricted for specific purposes, GASB Codification Sec. G60.109 requires that the grant revenue not be recognized until the expenditure has taken place inasmuch as the grant revenue has not been "earned" until the terms of the grant have been met through the expenditure. The receivable or cash asset is offset by a liability until the expenditure takes place. For example, assume that an irrevocable grant has been received from the state to fund a fine arts program, and a special revenue fund is created. When the grant is recognized, the special revenue fund entry would be:

|  | Debit | Credit |
|---|---|---|
| Grants Receivable—State . . . . . . . . . . . . . . . . | 50,000 |  |
| Deferred Revenues . . . . . . . . . . . . . . . . . . |  | 50,000 |

When the expenditure has taken place, the following would be recorded:

|  | Debit | Credit |
|---|---|---|
| Expenditures . . . . . . . . . . . . . . . . . . . . . | 50,000 |  |
| Vouchers Payable (or Cash) . . . . . . . . . . . . . |  | 50,000 |
| Deferred Revenues . . . . . . . . . . . . . . . . . . | 50,000 |  |
| Revenues . . . . . . . . . . . . . . . . . . . . . . |  | 50,000 |

This limitation does not apply to shared revenues and other situations where a great deal of flexibility is allowed in the expending of grant proceeds.

**Accounting and statements**   Special revenue fund accounting is exactly parallel to the accounting described for the General Fund in this chapter. Along with the General Fund, the total of the special revenue funds would be included in the Combined Balance Sheet, the Combined Statement of Revenues, Expenditures, and Changes in Fund Balances (All Governmental Fund Types), and the Combined Statement of Revenues, Expenditures, and Changes in Fund Balances—Budget and Actual. In addition, when more than one special revenue fund exists, combining operating and budget-actual statements are required for the Comprehensive Annual Finance Report.

## SELECTED REFERENCES

American Institute of Certified Public Accountants. *Audits of State and Local Governmental Units.* Rev. ed. New York, 1986.

Governmental Accounting Standards Board. *Codification of Governmental Accounting and Financial Reporting Standards.* 2nd ed. Norwalk, Conn., 1987.

## QUESTIONS AND EXERCISES

3–1.    Using the annual financial report obtained for Exercise 1–1, answer the following questions:

   a.  Are separate statements prepared for the General Fund? If so, what are they? What additional information is on the individual statements that is not in the combined statements?

   b.  Do the General Fund and the special revenue funds use an accrual basis of accounting? Read the note disclosure in the "Summary of Significant Accounting Policies." Does the Summary state that an accrual basis of accounting is used? Are property tax revenues recognized in conformity with the standards discussed in this text? Do the notes to the financial statements describe the property tax calendar and give other information so the reader can determine the governmental unit's accounting policies?

   c.  Do appropriations lapse at year-end? Can you tell from the financial report whether encumbrance accounting is appropriate?

   d.  Attempt to look at the General Fund statements from the point of view of a financial analyst. Is the Fund Balance as of balance sheet date larger or smaller than Fund Balance at the end of the preceding year? Are reasons for the increase/decrease clear from the statements? Did the expenditures stay within the budget in all categories? What is the government's position with respect to short-term debt? Review the Letter of Transmittal to study the relative increases in revenues and expenditures. Examine the statistical section to determine: *(a)* property tax collection history, *(b)* revenues per capita, (c) expenditures per capita, and (d) the recent history with regard to assessed valuation and property tax rates.

3–2.    Write the numbers 1 through 10 on a sheet of paper. Beside each number, write the letter corresponding to the best answer to each of the following questions.

Items 1 through 7 are based on the following information:

Maple Township uses encumbrance accounting, and formally integrates its budget into the accounting records for its general fund. For the year ending June 30, 19x8, the Township Council adopted a budget comprising estimated revenues of $10,000,000, appropriations of $9,000,000, and an estimated transfer of $300,000 to the debt service fund. The following additional information is provided:

- For the month of April 19x8, salaries and wages expense of $200,000 was incurred.
- On April 10, 19x8, an approved $1,500 purchase order was issued for supplies. The supplies were received on May 1, 19x8, and the $1,500 invoice was approved for payment.
- In November 19x7, an unexpected state grant of $100,000 was received to finance the purchase of school buses, and an additional grant of $5,000 was received for bus maintenance and operations. Only $60,000 of the capital grant was used in the current year for the purchase of buses, but the entire operating grant of $5,000 was disbursed in the current year. The remaining $40,000 of the capital grant is expected to be expended during the year ending June 30, 19x9. Maple's school bus system is appropriately accounted for in the capital projects fund.

1.  On adoption of the budget, the journal entry to record the budgetary fund balance should include a
    a.  Debit of $700,000.
    b.  Credit of $700,000.
    c.  Debit of $1,000,000.
    d.  Credit of $1,000,000.
2.  Budgeted revenues would be recorded by a
    a.  Debit to Estimated Revenues, $10,000,000.
    b.  Debit to Estimated Revenues Receivable, $10,000,000.
    c.  Credit to Estimated Revenues, $10,000,000.
    d.  Credit to Other Financing Sources, $10,000,000.
3.  Budgeted appropriations would be recorded by a
    a.  Debit to Estimated Expenditures, $9,300,000.
    b.  Credit to Appropriations, $9,300,000.
    c.  Debit to Estimated Expenditures, $9,000,000.
    d.  Credit to Appropriations, $9,000,000.
4.  What journal entry should be made on April 10, 19x8, to record the approved purchase order?

|  | Debit | Credit |
|---|---|---|
| a.  Expenditures . . . . . . . . . . . . . . . . . . . | $1,500 | |
|      Encumbrances . . . . . . . . . . . . . | | $1,500 |
| b.  Encumbrances . . . . . . . . . . . . . | 1,500 | |
|      Expenditures . . . . . . . . . . . . . | | 1,500 |

|                                                                 | Debit   | Credit  |
|-----------------------------------------------------------------|---------|---------|
| c. Encumbrances . . . . . . . . . . . . . . . . . . . . . . . . | $1,500  |         |
|        Fund Balance Reserved for Encumbrances . . . . .         |         | $1,500  |
| d. Encumbrances . . . . . . . . . . . . . . . . . . . . . . . . | 1,500   |         |
|        Appropriations . . . . . . . . . . . . . . . . . . . . . |         | 1,500   |

5. What journal entries should be made on May 1, 19x8, upon receipt of the supplies and approval of the invoice?

|                                                                 | Debit   | Credit  |
|-----------------------------------------------------------------|---------|---------|
| a. Encumbrances . . . . . . . . . . . . . . . . . . . . . . .   | $1,500  |         |
|        Appropriations . . . . . . . . . . . . . . . . . . . .   |         | $1,500  |
|     Supplies Expense . . . . . . . . . . . . . . . . . . . .    | 1,500   |         |
|        Vouchers Payable . . . . . . . . . . . . . . . . . .     |         | 1,500   |
| b. Fund Balance Reserved for Encumbrances . . . . . . .         | 1,500   |         |
|        Encumbrances . . . . . . . . . . . . . . . . . . . .     |         | 1,500   |
|     Expenditures . . . . . . . . . . . . . . . . . . . . . .    | 1,500   |         |
|        Vouchers Payable . . . . . . . . . . . . . . . . . .     |         | 1,500   |
| c. Appropriations . . . . . . . . . . . . . . . . . . . . .     | 1,500   |         |
|        Encumbrances . . . . . . . . . . . . . . . . . . . .     |         | 1,500   |
|     Expenditures . . . . . . . . . . . . . . . . . . . . . .    | 1,500   |         |
|        Vouchers Payable . . . . . . . . . . . . . . . . . .     |         | 1,500   |
| d. Expenditures . . . . . . . . . . . . . . . . . . . . . .     | 1,500   |         |
|        Encumbrances . . . . . . . . . . . . . . . . . . . .     |         | 1,500   |
|     Supplies Expense . . . . . . . . . . . . . . . . . . . .    | 1,500   |         |
|        Vouchers Payable . . . . . . . . . . . . . . . . . .     |         | 1,500   |

6. In connection with the grants for the purchase of school buses and bus maintenance and operations, what amount should be reported as grant revenues for the year ending June 30, 19x8?
   a. $5,000.
   b. $60,000.
   c. $65,000.
   d. $100,000.

7. What journal entry should be made to record the salaries and wages expense incurred for April?

|                                                                 | Debit     | Credit    |
|-----------------------------------------------------------------|-----------|-----------|
| a. Salaries and Wages Expense . . . . . . . . . . . . .         | $200,000  |           |
|        Vouchers Payable . . . . . . . . . . . . . . . . .       |           | $200,000  |
| b. Appropriations . . . . . . . . . . . . . . . . . . . .       | 200,000   |           |
|        Vouchers Payable . . . . . . . . . . . . . . . . .       |           | 200,000   |
| c. Encumbrances . . . . . . . . . . . . . . . . . . . . .       | 200,000   |           |
|        Vouchers Payable . . . . . . . . . . . . . . . . .       |           | 200,000   |
| d. Expenditures . . . . . . . . . . . . . . . . . . . . .       | 200,000   |           |
|        Vouchers Payable . . . . . . . . . . . . . . . . .       |           | 200,000   |

8. The following items were among Wood Township's expenditures from the General Fund during the year ended June 30, 19x7:

| Furniture for Township Hall . . . . . . . . . . . . . . . . . . . . . . . . . | $10,000 |
|-------------------------------------------------------------------------------|---------|
| Minicomputer for tax collector's office . . . . . . . . . . . . . . . . . .    | 15,000  |

The amount that should be classified as fixed assets in Wood's General Fund balance sheet at June 30, 19x7 is:

      *a.* $25,000.
      *b.* $15,000.
      *c.* $10,000.
      *d.* $0.

Items 9 and 10 are based on the following information:

The following balances appeared in the City of Reedsbury's General Fund at June 30, 19x1:

| *Account* | *Balance*<br>*Dr.  (Cr.)* |
|---|---|
| Encumbrances—current year | $ 200,000 |
| Expenditures: | |
|   Current year | 3,000,000 |
|   Prior year | 100,000 |
| Fund balance reserved for encumbrances: | |
|   Current year | (200,000) |
|   Prior year | None |

Reedsbury maintains its General Fund book in conformity with GASB standards. State law provides that the sum of current-year expenditures and encumbrances cannot exceed current year appropriations.

9. What total amount of expenditures (and encumbrances, if appropriate) should Reedsbury report in the General Fund column of its Combined Statement of Revenues, Expenditures, and Changes in Fund Balance for the year ended June 30, 19x1?
      *a.* $3,000,000.
      *b.* $3,100,000.
      *c.* $3,200,000.
      *d.* $3,300,000.

10. What total amount of expenditures (and encumbrances, if appropriate) should Reedsbury report in the General Fund "actual" column of its Combined Statement of Revenues, Expenditures, and Changes in Fund Balance—Budget and Actual for the year ended June 30, 19x1?
      *a.* $3,000,000.
      *b.* $3,100,000.
      *c.* $3,200,000.
      *d.* $3,300,000.

(AICPA, adapted)

**3–3.** As of June 30, 19x1, the last day of its fiscal year, the City of Briscoe had the following General Fund account balances:

| | Debit | Credit |
|---|---|---|
| Accounts Payable | | $ 193,000 |
| Appropriations | | 2,565,000 |
| Cash | $ 51,000 | |
| Due to Other Funds | | 30,000 |
| Encumbrances—19x1 | 42,000 | |
| Estimated Revenues | 2,566,000 | |
| Estimated Uncollectible Delinquent Taxes | | 62,000 |

| | | |
|---|---:|---:|
| Expenditures—19x1 . . . . . . . . . . . . . . . . . . . | 2,522,000 | |
| Fund Balance . . . . . . . . . . . . . . . . . . . . . | | 17,000 |
| Reserve for Encumbrances—19x1 . . . . . . . . . . . | | 42,000 |
| Revenues . . . . . . . . . . . . . . . . . . . . . . | | 2,570,000 |
| Taxes Receivable—Delinquent . . . . . . . . . . . . | 298,000 | |
| Totals . . . . . . . . . . . . . . . . . . . . . . . | $5,479,000 | $5,479,000 |

*Required:* (Show all necessary computations in good form.)

a. In the City of Briscoe's General Fund Statement of Revenues, Expenditures, and Changes in Fund Balance for the year ended June 30, 19x1, how much should be reported as the Excess of Revenues over (under) Expenditures?

b. In the City of Briscoe's General Fund Statement of Revenues, Expenditures, and Changes in Fund Balance—Budget and Actual for the year ended June 30, 19x1, how much should be reported as:
1. The *budgeted* Excess of Revenues over (under) Expenditures?
2. The *actual* Excess of Revenues over (under) Expenditures?

c. Explain why your answer to b2 differs from your answer to a, if it does.

3–4. On October 1, 19x6, the first day of its fiscal year, the City of Jackson received notification that a federal grant in the amount of $500,000 was approved. The grant was categorical; that is, it was restricted for the payment of wages to teenagers for summer employment. The terms of the grant permitted reimbursement only after payment was made; the grant could be used over a two-year period. The following data pertain to operations of the Summer Employment Grant Fund, a special revenue fund of the City of Jackson, during the year ended September 30, 19x7.

*Required:*

Show entries in general journal form to record the following events and transactions in the accounts of the Summer Employment Grant Fund:

1. The budget for fiscal year 19x7 was recorded. It provided for Estimated Revenues for the year in the amount of $250,000, and for Appropriations in the amount of $250,000.
2. The grant commitment from the federal government was recorded as a receivable.
3. A temporary loan of $250,000 was received from the General Fund.
4. During the year teenagers earned and were paid $246,000 under terms of the Summer Employment program.
5. A properly documented request for reimbursement was sent to the federal government; a check for $246,000 was received.
6. Necessary closing entries were made.

3–5. The Town of Parrishville's fiscal year ends on June 30. The following data relate to the property tax levy for the fiscal year ended June 30, 19x1.

*Required:*

Prepare journal entries for each of the dates as indicated.

a. On July 1, 19x0, property taxes in the amount of $10,000,000 were levied. It was estimated that 2 percent would be uncollectible. The property taxes were intended to finance the expenditures for the year ended June 30, 19x1.

*b.* On October 31, 19x0, $4,500,000 in property taxes were collected.

*c.* On December 31, 19x0, $4,800,000 additional property taxes were collected.

*d.* On January 1, 19x1, the uncollected property taxes became delinquent.

*e.* On October 31, 19x1, $500,000 in delinquent property taxes were collected.

*f.* On November 1, 19x1, the remaining delinquent property taxes were written off.

**3–6.** The Town of Northport has a July 1–June 30 fiscal year.

1. During the year ended 6/30/x1, goods and services were ordered in the amount of $1,000,000.
2. During the year, goods and services ordered in the amount of $950,000 were received; related invoices amounted to $951,000.
3. Make adjusting and closing entries related to the encumbrances and expenditures as of 6/30/x1. Debit Fund Balance for the full amount of the encumbrances and expenditures, recognizing that revenues will offset that debit in another closing entry not required in this problem.
4. On July 1, 19x1, reestablish the encumbrances (requirement *b* only).
5. During the fiscal year ended June 30, 19x2, goods related to the remaining purchase orders were received, along with invoices amounting to $52,000.
6. Make the closing entry related to these purchase orders and expenditures as of June 30, 19x2.

***Required:***

*a.* Record in general journal form the above transactions in the accounts of the General Fund of the Town of Northport, assuming that appropriations and encumbrances do **not** lapse at year-end. (This is the procedure illustrated in the chapter.)

*b.* Record in general journal form the above transactions on the books of the General Fund of the Town of Northport, assuming that both appropriations and encumbrances do lapse at year-end. Make the assumption that the Encumbrances and Reserve for Encumbrances accounts are closed at year-end and reestablished at the beginning of the following year.

**3–7.** The following information was abstracted from the accounts of the General Fund of the City of Rom after the books had been closed for the fiscal year ended June 30, 19x7.

| | Post-Closing Trial Balance June 30, 19x6 | Transactions July 1, 19x6 to June 30, 19x7 Debit | Transactions July 1, 19x6 to June 30, 19x7 Credit | Post-Closing Trial Balance June 30, 19x7 |
|---|---|---|---|---|
| Cash . . . . . . . . . . . . . | $700,000 | $1,820,000 | $1,852,000 | $668,000 |
| Taxes receivable  . . . . . . . . | 40,000 | 1,870,000 | 1,828,000 | 82,000 |
| | $740,000 | | | $750,000 |
| Allowance for uncollectible taxes . | $ 8,000 | 8,000 | 10,000 | $ 10,000 |
| Vouchers payable . . . . . . . . | 132,000 | 1,852,000 | 1,840,000 | 120,000 |
| Fund balance: | | | | |
|   Reserved for encumbrances  . . | — | 1,000,000 | 1,070,000 | 70,000 |
|   Unreserved . . . . . . . . . | 600,000 | 140,000 | 60,000 | 550,000 |
| | | | 30,000 | |
| | $740,000 | | | $750,000 |

**Additional information:**

The budget for the fiscal year ended June 30, 19x7, provided for estimated revenues of $2,000,000 and appropriations of $1,940,000.

**Required:**

Prepare journal entries to record the budgeted and actual transactions for the fiscal year ended June 30, 19x7.

(AICPA, adapted)

3–8.    The general fund trial balance of the City of Solna at December 31, 19x2, was as follows:

|  | Dr. | Cr. |
|---|---|---|
| Cash . . . . . . . . . . . . . . . . . . . . . . . . . | $ 62,000 | |
| Taxes receivable—delinquent . . . . . . . . . . . . . . | 46,000 | |
| Estimated uncollectible taxes—delinquent . . . . . . . . . . | | $  8,000 |
| Stores inventory—program operations . . . . . . . . . . | 18,000 | |
| Vouchers payable . . . . . . . . . . . . . . . . . . | | 28,000 |
| Fund balance reserved for stores inventory . . . . . . . . . . | | 18,000 |
| Fund balance reserved for encumbrances . . . . . . . . . . . | | 12,000 |
| Unreserved undesignated fund balance . . . . . . . . . . . | | 60,000 |
| | $126,000 | $126,000 |

Collectible delinquent taxes are expected to be collected within 60 days after the end of the year. Solna uses the "purchases" method to account for stores inventory. The following data pertain to 19x3 General Fund operations:

1. *Budget adopted:*

Revenues and other financing sources:

| | |
|---|---|
| Taxes . . . . . . . . . . . . . . . . . . . . . . . . . . . . . | $220,000 |
| Fines, forfeits, and penalties . . . . . . . . . . . . . . . . . . . | 80,000 |
| Miscellaneous revenues . . . . . . . . . . . . . . . . . . . . | 100,000 |
| Share of bond issue proceeds . . . . . . . . . . . . . . . . . | 200,000 |
| | $600,000 |

Expenditures and other financing uses:

| | |
|---|---|
| Program operations . . . . . . . . . . . . . . . . . . . . . . | $300,000 |
| General administration . . . . . . . . . . . . . . . . . . . . | 120,000 |
| Stores—program operations . . . . . . . . . . . . . . . . . . | 60,000 |
| Capital outlay . . . . . . . . . . . . . . . . . . . . . . . . | 80,000 |
| Periodic transfer to debt service fund . . . . . . . . . . . . . . | 20,000 |
| | $580,000 |

2. Taxes were levied at an amount that would result in revenues of $220,800, after deduction of 4 percent of the tax levy as uncollectible.

3. *Orders placed but not received:*

| | |
|---|---|
| Program operations . . . . . . . . . . . . . . . . . . . . . . . | $176,000 |
| General administration . . . . . . . . . . . . . . . . . . . . . | 80,000 |
| Capital outlay . . . . . . . . . . . . . . . . . . . . . . . . | 60,000 |
| | $316,000 |

4. The City Council designated $20,000 of the unreserved undesignated fund balance for possible future appropriation for capital outlay.

5. *Cash collections and transfer:*

Delinquent taxes . . . . . . . . . . . . . . . . . . . . . . . . . . . . $ 38,000
Current taxes . . . . . . . . . . . . . . . . . . . . . . . . . . . . . .   226,000
Refund of overpayment of invoice for purchase of equipment . . . . . .     4,000
Fines, forfeits, and penalties . . . . . . . . . . . . . . . . . . . . .    88,000
Miscellaneous revenues . . . . . . . . . . . . . . . . . . . . . . . .      90,000
Share of bond issue proceeds . . . . . . . . . . . . . . . . . . . . .     200,000
Transfer of remaining fund balance of a discontinued fund . . . . . . . .   18,000
                                                                         $664,000

6. *Purchase orders were filled in the following amounts:*

|  | Estimated | Actual |
|---|---|---|
| Program operations . . . . . . . . . . . . . . . . . . . | $156,000 | $166,000 |
| General administration . . . . . . . . . . . . . . . . | 84,000 | 80,000 |
| Capital outlay . . . . . . . . . . . . . . . . . . . . | 62,000 | 62,000 |
|  | $302,000 | $308,000 |

7. *Additional vouchers:*

Program operations . . . . . . . . . . . . . . . . . . . . . . . . . . $188,000
General administration . . . . . . . . . . . . . . . . . . . . . . . .    38,000
Capital outlay . . . . . . . . . . . . . . . . . . . . . . . . . . . .    18,000
Transfer to debt service fund . . . . . . . . . . . . . . . . . . . .     20,000
                                                                       $264,000

8. Albert, a taxpayer, overpaid his 19x3 taxes by $2,000. He applied for a $2,000 credit against his 19x4 taxes. The City Council granted his request.
9. Vouchers paid amounted to $580,000.
10. Stores inventory on December 31, 19x3, amounted to $12,000.

**Required:**
*a.* Prepare journal entries to record the effects of the foregoing data. Omit explanations and subsidiary accounts.
*b.* Prepare closing entries.

(AICPA, adapted)

## CONTINUOUS PROBLEM

3–C.    *Part 1.* Presented below are a number of transactions of the General Fund of the City of Everlasting Sunshine for which the budget was prepared in Continuous Problem 2–C. You are required to:
*a.* Record in the general journal the transactions given below for FY 19y1. Make any computations to the nearest dollar. Subsidiary accounts and explanations are not required.
   1. The 1/1/y1 balance of $20,000 in Deferred Revenues relates to property taxes levied for 19y1, but collected in 19y0. This amount should be recognized as 19y1 revenues (debit Deferred Revenues and credit Revenues).
   2. A general tax levy in the amount of $6,200,000 was made. It is estimated that 3 percent of the tax will be uncollectible.

3. Tax anticipation notes in the amount of $500,000 were issued.
4. Goods and supplies related to all encumbrances outstanding as of 12/31/y0 were received, along with invoices amounting to $30,000; the invoices were approved for payment.
5. All vouchers and the amount due other funds were paid.
6. The General Fund collected the following in cash: delinquent taxes, $180,000; interest and penalties receivable on taxes, $16,500; current taxes, $5,900,000; the amount due from the state government, and the operating transfer from the Street and Highway Fund, $500,000; licenses and permits, $800,000; sales taxes, $3,115,000; and miscellaneous revenues, $235,000.
7. Purchase orders, contracts, and other commitment documents were issued in the amount of $4,266,000.
8. Payrolls for the General Fund totaled $4,600,000. Of that amount $506,000 was withheld for employees' federal income taxes and $361,100 was withheld for employees' FICA tax liability; the balance was paid in cash. The encumbrance system is not used for payrolls.
9. The liability for the city's share of FICA taxes, $361,100, was recorded as was the liability for state unemployment taxes in the amount of $35,000.
10. Invoices for most of the supplies and services ordered in transaction 7 were received in the amount of $4,040,500 and approved for payment. The related commitment documents amounted to $4,038,200.
11. Tax anticipation notes were paid at maturity, along with interest in the amount of $22,000.
12. Notification was received that an unrestricted state grant in the amount of $288,000 will be received during the first month of 19y2.
13. The General Fund recorded a liability to the Water and Sewer Fund for services in the amount of $45,000 and to the Stores and Services Fund for supplies in the amount of $310,000; $290,000 of the amount due the Stores and Services Fund was paid.
14. The General Fund recorded an amount due of $35,000 from the Water and Sewer Fund as a contribution in lieu of taxes.
15. The General Fund paid vouchers in the amount of $3,980,000, and paid the amounts due the federal and state governments. The General Fund also transferred to the debt service funds cash in the amount of $1,280,000 for the recurring payment of principal and interest.
16. All required legal steps were accomplished to increase appropriations by the net amount of $360,000. Estimated revenues were increased by $330,000.
17. A physical inventory indicated that $85,000 of supplies were on hand. The purchases method of recording inventory is used for the General Fund.
18. The City Council authorized a write-off of $30,000 in delinquent property taxes and corresponding interest and penalties amounting to $4,000.
19. Current taxes receivable were transferred to the delinquent classification. Interest and penalties receivable on taxes were accrued in the amount of $33,000; $5,000 of this amount is expected to be uncollectible.

b. Post to the general ledger and prepare a trial balance. Remember to include the beginning balances.

c. Prepare and post the closing entries for the General Fund.

d. Prepare in good form a Balance Sheet for the General Fund as of the end of fiscal year, 12/31/y1.

e. Prepare a Statement of Revenues, Expenditures, and Changes in Fund Balance for the year ended December 31, 19y1. Assume the following detail:

| Revenues | | Expenditures | |
|---|---|---|---|
| | | **Authorized by 19y1** | |
| | | **Appropriations:** | |
| Property taxes . . . . . | .$ 6,034,000 | General government | .$1,692,300 |
| Sales taxes . . . . . . . | 3,115,000 | Public safety . . . . . | 3,258,700 |
| Interest and penalties | | Highways and streets | . 1,441,400 |
| on taxes . . . . . . | 28,000 | Sanitation . . . . . . | 591,400 |
| Licenses and permits . . . | 800,000 | Health . . . . . . . | 723,600 |
| Intergovernmental revenue . | 288,000 | Welfare . . . . . . . | 373,800 |
| Miscellaneous revenues . . | 270,000 | Culture and recreation . | 916,800 |
| | | Capital outlays . . . . | 416,600 |
| Total . . . . . . . . | .$10,535,000 | Total Expenditures of 19y1 | |
| | | Appropriations . . . . . | 9,414,600 |
| | | **Authorized by 19y0** | |
| | | **Appropriations:** | |
| | | Capital outlays . . . . | 29,000 |
| | | Total Expenditures . . . . | .$9,443,600* |

*Expenditures in this statement do not include encumbrances outstanding on December 31, 19y1.

f. Prepare in good form a Statement of Revenues, Expenditures, and Changes in Fund Balances—Budget and Actual for the General Fund as of December 31, 19y1. Assume the following detail:

| | Budget | Actual |
|---|---|---|
| *Revenues:* | | |
| Property taxes . . . . . . . . . . . . . . . . . . . | $ 6,030,000 | $ 6,034,000 |
| Sales taxes . . . . . . . . . . . . . . . . . . | 3,120,000 | 3,115,000 |
| Interest and penalties on taxes . . . . . . . . . . | 30,000 | 28,000 |
| Licenses and permits . . . . . . . . . . . | 805,000 | 800,000 |
| Intergovernmental revenue . . . . . . . . . . . | 285,000 | 288,000 |
| Miscellaneous revenues . . . . . . . . . . . . . | 260,000 | 270,000 |
| Total . . . . . . . . . . . . . . . . . . . | $10,530,000 | $10,535,000 |
| *Expenditures:* | | |
| Current: | | |
| General government . . . . . . . . . . . . . . | $ 1,800,000 | $ 1,797,620 |
| Public safety . . . . . . . . . . . . . . . . | 3,320,000 | 3,318,000 |
| Highway and streets . . . . . . . . . . . . . | 1,450,000 | 1,448,000 |
| Sanitation . . . . . . . . . . . . . . . . | 600,000 | 597,000 |
| Health . . . . . . . . . . . . . . . . . . | 730,000 | 728,500 |
| Welfare . . . . . . . . . . . . . . . . . | 380,000 | 379,500 |
| Culture and recreation . . . . . . . . . . . . | 920,000 | 919,720 |
| Capital outlay . . . . . . . . . . . . . . . . | 460,000 | 454,060 |
| Total . . . . . . . . . . . . . . . . . . . | $ 9,660,000 | $ 9,642,400* |

*This "actual" figure is on the budget basis; that is, it includes only expenditures of the 19y1 appropriation and does not include the $29,000 expended in 19y1 which was charged to Expenditures—19y0, but does include outstanding encumbrances of the 19y1 appropriation totaling $227,800.

*Part 2.* Presented below are a number of transactions of the Street and High-way Fund of the City of Everlasting Sunshine for which the budget was pre-pared in Continuous Problem 2–C. You are required to:

a. Record in the general journal the transactions given below. Make any com-putations to the nearest dollar. Subsidiary accounts and explanations are not required.

1. The state government notified the City that $975,000 will be available during 19y1. The funds are not considered restricted as defined by GASB standards.
2. Cash in the total amount of $950,000 was received from the state government.
3. Contracts for services, all eligible for payment from the Street and Highway Fund, were signed in the amount of $418,000.
4. An operating transfer of $500,000 was made to the General Fund, in accordance with the budget. This was to cover road maintenance by the Public Works Department; state policy required that the expendi-tures be included in the Highways and Street classification in the Gen-eral Fund.
5. Contractual services (see transaction 3) were received; the related con-tracts amounted to $386,500. Invoices amounting to $391,000 for these items were approved for payment. The goods and services all were for highways and streets.
6. Investment revenue of $4,000 was earned and received.
7. Vouchers were paid in the amount of $388,000.
8. All required legal steps were accomplished to increase appropriations in the amount of $2,500.

b. Post to the general ledger and prepare a trial balance.
c. Prepare and post the necessary closing entries for the Street and Highway Fund.
d. Prepare a Balance Sheet for the Street and Highway Fund as of December 31, 19y1.
e. Prepare a Statement of Revenues, Expenditures, and Changes in Fund Balances for the Street and Highway Fund for the fiscal year ended De-cember 31, 19y1.
f. Prepare a Statement of Revenues, Expenditures, and Changes in Fund Balances—Budget and Actual for the Street and Highway Fund for the fiscal year ended December 31, 19y1. Assume that the budgeted expendi-tures for highway and street maintenance amounted to $422,500 and that all the Estimated Revenues were classified as intergovernmental.

# Chapter 4

# CAPITAL PROJECTS FUNDS

Chapters 2 and 3 illustrate that long-lived assets such as office equipment, automobiles, and other items to be used by activities accounted for by governmental fund types may be acquired by expenditure of appropriations of the General Fund or one or more of the special revenue funds of a governmental unit. Long-lived assets used by activities accounted for by governmental funds are known as *general fixed assets* and are accounted for in the General Fixed Assets Account Group (GFAAG). Accounting and financial reporting for the GFAAG is discussed in Chapter 5.

Acquisitions of general fixed assets which require major amounts of money ordinarily cannot be financed from General Fund or special revenue fund appropriations. Major acquisitions of general fixed assets are usually financed, partially at least, from proceeds of issues of long-term debt. Long-term debt incurred for the acquisition of general fixed assets is accounted for in the General Long-Term Debt Account Group (GLTDAG), discussed in Chapter 7. Resources for repayment of general long-term debt are raised from tax levies and, in some cases, from special assessments against property deemed particularly benefited by the capital project for which the debt was incurred. Accounting for debt service is explained and illustrated in Chapter 6.

In addition to proceeds of issues of long-term debt, capital projects funds may receive grants from other governmental units, transfers from other funds, gifts from individuals or organizations, or from a combination of several of these sources. Capital projects funds are also used to account for the acquisition by a governmental unit of general fixed assets under capital lease agreements.

Capital projects funds differ from general and special revenue funds which have a year-to-year life, in that a capital project fund exists only for the duration of the project for which it is created. GASB standards do not require the utilization of Estimated Revenues and Appropriations accounts, although the encumbrance system is usually used to keep track of outstanding contracts and purchase orders. If state law or action of the governing board require adoption of annual budgets, budgetary accounts would be used as illustrated in Chapter 2. In such cases financial reporting standards require that a Capital Projects Funds column be included in the Combined Statement of Revenues, Expenditures, and Changes in Fund Balances—Budget and Actual, as discussed in Chapter 2. Neither the capital assets acquired nor any long-term debt incurred for the acquisition is accounted for by a capital projects fund; the GFAAG and the GLTDAG account for these items, as discussed in Chapters 5 and 7, respectively.

GASB standards require the same basis of accounting for capital projects funds, as for all other governmental funds. Proceeds of debt issues should be recognized by a capital projects fund at the time the debt is actually incurred, rather than the time it is authorized, because authorization of an issue does not guarantee its sale. Proceeds of debt issues should be recorded as **Proceeds of Bonds** or **Proceeds of Long-Term Notes** rather than as Revenues, and should be reported in the Other Financing Sources section of the Statement of Revenues, Expenditures, and Changes in Fund Balances. Similarly, revenues raised by the General Fund, or a special revenue fund, and transferred to a capital projects fund are recorded as Operating Transfers In and reported in the Other Financing Sources section of the operating statement. Taxes or other revenues raised specifically for a capital projects fund would be recorded as Revenues of the capital projects fund. Grants, entitlements, or shared revenues received by a capital projects fund from another governmental unit are considered as Revenues of the capital projects fund, as would be interest earned on temporary investments of the capital projects fund (assuming that the interest may be used by the capital projects fund—in some situations interest earned may have to be transferred to a debt service fund; in those cases interest receipts would be accounted for in the same manner as bond premium; see Entry 8 below).

## ILLUSTRATIVE CASE

In the following illustration of accounting for representative transactions of a capital projects fund, it is assumed that early in 19x6 the Village Council of the Village of Elizabeth authorized an issue of $1,200,000 of 8 percent tax-supported bonds to finance construction of a fire station. The total cost of the fire station was expected to be $2,000,000 with $600,000 to be financed by transfers from other governmental units, and $200,000 to be transferred from a special revenue fund of the Village of Elizabeth. The project, to utilize land already owned by the Village, was to be done partly by a private contractor and partly by the Village's own working force. Completion of the project was expected within 18 months. Transactions and entries are illustrated below. For economy of time and space, vouchering of liabilities and entries in subsidiary ledger accounts are not illustrated.

## Transactions and Events in 19x6

The $1,200,000 bond issue, which had received referendum approval by taxpayers, was officially approved by the Village Council.

No formal entry is required. A memorandum entry may be made to identify the approved project and the means of financing it.

The sum of $100,000 was borrowed from the National Bank for defraying engineering and other preliminary costs incurred before bonds could be sold.

| | | |
|---|---|---|
| 1. Cash | 100,000 | |
| Bond Anticipation Notes Payable | | 100,000 |

The receivables from the special revenue fund and the other governmental units were recorded; receipt was expected during 19x6 or early in 19x7.

| | | |
|---|---|---|
| 2. Due from Other Funds | 200,000 | |
| Due from Other Governmental Units | 600,000 | |
| Other Financing Sources—Operating | | |
| Transfers In | | 200,000 |
| Revenues | | 600,000 |

Total purchase orders and other commitment documents issued for supplies, materials, items of minor equipment, and labor required for the project amounted to $245,698.

| | | |
|---|---|---|
| 3. Encumbrances | 245,698 | |
| Reserve for Encumbrances | | 245,698 |

A contract was let for the major part of the work to be done by a private contractor in the amount of $1,500,000.

| | | |
|---|---|---|
| 4. Encumbrances | 1,500,000 | |
| Reserve for Encumbrances | | 1,500,000 |

Note that Entries 3 and 4 differ from entries illustrated in Chapters 2 and 3 to record encumbrances of general or special revenue funds in that those fund types operate under annual budgets (therefore the Encumbrances account and the Reserve for Encumbrances account are designated with the budget year) whereas capital projects funds operate under a project-life budget (so it is unnecessary to designate the Encumbrances and Reserve for Encumbrances accounts as being related to a certain year).

Special engineering and miscellaneous preliminary costs which had not been encumbered were paid in the amount of $97,500.

```
5. Construction Expenditures . . . . . . . . . . .        97,500
     Cash   . . . . . . . . . . . . . . . . . . . .                    97,500
```

When the project was approximately half finished, the contractor submitted billing for a payment of $750,000. The following entry records conversion of an estimated liability (recorded in Reserve for Encumbrances) to a firm liability, eligible for payment upon proper authentication. Contracts Payable records the status of a claim under a contract between the time of presentation and verification for vouchering or payment.

```
6. Reserve for Encumbrances . . . . . . . . . . .        750,000
     Construction Expenditures . . . . . . . . . . .     750,000
       Encumbrances  . . . . . . . . . . . . . . .                    750,000
       Contracts Payable   . . . . . . . . . . . .                    750,000
```

The transfer was received from the Special Revenue Fund, and $300,000 was received from the other governmental units.

```
7. Cash   . . . . . . . . . . . . . . . . . . . . .      500,000
     Due from Other Funds   . . . . . . . . . . .                     200,000
     Due from Other Governmental Units  . . . . .                     300,000
```

The bond issue, dated July 1, 19x6, was sold at a premium of $12,000 on that date. In this example, as is generally true, the premium must be used for debt service and is not available for use by the Capital Projects Fund. Normally one check is received for the proceeds. Since $1,200,000 is for use by the Capital Projects Fund, and $12,000 by the Debt Service Fund, it is logical to record the sale in the Capital Projects Fund as shown by Entry 8:

```
8. Cash   . . . . . . . . . . . . . . . . . . . . .    1,212,000
     Proceeds of Bonds   . . . . . . . . . . . . .                  1,200,000
     Due to Debt Service Fund . . . . . . . . . .                      12,000
```

When the Capital Projects Fund pays the $12,000 to the Debt Service Fund Entry 9 is made.

```
9. Due to Debt Service Fund . . . . . . . . . . .         12,000
     Cash   . . . . . . . . . . . . . . . . . . . .                    12,000
```

The account title "Premium on Bonds" is sometimes used instead of "Due to Debt Service Fund"; if the premium were available for use by the Capital Projects Fund the entire $1,212,000 should be credited to Proceeds of Bonds.

State statutes commonly prohibit the sale of government bonds at a discount. If bonds are sold at a discount, either the difference would be made up by a transfer from another fund, or the Capital Projects Fund would have less available for the project.

If bonds are sold between interest dates, the governmental unit must collect from the purchaser the amount of interest accrued to the date of sale, because a full six months' interest will be paid on the next interest payment date. Interest payments are the function of debt service funds; therefore, cash in the amount of accrued interest sold, although usually included in one check along with the other proceeds of the sale, should be recorded in the Capital Projects Fund as "Due to Debt Service Fund" as shown in Entry 8 for premium received by the Capital Projects Fund but which must be used by the Debt Service Fund. If cash in the amount of bond premium and/or accrued interest sold is received separately from cash for the face of the bonds, only the latter need be recorded in the Capital Projects Fund, and the former may be recorded directly in the Debt Service Fund.

When the Village of Elizabeth's Capital Projects Fund pays the bond anticipation notes and interest (assumed to amount to $2,500) Entry 10 is made:

```
10. Bond Anticipation Notes Payable . . . . . . . . .    100,000
    Interest Expenditures  . . . . . . . . . . . . .      2,500
        Cash  . . . . . . . . . . . . . . . . . . .                102,500
```

GASB standards allow governmental units the option of capitalizing net interest expenditures during the period of construction of general fixed assets. (Governments are **required** to capitalize net interest expense during the period of construction of assets to be used by **proprietary** funds.) Very few governments do capitalize net interest as an element of cost of general fixed assets; if a government wishes to capitalize net interest the interest expenditures should be charged to the Construction Expenditures account, rather than the Interest Expenditures account as shown in Entry 10.

The contractor's initial claim (see Entry 6) was paid, less a 5 percent retention. Retention of a contractually stipulated percentage from payments to a contractor is common until the construction is completed and has been inspected for conformity with specifications and plans.

```
11. Contracts Payable  . . . . . . . . . . . . . . .    750,000
        Cash  . . . . . . . . . . . . . . . . . . . .              712,500
        Contracts Payable—Retained Percentage  . . .               37,500
```

Upon final acceptance of the project, the retained percentage is paid. In the event that the governmental unit finds it necessary to spend money on correction of deficiencies in the contractor's performance, the payment is charged to Contracts Payable—Retained Percentage.

Disbursements for items ordered at an estimated cost of $215,000 (included in the amount recorded by Entry 3) amounted to $216,500.

```
12. Reserve for Encumbrances . . . . . . . . . . . .    215,000
    Construction Expenditures . . . . . . . . . . .    216,500
        Encumbrances  . . . . . . . . . . . . . . .                215,000
        Cash  . . . . . . . . . . . . . . . . . . .                216,500
```

Although the operations of a Capital Projects Fund are project-completion oriented, with slight reference to time, Encumbrances, Expenditures, Proceeds of Bonds, Operating Transfers In, and Revenues should be closed to Fund Balance at year-end in order to facilitate preparation of Capital Projects Fund financial statements for inclusion in the annual report on a basis consistent with year-end statements of other governmental funds. The closing entry for 19x6 would be:

| | | |
|---|---:|---:|
| 13. Revenues . . . . . . . . . . . . . . . . . . . | 600,000 | |
| Other Financing Sources—Operating Transfers In . . | 200,000 | |
| Proceeds of Bonds . . . . . . . . . . . . . | 1,200,000 | |
| Construction Expenditures . . . . . . . . . . | | 1,064,000 |
| Interest Expenditures . . . . . . . . . . . | | 2,500 |
| Encumbrances . . . . . . . . . . . . . . | | 780,698 |
| Fund Balance . . . . . . . . . . . . . . | | 152,802 |

The closing entry produces year-end Capital Projects Fund balance sheets which appear similar to those of the General and special revenue funds. The similarity of appearance and terminology may be misleading, however. The Fund Balance account of a General or special revenue fund represents net liquid assets available for appropriation, whereas the Fund Balance account of a multiple-period Capital Projects Fund represents net assets which have already been set aside for the acquisition of specified capital facilities. Because a year-end balance sheet for a Capital Projects Fund is really an interim statement in respect to the life of the project, its Fund Balance is comparable to the unexpended unencumbered appropriation at any given time during the fiscal year of a General or special revenue fund; it is **not** comparable to the year-end Fund Balance of those funds.

The Capital Projects Fund Balance Sheet for the Village of Elizabeth as of December 31, 19x6 is shown as Illustration 4–1. The Statement of Revenues, Expenditures, and Changes in Fund Balance for the Year

**ILLUSTRATION 4–1**

### VILLAGE OF ELIZABETH
#### Fire Station Capital Projects Fund
#### Balance Sheet
#### As of December 31, 19x6

#### Assets

| | | |
|---|---:|---:|
| Cash . . . . . . . . . . . . . . . . . . . . . . | | $671,000 |
| Due from other governmental units . . . . . . . . . . . | | 300,000 |
| Total Assets . . . . . . . . . . . . . . . . . . | | $971,000 |

#### Liabilities and Fund Equity

| | | |
|---|---:|---:|
| Liabilities: | | |
| Contracts payable—retained percentage . . . . . . . . | | $ 37,500 |
| Fund equity: | | |
| Reserve for encumbrances . . . . . . . . . . . . . | $780,698 | |
| Fund balance . . . . . . . . . . . . . . . . . | 152,802 | |
| Total Fund Equity . . . . . . . . . . . . . | | 933,500 |
| Total Liabilities and Fund Equity . . . . . . . . . . . . | | $971,000 |

Ended December 31, 19x6 is presented as Illustration 4–2. Note that the format in Illustration 4–2 is slightly different from the format for the General Fund Statement of Revenues, Expenditures, and Changes in Fund Balances (Illustration 3–2) in that Revenues and Other Financing Sources are grouped at the top of the Statement rather than reporting Other Financing Sources along with Other Financing Uses in a section following Expenditures. In this format Other Financing Uses would be grouped with Expenditures. GASB standards allow either the format used in Illustration 3–2 or that used in Illustration 4–2. (GASB Codification Sec. 2200.115.) Of course, when combined statements are prepared, the same format must be used for all fund types included in each statement.

## Transactions and Events in 19x7

As discussed in relation to Entry 13, the year-end closing entry artificially chops the accounts of a capital projects fund into fiscal year segments. Accordingly, it is desirable to reestablish the Encumbrances account at the beginning of the next fiscal year. In the Village of Elizabeth illustrative case the following entry should be made as of January 1, 19x7:

| | | |
|---|---|---|
| 14. Encumbrances . . . . . . . . . . . . . . . . . . | 780,698 | |
| Fund Balance . . . . . . . . . . . . . | | 780,698 |

After the above entry is made, subsequent receipt of goods or services encumbered in the prior year may be accounted for in the same

**ILLUSTRATION 4–2**

**VILLAGE OF ELIZABETH**
**Fire Station Capital Projects Fund**
**Statement of Revenues, Expenditures, and**
**Changes in Fund Balance**
**For the Year Ended December 31, 19x6**

| | | |
|---|---|---|
| Revenues and Other Financing Sources: | | |
| Revenues: | | |
| Financing provided by other governmental units . . . . | | $ 600,000 |
| Other Financing Sources: | | |
| Proceeds of bonds . . . . . . . . . . . . . . . . | $1,200,000 | |
| Transfer from special revenue fund . . . . . . . . . . | 200,000 | |
| Total Other Financing Sources . . . . . . . . . . . | | 1,400,000 |
| Total Revenues and Other Financing Sources . . . . | | 2,000,000 |
| Expenditures: | | |
| Construction . . . . . . . . . . . . . . . . . . . | 1,064,000 | |
| Interest . . . . . . . . . . . . . . . . . . . . . | 2,500 | |
| Total Expenditures . . . . . . . . . . . . . . . | | 1,066,500 |
| Excess of Revenues and Other Financing Sources over Expenditures . . . . . . . . . . . . . . . . . . . | | 933,500 |
| Fund Balance, January 1, 19x6 . . . . . . . . . . . | | — |
| (Increase) in Reserve for Encumbrances . . . . . . . . . | | (780,698) |
| Fund Balance, December 31, 19x6 . . . . . . . . . . | | $ 152,802 |

manner as if they had been ordered in the current year. Thus, when the contractor completes construction of the fire station and bills the Village of Elizabeth for the balance on the contract, the following entry is appropriate:

```
15. Reserve for Encumbrances . . . . . . . . . . . .    750,000
        Construction Expenditures . . . . . . . . . . .    750,000
            Encumbrances  . . . . . . . . . . . . . . .                750,000
            Contracts Payable  . . . . . . . . . . . . .                750,000
```

Assume the remaining amount from other governmental units was received:

```
16. Cash   . . . . . . . . . . . . . . . . . . . . . .    300,000
        Due from Other Governmental Units  . . . . .                300,000
```

Invoices for goods and services previously encumbered in the amount of $30,698 were received and approved for payment in the amount of $32,000. Additional construction expenditures, not encumbered, amounted to $115,000. The entire amount was paid in cash.

```
17. Reserve for Encumbrances . . . . . . . . . . . .     30,698
        Construction Expenditures . . . . . . . . . . .    147,000
            Encumbrances  . . . . . . . . . . . . . . .                 30,698
            Cash   . . . . . . . . . . . . . . . . . . .                147,000
```

Assuming that inspection revealed only minor imperfections in the contractor's performance and upon correction of these the contractor's bill and the amount previously retained was paid, Entry 18 should be made:

```
18. Contracts Payable—Retained Percentage  . . . . .     37,500
        Contracts Payable  . . . . . . . . . . . . . .    750,000
            Cash   . . . . . . . . . . . . . . . . . . .                787,500
```

When all requirements and obligations related to the project have been fulfilled, the expenditures account is closed.

```
19. Fund Balance   . . . . . . . . . . . . . . . . . .    897,000
        Construction Expenditures . . . . . . . . . .                897,000
```

After Entry 19 is recorded, the accounts of the Capital Projects Fund show balances of $36,500 in the Cash and Fund Balance accounts; all other accounts have been closed. Assume that, as is customary, the cash is transferred to a debt service fund for the future payment of bonds.

```
20. Equity Transfer Out . . . . . . . . . . . . . . .     36,500
        Cash   . . . . . . . . . . . . . . . . . . . . .                 36,500
```

Entry 21 records the closing of the Equity Transfer account and the Fund Balance account:

```
21. Fund Balance   . . . . . . . . . . . . . . . . . .     36,500
        Equity Transfer Out . . . . . . . . . . . . .                 36,500
```

Since all Balance Sheet accounts relating to the Fire Station Capital Projects Fund have been closed, it is not necessary to prepare a Balance Sheet as of December 31, 19x7. Illustration 4–3 presents the Statement of Revenues, Expenditures, and Changes in Fund Balances for the Year Ended December 31, 19x7.

**ILLUSTRATION 4–3**

**VILLAGE OF ELIZABETH**
**Fire Station Capital Projects Fund**
**Statement of Revenues, Expenditures and**
**Changes in Fund Balance**
**For the Year Ended December 31, 19x7**

| | |
|---|---:|
| Revenues and Other Financing Sources | $    — |
| Expenditures: | |
| Construction | 897,000 |
| Excess of Expenditures over Revenues and Other Financing Sources | (897,000) |
| Fund Balance, January 1, 19x7 | 152,802 |
| Equity Transfer to Debt Service Fund | (36,500) |
| Decrease in Reserve for Encumbrances | 780,698 |
| Fund Balance, December 31, 19x7 | —0— |

## ACQUISITION OF GENERAL FIXED ASSETS BY LEASE AGREEMENTS

FASB *SFAS No. 13* defines and establishes accounting and financial reporting standards for a number of forms of leases, only two of which, **operating** leases and **capital** leases, are of importance in governmental accounting. GASB Codification Sec. L20.101 accepts the *SFAS No. 13* definitions of these two forms of leases and prescribes accounting and financial reporting for lease agreements of state and local governmental units. If a particular lease meets any one of the following criteria, it is a **capital** lease:

1. The lease transfers ownership of the property to the lessee by the end of the lease term.
2. The lease contains an option to purchase the leased property at a bargain price.
3. The lease term is equal to or greater than 75 percent of the estimated economic life of the leased property.
4. The present value of rental or other minimum lease payments equals or exceeds 90 percent of the fair value of the leased property less any investment tax credit retained by the lessor.

If none of the criteria is met, the lease is classified as an **operating** lease by the lessee. Rental payments under an operating lease for assets used by governmental funds are recorded by the using fund as expenditures of the period.

If a governmental unit acquires general fixed assets under a capital lease agreement, the asset should be recorded in the GFAAG at the inception of the agreement at the lesser of (1) the present value of the minimum lease payments or (2) the fair value of the lease property. The debt should be recorded in the General Long-Term Debt Account Group at the present value of the minimum lease payments. GASB standards also require that a governmental fund (normally a capital projects fund) make the following entry at the inception of the lease:

```
Expenditures  . . . . . . . . . . . . . . . . . . . . . . . . . . . . . .  xx
     Other Financing Sources—Capital Lease Agreements  . . . . . .       xx
```

Rental payments during the life of the capital lease are recorded in a governmental fund, ordinarily a debt service fund, as illustrated in Chapter 6.

### Construction of General Fixed Assets Financed by Special Assessment Debt

For over 50 years standards for governmental accounting and financial reporting provided the special assessment fund type to account for the acquisition of capital improvements financed by special assessments against property deemed to be particularly benefited by the assets to be acquired. The special assessment fund type was also used to account for any long-term debt secured by the special assessments, and for the payment of interest on such debt and the repayment of the principal of the debt. Thus, the special assessment fund type combined the functions of capital projects funds and debt service funds, as well as accounting for special assessment long-term debt. In 1987 the Governmental Accounting Standards Board's *Statement No. 6* eliminated the special assessment fund type as a fund type to be reported in general purpose financial statements, effective with fiscal years beginning after June 15, 1987.

*GASB Statement No. 6* requires that transactions related to the construction phase of capital improvement projects financed wholly, or in part, by special assessments be reported in the same manner, and on the same basis of accounting, as any other capital improvement project—generally by a capital projects fund as described in this chapter. If a general governmental unit is obligated to assume debt service on special assessment debt in the event that collections of assessments are insufficient, transactions related to the debt service phase of such projects are to be reported in the same manner as debt service on tax-supported debt—generally by a debt service fund, as described in Chapter 6—and the long-term debt is to be reported in the GLTDAG (discussed in Chapter 7). If a general governmental unit has no obligation for debt service, but merely acts as an agent for the owners of the property against which the special assessments are levied for collection of the assessments, and as agent for the creditors for payment of interest and principal of the debt to the extent that collections of assessments are sufficient to do so, transactions related to the agency function are to be reported in the same manner as other agency transactions (see the discussion of agency funds in Chapter 9).

## SELECTED REFERENCES

Financial Accounting Standards Board. *Statement of Financial Accounting Standards No. 5: Accounting for Contingencies.* Norwalk, Conn., 1975.

_____. *Statement of Financial Accounting Standards No. 13: Accounting for Leases, as Amended and Interpreted to May 1980.* Norwalk, Conn., 1980.

Governmental Accounting Standards Board. *Codification of Governmental Accounting and Financial Reporting Standards.* 2nd ed. Norwalk, Conn., 1987.

## QUESTIONS AND EXERCISES

**4–1.**  Using the annual financial report obtained for Exercise 1–1, answer the following questions.

    *a.* List the names of the capital projects funds. Does your report have a divider page in front of the capital projects funds describing each fund?

    *b.* Does your report have a Combining Balance Sheet and a Combining Statement of Revenues, Expenditures, and Changes in Fund Balances for the capital projects funds? If an annual budget is adopted for capital projects funds, does the report have a Combining Statement of Revenues, Expenditures, and Changes in Fund Balances—Budget and Actual for the capital projects funds? Do the totals agree with the numbers in the combined statements?

    *c.* Does the accounting appear to conform with GASB standards for capital projects funds? Are Proceeds of Bonds shown as an "Other Financing Source" rather than as a revenue?

    *d.* Attempt to look at the capital projects funds from the point of view of a financial analyst. Compute the percentage of the sources of funding coming from bond sales, transfers from other funds, other governmental units, and other sources. Compute the percentage of capital outlay expenditures of total expenditures for all governmental funds. (See the Combined Statement of Revenues, Expenditures, and Changes in Fund Balances.)

    *e.* List any additional disclosures regarding capital outlays in your report. In particular, look at the Letter of Transmittal, the capital projects portion of the Financial Section, and the Statistical Section. Are these disclosures informative? List any items of information you would like to know about capital projects that are not furnished in your report.

**4–2.**  Write the numbers 1 through 10 on a sheet of paper. Beside each number, write the letter corresponding to the best answer to each of the following questions:

    1. Proceeds of General Obligation Bonds is an account of a governmental unit that would be included in the

      *a.* Enterprise Fund.

      *b.* Special Assessments Fund.

    *c.* Capital Projects Fund.

    *d.* Debt Service Fund.

2. Fixed assets used by a governmental unit should be accounted for in the

| | Capital Projects Fund | General Fund |
|---|---|---|
| *a.* | No | Yes |
| *b.* | No | No |
| *c.* | Yes | No |
| *d.* | Yes | Yes |

3. In 19x6, Menton City received $5,000,000 of bond proceeds to be used for capital projects. Of this amount, $1,000,000 was expended in 19x6. Expenditures for the $4,000,000 balance were expected to be incurred in 19x7. These bond proceeds should be recorded in Capital Projects Funds for

    *a.* $5,000,000 in 19x6.

    *b.* $5,000,000 in 19x7.

    *c.* $1,000,000 in 19x6 and $4,000,000 in 19x7.

    *d.* $1,000,000 in 19x6 and in the General Fund for $4,000,000 in 19x6.

4. Transactions related to the construction phase of General Fixed Assets whose acquisition is being financed by special assessments should be reported in the GPFS in the

    *a.* Special Assessment Fund column.

    *b.* Capital Projects Fund column.

    *c.* General Fixed Assets Account Group column.

    *d.* General Long-Term Debt Account Group column.

5. If a governmental unit acquires General Fixed Assets under a capital lease agreement, at the inception of the lease

    *a.* Entries are necessary in the GFAAG and in the GLTDAG, but not in any of the funds.

    *b.* Entries are necessary in a capital projects fund and in a debt service fund, but not in either account group.

    *c.* Entries are necessary in the GFAAG, the GLTDAG, and in a capital projects fund.

    *d.* No entries in any fund or account group are necessary, but the capital lease should be disclosed in the notes to the financial statements.

6. Short-term notes payable issued to finance a capital improvement pending the sale of long-term debt instruments should be:

    *a.* Reported as a Revenue of a Capital Projects Fund.

    *b.* Reported as an "Other Financing Source" of a Capital Projects Fund.

    *c.* Reported as a Liability of a Capital Projects Fund.

    *d.* Credited to the Construction Expenditures account of a Capital Projects Fund.

7. The proceeds of long-term debt issued to finance the acquisition or construction of General Fixed Assets should be:

    *a.* Reported as Revenue of a Capital Projects Fund.

    *b.* Reported as an "Other Financing Source" of a Capital Projects Fund.

    *c.* Reported as a Liability of a Capital Projects Fund.

    *d.* Reported in a Capital Projects Fund only if the debt is to be repaid by Tax Revenue, but not if it is to be repaid by Special Assessments.

8. Net interest expenditures during the period of construction of General Fixed Assets
   a. Must be capitalized as an element of the cost of the assets.
   b. May or may not be capitalized, depending on the choice of the governing body of the governmental unit.
   c. May not be capitalized as an element of the cost of the assets.
   d. None of the above; GASB standards relate to *gross* interest expenditures.
9. If bonds issued to finance the construction of general fixed assets are sold at a premium, state laws generally provide that:
   a. The premium must be donated to the governor's favorite charity.
   b. The premium must be expended for sculptures or paintings to beautify the fixed asset.
   c. The premium must be amortized over the life of the bonds by credits to the Interest Expenditures account.
   d. The premium must be used for debt service rather than for construction.
10. At the end of each fiscal year:
   a. All accounts of a Capital Projects Fund are left open because the fund has a project life, not a year-to-year life.
   b. The Budgetary and Operating Statement accounts are closed in order to facilitate the preparation of year-end Financial Statements.
   c. All accounts are closed in order to facilitate the preparation of year-end financial statements.
   d. None of the above.

(Items 1, 2, and 3, AICPA, adapted)

**4–3.** Write the numbers 1 through 10 on a sheet of paper. Beside each number, write the letter "T" or "F" indicating whether each of the following statements is true or false.

1. GASB standards require that all governmental expenditures for long-lived assets be accounted for by a capital projects fund
2. Capital projects funds should use the same basis of accounting as is used for the General Fund.
3. Although most capital projects funds do not use the Estimated Revenues and Appropriations control accounts, it is recommended that the Encumbrances control account be used.
4. Capital assets constructed or acquired through use of capital projects fund resources are recorded in the General Fixed Assets Account Group and are **not** recorded as assets of the Capital Projects Fund.
5. Proceeds of special assessment debt issued for the construction or acquisition of capital assets are recorded in Capital Projects Funds even though the liability is recorded in the General Long-Term Debt Account Group.
6. Proceeds of Bonds should, ordinarily, be credited only for the face amount of bonds sold, not for the total proceeds.
7. Premium (or discount) on tax-supported bonds issued should be amortized by a governmental unit in the same manner as bond premium (or discount) would be by a business which issues bonds.
8. If a bond sale occurs between interest dates, accrued interest sold should be credited to Due to Debt Service Fund.

9. Because year-end closings are artificial, it is desirable to debit Encumbrances on the first day of the new fiscal year in the amount which was closed at the end of the prior fiscal year.

10. After all liabilities are paid and the operating statement accounts closed, it is common to transfer any assets remaining in a capital projects fund to a debt service fund.

**4–4.** On July 1, 19x6, a five-year agreement was signed between the City of Jamestown and the Computer Leasing Corporation for the use of computer equipment. The cost of the lease was $20,000 per year. The first payment is to be made by the General Fund at the inception of the lease. The present value of lease payments is $77,384. Record all entries which should be made at the inception of the lease (including the first lease rental payment) in the General Fund and the Capital Projects Fund of the City of Jamestown under each of the two assumptions indicated below:

*a.* The agreement meets the criteria for a capital lease under the provisions of *SFAS No. 13*.

*b.* The agreement is an operating lease, as defined in *SFAS No. 13*.

**4–5.** The City of Garry established a City Hall Annex Construction Fund to account for a project which was expected to take approximately one and one-half years to complete. Record the following transactions in the City Hall Annex Construction Fund. Garry's fiscal year ends on April 30.

1. On May 1, 19x0, bonds were sold at par in the amount of $5,000,000 for the project.

2. On May 2, 19x0, a contract was signed with the Flybynite Construction Company in the amount of $4,895,000.

3. On April 30, 19x1, a progress bill was received from Flybynite in the amount of $2,400,000. The bill was paid, except for a 5 percent retainage.

4. On April 30, 19x1, the books were closed for the year.

5. On May 1, 19x1, the encumbrances were reestablished.

6. On November 30, 19x1, a final bill was received from Flybynite, which was paid, except for the 5 percent retainage. An appointment was made between the City Engineer and Fred Flybynite to inspect the building and to develop the "punch list" of items that need to be corrected.

7. On the day of the meeting, the City Engineer discovered that Flybynite had filed for bankruptcy and moved to California to establish a new construction firm. The City incurred a liability in the amount of $350,000 to have the defects corrected by the Goodguy Construction Co. (Charge the excess over the balance of Contracts Payable—Retained Percentage to Construction Expenditures.)

8. An equity transfer was made from the General Fund to cover the project deficit.

9. All vouchers were paid.

10. The accounts of the City Hall Annex Construction Fund were closed.

**4–6.** The voters of Pearl City authorized the sale of tax-supported serial bonds in the total face amount of $6,000,000 to finance the construction and equipping of a performing arts center on land already owned by the City. Owners of the property surrounding the performing arts center agreed to pay special assessments totaling $1,000,000 to finance improved street lighting and beautification of the area. The City Attorney stated that these related projects could legally be accounted for in a single capital projects fund. You are to record in general journal form the following transactions and events, as appropriate, in the Performing Arts Center Construction Fund using the following account titles, as needed:

| | |
|---|---|
| Cash | Interest Expenditures |
| Temporary Investments | Proceeds of Bonds |
| Special Assessments Receivable | Proceeds of Special Assessment Debt |
| Bond Anticipation Notes Payable | Revenues—Special Assessments |
| Due to Debt Service Fund | Encumbrances—Construction |
| Contracts Payable | Encumbrances—Furniture and Equipment |
| Contracts Payable—Retained Percentage | Encumbrances—Street Lighting Project |
| Vouchers Payable | Reserve for Encumbrances—Construction |
| Equity Transfers Out | Reserve for Encumbrances—Furniture and |
| Fund Balance | Equipment |
| Construction Expenditures | Reserve for Encumbrances—Street Lighting |
| Expenditures—Street Lighting Project | Project |

(Related entries are to be made in the General Fixed Assets Account Group, the Debt Service Fund, and the General Long-Term Debt Account Group in Exercises 5–6, 6–6, and 7–6, respectively.)

### Transactions during the year ended December 31, 19y1:

1. On January 3, 19y1, the first business day of the fiscal year, Pearl City borrowed $400,000 from local banks to provide working capital until the bond issue could be sold.
2. On January 5, preliminary architectural and engineering costs amounting to $375,000 were paid. These costs had not been encumbered.
3. As required by state law, the city advertised for bids on the construction of the Performing Arts Center. Newspapers charged $5,000 for the legal advertising. This amount was paid on January 31.
4. The bonds, dated February 15, 19y1, bearing interest at the annual rate of 7 percent were sold on March 1 at par, $6,000,000, plus accrued interest for one-half month. As required by state law, the accrued interest was transferred from the Performing Arts Center Construction Fund to the Debt Service Fund on March 1.
5. On March 4, local banks were repaid the amount borrowed in transaction 1, plus interest for 60 days at the annual rate of 9 percent. The remainder of bond proceeds and cash on hand were invested in U.S. Treasury securities.
6. Construction bids having been received and opened at a public hearing, the City Council voted on March 15 to accept the bid from the Bulldozer Construction Company. A contract in the amount of $4,600,000 was signed on that date.
7. On December 15, the Bulldozer Construction Company submitted a progress billing in the amount of $2,000,000. After the City Engineer inspected the work done, the billing was approved for payment.
8. On December 30, U.S. Treasury securities with a face value of $2,000,000 were sold at par plus accrued interest of $52,500. Proceeds in the amount of $1,900,000 were used to pay the Bulldozer Construction Company's December 15 billing, less a 5 percent retention; cash in the amount of the accrued interest sold was transferred to the Debt Service Fund.
9. Closing entries were made as of December 31, 19y1.

**4–7.**     This exercise continues Exercise 4–6.

*Required:*
   *a.* Prepare in good form a balance sheet for the Performing Arts Center Con-
        struction Fund of Pearl City as of December 31, 19y1.
   *b.* Prepare in good form a Statement of Revenues, Expenditures, and
        Changes in Fund Balance for the Performing Arts Center Construction
        Fund of Pearl City for the year ended December 31, 19y1.

**4–8.**     This exercise continues Exercise 4–6.

Record in general journal form the following transactions and events as
appropriate in the Pearl City Performing Arts Center Construction Fund, using the account titles listed in Exercise 4–6, as needed. (Related entries are
to be made in the General Fixed Assets Account Group, the Debt Service
Fund, and the General Long-Term Debt Account Group in Exercises 5–8,
6–8, and 7–8, respectively).

*Transactions during the year ended December 31, 19y2:*
   1. Encumbrances were reestablished as of January 1, 19y2.
   2. The city advertised for bids for furniture and equipment for the Perform-
      ing Arts Center. The legal advertising cost $2,000. This amount was paid
      on January 15.
   3. On February 1, all legal steps were completed for the $1,000,000 special
      assessment against the property surrounding the Performing Arts Center.
      The owners of the property were allowed to pay the assessment in five
      equal annual installments, the first of which is noninterest bearing if it is
      paid to the Performing Arts Center Construction Fund by March 1, 19y2.
      The receivable is recorded by the Construction Fund on February 1. The
      remaining four installments bear interest at the rate of 10 percent and are
      to be paid to the Debt Service Fund on March 1 of 19y3, 19y4, 19y5, and
      19y6, respectively.
   4. Furniture and equipment bids were received and opened at a public hear-
      ing. The City Council voted on March 1 to accept the bid of the Artis-
      tique Company. A contract in the amount of $1,005,000 was signed on that
      date.
   5. Also on March 1, the first installment of the special assessment was col-
      lected in full.
   6. Contracts totaling $990,000 for the street lighting and beautification proj-
      ect were signed on March 2.
   7. On November 1, the Bulldozer Construction Company submitted its final
      billing in the amount of $2,600,000. After inspection of the work done,
      that amount plus the amount retained in 19y1 was approved for payment.
      U.S. Treasury securities with a face value of $2,700,000 were sold at par
      plus accrued interest of $39,400. Cash in the amount of accrued interest
      sold was transferred to the Debt Service Fund. The amount owed to Bull-
      dozer Construction Company was paid in full.
   8. The Artistique Company completed installation of furniture and equip-
      ment in the Performing Arts Center on December 20 and submitted a bill
      for $1,010,000. The city agreed to pay the entire amount because certain
      items not included in the contract had been installed with the approval of
      a committee of the City Council.

9. The street lighting and beautification project was completed. Contractors' bills in the amount of $1,000,000 were approved for payment on December 30.

10. On December 30, representatives of owners of property surrounding the Performing Arts Center borrowed $800,000 from local banks to be repaid from collections of the second, third, fourth, and fifth installments of the special assessment; the City Council of Pearl City voted to guarantee to repay the banks if collections from property owners proved to be insufficient.

11. On December 31, 19y2, remaining U.S. Treasury securities were sold at par plus $24,000 accrued interest. All outstanding liabilities recorded in the Performing Arts Center Construction Fund were paid. Since all projects had been completed, cash remaining in the Construction Fund was transferred to the Debt Service Fund and all accounts of the Performing Arts Center Construction Fund were closed.

**4–9.** This exercise continues Exercise 4–8.

Record in good form a Statement of Revenues, Expenditures, and Changes in Fund Balance for the Performing Arts Center Construction Fund of Pearl City for the year ended December 31, 19y2.

**4–10.** The City of Westgate's fiscal year ends on June 30. During the fiscal year ended June 30, 19x6, the City authorized the construction of a new library and sale of general obligation term bonds to finance the construction of the library. The authorization imposed the following restrictions:

The construction cost was not to exceed $5,000,000.

The annual interest rate on bonds issued was not to exceed 8½ percent. The following transactions relating to the financing and construction of the library occurred during the fiscal year ended June 30, 19x7:

1. On July 1, 19x6, the City issued $5,000,000 of 30-year 8 percent general obligation bonds for $5,100,000. The semiannual interest dates are December 31 and June 30. The premium of $100,000 was transferred to the Library Debt Service Fund.

2. On July 3, 19x6, the Library Capital Projects Fund invested $4,900,000 in short-term commercial paper. These purchases were at face value with no accrued interest. Interest on cash invested by the Library Capital Projects Fund must be transferred to the Library Debt Service Fund.

3. On July 5, 19x6, the City signed a contract with F&A Construction Company to build the library at a total cost of $4,980,000.

4. On January 15, 19x7, the Library Capital Projects Fund received $3,040,000 from the maturity of short-term notes purchased on July 3. The cost of these notes was $3,000,000. The interest of $40,000 was transferred to the Library Debt Service Fund.

5. On January 20, 19x7, F&A Construction Company properly billed the City $3,000,000 for work performed on the new library. The contract calls for 10 percent retention until final inspection and acceptance of the building. The Library Capital Projects Fund paid F&A $2,700,000.

6. On June 30, 19x7, the Library Capital Projects Fund made the proper adjusting entries (including accrued interest receivable of $103,000) and closing entries.

*Required:*

a. Prepare in good form journal entries to record the six preceding sets of facts in the Library Capital Projects Fund. List the transaction numbers (1 to 6) and give the necessary entry or entries. Do not record journal entries in any other fund or group of accounts.

b. Prepare in good form a Balance Sheet for the City of Westgate Library Capital Projects Fund as of June 30, 19x7.

(AICPA, adapted)

## CONTINUOUS PROBLEM

4–C.  The voters of the City of Everlasting Sunshine approved the issuance of tax-supported bonds in the face amount of $4,000,000 for the construction and equipping of a new annex to the City Hall. Architects were to be retained, and construction was to be completed by outside contractors. In addition to the bond proceeds, a $500,000 grant was expected from the state government. You are required to:

a. Open a general journal for the City Hall Annex Construction Fund. Record the transactions below, as necessary. Use account titles listed under requirement (b).

   (1) On January 1, 19y1, the total face amount of bonds bearing an interest rate of 8 percent were sold at a $50,000 premium. The bonds are to mature in blocks of $200,000 each year over a 20-year period commencing January 1, 19y2. Interest payment dates are July 1 and January 1. The first interest payment will be July 1, 19y1. The premium was transferred by the City Hall Annex Construction Fund to the City Hall Annex Debt Service Fund for the future payment of principal on the bonds.

   (2) The receivable from the state government was recorded.

   (3) Legal and engineering fees early in the project were paid in the amount of $53,000. This amount had not been encumbered.

   (4) Architects were engaged at a fee of $210,000.

   (5) Preliminary plans were approved, and the architect was paid 20 percent of the fee.

   (6) The complete plans and specifications were received from the architect and approved. A liability in the amount of $126,000 to the architect was approved and paid.

   (7) Bids were received and opened in public session. After considerable discussion in City Council, the low bid from Hardhat Construction Company in the amount of $3,800,000 was accepted, and a contract was signed.

   (8) The contractor requested partial payment of $2,000,000. Payment was approved and vouchered with the exception of a 5 percent retainage.

   (9) Cash in the full amount of the grant was received from the state government.

   (10) Furniture and equipment for the annex were ordered at a total cost of $300,000.

   (11) Payment was made to the contractor for the amount vouchered (see transaction 8).

(12) The contractor completed construction and requested payment of the balance due on the contract. After inspection of the work, the amount, including the past retainage, was vouchered and paid.

(13) Furniture and equipment were received at a total actual installed cost of $305,550. Invoices were approved for payment.

(14) The remainder of the architect's fee was approved for payment.

(15) The City Hall Annex Construction Fund paid all outstanding liabilities on December 31, 19y1.

b. Open a general ledger for the City Hall Annex Construction Fund. Use the account titles shown below. Allow five lines unless otherwise indicated. Post the entries to the City Hall Annex Construction Fund general ledger.

> Cash—11 lines
> Due from Other Governmental Units
> Revenues
> Other Financing Sources—Proceeds of Bonds
> Vouchers Payable—11 lines
> Contracts Payable—Retained Percentage
> Due to Other Funds
> Construction Expenditures—10 lines
> Encumbrances—12 lines
> Reserve for Encumbrances—12 lines
> Equity Transfers Out
> Fund Balance

c. The City Hall Annex Construction Fund was closed. Prepare and post an entry closing all nominal accounts to Fund Balance. Then record and post as of December 31, 19y1, an Equity Transfer Out of the remaining Cash to the City Hall Annex Debt Service Fund. Finally, record and post the entry to close the remaining accounts.

d. Prepare a Statement of Revenues, Expenditures, and Changes in Fund Balances for the City Hall Annex Construction Fund for the Year Ended December 31, 19y1.

# Chapter 5

# GENERAL FIXED ASSETS ACCOUNT GROUP

**O**nly enterprise and internal service funds routinely account for property, plant, and equipment used in their operations. Trust funds that use fixed assets for the production of income also account for property, plant, and equipment. All other funds account only for assets that will be turned into cash during the regular operations of the fund. Thus, property, plant, and equipment acquired by general, special revenue, and capital projects funds are brought under accounting control by the creation of a General Fixed Assets Account Group (GFAAG).

In conformity with GASB standards, general fixed assets are recorded at acquisition cost (or fair value at time of receipt if assets are received by donation). If the cost of fixed assets was not recorded when the assets were acquired and is unknown when accounting control over the assets is established, it is acceptable to record them at estimated cost. The General Fixed Assets Account Group is only an accounting entity, not a fiscal entity (therefore not a fund). It records no current assets and no liabilities of any kind. The offset to the fixed asset accounts is the set of equity accounts that indicate the sources from which the fixed assets were acquired. "Investment in General Fixed Assets—Capital Projects Funds—Tax-Supported Bonds," or "Investment in General Fixed Assets—General Fund Revenues," are examples of typical equity accounts of a General Fixed Assets Account Group. Balance sheets of this account group display to interested parties the total cost of each category of general fixed asset and the total amount contributed by each source. Customarily, a balance sheet is supplemented by a schedule showing the description of and dollar amount of additions to and deductions from each fixed asset category during the year.

Since the measurement focus of governmental funds is the flow of financial resources, not the determination of net income, depreciation of general fixed assets is not recorded in the General, special revenue, capital projects, or debt service funds. Accumulated depreciation may be recorded in the GFAAG by reducing the "Investment" accounts, but this is seldom done. GASB standards allow depreciation expense to be computed for cost-finding purposes and cost reimbursement claims under grants and contracts; even when this is done the expense is not recorded in the accounts of any governmental fund, nor in the GFAAG.

General fixed assets may be thought of as those not used exclusively in the operations of any one fund nor belonging to any one fund. They include courthouses and city halls, public buildings generally, the land on which they are situated, highways, streets, sidewalks, equipment, motor vehicles, and other tangible assets with a life longer than one fiscal year that are not used by an enterprise, nonexpendable trust, or internal service fund. A Statement of General Fixed Assets might appear as shown in Illustration 5–1.

## General Fixed Assets

The asset accounts shown in Illustration 5–1 are those commonly found in Statements of General Fixed Assets. Additional categories may be used for motor vehicles or other assets which the governmental unit wishes to separately identify. In addition to the "Investment" accounts shown in Illustration 5–1, Investment in General Fixed Assets—Special Assessments would be used if general fixed assets are constructed or acquired through use of special assessment financing.

**Land**  The cost of land acquired by a governmental unit through purchase should include not only the contract price but also such other

**ILLUSTRATION 5–1**

**CITY OF ANYWHERE**
**Statement of General Fixed Assets—By Source**
**June 30, 19x5**

General Fixed Assets:

| | |
|---|---:|
| Land . . . . . . . . . . . . . . . . . . . . . . . . . . . . . . . . . | $ 4,322,561 |
| Buildings . . . . . . . . . . . . . . . . . . . . . . . . . . . . . . | 9,167,822 |
| Improvements other than buildings . . . . . . . . . . . . . . . . . | 3,146,951 |
| Equipment . . . . . . . . . . . . . . . . . . . . . . . . . . . . | 6,145,996 |
| Total General Fixed Assets . . . . . . . . . . . . . . . . . . . . | $22,783,330 |

Investment in General Fixed Assets from:
Capital projects funds:

| | |
|---|---:|
| Tax-supported bonds . . . . . . . . . . . . . . . . . . . . . . . | $12,556,981 |
| Federal grants . . . . . . . . . . . . . . . . . . . . . . . . . | 3,166,513 |
| State grants . . . . . . . . . . . . . . . . . . . . . . . . . . | 1,981,224 |
| General fund revenues . . . . . . . . . . . . . . . . . . . . . . | 4,156,776 |
| Special revenue fund revenues . . . . . . . . . . . . . . . . . . | 921,836 |
| Total Investment in General Fixed Assets . . . . . . . . . . . . . | $22,783,330 |

related costs as taxes and other liens assumed, title search costs, legal fees, surveying, filling, grading, drainage, and other costs of preparation for the use intended. Land acquired through forfeiture should be capitalized at the total amount of all taxes, liens, and other claims surrendered, plus all other costs incidental to acquiring ownership and perfecting title. Land acquired through donation should be recorded on the basis of fair value at the date of acquisition.

**Buildings and improvements other than buildings**  "Buildings" consist of those structures erected above ground for the purpose of sheltering persons or property. "Improvements Other than Buildings" consists of land attachments of a permanent nature, other than buildings, and includes infrastructure assets such as roads, bridges, tunnels, walks, walls, parking lots, and sidewalks.

The cost of these assets includes the cost of the purchase or contract, legal costs, and expenditures necessary to put the property into acceptable condition for its intended use. If the governmental unit so chooses, cost may also include net interest expenditures during construction. Buildings and improvements acquired by donation should be recorded at fair value at the date of acquisition.

GASB standards allow governmental units to elect not to report the cost of infrastructure assets such as roads, bridges, curbs and gutters, streets, sidewalks, drainage systems, and lighting systems in the Statement of General Fixed Assets. Current standards require only that each government disclose its policy of reporting the cost of infrastructure assets, or not reporting the cost of those assets, and follow that policy consistently.

**Equipment, or machinery and equipment**  The cost of machinery and equipment purchased should include purchase price, transportation costs, installation cost, and other direct costs of readying for use. Donated equipment should be recorded at fair value at the date of donation.

**Construction work in progress**  The Construction Work in Progress account is needed to account for construction expenditures accumulated to balance sheet date on projects financed by governmental funds. The amount added to this account during a given fiscal year would be equal to the Construction Expenditures recorded in the capital projects funds and any other governmental funds used to account for the construction of general fixed assets. When a project is completed the balance in the Construction Work in Progress account is transferred to the appropriate fixed asset account or accounts.

**Leased assets**  State and local governmental units generally are subject to constitutional or statutory limits on the amount of long-term debt that they may issue. It has been customary for governmental units that have reached (or nearly reached) their legal debt limit to acquire the use of capital assets through a lease agreement. Chapter 4 describes the accounting entries in a capital projects fund when general fixed assets are acquired under a capital lease. At the inception of a capital lease for general fixed assets the following entry would also need to be recorded in the GFAAG, assuming that the assets acquired were classified as equipment:

Equipment . . . . . . . . . . . . . . . . . . . . . . . . . . . . . . . . xxx
    Investment in General Fixed Assets—Capital Leases . . . . . .         xxx

**Disposition of general fixed assets**   When assets are sold, demolished, or traded their carrying value must be removed from the GFAAG. Since accumulated depreciation is seldom recorded, removal from the records is accomplished by debiting the related "Investment" accounts and crediting the asset accounts. If disposal of the asset gives rise to revenues or expenditures, the revenues or expenditures would be recorded in the governmental fund receiving the revenue or incurring the expenditure. In the event that accumulated depreciation is recorded in the GFAAG, disposal of a general fixed asset would require a debit to the Accumulated Depreciation account as well as to the Investment account.

## ILLUSTRATIVE ENTRIES

Acquisition of general fixed assets requires a debit to the appropriate General Fixed Assets general ledger asset account and credit to an equity account indicating the source from which provided. Thus, if office equipment is purchased for the Finance Director's office from General Fund resources, the **General Fixed Assets Account Group** entry would be:

Equipment . . . . . . . . . . . . . . . . . . . . . . . . . . . . . . . . 1,245
    Investment in General Fixed Assets—
      General Fund Revenues . . . . . . . . . . . . . . . . . .        1,245

Although purchased for immediate use of one department, the equipment belongs to the general government and could, if desired, be transferred to other use. On the **General Fund** books, the entry would be:

Expenditures . . . . . . . . . . . . . . . . . . . . . . . . . . . . . . 1,245
    Vouchers Payable . . . . . . . . . . . . . . . . . . . . . . .        1,245

General fixed assets purchased or constructed by a capital projects fund would be recorded in the same manner as if acquired from resources of the General Fund, the only difference being that the title of the Investment in General Fixed Assets account credited would identify the source as "Capital Projects Fund." It is conceivable that two or more funds might contribute to the total cost of a general fixed asset or that two or more sources (such as bonds and federal grants) might contribute to the total cost of a general fixed asset. Any such situation would require only that the credits clearly reveal the amount contributed by each source.

General fixed assets constructed by a capital projects fund are accounted for in the General Fixed Assets Account Group in the same manner as though purchased, if construction is initiated and completed in the same fiscal period. If two or more periods are involved, additional steps are necessary. Continuing the fire station example for the Village of Elizabeth in Chapter 4, the entry in the GFAAG to capitalize construction expenditures of 19x6 (see Entry 13 in Chapter 4) would be:

```
Construction Work in Progress . . . . . . . . . . .  1,064,000
     Investment in General Fixed Assets—Capital
        Projects Fund—Other Governmental Units   . . .              600,000
     Investment in General Fixed Assets—Special
        Revenue Fund Revenues . . . . . . . . . . . .                200,000
     Investment in General Fixed Assets—Capital
        Projects Fund—Tax-Supported Bonds  . . . . . .              264,000
```

As described in Chapter 4 the project is completed in the second year for additional expenditures amounting to $897,000. The entry in the GFAAG, corresponding with Entry 19 in Chapter 4, would be (assuming that $50,000 of construction expenditures were for equipment):

```
Buildings   . . . . . . . . . . . . . . . . . . . .  1,911,000
Equipment . . . . . . . . . . . . . . . . . . . .       50,000
     Construction Work in Progress . . . . . . . . .             1,064,000
     Investment in General Fixed Assets—Capital
        Projects Fund—Tax-Supported Bonds  . . . . . .             897,000
```

An assumption was made that the transfers from other governmental units and from the special revenue fund were used in total and the unused cash (transferred to the Debt Service Fund in the amount of $36,500) came from the bond sale.

## Fixed Assets Acquired by Proprietary Fund

If depreciable fixed assets constructed or acquired by a proprietary fund are transferred to a department accounted for by a governmental fund, at what figure should they be recorded in the accounts of the General Fixed Assets Account Group—book value as shown by the transferring fund, historical cost, or fair value at the date of transfer? The answer at present appears to be book value. Thus, assuming that a building carried on the books of a proprietary fund at $300,000 cost, less accumulated depreciation of $230,000, is permanently transferred to the general government, the following entry would be made in the **GFAAG:**

```
Buildings   . . . . . . . . . . . . . . . . . . . .     70,000
     Investment in General Fixed Assets—Water Utility
        Fund  . . . . . . . . . . . . . . . . . . . .                 70,000
```

The **proprietary fund's** accounting treatment of this transaction would be:

Accumulated Provision for Depreciation of Utility Plant       230,000
Loss on Disposal of Building . . . . . . . . . . . . .       70,000
   Utility Plant in Service  . . . . . . . . . . . . . .                   300,000

If the above transaction were modified to include a cash reimbursement to the proprietary fund, the entry in the GFAAG would be unchanged, the governmental fund would report an expenditure, and the proprietary fund would modify the loss shown above.

## Disposal of General Fixed Assets

Disposal of general fixed assets involves no accounting problem if no cash or other current assets are involved in the liquidation. The requirement is elimination of the fixed asset and reduction of the equity account that records its sources. Assuming that a building that cost $50,000, provided by a capital projects fund from resources derived from a federal grant, is retired without transfer of any other assets by a governmental unit, the following entry in the **GFAAG** would suffice:

Investment in General Fixed Assets—Capital Projects Fund—
   Federal Grant  . . . . . . . . . . . . . . . . . . . . . . . . 50,000
   Buildings  . . . . . . . . . . . . . . . . . . . . . .            50,000

In the event that cash is disbursed or received in connection with the disposal of general fixed assets there would be no effect on the entry to be made in the GFAAG. Cash disbursements in connection with the removal of an asset would be recorded as an expenditure of the disbursing fund. For example, assuming that building demolition charges of $2,000 were paid by the General fund, the entry in the **General Fund** books would be:

Expenditures . . . . . . . . . . . . . . . . . . . . . . . . . 2,000
   Cash  . . . . . . . . . . . . . . . . . . . . . . . . . .          2,000

If cash is received from the disposal of a fixed asset, the governmental fund would record the cash with an offsetting credit to Revenues.

## Detailed Property Records

As is true for business enterprises, governmental units should keep detailed property records for fixed assets. A common exception cited in auditors' reports on governmental financial statements is the lack of property records to substantiate the amounts shown in the Statement of General Fixed Assets (or omission of the GFAAG entirely). Detailed property records are vital for purposes of insurance coverage, determining costs of providing services, assisting in maintenance planning, fixing accountability of government officials, and assisting in long-range capital planning. Subsidiary records should be kept for land, buildings, improvements, and equipment. The records would be in whatever form (computerized or not) that is useful and available. Records should provide a complete description of the department or location to which the asset is assigned, cost data, maintenance data, and, if desired, memorandum entries for depreciation. Periodic inventories should be taken of the fixed assets, and the inventories reconciled with the subsidiary and general ledger records. Identification tags should be affixed to equipment, automobiles, trucks, and similar items.

## Statements of General Fixed Assets

For general fixed assets, the basic financial statement is the Statement of General Fixed Assets or, as it is sometimes called, the General Fixed Assets Balance Sheet. Its special contribution is to show the total cost of assets of the various groups in use by the general government and the sources from which they were derived. An example of this statement is shown as Illustration 5–1.

The purposes for which fixed assets were being used at a given date, ordinarily the end of a fiscal period, and the program, function, department, or activity to which the assets are assigned are set forth in a Schedule of General Fixed Assets—By Function and Activity. Illustration 5–2, which is taken from an annual report of a small city, is a good example of a Schedule of General Fixed Assets—By Function and Activity.

Another schedule commonly presented is one that shows changes in general fixed assets during a period of time. Illustration 5–3, taken from an annual report of the same city as Illustration 5–2, is an example of a Schedule of Changes in General Fixed Assets—By Function and Activity.

## SELECTED REFERENCES

American Institute of Certified Public Accountants. *Audits of State and Local Governmental Units.* Rev. ed. New York, 1986.

Governmental Accounting Standards Board. *Codification of Governmental Accounting and Financial Reporting Standards.* 2nd ed. Norwalk, Conn., 1987.

## QUESTIONS AND EXERCISES

5–1.   Using the annual financial report obtained for Exercise 1–1, answer the following questions.
   *a.* Does your financial report have the three statements and schedules illustrated in the chapter? If so, where are they presented? Are additional statements and schedules relating to general fixed assets included in the report? If so, list and describe them.

**ILLUSTRATION 5–2**

**CITY OF BEEHIVE**
**Schedule of General Fixed Assets—By Function and Activity**
**Year Ended June 30, 19x7**

| Function and Activity | Total | Land | Buildings | Improvements Other than Buildings | Machinery and Equipment |
|---|---|---|---|---|---|
| **General government:** | | | | | |
| Control: | | | | | |
| Legislative . . . . . . . | $    2,825 | $    — | $    — | $  — | $    2,825 |
| Executive . . . . . . . | 600 | — | — | — | 600 |
| Judicial . . . . . . . | 5,070 | — | 793 | — | 4,277 |
| Total Control . . . . . | 8,495 | — | 793 | — | 7,702 |
| Staff agencies: | | | | | |
| Purchasing . . . . . . | 10,245 | — | — | — | 10,245 |
| Finance . . . . . . . | 3,268 | — | — | — | 3,268 |
| Data processing . . . . . | 179,875 | — | — | — | 179,875 |
| Treasurer . . . . . . . | 1,475 | — | — | — | 1,475 |
| Recorder . . . . . . . | 1,366 | — | — | — | 1,366 |
| Attorney . . . . . . . | 1,924 | — | — | — | 1,924 |
| Community | | | | | |
| development . . . . . | 592,991 | 237,364 | 351,888 | — | 3,739 |
| Taxi . . . . . . . . . | 5,300 | — | — | — | 5,300 |
| Garage . . . . . . . . | 12,188 | — | — | — | 12,188 |
| Personnel . . . . . . | 1,330 | — | — | — | 1,330 |
| Government | | | | | |
| buildings . . . . . . . | 1,640,862 | 525,113 | 1,025,569 | 6,153 | 84,027 |
| Billing . . . . . . . . | 12,013 | — | — | — | 12,013 |
| Total Staff Agencies . . | 2,462,837 | 762,477 | 1,377,457 | 6,153 | 316,750 |
| Public safety: | | | | | |
| Police department . . . . . | 341,067 | — | 1,665 | 676 | 338,726 |
| Fire department . . . . . . | 940,715 | — | 444,541 | 92,427 | 403,747 |
| Total Public Safety . . . | 1,281,782 | — | 446,206 | 93,103 | 742,473 |
| Public works: | | | | | |
| Streets and highways . . . | 1,458,257 | — | 51,463 | 553,985 | 852,809 |
| Engineering . . . . . . . . | 93,554 | — | — | — | 93,554 |
| Planning and zoning . . . . | 5,050 | — | — | — | 5,050 |
| Total Public Works . . | 1,556,861 | — | 51,463 | 553,985 | 951,413 |
| Mosquito abatement . . . . . | 8,588 | — | — | — | 8,588 |
| Parks . . . . . . . . . . | 1,872,919 | 1,612,402 | 22,299 | 39,889 | 198,329 |
| Recreation . . . . . . . . . | 2,005,988 | 66,550 | 1,619,236 | 235,416 | 84,786 |
| Cemetery . . . . . . . . | 20,414 | — | — | — | 20,414 |
| Library . . . . . . . . . . | 71,079 | 4,000 | 30,320 | 10,980 | 25,779 |
| Airport . . . . . . . . . . | 9,604 | 9,604 | — | — | — |
| Total General Fixed | | | | | |
| Assets . . . . . . . | $9,298,567 | $2,455,033 | $3,547,774 | $939,526 | $2,356,234 |

b. Is the Statement of General Fixed Assets in the format illustrated in the chapter? Are source classifications clearly shown? Is Accumulated Depreciation deducted from the cost of the assets?

c. Does note disclosure describe the accounting policy for acquisitions of general fixed assets? Does the disclosure clearly indicate that depreciation expense is not recorded in governmental funds? Do the notes disclose the

## ILLUSTRATION 5–3

### CITY OF BEEHIVE
### Schedule of Changes in General Fixed Assets—By Function and Activity
### Year Ended June 30, 19x7

| Function and Activity | General Fixed Assets June 30, 19x6 | Additions | Deductions | General Fixed Assets June 30, 19x7 |
|---|---|---|---|---|
| **General government:** | | | | |
| **Control:** | | | | |
| Legislative . . . . . . . . . | $ 1,430 | $ 1,395 | $ — | $ 2,825 |
| Executive . . . . . . . . | 600 | — | — | 600 |
| Judicial . . . . . . . . . | 5,070 | — | — | 5,070 |
| Total Control . . . . . . | 7,100 | 1,395 | — | 8,495 |
| **Staff agencies:** | | | | |
| Purchasing . . . . . . . . | 10,245 | — | — | 10,245 |
| Finance . . . . . . . . . | 2,493 | 775 | — | 3,268 |
| Data processing . . . . . | 67,371 | 112,504 | — | 179,875 |
| Treasurer . . . . . . . . . | 700 | 775 | — | 1,475 |
| Recorder . . . . . . . . . | 1,366 | — | — | 1,366 |
| Attorney . . . . . . . . . | 1,924 | — | — | 1,924 |
| Community development . . | 592,991 | — | — | 592,991 |
| Taxi . . . . . . . . . . . | 5,300 | — | — | 5,300 |
| Garage . . . . . . . . . | 12,188 | — | — | 12,188 |
| Personnel . . . . . . . . | 1,330 | — | — | 1,330 |
| Government buildings . . . . | 777,814 | 865,515 | (2,467) | 1,640,862 |
| Billing . . . . . . . . . . | 12,013 | — | — | 12,013 |
| Total Staff Agencies . . . . | 1,485,735 | 979,569 | (2,467) | 2,462,837 |
| **Public safety:** | | | | |
| Police department . . . . . . . | 340,222 | 39,712 | (38,867) | 341,067 |
| Fire department . . . . . . . . | 923,056 | 17,659 | — | 940,715 |
| Total Public Safety . . . . | 1,263,278 | 57,371 | (38,867) | 1,281,782 |
| **Public works:** | | | | |
| Streets and highways . . . . . | 1,349,142 | 109,189 | (74) | 1,458,257 |
| Engineering . . . . . . . . | 89,221 | 4,333 | — | 93,554 |
| Planning and zoning . . . . . | 5,050 | — | — | 5,050 |
| Total Public Works . . . . | 1,443,413 | 113,522 | (74) | 1,556,861 |
| Mosquito abatement . . . . . | 8,588 | — | — | 8,588 |
| Parks . . . . . . . . . . . | 1,845,283 | 28,446 | (810) | 1,872,919 |
| Recreation . . . . . . . . . | 1,981,573 | 24,415 | — | 2,005,988 |
| Cemetery . . . . . . . . . | 20,414 | — | — | 20,414 |
| Library . . . . . . . . . . . | 23,191 | 49,080 | (1,192) | 71,079 |
| Airport . . . . . . . . . . | 9,604 | — | — | 9,604 |
| Total General Fixed Assets . . . . . . . . | $8,088,179 | $1,253,798 | $(43,410) | $9,298,567 |

policy regarding reporting of infrastructure assets? Do you believe infrastructure should be capitalized? Why or why not? What other note disclosures are made regarding fixed assets?

d. Look at the fixed asset disclosure from the point of view of a financial
analyst. Does your report disclose the condition or age of general fixed
assets? Can you tell the extent to which the governmental unit is replacing

its fixed assets as needed? Does the letter of transmittal or other narrative in the financial report give any information about condition of general fixed assets, including infrastructure and replacement policies? What changes would you recommend in financial reporting to provide some of the information you might need?

**5–2.** Write the numbers 1 through 10 on a sheet of paper. Beside each number, write the letter corresponding to the best answer to each of the following questions:

1. Fixed assets should be accounted for in the General Fixed Assets Account Group for the

|  | Capital Projects Fund | Internal Service Fund |
|---|---|---|
| a. | Yes | Yes |
| b. | Yes | No |
| c. | No | No |
| d. | No | Yes |

2. Which of the following accounts would be included in the fund equity section of the Combined Balance Sheet of a governmental unit for the General Fixed Asset Account Group?

|  | Investment in General Fixed Assets | Fund Balance Reserved for Encumbrances |
|---|---|---|
| a. | Yes | Yes |
| b. | Yes | No |
| c. | No | No |
| d. | No | Yes |

3. Dodd Village received a gift of a new fire engine from a local resident. The fair market value of this fire engine was $200,000. The entry to be made in the general fixed assets account group for this gift is

|  | Debit | Credit |
|---|---|---|
| a. Machinery and equipment . . . . . . . . . . . . . . . . | $200,000 | |
| Investment in general fixed assets from private gifts . | | $200,000 |
| b. Investment in general fixed assets . . . . . . . . . . . | $200,000 | |
| Gift revenue . . . . . . . . . . . . . . . . . . | | $200,000 |
| c. General fund assets . . . . . . . . . . . . . . . . . | $200,000 | |
| Private gifts . . . . . . . . . . . . . . . . . | | $200,000 |
| d. Memorandum entry only . . . . . . . . . . . . . . . . | — | — |

4. A capital projects fund of a city is an example of what type of fund?
   a. Internal Service.
   b. Governmental.
   c. Proprietary.
   d. Fiduciary.

5. Which of the following would be included in the Combined Statement of Revenues, Expenditures, and Changes in Fund Balances—Budget and Actual in the comprehensive annual financial report (CAFR) of a governmental unit?

|     | General<br>Fund | General Fixed Assets<br>Account Group |
| --- | --- | --- |
| a.  | Yes | Yes |
| b.  | Yes | No  |
| c.  | No  | Yes |
| d.  | No  | No  |

6. Fixed assets of a city-owned utility are accounted for in which of the following?

|     | General<br>Fund | General Fixed Assets<br>Account Group |
| --- | --- | --- |
| a.  | No  | No  |
| b.  | No  | Yes |
| c.  | Yes | No  |
| d.  | Yes | Yes |

7. When a capital project is financed entirely from a single bond issue, and the proceeds of the bond issue equal the par value of the bonds, the Capital Projects Fund would record this transaction by debiting Cash and crediting:
   a. Bond Issue Proceeds.
   b. Fund Balance.
   c. Appropriations.
   d. Bonds Payable.

8. Equipment in general governmental service that had been constructed 10 years before by a capital projects fund was sold. The receipts were accounted for as unrestricted revenue. Entries are necessary in the:
   a. General Fund and Capital Projects Fund.
   b. General Fund and the General Fixed Assets Account Group.
   c. General Fund, Capital Projects Funds, and Enterprise Fund.
   d. General Fund, Capital Projects Fund, and General Fixed Assets Account Group.

9. The following assets are among those owned by the City of Foster:

| | |
| --- | --- |
| Apartment building (part of the principal of a nonexpendable trust fund) | $  200,000 |
| City Hall | 800,000 |
| Three fire stations | 1,000,000 |
| City streets and sidewalks | 5,000,000 |

How much should be included in Foster's General Fixed Assets Account Group?
   a. $1,800,000 or $6,800,000.
   b. $2,000,000 or $7,000,000.
   c. $6,800,000, without election of $1,800,000.
   d. $7,000,000, without election of $2,000,000.

10. The following items were among Kew Township's expenditures during the year ended July 31, 19x1:

| | |
| --- | --- |
| Minicomputer for tax collector's office | $22,000 |
| Furniture for Township Hall | 40,000 |

How much should be classified as fixed assets in Kew's General Fund
balance sheet at July 1, 19x1?
a. $0.
b. $22,000.
c. $40,000.
d. $62,000.

(AICPA, adapted)

5–3.     The statement and two schedules shown in the annual report of the City of
Bolivar for the year ended June 30, 19y1, which present information about
general fixed assets, are shown below and on the following page.

**Required:**
a. To what extent does the information about general fixed assets satisfy the
information needs of (1) a new member of the City Council and (2) a resident interested in the financial management of fixed assets of the City.
b. If you were a CPA auditing the City, should you give a clean opinion on
the statements as they exist? If not, are there any changes the client could
make that would enable you to give a clean opinion?

**CITY OF BOLIVAR**
**Statement of General Fixed Assets**
**June 30, 19y1**
**(in thousands)**

**General Fixed Assets**

| | |
|---|---:|
| Land . . . . . . . . . . . . . . . . . . . . . . . . . . . . . . . . . . | $ 6,172 |
| Building and structures . . . . . . . . . . . . . . . . . . . . . . . | 16,426 |
| Furniture and equipment . . . . . . . . . . . . . . . . . . . . . . | 5,799 |
| Streets, sidewalks, and other infrastructure . . . . . . . . . . . . | 11,541 |
| Total General Fixed Assets . . . . . . . . . . . . . . . . . . | $39,938 |

**Investment in General Fixed Assets**

| | |
|---|---:|
| Tax-supported bonds . . . . . . . . . . . . . . . . . . . . . . . | $15,000 |
| Special assessment bonds . . . . . . . . . . . . . . . . . . . . . | 3,795 |
| General Fund revenues . . . . . . . . . . . . . . . . . . . . . . | 9,363 |
| Special Revenue Fund revenues . . . . . . . . . . . . . . . . . . | 8,600 |
| Capital leases . . . . . . . . . . . . . . . . . . . . . . . . . . | 3,180 |
| Total Investment in General Fixed Assets . . . . . . . . . . . . | $39,938 |

**CITY OF BOLIVAR**
**Schedule of General Fixed Assets—**
**By Function and Activity**
**June 30, 19y1**
**(in thousands)**

| Function | Total | Land | Buildings | Furniture and Equipment | Streets and Other |
|---|---:|---:|---:|---:|---:|
| General Government . . | $ 8,484 | $ 762 | $ 6,885 | $ 807 | $ 30 |
| Public Safety . . . . . | 4,416 | 238 | 2,230 | 1,855 | 93 |
| Public Works . . . . . | 10,555 | — | 251 | 2,380 | 7,924 |
| Parks and Recreation . . | 16,483 | 5,172 | 7,060 | 757 | 3,494 |
| Total . . . . . . | $39,938 | $6,172 | $16,426 | $5,799 | $11,541 |

**CITY OF BOLIVAR**
**Schedule of Changes in General Fixed Assets—**
**By Function and Activity**
**For the Year Ended June 30, 19y1**
**(in thousands)**

| | General Fixed Assets June 30, 19y0 | Additions | Deductions | General Fixed Assets June 30, 19y1 |
|---|---|---|---|---|
| General Government . . | $ 8,049 | $ 502 | $ 67 | $ 8,484 |
| Public Safety . . . . . . | 3,979 | 476 | 39 | 4,416 |
| Public Works . . . . . . | 10,051 | 696 | 192 | 10,555 |
| Parks and Recreation . . | 15,722 | 761 | — | 16,483 |
| Total . . . . . . | $37,801 | $2,435 | $298 | $39,938 |

**5–4.** Assume the City of St. John had, as of January 1, 19x1, land costing $1,000,000, buildings costing $10,000,000, and equipment costing $4,000,000, purchased at the end of the previous year. The land and buildings were acquired from the proceeds of a tax-supported bond issue; the purchase was accounted for by a capital projects fund. General Fund revenues in the amount of $3,000,000 were used to acquire equipment; the remainder of the equipment was purchased from revenues of a special revenue fund.

*Required:*
a. Assuming that a decision has been made to record depreciation in the GFAAG, show in general journal form the entry on December 31, 19x1, to record depreciation of the building at the rate of 3 percent per year and depreciation of the equipment at the rate of 15 percent per year.
b. Prepare in good form a Statement of General Fixed Assets as of December 31, 19x1.

**5–5.** Below are described a number of transactions, each of which had an effect on the General Fixed Assets Account Group of a certain city. You are required to make an entry or entries for each transaction as it should have been recorded in the GFAAG. Explanations are not required.
1. During the year a capital projects fund completed a building project which had been initiated in the preceding year. The total cost of the project was $3,850,000, of which $2,140,000 had been expended in the preceding year; the correct entry was made in the GFAAG at the end of that year. Current-year expenditures on the project consisted of $800,000 from a federal grant, with the balance coming from the proceeds of a tax-supported bond issue.
2. An electric typewriter was traded in on a new word processor with a cash payment of $3,150. Price of the new machine to governmental bodies is $3,500. The electric typewriter had been purchased from General Fund revenue for $550. Cash for the new machine was furnished by a special revenue fund.
3. A tract of land and a building located upon it were on the required right-of-way of an interstate highway and were sold to the state for $250,000 by the City. Cost of the building when erected was $110,000, and the cost of the land was $20,000, both purchased from General Fund revenue.

    4. A subdivision annexed by the City contained privately financed streets and sidewalks and a system of sewers. The best available information showed a cost of $900,000 for the sewer system and $850,000 for the streets and sidewalks, of which $80,000 was estimated cost of the land. Both types of improvements were provided by the developers. The City records the cost of infrastructure assets in the GFAAG.

    5. The cost of remodeling the interior of the City Hall was $856,500; $134,200 of this amount was classified as maintenance rather than improvement. In the remodeling process, walls, partitions, floors, and so on, which were estimated to have cost $147,300, were removed and replaced. Cost of the total operation was provided by the General Fund. The building had been built from tax-supported bonds sold by a capital projects fund.

    6. The street department, part of the General Fund, acquired new equipment for a cash outlay of $235,000 and a trade-in of old equipment on which an allowance of $25,000 was received. The equipment traded in had cost $75,000. Equipment which had cost $15,000 was scrapped.

    7. An insurance settlement of $120,000 was received for the total loss of a building which had cost $142,614; a settlement of $42,141 was received for the total loss of equipment which had cost $39,644. These assets had originally been purchased with General Fund revenues.

**5–6.** Expenditures of the Pearl City Performing Arts Center Construction Fund for the year ended December 31, 19y1, are given in Exercise 4–6. Prepare an entry in general journal form to record in the Pearl City General Fixed Assets Account Group the amount that should be capitalized as Construction Work in Progress, as of December 31, 19y1. (Pearl City does not capitalize net interest expenditures during the period of construction of General Fixed Assets.)

**5–7.** Assuming that as of December 31, 19y1, Pearl City has the following investment in general fixed assets, in addition to the performing arts center which is not yet complete (see Exercise 5–6): Land, $322,000; Buildings, $9,000,000; Improvements Other Than Buildings, $4,000,000; and Furniture and Equipment, $6,000,000. The sources of the investment in these General Fixed Assets were: Capital Projects Funds—Tax-Supported Bonds, $10,250,000; Capital Projects Funds—Federal Grants, $5,000,000; General Fund Revenues, $2,072,000; and Special Revenue Fund Revenues, $2,000,000. Prepare in good form a Statement of General Fixed Assets—By Source, as of December 31, 19y1, for Pearl City. Be sure to include all fixed assets listed in this problem and, also, the amount you capitalized in your solution to Exercise 5–6.

**5–8.** Information is given in Exercises 4–6 and 4–8 about expenditures of the Pearl City Performing Arts Center Construction Fund for the years ended December 31, 19y1, and December 31, 19y2. Prepare an entry in general journal form to record in the Pearl City General Fixed Assets Account Group the amounts that should be capitalized as Buildings, Improvements Other Than Buildings, and Furniture and Equipment, as of December 31, 19y2. (Expenditures for the street lighting project should be capitalized as Improvements Other Than Buildings.)

**5–9.** Prepare in good form a Statement of General Fixed Assets—By Source, as of December 31, 19y2, for Pearl City, from information recorded in your solutions to Exercises 5–7 and 5–8.

## CONTINUOUS PROBLEM

5–C.    As of December 31, 19y0, the City of Everlasting Sunshine presented the following Statement of General Fixed Assets:

General Fixed Assets:
Land . . . . . . . . . . . . . . . . . . . . . . . . . . . . . . . . . . . . $ 5,125,141
Buildings . . . . . . . . . . . . . . . . . . . . . . . . . . . . . . . . 30,192,468
Improvements other than buildings . . . . . . . . . . . . . . . . 18,987,493
Equipment . . . . . . . . . . . . . . . . . . . . . . . . . . . . . .     8,344,169

    Total General Fixed Assets . . . . . . . . . . . . . . . . . . . $62,649,271

Investment in General Fixed Assets:
Capital projects funds:
    Tax-supported bonds    . . . . . . . . . . . . . . . . . . . . . $32,498,333
    Federal grants    . . . . . . . . . . . . . . . . . . . . . . . .     4,916,167
    State grants . . . . . . . . . . . . . . . . . . . . . . . . . . .     4,342,768
General fund revenues    . . . . . . . . . . . . . . . . . . . . . .     8,124,619
Special revenue fund revenues . . . . . . . . . . . . . . . . . . .     5,691,111
Special assessments . . . . . . . . . . . . . . . . . . . . . . . . .     7,076,273

    Total Investment in General Fixed Assets . . . . . . . . . . . . $62,649,271

### Transactions:

1. During 19y1, General Fund revenues were used for the acquisition of $523,146 in equipment and $68,469 in improvements other than buildings. An additional $46,199 in equipment was purchased with resources provided from special revenue fund revenues.
2. Also, during 19y1, equipment initially costing $614,231 was retired as were improvements in the amount of $1,142,613. All retirements were of assets originally financed by General Fund departments.
3. Sidewalk projects costing $613,469, financed by special assessments, were completed during 19y1.
4. The City Hall Annex and new furniture (see Problem 4–C) were recorded in GFAAG accounts.

### Required:

a. Open a general journal for the General Fixed Assets Account Group for the City of Everlasting Sunshine. Record the transactions above, as necessary. Use account titles shown in the December 31, 19y0, Statement of General Fixed Assets.
b. Open a general ledger for the GFAAG, providing three lines for each account. Enter the amounts shown in the December 31, 19y0, Statement of General Fixed Assets in each account. Date these amounts as "1/1/y1." Post to the accounts the entries you made as your solution to requirement a of this problem.
c. Prepare a Statement of General Fixed Assets as of December 31, 19y1.

# Chapter 6

# DEBT SERVICE FUNDS

The principal of long-term debt incurred to finance the construction or acquisition of general fixed assets, or for any other purpose, and interest on that debt, is usually paid from collections of tax levies specifically designated for debt service. Another source of revenue sometimes utilized by governmental units to pay principal and interest on long-term debt incurred for construction or acquisition of general fixed assets is collections of special assessments levied against property deemed to be particularly benefited by the fixed assets constructed or acquired. GASB standards provide a fund type called, unsurprisingly, the **debt service fund** type to account for revenue and other financing sources raised to service long-term debt, and for expenditures for debt service. Earlier in this century, governmental issues of long-term debt commonly matured in total on a given date. In that era, bond indentures often required the establishment of a "sinking fund," sometimes operated on an actuarial basis. Some sinking fund term bond issues are still outstanding, but they are dwarfed in number and amount by serial bond issues, in which the principal matures in installments.

If taxes and/or special assessments for payment of interest and principal on long-term debt are levied specifically for the debt service fund, they are recognized as revenues of the debt service fund. If taxes and/or special assessments are levied by another fund and transferred to the debt service fund, they must be included in the revenues budget of the fund that will levy the taxes or special assessments (often the General Fund) and also budgeted by that fund as operating transfers to the debt service fund. The debt service fund should prepare a budget that includes operating transfers from other funds as well as revenues that it will raise directly or that will be earned on its investments. Also, debt service funds generally receive premium on debt issues sold and accrued interest on debt issues sold. Similarly, as illustrated in Chapter 4, if capital projects are completed with total expenditures less than total revenues and other financing sources, the residual equity is ordinarily transferred to the appropriate debt service fund. The appropriations budget of a debt service fund should include amounts that will be required during the budget period to pay interest on outstanding long-term debt and to repay any maturing issues or installments.

## The Accrual Basis—Meaning for Debt Service

GASB standards require debt service accounting to be on the same basis of accounting as General, special revenue, and capital project funds. One peculiarity of the accrual basis as applied to debt service accounting is that interest on long-term debt is not accrued; it is recognized as an expenditure in the year in which payment of the interest is authorized by the Appropriations budget (generally the year in which the interest is legally due). For example, if the fiscal year of a government ends on December 31, 19x5, and the interest on its bonds is payable on January 1 and July 1 of each year, interest payable on January 1, 19x6, would not be reported as a liability in the balance sheet of the debt service fund prepared as of December 31, 19x5. The rationale is that, since interest is not legally due until January 1, 19x6, resources need not be appropriated until 19x6. Consequently, the expenditure and liability would be recognized in the same year as the appropriation. The same reasoning applies to principal amounts that mature early in the next fiscal year; expenditures and liabilities are recognized in the year for which the appropriation is made. If appropriations are made in 19x5 for interest and/or principal due in 19x6, expenditures and related liabilities should be recorded in 19x5.

## Additional Uses of Debt Service Funds

In addition to term bonds and serial bonds, debt service funds may be required to service debt arising from the use of notes or warrants having a maturity more than one year after date of issue. Although each issue of long-term or intermediate-term debt is a separate obligation and may have legal restrictions and servicing requirements that differ from other issues, all debts to be serviced from tax revenues should be accounted for by a single debt service fund, if permitted by state laws and covenants with creditors. If more than one debt service fund is required by law, as few funds of this type should be created as possible. Subsidiary records of a debt service fund can provide needed assurance that restrictions and requirements relating to each debt issue are properly budgeted and accounted for. Debt service funds are not created for proprietary funds because debt service activities of such funds are accounted for within those funds.

If a governmental unit enters into a lease agreement that meets the criteria of a capital lease (see Chapter 4), a debt service fund may be used to account for the payments required by the lease agreement. Accounting for capital lease payments is discussed in a later section of this chapter.

In some jurisdictions statutes do not require the debt service function to be accounted for by a debt service fund. Whether or not required by statute or local ordinance, bond indentures, or other agreements with creditors, are often construed as requiring the use of a debt service fund. Unless the debt service function is very simple, it may be argued that good financial management would dictate the establishment of a debt service fund even though not legally required. If neither law nor sound financial administration require the use of debt service funds, the function may be performed within the accounting and budgeting framework of the General Fund. In such cases, the accounting and financial reporting standards discussed in this chapter should be followed for the debt service activities of the General Fund.

## Debt Service Accounting for Regular Serial Bonds

Accounts recommended for use by debt service funds created to account for resources to be used for the payment of interest and principal of serial bond issues are similar to those recommended for use by General and special revenue funds. The use of budgetary accounts is recommended, except that encumbrance accounting need not be used (since the debt service function does not require the use of purchase orders). Usually the government designates a bank as "Fiscal Agent" to handle interest and principal payments for each issue. The assets of a debt service fund may, therefore, include "Cash with Fiscal Agent," and the appropriations, expenditures, and liabilities may include amounts for the service charges of fiscal agents.

There are four types of serial bonds: *regular, deferred, annuity,* and *irregular.* If the total principal of an issue is repayable in a specified number of equal installments over the life of the issue, it is a **regular** serial bond issue. If the first installment is delayed for a period of more than one year after the date of the issue, but thereafter installments fall due on a regular basis, the bonds are known as **deferred** serial bonds. If the amount of annual principal repayments is scheduled to increase each year by approximately the same amount that interest payments decrease (interest decreases, of course, because the amount of outstanding bonds decreases) so that the total debt service remains reasonably level over the term of the issue, the bonds are called **annuity** serial bonds. **Irregular** serial bonds may have any pattern of repayment that does not fit the other three categories.

Accounting for regular serial bonds is illustrated by a debt service fund created to pay principal and interest for the fire station project for the Village of Elizabeth discussed in Chapter 4. Recall that, early in 19x6, the Village Council of the Village of Elizabeth authorized an issue of $1,200,000 of 8 percent tax-supported bonds. At the time of authorization, no formal entry is required in the capital projects fund; at that time a memorandum entry may be made in the capital projects fund, and provision made to account for debt service of the new debt issue in a debt service fund.

Assume that the bonds in this example are dated July 1, 19x6, that interest payment dates are January 1 and July 1, and that the first of the equal annual principal payments will be on July 1, 19x7. Since no interest or principal of these bonds becomes legally due in calendar year 19x6, the fiscal year of the Village of Elizabeth, no appropriations for 19x6 must be budgeted by the debt service fund. However, the debt service fund will be required to expend $48,000 for interest on the first day of 19x7. (Revenues for debt service are being raised by the General Fund in this example, therefore it would be prudent for the General Fund to raise in 19x6 the $48,000 it will need to transfer in cash on the first day of 19x7 to the debt service fund.)

The bonds were sold on July 1, 19x6 for a premium of $12,000. The face amount of the liability for the bonds is recorded in the General Long-Term Debt Account Group (GLTDAG); GLTDAG entries are illustrated in Chapter 7. Cash in the amount of premium on bonds sold must be used by the Debt Service Fund, not by the Capital Projects Fund (see Entry 8 in Chapter 4). The entry in **Debt Service Fund** accounts is:

```
1.  Due from Capital Projects Fund  . . . . . . . . . . .   12,000
        Revenues   . . . . . . . . . . . . . . . . . . .            12,000
```

The entry to record cash transferred to the Debt Service Fund from the Capital Projects Fund is:

```
2.  Cash  . . . . . . . . . . . . . . . . . . . . . . . .   12,000
        Due from Capital Projects Fund  . . . . . . . . .            12,000
```

The only other Debt Service Fund entry in 19x6 would be an entry to close Revenues to Fund Balance. The 19x6 Balance Sheet (not illustrated) would show the asset, Cash, in the amount of $12,000, offset by Fund Balance. The Statement of Revenues, Expenditures, and Changes in Fund Balances (also not illustrated) would show only Revenues of $12,000; Excess of Revenues over Expenditures, $12,000; Fund Balance at beginning of year, $0; and Fund Balance at end of year, $12,000.

As of January 1, 19x7, an entry would be made to record the appropriation for principal and interest to be paid in 19x7, and to record the estimated revenues and other financing sources for 19x7. Assuming the resources are to come as an operating transfer from the General Fund and assuming the $12,000 (see Entry 2) may be used for payments due in 19x7, the computation of the amount to be appropriated, and the amount to be transferred from the General Fund in 19x7, would be:

Interest, January 1 ($1,200,000 × .08 × ½) . . . . . . . . . . . . . $ 48,000
Interest, July 1 ($1,200,000 × .08 × ½) . . . . . . . . . . . . . . . 48,000
Principal, July 1 ($1,200,000 ÷ 10) . . . . . . . . . . . . . . . . . 120,000

Total amount to be appropriated for 19x7 . . . . . . . . . . . . $216,000
Less cash available on January 1, 19x7 . . . . . . . . . . . . . . . 12,000

Operating transfer in required for 19x7 . . . . . . . . . . . . . . . $204,000

The entry to record the budget, therefore, would be:

3.  Estimated Other Financing Sources . . . . . . . . . . 204,000
    Fund Balance . . . . . . . . . . . . . . . . . . . . . 12,000
        Appropriations . . . . . . . . . . . . . . . . . .              216,000

Assume that on January 1 the General Fund transferred $36,000 cash
to the Debt Service Fund, and, on that date the Debt Service Fund
transferred $48,000 cash to the bank which acts as the Village of Eliza-
beth's fiscal agent for the payment of interest due January 1. The **Debt
Service Fund** entries would be:

4a. Cash . . . . . . . . . . . . . . . . . . . . . . . . 36,000
        Operating Transfers In . . . . . . . . . . . . .              36,000
4b. Cash with Fiscal Agent . . . . . . . . . . . . . . 48,000
        Cash . . . . . . . . . . . . . . . . . . . . . . . . .        48,000

The Debt Service Fund entry to record the liability for the interest
payment due January 1, 19x7, is:

5.  Expenditures . . . . . . . . . . . . . . . . . . . . 48,000
        Matured Interest Payable . . . . . . . . . . . .              48,000

When the fiscal agent reports that checks have been issued to all
bondholders Entry 6 is made:

6.  Matured Interest Payable . . . . . . . . . . . . . . 48,000
        Cash with Fiscal Agent . . . . . . . . . . . . .              48,000

On July 1, 19x7, the next interest payment of $48,000 is due; also on
that date a principal payment of $120,000 is due. Immediately prior to
that date the General Fund transfers $168,000 to the Debt Service Fund
and the Debt Service Fund transfers the cash to the fiscal agent:

7a. Cash . . . . . . . . . . . . . . . . . . . . . . . . 168,000
        Operating Transfers In . . . . . . . . . . . . .              168,000
7b. Cash with Fiscal Agent . . . . . . . . . . . . . . 168,000
        Cash . . . . . . . . . . . . . . . . . . . . . . . . .        168,000

The Debt Service Fund records the liability for the interest payment
and the principal payment on the date they are legally due, July 1:

8.  Expenditures . . . . . . . . . . . . . . . . . . . . 168,000
        Matured Interest Payable . . . . . . . . . . . .              48,000
        Matured Bonds Payable . . . . . . . . . . . . .              120,000

Payment by the fiscal agent of interest and principal is recorded in the Debt Service Fund as:

```
9.  Matured Interest Payable . . . . . . . . . . . . . .   48,000
    Matured Bonds Payable . . . . . . . . . . . . . . .  120,000
       Cash with Fiscal Agent  . . . . . . . . . . . . .            168,000
```

Obviously, the net effect of Entries 4a, 4b, 5, and 6 is a debit to Expenditures in the amount of $48,000, and credits to Operating Transfers In, $36,000, and Cash, $12,000. The net effect of Entries 7a, 7b, 8, and 9 is a debit to Expenditures, $168,000, and a credit to Operating Transfers In, $168,000.

Entry 20 of Chapter 4 records the effect on the Capital Projects Fund of the transfer of the residual equity of that fund to the Debt Service Fund. The corresponding entry in the Debt Service Fund would be:

```
10. Cash  . . . . . . . . . . . . . . . . . . . . . . .   36,500
       Equity Transfers In  . . . . . . . . . . . . . . .            36,500
```

At the end of 19x7 the Debt Service Fund should close the budgetary and operating statement accounts for the year:

```
11. Operating Transfers In  . . . . . . . . . . . . . .  204,000
    Equity Transfers In  . . . . . . . . . . . . . . . .   36,500
    Appropriations . . . . . . . . . . . . . . . . . . .  216,000
       Estimated Other Financing Sources . . . . . . . .            204,000
       Expenditures . . . . . . . . . . . . . . . . . . .            216,000
       Fund Balance  . . . . . . . . . . . . . . . . . .             36,500
```

The Balance Sheet for the Fire Station Debt Service Fund as of December 31, 19x7 is shown as Illustration 6–1. The Statement of Revenues, Expenditures, and Changes in Fund Balance for the Fire Station Debt Service Fund for the Year Ended December 31, 19x7 is shown as Illustration 6–2. Note that Revenues and Other Financing Sources are shown together as was true for the Fire Station Capital Projects Fund in Illustration 4–2. The alternate procedure of showing Other Financing Sources and Uses after Expenditures is also acceptable.

**ILLUSTRATION 6–1**

**VILLAGE OF ELIZABETH**
**Fire Station Debt Service Fund**
**Balance Sheet**
**As of December 31, 19x7**

**Assets**

| | |
|---|---|
| Cash . . . . . . . . . . . . . . . . . . . . . . . . . . . . . . . . . . . . . . . . | $36,500 |
| Total Assets . . . . . . . . . . . . . . . . . . . . . . . . . . . . . . . . . | $36,500 |

**Fund Equity**

| | |
|---|---|
| Fund Balance . . . . . . . . . . . . . . . . . . . . . . . . . . . . . . . . . | $36,500 |
| Total Fund Equity . . . . . . . . . . . . . . . . . . . . . . . . . . . . . | $36,500 |

**ILLUSTRATION 6–2**

**VILLAGE OF ELIZABETH**
**Fire Station Debt Service Fund**
**Statement of Revenues, Expenditures, and**
**Changes in Fund Balance**
**For the Year Ended December 31, 19x7**

| | | |
|---|---:|---:|
| Revenues and Other Financing Sources: | | |
| Other Financing Sources: | | |
| Operating transfers from General Fund . . . . . . . . . . | | $204,000 |
| Expenditures: | | |
| Principal . . . . . . . . . . . . . . . . . . . . . . . . . | $120,000 | |
| Interest . . . . . . . . . . . . . . . . . . . . . . . . . | 96,000 | |
| Total Expenditures . . . . . . . . . . . . . : . . . . . | | 216,000 |
| Excess of Revenues and Other Financing Sources over (under) Expenditures . . . . . . . . . . . . . . . . . . | | (12,000) |
| Fund Balance, January 1, 19x7 . . . . . . . . . . . . . | | 12,000 |
| Equity Transfer from Capital Projects Fund . . . . . . . . . | | 36,500 |
| Fund Balance, December 31, 19x7 . . . . . . . . . . . | | $ 36,500 |

## Debt Service Accounting for Deferred Serial Bonds

If a government issues bonds other than regular serial bonds, debt service fund accounting is somewhat more complex than illustrated above. A government that issues deferred serial bonds will normally have several years without principal repayment during which, if it is fiscally prudent, amounts will be accumulated in the Debt Service Fund for payment when the bonds mature. If this is the case, debt service fund cash should be invested in order to earn interest revenues. Material amounts of interest receivable on investments should be accrued at year-end, and interest revenues should be budgeted.

## Debt Service Accounting for Term Bonds

Term bond issues mature in their entirety on a given date, in contrast to serial bonds which mature in installments. Required revenues of term bond debt service funds may be determined on an "actuarial" basis or on less sophisticated bases designed to produce approximately level contributions during the life of the issue. The annuity tables used for an "actuarial" basis assume that the investments of a debt service fund earn interest at a given percentage. Accounting for a term bond debt service fund would be similar to that described for a deferred serial bond issue. In addition, if investments are made in securities with a fixed maturity date, and if the intention is that those securities be held to maturity, premiums and discounts on investments should be amortized (in the same manner as is done in business organizations). Also in debt service accounting for term bonds the budgetary accounts, "Estimated Revenues," may be replaced by two budgetary accounts: "Required Additions," to record the amount which must be added to the fund each year and "Required Earnings," to record the amount which must be earned on the investments and reinvested. Over the life of the term bonds the sum of Required Additions and Required Earnings is expected to equal the face amount of bonds to be paid at maturity.

### Debt Service Accounting for Capital Lease Payments

In Chapter 4, in the section "Acquisition of General Fixed Assets by Lease Agreements," an example is given of the necessary entry in a governmental fund at the inception of a capital lease.

In Chapter 5, in the subsection "Leased Assets," the example is continued to illustrate the entry required in the General Fixed Assets Account Group when an asset is acquired by a capital lease agreement. Commonly, governmental units use a debt service fund to record capital lease payments because the annual payments are merely installment payments of long-term debt. Part of each payment is interest at a constant rate on the unpaid balance of the lease obligation, and part is a payment on the principal. If the annual payment on a capital lease amounted to $10,000, of which $5,759 is payment of interest, and $4,241 is payment on principal, the entry in the Debt Service Fund would be:

Expenditures . . . . . . . . . . . . . . . . . . . . . . . . . 10,000
    Cash . . . . . . . . . . . . . . . . . . . . . . . . . .            10,000

The detail records in the Debt Service Fund should show how much of the expenditure was for interest and how much for principal. The General Long-Term Debt Account Group (discussed in Chapter 7) should record the decrease of $4,241 in the principal amount of the capital lease obligation.

## COMBINING STATEMENTS FOR DEBT SERVICE FUNDS

Statements for deferred serial and term bond debt service funds are similar to those shown for regular serial bond debt service funds in Illustrations 6–1 and 6–2. If a governmental unit has several debt service funds combining financial statements should be prepared. Combining statements for the debt service funds of a large city are reproduced here as Illustrations 6–3 and 6–4.

Illustration 6–3 presents the Combining Balance Sheet of the four debt service funds that must be maintained in compliance with pertinent laws and agreements. The total column is provided to support the Debt Service Funds column in the Combined Balance Sheet—All Fund Types and Account Groups in the General Purpose Financial Statements section of the annual report.

Illustration 6–4 presents the Combining Statement of Revenues, Expenditures, and Changes in Fund Balances. The total column supports the Debt Service Fund column in the Combined Statement of Revenues,

**ILLUSTRATION 6–3**

**CITY OF ESSEXVILLE**
**Debt Service Fund Types**
**Combining Balance Sheet**
**June 30, 19x8**

| | General Services District | | | Urban Services District | Total Debt Service Funds |
|---|---|---|---|---|---|
| | General Obligation Bonds | | | General Obligation Bonds | |
| | General Purposes | Convention Center | School Purposes | | |
| **ASSETS** | | | | | |
| Cash . . . . . . . . . | $ 30,176 | $ 87,698 | $ 17,308 | $ 114,832 | $ 250,014 |
| Cash with fiscal agent . | 1,930,544 | — | 82,480 | 116,019 | 2,129,043 |
| Investments . . . . . | 11,167,467 | 7,983,789 | 1,302,563 | 8,629,059 | 29,082,878 |
| Accrued interest receivable . . . . . | 187,733 | 44,393 | 124,188 | 164,602 | 520,916 |
| Due from other funds . | 27,422 | 2,210 | — | — | 29,632 |
| Delinquent taxes receivable . . . . . | 523,942 | — | — | 242,756 | 766,698 |
| Total Assets . . . . . | $13,867,284 | $8,118,090 | $1,526,539 | $9,267,268 | $32,779,181 |
| **LIABILITIES AND FUND EQUITY** | | | | | |
| LIABILITIES: | | | | | |
| Accounts payable . . | $ 706 | $ — 7 | $ — | $ 1,708 | $ 2,421 |
| Due to other funds . . | 688,938 | — | — | 1 | 688,939 |
| Deferred revenue . . | 523,942 | — | — | 242,756 | 766,698 |
| Total liabilities . . | 1,213,586 | 7 | — | 244,465 | 1,450,050 |
| FUND BALANCE: | | | | | |
| To be used for debt service . . . . . . | 12,653,698 | 8,118,083 | 1,526,539 | 9,022,803 | 31,321,123 |
| Total Fund Balance . . . | 12,653,698 | 8,118,083 | 1,526,539 | 9,022,803 | 31,321,123 |
| Total Liabilities and Fund Balance . . . . . . | $13,867,284 | $8,118,090 | $1,526,539 | $9,267,268 | $32,779,181 |

Expenditures, and Changes in Fund Balance—All Governmental Fund Types. A Combining Statement of Revenues, Expenditures, and Changes in Fund Balance—Budget and Actual would also be required if the budget for the Debt Service Fund is legally required rather than prepared by choice of the administrators to facilitate financial management.

## SELECTED REFERENCES

American Institute of Certified Public Accountants. *Audits of State and Local Governmental Units.* Rev. ed. New York, 1986.

Governmental Accounting Standards Board. *Codification of Governmental Accounting and Financial Reporting Standards.* 2nd ed. Norwalk, Conn., 1987.

**ILLUSTRATION 6–4**

**CITY OF ESSEXVILLE**
**Combining Statement of Revenues, Expenditures,**
**and Changes in Fund Balances**
**Debt Service Fund Types**
**For the Year Ended June 30, 19x8**

| | General Services District | | | Urban Services District | Total Debt Service Funds |
|---|---|---|---|---|---|
| | General Obligation Bonds | | | General Obligation Bonds | |
| | General Purposes | Convention Center | School Purposes | | |
| REVENUES: | | | | | |
| Taxes . . . . . . . . | $ 8,740,740 | $ — | $6,537,325 | $3,849,992 | $19,128,057 |
| Revenue from the use of money or property . . . . | 5,156,620 | 668,273 | 986,052 | 2,675,808 | 9,486,753 |
| Revenues from other governmental agencies . . . . . | 326,298 | — | — | — | 326,298 |
| Total Revenues . . | 14,223,658 | 668,273 | 7,523,377 | 6,525,800 | 28,941,108 |
| EXPENDITURES: | | | | | |
| Debt service: | | | | | |
| Principal retirement. | 6,650,495 | — | 4,849,000 | 3,049,000 | 14,548,495 |
| Interest and fiscal charges . . . . . | 6,515,348 | 2,073,750 | 2,983,586 | 2,595,120 | 14,167,804 |
| Total Expenditures | 13,165,843 | 2,073,750 | 7,832,586 | 5,644,120 | 28,716,299 |
| Excess (deficiency) of revenues over expenditures . . . | 1,057,815 | (1,405,477) | (309,209) | 881,680 | 224,809 |
| OTHER FINANCING SOURCES (USES): | | | | | |
| Transfers from other funds . . . . . . | 168,564 | — | 105,858 | 873,297 | 1,147,719 |
| Transfer to other funds | (105,858) | — | — | — | (105,858) |
| Total Other Financing Sources (Uses) . | 62,706 | — | 105,858 | 873,297 | 1,041,861 |
| Excess (deficiency) of revenues and other sources over expenditures and other uses . . . . . | 1,120,521 | (1,405,477) | (203,351) | 1,754,977 | 1,266,670 |
| Equity transfer from (to) Capital Projects Funds . . . . . . . | (687,868) | 9,523,560 | — | — | 8,835,692 |
| FUND BALANCE, beginning of year . . | 12,221,045 | — | 1,729,890 | 7,267,826 | 21,218,761 |
| FUND BALANCE, end of year . . . . . | $12,653,698 | $8,118,083 | $1,526,539 | $9,022,803 | $31,321,123 |

## QUESTIONS AND EXERCISES

**6–1.** Using the annual financial report obtained for Exercise 1–1, answer the following questions.

 *a.* If there is more than one debt service fund, list the name of each and describe the purpose for which it exists. Does your report have a divider page in front of the Debt Service Funds section describing each debt service fund included in the report?

 *b.* Does your report have a Combining Balance Sheet and a Combining Statement of Revenues, Expenditures, and Changes in Fund Balance for the debt service funds? If an annual budget is legally required for debt service funds, does the report have a Combining Statement of Revenues, Expenditures, and Changes in Fund Balances—Budget and Actual for the debt service funds? Do the totals agree with the numbers in the combined statements? Are any individual fund statements presented for debt service funds?

 *c.* Does the accounting appear to conform with GASB standards for debt service funds as described in this chapter? Are expenditures for interest on long-term debt recorded when legally due, rather than being recognized on the full accrual basis? Does note disclosure clearly describe the treatment of interest expenditures?

 *d.* Do the debt service funds statements report resources for the payment of capital leases? Does the Statement of Revenues, Expenditures, and Changes in Fund Balances show expenditures for capital lease payments?

 *e.* Attempt to look at the debt service expenditures from the viewpoint of a financial analyst. Compute the percentage of total debt service expenditures to total expenditures of all governmental fund types. A Schedule of Debt Service Requirements to Maturity should appear in the "Statistical" section of the report. Do the future payments appear reasonable, considering the size of the community, and revenues which are currently being raised?

 *f.* List any additional disclosures regarding general obligation debt service requirements in the Letter of Transmittal, the debt service portion of the Financial Section, and the Statistical Tables. What additional disclosures would be helpful to you in analyzing this function?

**6–2.** Write the numbers 1 through 10 on a sheet of paper. Beside each number, write the letter "T" or "F" indicating whether each of the following statements is true or false.

 1. Expenditures for interest on tax-supported long-term debt are not accrued, even though debt service funds are accounted for on an accrual basis.

 2. Debt service funds are established only for bonded debt, not for debt arising from use of notes or warrants.

 3. Budgetary accounts for Estimated Revenues and Appropriations are used by debt service funds, but Encumbrances is not used.

 4. Payment of debt service interest and payment of matured debt principal is ordinarily handled through the banking system.

 5. Four types of serial bonds are: regular, irregular, deferred, and ordinary.

6. If all financial resource inflows have been collected, and all debt interest and principal legally due has been paid, a regular serial bond debt service fund may have no assets, no liabilities, and no Fund Balance at year-end.

7. At year-end, budgetary and operating statement accounts of a debt service fund are closed in the same manner as is true for general funds or special revenue funds.

8. If all outstanding bonds are registered as to interest and principal it would be inappropriate for the Debt Service Fund to have a year-end balance in a liability account, "Accrued Interest Payable."

9. If capital lease payments are made through debt service funds, only the principal portion of the payments would be recorded as "Expenditures."

10. If the budgetary basis for debt service funds differs from the accrual basis used for financial reporting, the Combining Statement of Revenues, Expenditures, and Changes in Fund Balances—Budget and Actual for the debt service funds should be on the budgetary basis.

**6–3.** GASB standards provide that expenditures for interest on long-term debt due on the day following the balance sheet date be recorded on the date that it becomes legally due, unless payment of the interest is authorized by an appropriation for the year ended on the balance sheet date. Critics feel that interest on long-term debt should be accrued, as is done in full accrual accounting. Present arguments on both sides of this issue.

**6–4.** On July 1, 19x0, the Village of Campbell issued $10,000,000 in 7 percent tax-supported regular serial bonds at par. The bonds pay interest on July 1 and January 1 of each year. The first of 10 equal annual principal payments is due on July 1, 19x1.

*Required:*

a. Assuming Campbell's fiscal year ends on June 30, prepare the budgetary entries for the Debt Service Fund for the fiscal years ending June 30, 19x1, and June 30, 19x2. Assume that Estimated Revenues and Appropriations will be just enough to make principal and interest payments legally due each year.

b. Assuming Campbell's fiscal year ends on September 30, prepare the budgetary entries for the Debt Service Fund for the fiscal years ending September 30, 19x0, and September 30, 19x1. Assume that Estimated Revenues and Appropriations will be just enough to make principal and interest payments legally due each year.

**6–5.** Elburn County's Debt Service Fund Balance Sheet as of December 31, 19x5, is presented below:

**ELBURN COUNTY**
**Balance Sheet—Debt Service Fund**
**As of December 31, 19x5**

**Assets**

| | |
|---|---:|
| Investments | $2,500,000 |
| Interest receivable on investments | 50,000 |
| Total Assets | $2,550,000 |

**Fund Equity**

| | |
|---|---:|
| Fund Balance | $2,550,000 |
| Total Fund Equity | $2,550,000 |

***Required:***

*a.* Prepare entries in general journal form to reflect, as necessary, the following information. Explanations are not required:

(1) The Revenues budget for serial bond debt service for 19x6 consists
of estimated revenues from a direct tax levy of $350,000, and esti-
mated revenues of $200,000 from earnings on investments. The Ap-
propriations budget consists of bond interest to be paid by the
fiscal agent on January 1, 19x6, $150,000; and bond interest of
$150,000 and bond principal of $275,000 to be paid by the fiscal agent
on July 1, 19x6.

(2) The tax levy in the amount of $350,000 was recorded. Assume no
estimated uncollectibles.

(3) On January 2, 19x6, investments in the amount of $150,000, were sold
at par, plus accrued interest of $3,000.

(4) Matured interest payable as of January 1, 19x6 is recorded as a
liability.

(5) Cash is transferred to the fiscal agent in the amount of the interest
due on January 1.

(6) The fiscal agent reported that it has paid interest of $150,000.

(7) The property tax levy was collected in full.

(8) Interest on investments was received in the amount of $94,000, in-
cluding the remainder of the amount accrued at the beginning of the
year.

(9) Matured interest and matured bonds payable as of July 1 are recorded
as liabilities of the Debt Service Fund.

(10) Cash in the amount of $425,000 is transferred to the fiscal agent.

(11) Interest on investments is received in cash in the amount of $94,000.
This amount is invested.

(12) Notice is received from the fiscal agent that it has paid interest,
$150,000, and bonds, $275,000.

(13) Accrued interest receivable on investments at year-end is computed
as $48,880.

(14) Budgetary and operating statement accounts for 19x6 are closed.

*b.* Prepare a Balance Sheet for the Elburn County Debt Service Fund as of
December 31, 19x6.

*c.* Prepare a Statement of Revenues, Expenditures, and Changes in Fund
Balance for the year ended December 31, 19x6.

*d.* Prepare a Statement of Revenues, Expenditures, and Changes in Fund
Balance—Budget and Actual for the fund for the year ended December 31,
19x6.

6–6.     This exercise is related to Exercises 4–6 and 5–6.

Pearl City maintains one debt service fund. Prepare entries in general journal form to record in the Pearl City Debt Service Fund transactions and events shown below. The bonds sold to finance the construction
of the Performing Arts Center bear interest at the annual rate of 7 percent, payable semiannually on February 15 and August 15. The first semiannual interest payment is due August 15, 19y1. Bonds with a face value
of $300,000 will mature on the second interest payment date, Febru-
ary 15, 19y2.

**Transactions during the year ended December 31, 19y1:**

1. As of the date of sale of the bonds, March 1, the Debt Service Fund is required to prepare and record its budget for the remainder of 19y1. The revenues budget provided for estimated revenues in the amount of $320,000 from interest earned on temporary investment of the bond proceeds and estimated other financing sources in the amount of $400,000 operating transfers from the General Fund. The appropriations budget provided for interest legally due in 19y1.

2. Also on March 1, the Debt Service Fund received $17,500 cash from the Performing Arts Center Construction Fund—the amount of interest accrued on bonds sold.

3. On August 15, the Debt Service Fund received $180,000 interest on bond proceeds which had been temporarily invested by the Performing Arts Center Construction Fund.

4. The Debt Service Fund also received on August 15 a $200,000 operating transfer from the General Fund.

5. Checks dated August 15, totaling $210,000, were mailed to bondholders in payment of interest due that day. On the same day, remaining cash was invested in six-month Certificates of Deposit bearing an annual rate of 6 percent.

6. On December 30, the Debt Service Fund received $52,500 from the Performing Arts Center Construction Fund as accrued interest on temporary investments sold that day. This amount was invested in CDs maturing February 15, 19y2.

7. On December 31, a receivable from the General Fund was recorded for the portion of the 19y1 operating transfer not yet made.

8. Accrued interest on temporary investments of bond proceeds held on December 31, amounted to $94,800, and accrued interest on CDs purchased on August 15 amounted to $4,200 on December 31. The total of these amounts was recorded as 19y1 revenue of the Debt Service Fund.

9. Budgetary and operating statement accounts for 19y1 were closed.

**6–7.** This exercise continues Exercise 6–6.

**Required:**

*a.* Prepare in good form a Balance Sheet as of December 31, 19y1, for the Pearl City Debt Service Fund.

*b.* Prepare in good form a Statement of Revenues, Expenditures, and Changes in Fund Balance for the Pearl City Debt Service Fund for the year ended December 31, 19y1.

*c.* Prepare in good form a Statement of Revenues, Expenditures, and Changes in Fund Balance—Budget and Actual for the Pearl City Debt Service Fund for the year ended December 31, 19y1.

**6–8.** This exercise continues Exercise 6–6.

Record in general journal form the following transactions in the Pearl City Debt Service Fund, as appropriate.

**Transactions during the year ended December 31, 19y2:**

1. The Debt Service Fund budget for 19y2 provided for Estimated Revenues of $425,000 ($225,000 from interest on temporary investments, and $200,000 from special assessments), Estimated Other Financing Sources of $475,000 from operating transfers from the General Fund, and Appro-

priations for interest payments due on February 15 and August 15 and for the $300,000 of principal of the bonds which mature on February 15. Record the budget as of January 1, 19y2.

2. On February 1, the four installments of the special assessment to be paid to the Debt Service Fund on March 1, 19y3, 19y4, 19y5, and 19y6, were recorded as receivables (credit Deferred Revenues).

3. On February 15, the Debt Service Fund received the following in cash: (a) the amount due from the General Fund for the second half of the 19y1 operating transfer, (b) interest on the temporary investment of bond proceeds, $126,500—this includes the amount accrued on December 31, 19y1, and (c) the face of all CDs maturing on February 15, plus interest on the CDs in the amount of $6,025—this includes the amount accrued on December 31, 19y1.

4. Checks dated February 15 were mailed to bondholders in payment of interest due that date. Checks dated February 15 were also mailed to the owners of bonds maturing on that date. Remaining cash on hand was invested in six-month CDs bearing interest at the annual rate of 6 percent.

5. On August 15, the Debt Service Fund received in cash (a) interest on temporary investment of bond proceeds, $126,500, (b) the face amount of CDs maturing on that date plus interest on the CDs, $1,875, and (c) $200,000 as part payment by the General Fund of its operating transfer for 19y2.

6. Checks dated August 15 were mailed to bondholders in payment of interest due that date. On the same day, remaining cash on hand was invested in six-month CDs bearing interest at the annual rate of 6.25 percent.

7. On November 1, cash in the amount of $39,400 was transferred from the Performing Arts Center Construction Fund representing accrued interest on temporary investments sold.

8. On December 31, cash in the amount of $26,000 was transferred from the Performing Arts Center Construction Fund—$24,000 of this representing accrued interest on temporary investments sold, and $2,000 the residual equity of the Construction Fund.

9. On December 31, a receivable from the General Fund was recorded for the portion of the 19y2 operating transfer not yet made. Accrued interest on CDs was recorded in the amount of $4,500. The installment of the special assessment due on March 1, 19y3, was transferred to the current category, and an equivalent amount was transferred from Deferred Revenues to Revenues.

10. Budgetary and operating statement accounts for 19y2 were closed.

6–9.    This exercise continues Exercise 6–8.

*Required:*

a. Prepare in good form a Balance Sheet as of December 31, 19y2, for the Pearl City Debt Service Fund.

b. Prepare in good form a Statement of Revenues, Expenditures, and Changes in Fund Balance for the Pearl City Debt Service Fund for the year ended December 31, 19y2.

c. Prepare in good form a Statement of Revenues, Expenditures, and Changes in Fund Balance—Budget and Actual for the Pearl City Debt Service Fund for the year ended December 31, 19y2.

## CONTINUOUS PROBLEM

**6–C.**  The City Hall Debt Service Fund of the City of Everlasting Sunshine has been open for five years; it was created to service an $8,000,000, 6 percent tax-supported bond issue. As of December 31, 19y0, this serial bond issue has a balance of $6,000,000. Semiannual interest payments are made on January 1 and July 1, and a principal payment of $400,000 is due on January 1 of each year. As this is a regular serial bond debt service fund, the only accounts with balances as of January 1, 19y1 were "Cash with Fiscal Agent" and "Fund Balance," each with balances of $580,000. (Revenues were raised and collected in cash in 19y0 in order to be able to pay bond principal and interest due on January 1, 19y1.)

*Required:*

*a.* Open a general journal for the City Hall Debt Service Fund and prepare journal entries for the following transactions. Use account titles listed under requirement *(b)*. One page will suffice.

  (1) The budget was enacted as of January 1, 19y1. It provided for a planned operating transfer of $736,000 from the General Fund and for appropriations as necessary to make the principal and interest payments due in 19y1.

  (2) The fiscal agent reported that checks had been mailed to bondholders for interest due on January 1, $180,000, and for bonds maturing that day, $400,000.

  (3) Cash in the amount of $168,000 was received from the General Fund on June 30 and was transferred to the fiscal agent.

  (4) The fiscal agent reported that checks dated July 1 had been mailed to bondholders for interest due that day.

  (5) Cash in the amount of $568,000 was received from the General Fund on December 31 and transferred to the fiscal agent to be used for the interest and principal payments due on January 1, 19y2.

  (6) Closing entries were made.

*b.* Open a general ledger for the City Hall Debt Service Fund. Use the account titles shown below. Allow five lines for each account. Enter the beginning balances. Post the entries made for requirement *(a)* to the ledger accounts.

> Cash
> Cash with Fiscal Agent
> Estimated Other Financing Sources
> Operating Transfers In
> Appropriations
> Expenditures—Interest on Bonds
> Expenditures—Principal of Bonds
> Fund Balance

*c.* On the advice of the City Attorney, a City Hall Annex Debt Service Fund is opened to account for debt service transactions related to the bond issue sold on January 1, 19y1 (see Continuous Problem 4–C). Open a general journal for the City Hall Annex Debt Service Fund. Record the transactions below, as necessary. Use account titles listed under requirement *(d)*.

(1) The budget for the City Hall Annex Debt Service Fund was enacted. It provided for a planned operating transfer from the General Fund in the amount of $520,000 and appropriations for payment of interest due in 19y1.

(2) The premium described in transaction (1) of Problem 4–C was received. Record as a Revenue.

(3) Cash in the amount of $160,000 was received from the General Fund on June 30 and was transferred to the fiscal agent.

(4) The fiscal agent reported that checks dated July 1 had been mailed to bondholders for interest due that day.

(5) The equity transfer described in part (c) of Problem 4–C was received and invested for use for bond principal repayment in future years.

(6) Cash in the amount of $360,000 was received from the General Fund on December 31 and transferred to the fiscal agent to be used for interest and principal payments due on January 1, 19y2. The remaining cash on hand was invested.

(7) Closing entries were made.

d. Open a general ledger for the City Hall Annex Debt Service Fund. Use the account titles shown below. Allow five lines unless otherwise indicated. Post the entries to the City Hall Annex Debt Service Fund general ledger.

> Cash—seven lines
> Cash with Fiscal Agent
> Investments
> Estimated Other Financing Sources
> Revenues
> Operating Transfers In
> Appropriations
> Expenditures—Interest on Bonds
> Equity Transfers In
> Fund Balance

e. Prepare a Combining Balance Sheet for the Debt Service Funds for the City of Everlasting Sunshine as of December 31, 19y1.

f. Prepare a Combining Statement of Revenues, Expenditures, and Changes in Fund Balances for the Debt Service Funds of the City of Everlasting Sunshine for the year ended December 31, 19y1.

g. Prepare a Combining Statement of Revenues, Expenditures, and Changes in Fund Balances—Budget and Actual for the Debt Service Funds for the year ended December 31, 19y1.

# Chapter 7

# GENERAL LONG-TERM DEBT ACCOUNT GROUP

**L**ong-term debt which is to be repaid from the revenues of an enterprise fund of a governmental unit is known as **revenue** debt and is reported as debt of the enterprise fund which services the debt, whereas long-term debt backed by the taxing power of a governmental unit is considered to be debt of the unit as a whole and not of any individual fund. In order to bring such debt under accounting control the General Long-Term Debt Account Group (GLTDAG) was created. The GLTDAG accounts for debt backed by the "full faith and credit," or general tax revenues of the government (called **general obligation**, or G.O., debt), debt backed only by certain taxes (called **limited obligation** debt), and debt backed only by a specified portion of a certain tax—for example, 1 cent of a 5 cent sales tax (called **tax increment** debt). Debt backed by special assessments against property deemed to be particularly benefited by a capital project for which the debt was incurred (called **special assessment** debt) is accounted for in the GLTDAG if the government is obligated to assume payment of debt service if collections of special assessments are not sufficient to repay the debt and pay the interest thereon. Long-term debt may be evidenced by bonds, notes, or time warrants.[1]

---

[1]Under current GASB standards the GLTDAG is also used to account for the present value of capital lease payments; the noncurrent portion of claims, judgments, and compensated absences to be paid when due by use of the resources of governmental funds; and any unfunded liability for pensions of employees of activities accounted for by governmental funds. In its proposed statement on measurement focus and basis of accounting for governmental funds, the GASB proposes that the GLTDAG be utilized to account only for long-term debt related to the acquisition of general fixed assets; other long-term debt would be accounted for by the appropriate governmental funds. If the proposed standards become actual standards, the publisher will send an Update Bulletin to adopters of this text.

The GLTDAG accounts only for liabilities; it does not account for any assets. Therefore it is not a fund, merely an account group. Liability accounts have credit balances; in order for the GLTDAG to be self-balancing it is necessary to create accounts that have debit balances. The debit balance accounts that offset the long-term liabilities are of two categories: (1) Amounts Accumulated in Debt Service Funds (for repayment of general long-term debt) and (2) Amounts to Be Provided in Future Years (for repayment of general long-term debt). The sum of the two categories of debit balance accounts, therefore, equals the total amount of outstanding general long-term debt, carried in credit-balance accounts.

Long-term debt of enterprise funds may be issued with covenants that give it the status of tax-supported debt, although the intent is that the debt be serviced from the resources of the issuing fund. As discussed in subsequent chapters, the liability should be displayed in the body of the statement of the issuing fund as long-term debt, and the contingent liability should be disclosed by a note to the financial statements. If before the maturity of the debt it is determined that revenues of the enterprise fund are insufficient to repay debt which bears contingent tax-supported backing, the amount of unpaid debt should be recorded in the GLTDAG; at the same time the same amount should be removed from the liability accounts of the enterprise fund and credited to a Contributed Equity account of that fund. Similarly, if at date of issue there is no expectation that tax-supported debt issued for the benefit of an enterprise fund will ever be serviced from the revenues of such fund, the entire debt issue should be recorded as a liability in the GLTDAG and as Contributed Equity of the fund which receives the proceeds of the debt issue.

Entries are ordinarily made in the accounts of the GLTDAG only as a result of transactions and events that also require entries in the accounts of one or more of the funds. If the incurrence of long-term debt is for the purpose of acquisition of general fixed assets, an entry is required in a capital projects fund (see Chapter 4) and a related entry is required in the General Long-Term Debt Account Group. The following section illustrates the entries required in the GLTDAG of the Village of Elizabeth to correspond with the Capital Projects Fund entries illustrated in Chapter 4 for the issue of regular serial bonds, and in Chapter 6 for debt service fund activities.

A subsequent section of this chapter illustrates the entries required in the General Long-Term Debt Account Group to correspond with the entries in a Capital Projects Fund (Chapter 4), in the General Fixed Assets Account Group (Chapter 5), and a Debt Service Fund (Chapter 6), for obligations arising under a capital lease agreement.

## ILLUSTRATIVE CASE

Entries in the General Long-Term Debt accounts may be made on a current basis throughout the fiscal period as long-term debt is issued, as it is repaid, and as assets are added to debt service funds; or all the events of the period may be cumulated and appropriate entries made at period-end for the net effect of all events. In order to make the illustrative entries in this chapter correspond with the illustrative entries in Chapters 4, 5, and 6, it is assumed that the Village Accountant elects to record in the General Long-Term Debt Group events as they occur.

The illustrative case, originally developed in Chapter 4, provided that $1,200,000 of 8 percent tax-supported bonds were sold at a premium during 19x6 to help finance the construction of a fire station. The premium of $12,000 was transferred to the Debt Service Fund to be used for payment of interest on the bonds. The $1,200,000 cash was recorded in the Capital Projects Fund by crediting "Proceeds of Bonds," and the $12,000 was recorded in the Debt Service Fund as a Revenue. The entry in the GLTDAG to reflect the issuance of the bonds would be:

1. Amount to Be Provided for Payment of Regular
   Serial Bonds . . . . . . . . . . . . . . . . . 1,200,000
       8% Regular Serial Bonds Payable . . . . . . .                1,200,000

No other transactions took place during 19x6 that would affect the GLTDAG. The Statement of General Long-Term Debt as of December 31, 19x6 (not illustrated) would show the account debited in Entry 1 as an "asset" and the account credited in Entry 1 as a liability. Note that although the Fund Balance of the Debt Service Fund as of December 31, 19x6, is $12,000 (see Chapter 6), no "Amount Available in Debt Service Funds" is reported in the Statement of General Long-Term Debt as of that date because the $12,000 is to be used on the day following the balance sheet date for payment of interest due on that date. Obviously, therefore it is **not** available for repayment of bond principal.

In 19x7 the Debt Service Fund budget provided for $204,000 to be transferred from the General Fund for the payment of interest on January 1 and July 1, 19x7, and payment of principal maturing on July 1, 19x7. Principal transactions only (not interest transactions) are recorded in the GLTDAG. On July 1, 19x7, the transfer of $168,000 from the General Fund to the Debt Service Fund ($48,000 for interest and $120,000 for principal; see Entry 7, Chapter 6) would be recorded in the GLTDAG as:

2. Amount Available in Debt Service Fund for Payment
   of Regular Serial Bonds . . . . . . . . . . . . .        120,000
       Amount to Be Provided for Payment of Regular
       Serial Bonds . . . . . . . . . . . . . . .                   120,000

On the same date (July 1) the bonds matured and were recorded as a liability of the Debt Service Fund (see Entry 8, Chapter 6). The matured bonds, therefore, are no longer long-term debt and should be removed from the books of the GLTDAG by the following entry, which also reflects the fact that cash of the Debt Service Fund has been transferred to the fiscal agent to be used for redemption of the matured bonds.

| | | |
|---|---|---|
| 3. 8% Regular Serial Bonds Payable . . . . . . . . . | 120,000 | |
| Amount Available in Debt Service Fund for Payment of Regular Serial Bonds . . . . . . . . | | 120,000 |

Finally, when the capital project was completed in 19x7, the remaining balance was sent as an Equity Transfer to the Debt Service Fund for the future payment of principal (see Entry 10, Chapter 6). The corresponding entry in the GLTDAG is:

| | | |
|---|---|---|
| 4. Amount Available in Debt Service Fund for Payment of Regular Serial Bonds . . . . . . . . . . . . . | 36,500 | |
| Amount to Be Provided for Payment of Regular Serial Bonds . . . . . . . . . . . . . . . . | | 36,500 |

Illustration 7–1 presents the Statement of General Long-Term Debt for the Village of Elizabeth as of December 31, 19x7. In order to introduce some complexity, one additional bond issue and a capital lease obligation are assumed to exist, as shown in the statement.

**ILLUSTRATION 7–1**

### VILLAGE OF ELIZABETH
### Statement of General Long-Term Debt
### December 31, 19x7

**Amount Available and to Be Provided
for Payment of General Long-Term Debt**

| | | |
|---|---|---|
| Regular Serial Bonds: | | |
| Amount available in debt service fund . . . . . . . . | $ 36,500 | |
| Amount to be provided . . . . . . . . . . . . . . | 1,043,500 | |
| Total Regular Serial Bonds . . . . . . . . . . . . | | $1,080,000 |
| Deferred Serial Bonds: | | |
| Amount available in debt service fund . . . . . . . . | 535,000 | |
| Amount to be provided . . . . . . . . . . . . . . | 425,000 | |
| Total Deferred Serial Bonds . . . . . . . . . . . | | 960,000 |
| Capital Lease Obligations: | | |
| Amount to be provided . . . . . . . . . . . . . . | | 350,000 |
| Total Available and to Be Provided . . . . . . . . | | $2,390,000 |

**General Long-Term Debt Payable**

| | |
|---|---|
| Regular serial bonds, 8%, J and J1, final maturity 7/1/y6 . . | $1,080,000 |
| Deferred serial bonds, 6%, J and J1, final maturity 7/1/y8 . | 960,000 |
| Capital lease obligations, monthly, final payment 1/1/x9 . . | 350,000 |
| Total General Long-Term Debt Payable . . . . . . . | $2,390,000 |

## General Long-Term Debt Arising from Capital Lease Agreements

In Chapter 4, under the caption "Acquisition of General Fixed Assets by Lease Agreements," a brief example of the entry in the Capital Projects Fund for the acquisition of a capital asset through a capital lease was given. Chapter 5 illustrated the entry recording the fixed asset in the General Fixed Assets Account Group, and Chapter 6 illustrated the accounting by the Debt Service Fund for the total payment, including the interest. At the inception of a capital lease for a general fixed asset, it is necessary to record a lease obligation in the GLTDAG in the amount of the present value of capital lease rentals. The entry to record the lease would be:

Amount to Be Provided for Payment of Capital Lease Obligation . . xxx
    Capital Lease Obligations Payable . . . . . . . . . . . . . . .                 xxx

When periodic lease rental payments are made, part of each payment is considered to be for interest on the unpaid balance of lease obligations, and part for principal. The amount considered to be a payment of **principal only** would be recorded in the GLTDAG:

Capital Lease Obligations Payable . . . . . . . . . . . . . . 4,241
    Amount to Be Provided for Payment of
      Capital Lease Obligations . . . . . . . . . . . . . . .              4,241

The credit in the entry above would have been to Amount Available in Debt Service Funds if that account had been debited and the Amount to Be Provided account had been credited when resources were made available in a debt service fund for payment of the lease rental.

## Claims, Judgments, Compensated Absences, and Other Long-Term Debt Not Evidenced by Bonds or Notes[2]

GASB standards require that a governmental fund record only liabilities which will be paid from expendable resources of the fund. Governmental bodies, however, commonly incur liabilities under employment contracts for amounts to be paid in future years to employees who have accumulated vacation time and/or other leave time, and who elect to take cash rather than vacation time or leave time—such payments are known as compensated absences. (Governments traditionally have had much more liberal policies than have business organizations with regard to accumulation of vacation and other leave time by employees.) Liabilities to be paid in future years from resources to be raised in future years by one or more governmental funds must be recorded in the GLTDAG. In addition to compensated absences, governments also may have liabilities for claims and judgments in excess of amounts which may

---

[2]See footnote 1 of this chapter for proposed changes in GASB standards relating to accounting and financial reporting for these items.

be reported as fund liabilities. Also governments may have pension plans which have not been funded to the extent required by actuarial computations made in conformity with GASB standards. To the extent that liabilities for claims and judgments, and for unfunded pensions, will not be liquidated by existing assets of governmental funds, the excess amount must be recorded in the GLTDAG and disclosed in the Statement of General Long-Term Debt.

## Changes in Long-Term Debt

GASB standards currently require the presentation in the comprehensive annual financial report of a Schedule of Changes in Long-Term Debt, unless notes to the financial statements provide sufficient disclosure. Illustration 7–1, the Statement of General Long-Term Debt, presents only ending balances and would not inform the reader of additions to long-term debt during the year, debt retirements during the year, capital lease transactions, and so on. Illustration 7–2 presents a schedule taken from the annual report of the City of Anywhere, USA, which reports for each general obligation debt issue the interest rates, interest payment dates, issue dates, final maturity date, annual serial payments, original amount of issue, balance at the beginning of the fiscal year, new issues, retirements, and principal balance at year-end, as well as interest expenditures for the year. Note that the present value of lease rentals is shown in this statement in conformity with GASB Codification Sec. L20.111.

## Principal and Interest Payable in Future Years

In order to disclose the future demands on resources resulting from the maturing of debt principal and the payment of interest, a schedule showing the debt service payments to maturity is often included in the annual report. An example of one form of this schedule is shown as Illustration 7–3.

## Debt Limit and Debt Margin

Another matter of importance in relation to long-term indebtedness is the legal limitation upon the amount of long-term indebtedness which may be outstanding at a given time, in proportion to the assessed value of property within the jurisdiction represented. This type of restriction is of importance as a protection of taxpayers against possible confiscatory tax rates. Even though tax rate limitation laws may be in effect for a government unit, the limitation upon bonded indebtedness is usually needed because the prevailing practice is to exempt the claims of bondholders from the barrier of tax-rate restrictions. This is to say that, even though a law establishing maxima for tax rates exists, such laws usually

**ILLUSTRATION 7–2**

### CITY OF ANYWHERE, USA
**General Long-Term Debt**
**Schedule of Bonds and Warrants Payable**
**Year Ended September 30, 19y2**

|  | Interest Rates Percent | Interest Payment Dates | Issue Dates | Final Maturity Date | Annual Serial Payments |
|---|---|---|---|---|---|
| General Obligation Bonds: |  |  |  |  |  |
| Auditorium and Hospital . | 4.00 | 2/1–8/1 | 8/1/w1 | 8/1/z0 | $330,000 in 19y3 to $360,000 in z0 |
| General Obligation Warrants: |  |  |  |  |  |
| State Gasoline . . . . . . | 4.00–5.25 | 3/1–9/1 | 3/1/x3 | 3/1/z3 | $140,000 in 19y3 to $240,000 in z3 |
| Debt Refunding  . . . . | 5.70–6.20 | 2/15–8/15 | 4/15/x8 | 2/15/a7 | (A) |
| Capital Improvement and |  |  |  |  |  |
| Master Drainage . . . . | 6.30–6.40 | 2/1–8/1 | 8/1/x8 | 8/1/a3 | $500,000 in 19z3 to $1,500,000 in 20a3 |
| Capital Improvement and |  |  |  |  |  |
| Master Drainage . . . . | 6.25–7.50 | 2/1–8/1 | 6/1/x9 | 8/1/a3 | $500,000 in 19z1 to $2,300,000 in 20a3 |
| Property Acquisition  . . . | 7.90–10.75 | (B) | (B) | (B) | (B) |
| Property Acquisition  . . . | 8.00 | 3/1–9/1 | 3/1/y0 | 3/1/y2 |  |
| Drainage Improvements . . | 10.50 | (B) | (B) | (B) | (B) |
| Capital Improvement and |  |  |  |  |  |
| Master Drainage . . . . | 11.5 | 4/1–10/1 | 4/8/y1 | 10/1/y6 | $15,000,000 in 19y6 |
| Property Acquisition  . . . | 12.0 | 6/1–12/1 | 1/5/y2 | 12/1/y6 | $255,000 in 19y3 to 19y5 with final payment in 19y6 of $230,000 |

Total General Obligation Warrants

General Obligation Leases:                                                                          (C)

Public Building Authority Lease

Note: (A) Principal is payable in annual installments ranging from $3,945,000 in 19z2 to $935,000 in 20a2 with a final payment of $38,355,000 in 20a7.

(B) Retired in October 19y1.

(C) The City of Anywhere's lease with the Public Building Authority calls for annual lease payments ranging from $646,263 in 19y2 to $779,700 in 20a2.

exclude debt service requirements from the restrictions of the law. This exclusion would be reiterated, in effect, in the bond indentures.

The meanings of the terms **debt limit** and **debt margin** should be clarified. **Debt limit** means the total amount of indebtedness of specified kinds that is allowed by law to be outstanding at any one time. The limitation is likely to be in terms of a stipulated percentage of the assessed valuation of property within the government's jurisdiction. It may relate to either a gross or a net valuation. Taxpaying property only should be used in regulating maximum indebtedness. In many governmental jurisdictions, there is much property that is legally excluded even from assessment. This includes property owned by governments, churches, charitable organizations, and some others depending upon state laws. Exemptions, which apply to property subject to assessment,

**ILLUSTRATION 7–2 (concluded)**

| Original Amount of Issue | Balance at October 1, 19y1 | Year Ended September 30,19y2 | | Balance at 9/30/y2 | Interest for Year Ended 9/30/y2 |
|---|---|---|---|---|---|
| | | New Issues | Retirements | | |
| $ 8,000,000 | $ 3,105,000 | $ | $ 320,000 | $ 2,785,000 | $ 124,200 |
| 3,075,000 | 2,205,000 | | 135,000 | 2,070,000 | 107,925 |
| 68,845,000 | 68,845,000 | | | 68,845,000 | 4,151,233 |
| 14,500,000 | 14,500,000 | | | 14,500,000 | 915,000 |
| 12,300,000 | 12,300,000 | | | 12,300,000 | 783,000 |
| 3,720,000 | 3,720,000 | | 3,720,000 | | 165,514 |
| 500,000 | 500,000 | | 500,000 | | 20,000 |
| 10,525,000 | 10,525,000 | | 10,525,000 | | 165,769 |
| 15,000,000 | –0– | 15,000,000 | | 15,000,000 | 737,916 |
| 1,075,000 | –0– | 1,075,000 | 80,000 | 995,000 | 49,833 |
| 129,540,000 | 112,595,000 | 16,075,000 | 14,960,000 | 113,710,000 | 7,096,190 |
| 5,200,000 | –0– | 5,200,000 | | 5,200,000 | |
| $142,740,000 | $115,700,000 | $21,275,000 | $15,280,000 | $121,695,000 | $7,220,390 |

are based on homestead or mortgage exemption laws, military service, economic status, and possibly some others. Both exclusions and exemptions reduce the amount of taxpaying property.

**Debt margin,** sometimes referred to as "borrowing power," is the difference between the amount of debt limit calculated as prescribed by law and the net amount of outstanding indebtedness subject to limitation. The net amount of outstanding indebtedness subject to limitation differs from total general long-term indebtedness because certain debt issues may be exempted by law from the limitation, and the amount available in debt service funds for debt repayment is deducted from the outstanding debt in order to determine the amount subject to the legal debt limit. Total general long-term indebtedness must, in some jurisdictions, include debt serviced by enterprise funds if such debt was issued

**ILLUSTRATION 7–3**

**CITY OF ANYWHERE, USA**
**Notes to the Financial Statements**
**September 30, 19y2**

7. *General long-term debt*
The annual requirements to amortize all debt outstanding as of September 30, 19y2, including interest payments are as follows:

| September 30, | Principal | Interest | Sinking Fund | Total |
|---|---|---|---|---|
| 19y3 . . . . . . . . | $    645,000 | $   8,547,245 | $  1,385,554 | $ 10,577,799 |
| 19y4 . . . . . . . . | 760,000 | 8,505,194 | 1,493,282 | 10,758,476 |
| 19y5 . . . . . . . . | 810,000 | 8,452,207 | 1,419,169 | 10,681,376 |
| 19y6 . . . . . . . . | 860,000 | 8,394,301 | 1,525,334 | 10,779,635 |
| 19y7 . . . . . . . . | 18,755,000 | 33,488,580 | 7,232,246 | 59,475,826 |
| 19y7–z1 . . . . . . | 27,135,000 | 28,570,553 | (14,622,844) | 41,082,709 |
| 19z2–z6 . . . . . . | 25,950,000 | 19,916,475 | (14,622,844) | 31,243,631 |
| 19z7–20a1 . . . . . | 8,425,000 | 12,750,850 | (14,622,844) | 6,553,006 |
| 20a2–a6 . . . . . . | 38,355,000 | 1,189,005 | (39,817,284) | (273,279) |
| | $121,695,000 | $129,814,410 | $(70,630,231) | $180,879,179 |

The 19x8 Debt Refunding Warrants require payments into a sinking fund. Payments by the City to the Sinking Fund differ from the actual debt service cost on the bond issue. From February 19x9 through August 19z1 the City's required payments to the Sinking Fund will exceed the debt service cost on the bond issue allowing the Sinking Fund to accumulate a principal balance. From February 19z2 through August 20a2 the City's required payments to the Sinking Fund will be less than the debt service cost on the bond issue. Income from the Sinking Fund's principal balance makes up the difference between the City's payments and the actual debt service cost on the bond issue. From February 20a3 through August 20a7 (final maturity date) the City will receive payments from the Sinking Fund because income from the Sinking Fund will exceed the debt service cost on the bond issue.

with covenants that give the debt tax-supported status in the event resources of the issuing fund are insufficient to meet required interest or principal payments. Although it would be in keeping with the purpose of establishing a legal debt limit to include the present value of capital lease obligations along with bonded debt in the computation of legal debt margin, generally state statutes do not specify that the liability for capital lease obligations is subject to the legal debt limit. The computations of legal debt limit and legal margin for the City of Anywhere, USA, are shown in Illustration 7–4.

## Direct and Overlapping Debt

Debt limitation laws ordinarily establish limits that may not be exceeded by each separate governmental unit affected by the laws. This means that the county government may incur indebtedness to the legal limit, a township within that county may do likewise, and a city within the township may become indebted to the legal limit, with no restriction because of debt already owed by larger territorial units in which it is located. As a result, a given parcel of real estate or object of personal property may be the basis of debt beyond the so-called legal limit and

**ILLUSTRATION 7–4**

CITY OF ANYWHERE, USA
Computation of Legal Debt Margin
September 30, 19y2
(Not Reported on by Certified Public Accountants)

| | | | |
|---|---|---|---|
| Assessed value of real property, September 30, 19y2 . . . . . . . . . . . . . . . . . . . . | | | $694,147,340 |
| Assessed value of personal property, September 30, 19y2 . . . . . . . . . . . . . . . . . | | | 53,012,260 |
| Total Assessed Value of Real and Personal Property . . . . . . . . . . . . . . | | | $747,159,600 |
| Debt limit, 20% of assessed value . . . . . . . | | | $149,431,920 |
| Amount of debt applicable to debt limit: | | | |
| General obligation bonds and warrants . . . . | | $121,695,000 | |
| Notes and mortgages payable . . . . . . . . | | 125,256 | |
| Other . . . . . . . . . . . . . . . . . . . | | 4,618,363 | |
| | | 126,438,619 | |
| Less: | | | |
| Net assets in Debt Service Funds applicable to bonds and warrants included in legal debt limit . . . . . . . . . . . . . . . . . . . . | $ 9,446,524 | | |
| Items excluded from legal debt limit: | | | |
| General Obligation Warrants applicable to sewer improvements . . . . . . . . . . | 31,190,000 | | |
| General obligation lease with Public Building Authority . . . . . . . . . . | 5,200,000 | 45,836,524 | |
| Total amount of debt applicable to debt limit | | | 80,602,095 |
| Legal Debt Margin . . . . . . . . . . . | | | $ 60,029,825 |

also may be subject at a given time to levies for the payment of taxes to retire bonds issued by two or more governmental units. When this situation exists, it is described as "overlapping debt."

To show the total amount of long-term debt against property located within a given jurisdiction, a Schedule of Direct and Overlapping Debt should be prepared. A statement of this type begins with the direct debt, which is that owed by the reporting entity. To this direct debt are added amounts owing by other units and authorities which levy taxes against the same property on which the direct debt is based. A Schedule of Direct and Overlapping Debt is shown as Illustration 7–5. Notes included as a part of Illustration 7–5 disclose the relation of direct debt and overlapping debt to assessed valuation of real property within the City of Anywhere, USA, and, also, the amount of direct and overlapping debt borne by each resident of the City.

Information shown in this chapter as Illustrations 7–2, 7–3, 7–4, and 7–5 may be disclosed in the Notes to the Financial Statements at the option of the reporting entity. GASB standards state that the following should be disclosed for long-term debt in whatever manner the issuer deems to be the most meaningful presentation:

**ILLUSTRATION 7–5**

CITY OF ANYWHERE, USA
Schedule of Direct and Overlapping Debt
September 30, 19y2
(Not Reported on by Certified Public Accountants)

| | Gross Debt Less Debt Service Assets | Percentage of Debt Applicable to City of Anywhere | Amount of Debt Applicable to City of Anywhere |
|---|---|---|---|
| City of Anywhere: | | | |
| Gross debt . . . . . . . . . . . . . . . . . | $121,695,000 | | |
| Less debt service assets . . . . . . . . . . . | 13,665,319 | | |
| Direct Net Debt . . . . . . . . . . . . | 108,029,681 | 100.00% | $108,029,681* |
| Overlapping debt | | | |
| Anywhere County: | | | |
| Special highway fund . . . . . . . . . | 20,553,000 | 56.23 | 11,556,952 |
| Road and bridge fund: | | | |
| General obligation . . . . . . . . . . | 57,000 | 56.23 | 32,051 |
| State gasoline . . . . . . . . . . . | 60,000 | 33.41 | 20,046 |
| Medical school . . . . . . . . . . . | 2,200,000 | 56.23 | 1,237,060 |
| Total Anywhere County . . . . . . . | 22,870,000 | 56.17 | 12,846,109 |
| Board of School Commissioners . . . . . . | 25,285,000 | 56.23 | 14,217,755 |
| Anywhere Hospital Board . . . . . . . . | 2,665,000 | 56.23 | 1,498,529 |
| Total Overlapping Debt . . . . . . . . | 50,820,000 | 56.20 | 28,562,393† |
| Total Direct and Overlapping Debt . . . . . . | $158,849,681 | 85.99% | $136,592,074‡ |

*Direct net debt, 15.56 percent of assessed value of real property; $541.64 per capita.
†Overlapping debt, 4.11 percent of assessed value of real property; $143.23 per capita.
‡Direct and overlapping debt, 19.68 percent of assessed value of real property; $684.98 per capita.

Long-Term Debt
a. Description of individual bond issues and leases outstanding.
b. Changes in general long-term debt.
c. Summary of debt service requirements to maturity.
d. Disclosure of legal debt margin.
e. Bonds authorized but unissued.
f. Synopsis of revenue bond covenants.

## SELECTED REFERENCES

American Institute of Certified Public Accountants. *Audits of State and Local Governmental Units.* Rev. ed. New York, 1986.

Governmental Accounting Standards Board. *Codification of Governmental Accounting and Financial Reporting Standards.* 2nd ed. Norwalk, Conn., 1987.

## QUESTIONS AND EXERCISES

7–1.     Using the annual financial report obtained for Exercise 1–1, answer the following questions.

a. Analyze the Combined Balance Sheet and determine the total amount available and to be provided as well as the nature of the general long-term debt outstanding. What relationship does the "Amount Available" have to the Fund Balance reported in the Debt Service Funds column?

b. Review the Notes to the Financial Statements and list or describe all disclosures related to long-term debt. Distinguish between tax-supported long-term debt and debt of proprietary funds. Review the Statistical Tables and list all disclosures related to debt. Where, if at all, does the CAFR include a Statement of Long-Term Debt, a Schedule of Changes in Long-Term Debt, a Schedule of Debt Service to Maturity, a Schedule of Direct and Overlapping Debt, and a Schedule of Debt Limit and Margin?

c. As a financial analyst, do you think the information presented in the report would help you decide if you would invest in additional tax-supported debt of the city? Would you? Does the debt margin appear reasonable? Does your report clearly indicate the existence or absence of capital leases? What about compensated absences (sick and vacation pay), unpaid pension contributions, and claims and judgments payable in future years?

d. Does the report you have disclose the rating of each debt issue? If so, are all issues rated the same? If not, attempt to determine the reason. For further information, check your library for Moody's or Standard and Poor's ratings.

7–2.     This exercise provides a review of Chapters 4 through 7. Write the numbers 1 through 10 on a sheet of paper. Beside each number, write the letter corresponding to the best answer to each of the following questions:

Items 1 through 6 are based on the following information:

The City of Friesland issued tax-supported bonds in the amount of $10,000,000 to finance a street and storm sewer improvement project. Property owners in a certain area affected by this project wanted additional levels of street lighting than were called for in the project specifications and agreed to pay special assessments totaling $1,000,000 to finance installation of lighting at desired levels. The City agreed to guarantee any debt incurred which was backed primarily by collections by the special assessments.

1. The par value of the tax-supported bonds sold should be:
    a. Credited to Bonds Payable in the GLTDAG.
    b. Credited to Bonds Payable in the Capital Projects Fund.
    c. Credited to Bonds Payable in the Debt Service Fund.
    d. Debited to Buildings in the GFAAG.

2. If the tax-supported bonds are sold at 101, the total amount would be debited to Cash of the Capital Projects Fund and the credit(s) in that fund would most likely be to:
    a. Revenues in the same amount as the debit to Cash.
    b. Other Financing Sources in the same amount as the debit to Cash.
    c. Revenues in the amount of the face value of the bonds, and Due to Debt Service Fund in the amount of the premium.
    d. Other Financing Sources in the amount of the face value of the bonds, and Due to Debt Service Fund in the amount of the premium.

3. The construction phase and the debt service phase of the street lighting project financed by special assessments should be accounted for:
    a. Both in the Special Assessments Fund of the City of Friesland.

    *b.* Both in the accounts of a special district, not in any funds of the City of Friesland.

    *c.* The construction phase should be accounted for in a capital projects fund and the debt service phase should be accounted for in a debt service fund of the City of Friesland.

    *d.* None of the above.

4. If expenditures of the City of Friesland's Capital Projects Fund totaled $4,200,000 at the end of the first fiscal year, $4,000,000 of which had been financed from bond proceeds and $200,000 of which had been financed from collections of special assessments, the correct entry in the GFAAG would be:

    *a.* None; all assets under construction are classified as infrastructure which is not recorded in the GFAAG under GASB standards.

    *b.* Construction Work in Progress . . . . . . . . . . 4,000,000
        Investment in General Fixed Assets—Capital
          Projects Funds, Bonds . . . . . . . . . . . .            4,000,000

    *c.* Construction Work in Progress . . . . . . . . . .   200,000
        Investment in General Fixed Assets—Capital
          Projects Funds—Special Assessments  . . . . .        200,000

    *d.* Both (*b*) and (*c*).

5. At the time the tax-supported bonds are sold:

    *a.* The present value of the bond issue should be recorded as a liability in the GLTDAG.

    *b.* The par value of the bond issue should be recorded as a liability in the GLTDAG.

    *c.* The entire proceeds should be recorded as a liability in the GLTDAG; premium on bonds sold should be amortized over the life of the issue.

    *d.* The face value of bonds due within one year from date of issue should be recorded in the Debt Service Fund as a liability. The remainder of the issue should be recorded at par in the GLTDAG.

6. At the time the special assessment is legally approved and the amount to be paid by each property owner becomes definite, the entry in the Capital Projects Fund should be (assuming the entire assessment is due within 30 days):

    *a.* Special Assessments Receivable—Current . . . . . . 1,000,000
        Revenues  . . . . . . . . . . . . . . . . . . . .       1,000,000

    *b.* Special Assessments Receivable—Current . . . . . . 1,000,000
        Other Financing Sources—Special Assessments . .     1,000,000

    *c.* Special Assessments Receivable—Current . . . . . . 1,000,000
        Deferred Revenues  . . . . . . . . . . . . . .      1,000,000

    *d.* No entry is necessary.

7. Ariel Village issued the following bonds during the year ended June 20, 19x1:

Revenue bonds to be repaid from admission fees collected by the Ariel
    Zoo Enterprise Fund . . . . . . . . . . . . . . . . . . . . . . . . . . . . . $200,000
General obligation bonds issued for the Ariel Water and Sewer Enterprise
    Fund which will service the debt  . . . . . . . . . . . . . . . . . . . . $300,000

How much of these bonds should be accounted for in Ariel's General Long-Term Debt Account Group?

a. $0.

b. $200,000.

c. $300,000.

d. $500,000.

8. The Amount to be Provided for Retirement of General Long-Term Debt of a governmental unit would be reported in the:

a. Asset section of the Statement of General Long-Term Debt.

b. Asset section of the Debt Service Fund Balance Sheet.

c. Liability section of the Statement of General Long-Term Debt.

d. Liability section of the Debt Service Fund Balance Sheet.

9. Interest on bonds payable should be recorded as an expenditure by a debt service fund:

a. At the end of the fiscal period if the interest due date does not coincide with the end of the fiscal period.

b. When bonds are issued.

c. When legally payable.

d. When paid.

10. On December 31, 19x0, the last day of the fiscal year, the City of Englewood's Debt Service Fund holds $150,000 for payment of interest due January 1, 19x1, and $200,000 for payment of matured principal on January 1, 19x1. The Statement of General Long-Term Debt as of December 31, 19x0, should show:

a. Amount Available in Debt Service Funds . . . . . . . . . . . . . $150,000

b. Amount Available in Debt Service Funds . . . . . . . . . . . . . $200,000

c. Amount Available in Debt Service Funds . . . . . . . . . . . . . $350,000

d. None of the above.

(Items 7, 8, 9, AICPA, adapted)

7–3. Below are stated a number of unrelated transactions that affect a General Long-Term Debt Account Group, none of which have yet been recorded in that group. You are to prepare journal entries to record each transaction in the GLTDAG.

a. A capital lease was signed with the Ace Computer Company for a network of PCs. The present value of the lease rental payments was $28,667.

b. A payment was made on another capital lease. The total payment was $18,888, of which $13,333 was a payment of interest.

c. A $4,000,000 issue of serial bonds was sold at 103. The premium was transferred to a debt service fund to be held for the payment of principal.

d. A special tax levy of $600,000, designated to provide cash for retirement of serial bonds that had been issued some years previously, was recorded by a debt service fund. It was estimated that $12,000 of the levy would be uncollectible.

e. The Fund Balance of a debt service fund increased $240,000 during the year; $130,000 of the increase is to be held for debt repayment and $110,000 for interest payment.

7–4. You are asked to prepare a Statement of Legal Debt Margin for the Village of Happy Hollow as of December 31, 19x7. You ascertain that the following bond issues were outstanding:

General obligation serial bonds . . . . . . . . . . . . . . . . . . . . . . . $10,500,000
Water utility bonds . . . . . . . . . . . . . . . . . . . . . . . . . . . . . 33,000,000
Special assessment bonds . . . . . . . . . . . . . . . . . . . . . . . . .  3,500,000
Village auditorium bonds . . . . . . . . . . . . . . . . . . . . . . . . .  3,500,000
Street improvement bonds . . . . . . . . . . . . . . . . . . . . . . . . .  8,400,000
Electric utility bonds . . . . . . . . . . . . . . . . . . . . . . . . . . . 14,200,000
Golf course clubhouse bonds . . . . . . . . . . . . . . . . . . . . . . .    550,000

Other information obtained by you included the following items:
1. Assessed valuation of real and taxable property in the Village totaled $660,000,000.
2. The rate of debt limitation applicable to the Village of Happy Hollow was 10 percent of total real and taxable personal property valuation.
3. No general liability existed in connection with the special assessment bonds.
4. Electric utility, water utility, and golf clubhouse bonds were all serviced by enterprise revenues, but each carried a full faith and credit contingency provision and by law was subject to debt limitation.
5. The Village auditorium bonds and street improvement bonds were general obligation issues.
6. The amount of assets segregated for debt retirement at December 31, of the current year, was $6,500,000.
7. None of the bonds matured during the following year.

**7–5.**  At December 31, 19x0, all property inside the limits of the City of Balcom was situated within four governmental units, each authorized to incur long-term debt. At that date, net long-term debt of the four units was as follows:

Balcom County . . . . . . . . . . . . . . . . . . . . . . . . . . . . . . $23,555,000
City of Balcom . . . . . . . . . . . . . . . . . . . . . . . . . . . . . .  9,444,000
Balcom School District . . . . . . . . . . . . . . . . . . . . . . . . . . 14,998,000
Balcom Library District . . . . . . . . . . . . . . . . . . . . . . . . . .  1,200,000

Assessed values of property at the same date were: County and Library District, $900,560,000; City, $360,224,000; and School District, $495,308,000.

*Required:*
a. Prepare a Schedule of Direct and Overlapping Debt for the City of Balcom. (Round the percentages to nearest whole percent.)
b. Compute the actual ratio (round percentages to nearest tenth of a percent) of total debt applicable to the property within the City of Balcom.
c. Compute the share of the City's direct and overlapping debt which pertained to your home, which has an assessed valuation of $33,000 at December 31, 19x0.

**7–6.**  Record in general journal form the entries that should be made in the Pearl City General Long-Term Debt Account Group to record the effect on accounts of the GLTDAG of events and transactions given in Exercises 4–6, 5–6, and 6–6 for the year ended December 31, 19y1.

**7–7.**  Assuming that Pearl City has no outstanding general long-term debt as of December 31, 19y1, other than that recorded in the GLTDAG in your solution to Exercise 7–6, prepare a Statement of General Long-Term Debt for Pearl City as of December 31, 19y1.

7–8.    Record in general journal form the entries that should be made in the Pearl City General Long-Term Debt Account Group to record the effect on the accounts of the GLTDAG of events and transactions given in Exercises 4–8, 5–8, and 6–8 for the year ended December 31, 19y2.

7–9.    Assuming that Pearl City has no outstanding general long-term debt other than that recorded in the GLTDAG in your solutions to Exercises 7–6 and 7–8, prepare a Statement of General Long-Term Debt for Pearl City as of December 31, 19y2.

## CONTINUOUS PROBLEM

7–C.    As of December 31, 19y0, the General Long-Term Debt Account Group of the City of Everlasting Sunshine had the following trial balance (all accounts relate to the City Hall bond issue described in Problem 6–C):

|  | Debit | Credit |
|---|---|---|
| Amount to Be Provided for Payment of 6% Serial Bonds . . | $5,600,000 | |
| Amount Available in Debt Service Fund for Payment of 6% Serial Bonds . . . . . . . . . . . . . . . . . . . . . . | 400,000 | |
| 6% Serial Bonds Payable . . . . . . . . . . . . . . . . | | $6,000,000 |
| Totals . . . . . . . . . . . . . . . . . . . . . . . | $6,000,000 | $6,000,000 |

*Required:*

a. Open a general journal for the General Long-Term Debt Account Group and prepare journal entries for the following transactions. Use account titles listed above; add other accounts as necessary.

   (1) On January 1, 19y1, 6 percent serial bonds maturing that day were paid (see Problem 6–C, transaction a2).

   (2) On January 1, 19y1, 8 percent serial bonds in the face amount of $4,000,000 were sold at $50,000 premium. The premium was to be held by the Debt Service Fund for future payment of principal (see Problem 4–C, transaction a1).

   (3) On December 31, 19y1, the City Hall Debt Service Fund received $400,000 for payment of principal of 6 percent serial bonds on January 1, 19y2 (see Problem 6–C, transaction a5), and the City Hall Annex Debt Service Fund received $200,000 for payment of principal of 8 percent serial bonds on January 1, 19y2 (see Problem 6–C, transaction c6).

   (4) On December 31, 19y1, the residual equity of the City Hall Annex Construction Fund was transferred to the City Hall Annex Debt Service Fund for future payment of bond principal (see Problem 4–C, transaction c, and Problem 6–C, transaction c5).

b. Prepare a Statement of General Long-Term Debt as of December 31, 19y1.

# Chapter 8

# PROPRIETARY FUNDS

**A**ll of the funds discussed in previous chapters (general, special revenue, capital projects, and debt service) are classified as governmental funds, and owe their existence to legal constraints placed upon the
raising of revenue and/or the use of resources for the provision of services to the public or segments thereof, and the acquisition of facilities
to aid in the provision of services. Funds discussed in previous chapters
are expendable: they record only assets which will be converted into
cash and record only liabilities to be paid from fund cash. Governmental
funds recognize revenues and expenditures, not expenses. Fixed assets
are recorded in a separate account group (the GFAAG), and long-term
debt is accounted for in a separate account group (the GLTDAG).[1]

A second fund classification, **proprietary funds,** is used to describe
funds which are nonexpendable. Proprietary funds are used to account
for activities similar to those often engaged in by profit-seeking businesses. Such activities, when engaged in by a governmental body are not
profit seeking, but usually are intended to be cost covering. That is,
users of goods or services produced by a proprietary fund are charged
amounts directly related to the costs of providing the goods or services.
Thus, in the pure case, proprietary funds are self-supporting. Revenues
and *expenses* (not expenditures) are recognized on the full accrual basis,
so that financial statements of proprietary funds are similar in all respects to those of business organizations. Fixed assets used in fund operations and long-term debt serviced from fund revenues are recorded
in the accounts of each proprietary fund. Depreciation on fixed assets
is recognized as an expense, and all other accruals and deferrals common to business accounting are recorded in proprietary funds. Budgets
should be prepared for proprietary funds to facilitate management of

---

[1]See footnote 1 of Chapter 7 for proposed changes in GASB standards. When the
GASB issues standards in final form the publisher will distribute an Update Bulletin to
adopters of this text.

fund activities, but, in most states, proprietary funds are not required to adopt legal budgets. Consequently, GASB standards do not require the incorporation of budgetary accounts into the accounting systems of proprietary funds.

The use of full accrual accounting should disclose whether or not the objective of capital maintenance is achieved. The full accrual basis of accounting requires revenues to be recognized when earned, and expenses to be recognized when incurred. Operating revenues are distinguished from nonoperating revenues. Grants, entitlements, and shared revenues received for operating purposes (or which the grantor permits the recipient to use for either operating or capital purposes) are recognized as nonoperating revenues when earned. However, grants restricted for capital outlay are recorded as contributed capital of proprietary funds—not as any sort of revenue. (Recall that governmental funds record capital grants, as well as operating grants, as credits to Revenues when earned.)

Two types of funds are classified as proprietary funds: internal service funds and enterprise funds. Accounting and financial reporting for these fund types is described and illustrated in the following sections of this chapter.

## INTERNAL SERVICE FUNDS

As governmental units become more complex, efficiency can be improved if services used by several departments or funds, or even by several governmental units, are combined in a single administrative unit. Purchasing, computer services, and motor pools are common examples. Activities that produce goods or services to be provided to **other departments or other governmental units** on a cost reimbursement basis are accounted for by internal service funds. (Internal service funds are also called intragovernmental service funds, working capital funds, revolving funds, and other similar names.)

Internal service funds recognize revenues and expenses on the full accrual basis. They account for all fixed assets used in their operations and for long-term debt to be serviced from revenues generated from their operations, as well as for all current assets and current liabilities. Distinction should be made in the equity accounts of an internal service fund between equity contributed to the fund and retained earnings resulting from operations of the fund.

### Establishment and Operation of Internal Service Funds

The establishment of an internal service fund is normally subject to legislative approval. The original allocation of resources to the fund may be derived from a transfer of assets of another fund, such as the General

Fund or an enterprise fund, intended as a **contribution** not to be repaid, or a transfer that is in the nature of a long-term **advance** to be repaid by the internal service fund over a period of years.

Since internal service funds are established to improve the management of resources, it is generally considered that they should be operated, and accounted for, on a business basis. For example, assume that administrators request the establishment of a fund for the purchasing, warehousing, and issuing of supplies used by a number of funds and departments. A budget should be prepared for the internal service fund (but not recorded in the accounts) to demonstrate that fund management has realistic plans to generate sufficient revenues to cover the cost of goods issued and such other expenses, including depreciation, which the governing body intends fund operations to recover. Departments and units expected to purchase goods and services from internal service funds should include in their budgets the anticipated outlays for goods and services. During the year, as supplies are issued or services are rendered, the internal service fund records revenues ("Billings to Departments" is an account title commonly used instead of "Sales") and the using departments accounted for by governmental funds record expenditures. Periodically, and at year-end, an operating statement should be prepared for each internal service fund to compare revenues and related expenses; these operating statements, called Statement of Revenues, Expenses, and Changes in Retained Earnings, are similar to income statements prepared for investor-owned businesses.

### Illustrative Case—Supplies Fund

Assume that the administrators of the Village of Elizabeth obtain approval from the Village Council in early 19x6 to centralize the purchasing, storing, and issuing functions and to administer and account for these functions in a Supplies Fund. An equity transfer of $100,000 cash is made from the General Fund as a contribution not to be repaid by the Supplies Fund. Additionally, a long-term advance of $200,000 is made from the Water Utility Fund. The advance is to be repaid in 20 equal annual installments, with no interest. The receipt of the equity transfer in and the liability to the Water Utility Fund would be recorded in the Supplies Fund accounts in the following manner:[2]

```
1. Cash . . . . . . . . . . . . . . . . . . . . . . . . . .   300,000
        Equity Transfers In . . . . . . . . . . . . . . . .            100,000
        Advance from Water Utility Fund . . . . . . . . .              200,000
```

Assume that early in 19x6 a satisfactory warehouse building is purchased for $150,000; $20,000 of the purchase price is considered as a

---

[2]The corresponding entry in the General Fund is Entry 21 in Chapter 3. The corresponding entry in the Water Utility Fund is Entry 4 in the "Illustrative Case—Water Utility Fund" in a later section of this chapter.

cost of the land. Necessary warehouse machinery and equipment is purchased for $60,000. Delivery equipment is purchased for $18,000. If the purchases are made for cash, the acquisition of the assets would be recorded in the books of the Supplies Fund as:

```
2. Land . . . . . . . . . . . . . . . . . . . . . . . . . . .    20,000
   Building . . . . . . . . . . . . . . . . . . . . . . . .   130,000
   Machinery and Equipment—Warehouse . . . . . . . .         60,000
   Equipment—Delivery . . . . . . . . . . . . . . . .        18,000
      Cash . . . . . . . . . . . . . . . . . . . . . . . .               228,000
```

Supplies are ordered to maintain inventories at a level commensurate with expected usage. No entry is needed because proprietary funds accounted for in conformity with GASB standards are not required to record encumbrances. During 19x6, it is assumed that supplies are received and related invoices are approved for payment in the amount of $323,500; the entry needed to record the asset and the liability is:

```
3. Inventory of Supplies . . . . . . . . . . . . . . .    323,500
      Vouchers Payable . . . . . . . . . . . . . . .                 323,500
```

Governmental funds which maintain relatively minor inventories of supplies usually account for them on the physical inventory basis, as illustrated in Chapter 3. The Supplies Fund, however, should account for its inventories on the perpetual inventory basis since the information is needed for proper performance of its primary function. Accordingly, when supplies are issued, the Inventory Account must be credited for the cost of the supplies issued. Since the using fund will be charged an amount in excess of the inventory carrying value, the Receivable and Revenue accounts must reflect the selling price. The markup above cost should be determined on the basis of budgeted expenses and other items to be financed from net income. If the budget for the Village of Elizabeth's Supplies Fund indicates that a markup of 30 percent on cost is needed, issues to General Fund departments of supplies costing $290,000 would be recorded by the following entries:

```
4a. Cost of Supplies Issued . . . . . . . . . . . . . .    290,000
       Inventory of Supplies . . . . . . . . . . . . . .                290,000
4b. Due from General Fund . . . . . . . . . . . . . . .    377,000
       Billings to Departments . . . . . . . . . . . .                377,000
```

During the year it is assumed that purchasing expenses totaling $19,000, warehousing expenses totaling $12,000, administrative expenses totaling $11,000, and delivery expenses totaling $13,000 were incurred. If all liabilities are vouchered before payment, the entry would be:

```
5. Purchasing Expenses . . . . . . . . . . . . . . . . . . .    19,000
   Warehousing Expenses . . . . . . . . . . . . . . . . .     12,000
   Administrative Expenses . . . . . . . . . . . . . . . .     11,000
   Delivery Expenses . . . . . . . . . . . . . . . . . . .     13,000
      Vouchers Payable . . . . . . . . . . . . . . . . . .                55,000
```

If collections from the General Fund during 19x6 totaled $322,000, the entry would be:

```
6. Cash . . . . . . . . . . . . . . . . . . . . . . .   322,000
      Due from General Fund  . . . . . . . . . . . .              322,000
```

Assuming that payment of vouchers during the year totaled $368,500, the entry is made:

```
7. Vouchers Payable . . . . . . . . . . . . . . . .   368,500
      Cash . . . . . . . . . . . . . . . . . . . . .              368,500
```

The advance from the Water Utility Fund is to be repaid in 20 equal annual installments; repayment of one installment at the end of 19x6 is recorded as:

```
8. Advance from Water Utility Fund . . . . . . . . . .   10,000
      Cash . . . . . . . . . . . . . . . . . . . . .              10,000
```

At the time depreciable assets were acquired, the building used as a warehouse had an estimated useful life of 20 years; the warehouse machinery and equipment had an estimated useful life of 10 years; the delivery equipment had an estimated useful life of 5 years; and none of the assets was expected to have any salvage value at the expiration of its useful life. Under these assumptions straight-line depreciation of the building would be $6,500 per year; depreciation of machinery and equipment, $6,000 per year; and depreciation of delivery equipment, $3,600 per year. (Since governmental units are not subject to income taxes, there is no incentive to use any depreciation method other than straight line.)

If the administrative and clerical office space occupies 10 percent of the area of the warehouse, 10 percent of the depreciation of the warehouse, $650, should be considered as administrative expense; similarly, if the purchasing office occupies 10 percent of the space in the warehouse building, 10 percent of the building depreciation, $650, should be considered purchasing expense. The remainder of the building is devoted to warehousing, therefore 80 percent of the total building depreciation, $5,200, is to be charged to Warehousing Expense. The latter account is also charged $6,000 for warehouse machinery and equipment depreciation expense. Delivery Expense is charged $3,600 for delivery equipment depreciation for the year:

```
9. Administrative Expenses . . . . . . . . . . . . . .       650
     Purchasing Expenses . . . . . . . . . . . . . . .       650
     Warehousing Expenses . . . . . . . . . . . . . .    11,200
     Delivery Expenses . . . . . . . . . . . . . . . .     3,600
        Allowance for Depreciation—Building . . . . . . .              6,500
        Allowance for Depreciation—Machinery and
           Equipment—Warehouse  . . . . . . . . . . .              6,000
        Allowance for Depreciation—Equipment—Delivery .              3,600
```

Organizations which keep perpetual inventory records must adjust the records periodically to reflect shortages, overages, or out-of-condition stock disclosed by physical inventories. Adjustments to the Inventory account are also considered to be adjustments to the warehousing expenses of the period. In this illustrative case it is assumed that no adjustments were found to be necessary at year-end.

Assuming that all revenues and expenses applicable to 19x6 have been properly recorded by the entries illustrated above, the nominal accounts should be closed as of December 31, 19x6:

```
10. Billings to Departments . . . . . . . . . . . . . .  377,000
        Cost of Supplies Issued . . . . . . . . . . . .            290,000
        Purchasing Expenses  . . . . . . . . . . . . .              19,650
        Warehousing Expenses  . . . . . . . . . . . .              23,200
        Administrative Expenses  . . . . . . . . . . .              11,650
        Delivery Expenses  . . . . . . . . . . . . . .              16,600
        Excess of Net Billings to Departments over Costs  .         15,900
```

Excess of Net Billings to Departments over Costs (or Excess of Costs over Net Billings to Departments, if operations resulted in a loss) is the account title used here in place of "Income Summary"—the title commonly found in profit-seeking businesses. Whatever title is used for the account summarizing the results of operations for the period, the account should be closed at year-end. The title of the account that records earnings retained in an internal service fund is the same as the title commonly used for profit-seeking businesses, Retained Earnings.

```
11. Excess of Net Billings to Departments over Costs   . . .   15,900
        Retained Earnings  . . . . . . . . . . . . . .              15,900
```

The Equity Transfers In account credited in Entry 1 would be closed to Fund Balance if the Supplies Fund were a governmental fund. The Supplies Fund, however, is a proprietary fund and proprietary funds utilize two equity accounts in order to disclose to the readers of their financial statements the amount of equity contributed to the fund and the amount of equity resulting from fund operations. Entry 11 records the latter; in order to record the former the following entry is made:

```
12. Equity Transfers In  . . . . . . . . . . . . . . . .  100,000
        Contribution from General Fund . . . . . . . . .           100,000
```

## Illustrative Financial Statements—Supplies Fund

The Balance Sheet of the Supplies Fund of the Village of Elizabeth for December 31, 19x6 is shown as Illustration 8–1. Illustration 8–2 presents a Statement of Revenues, Expenses, and Changes in Retained Earnings for the Year Ended December 31, 19x6. Illustration 8–3 presents the Statement of Cash Flows for the Supplies Fund for the Year Ended December 31, 19x6.

**ILLUSTRATION 8–1**

**VILLAGE OF ELIZABETH**
**Supplies Fund**
**Balance Sheet**
**As of December 31, 19x6**

**Assets**

| | | | |
|---|---|---|---|
| Current Assets: | | | |
| Cash . . . . . . . . . . . . . . . . . . . . . . . . . . . | | | $ 15,500 |
| Due from General Fund . . . . . . . . . . . . . . | | | 55,000 |
| Inventory of supplies . . . . . . . . . . . . . . . | | | 33,500 |
|     Total Current Assets . . . . . . . . . . . . . . | | | 104,000 |
| Fixed Assets: | | | |
| Land . . . . . . . . . . . . . . . . . . . . . . . . . | | $ 20,000 | |
| Building . . . . . . . . . . . . . . . . . . . . . . | $130,000 | | |
|     Less allowance for depreciation . . . . . . . . . . . | 6,500 | 123,500 | |
| Machinery and equipment—Warehouse . . . . . . . | 60,000 | | |
|     Less allowance for depreciation . . . . . . . . . . . | 6,000 | 54,000 | |
| Equipment—delivery . . . . . . . . . . . . . . | 18,000 | | |
|     Less allowance for depreciation . . . . . . . . . . . | 3,600 | 14,400 | |
|     Total Fixed Assets . . . . . . . . . . . . . . | | | 211,900 |
| Total Assets . . . . . . . . . . . . . . . . . . | | | $315,900 |

**Liabilities and Fund Equity**

| | | | |
|---|---|---|---|
| Current Liabilities: | | | |
| Vouchers payable . . . . . . . . . . . . . . . . | | | $ 10,000 |
| Long-Term Debt: | | | |
| Advance from Water Utility Fund . . . . . . . . . . . | | | 190,000 |
|     Total Liabilities . . . . . . . . . . . . . . . | | | 200,000 |
| Fund Equity: | | | |
| Contribution from General Fund . . . . . . . . . | | $100,000 | |
| Retained earnings . . . . . . . . . . . . . . . . | | 15,900 | |
|     Total Fund Equity . . . . . . . . . . . . . . | | | 115,900 |
| Total Liabilities and Fund Equity . . . . . . . . . . . . . | | | $315,900 |

**ILLUSTRATION 8–2**

**VILLAGE OF ELIZABETH**
**Supplies Fund**
**Statement of Revenues, Expenses, and**
**Changes in Retained Earnings**
**For the Year Ended December 31, 19x6**

| | | |
|---|---|---|
| Billings to departments . . . . . . . . . . . . . . . . . . . . . . . . . . | | $377,000 |
|     Less: Cost of supplies issued . . . . . . . . . . . . . . . . . . . . | | 290,000 |
| Gross Margin . . . . . . . . . . . . . . . . . . . . . . . . . . | | 87,000 |
| Less: | | |
| Purchasing expenses . . . . . . . . . . . . . . . . . . . . . . . . | $19,650 | |
| Warehousing expenses . . . . . . . . . . . . . . . . . . . . . . . | 23,200 | |
| Administrative expenses . . . . . . . . . . . . . . . . . . . . . | 11,650 | |
| Delivery expenses . . . . . . . . . . . . . . . . . . . . . . . . | 16,600 | |
|     Total Operating Expenses . . . . . . . . . . . . . . . . . . . | | 71,100 |
| Excess of Net Billings to Departments over Costs for the year . . . . . . . | | 15,900 |
| Retained Earnings, January 19x6 . . . . . . . . . . . . . . . . . . . . | | –0– |
| Retained Earnings, December 31, 19x6 . . . . . . . . . . . . . . . . . . | | $ 15,900 |

**ILLUSTRATION 8–3**

**VILLAGE OF ELIZABETH**
**Supplies Fund**
**Statement of Cash Flows**
**For the Year Ended December 31, 19x6**

| | |
|---|---:|
| Cash flows from operating activities: | |
| Cash received from customers . . . . . . . . . . . . . . . . . . . | $322,000 |
| Cash paid to suppliers and employees . . . . . . . . . . . . . . . | (368,500) |
| Net cash used for operating activities . . . . . . . . . . . . . . | (46,500) |
| Cash flows from capital and related financing activities: | |
| Advance from Water Utility Fund . . . . . . . . . . . . . . . . | 200,000 |
| Partial repayment of advance from Water Utility Fund . . . . . . . . | (10,000) |
| Equity transfer from General Fund . . . . . . . . . . . . . . . . | 100,000 |
| Acquisition of capital assets . . . . . . . . . . . . . . . . . . . | (228,000) |
| Net cash provided by capital and related financing activities . . . . . | 62,000 |
| New increase in cash and cash equivalents . . . . . . . . . . . . . | 15,500 |
| Cash and cash equivalents, January 1, 19x6 . . . . . . . . . . . . | -0- |
| Cash and cash equivalents, December 31, 19x6 . . . . . . . . . . . . | $ 15,500 |

**Reconciliation of Excess of Net Billings**
**to Departments over Costs to Net Cash Used**
**for Operating Activities**

| | | |
|---|---:|---:|
| Excess of Net Billings to Departments over Costs . . . . . . | | $ 15,900 |
| Adjustments: | | |
| Depreciation expense . . . . . . . . . . . . . . . . . | $16,100 | |
| Increase in receivables from other funds . . . . . . . . . | (55,000) | |
| Increase in inventory . . . . . . . . . . . . . . . . | (33,500) | |
| Increase in vouchers payable . . . . . . . . . . . . . | 10,000 | |
| Total adjustments . . . . . . . . . . . . . . . . . . | | (62,400) |
| Net cash used for operating activities . . . . . . . . . . . . | | $ 46,500 |

# ENTERPRISE FUNDS

Enterprise funds are used by governmental units to account for services provided **to the general public** on a user charge basis. Enterprise
funds may also be used to account for any operations for which the
governmental unit wishes to determine net income for purposes of public policy or administrative control. From this description, and from the
fact that the word *enterprise* is often used as a synonym for **business,**
it may be apparent that enterprise funds should use full accrual accounting and account for all assets used in the production of goods or services
offered by the fund, just as internal service funds do. Similarly,

if long-term debt is to be serviced by the fund, it is accounted for by the fund. Distinction should be made in fund equity accounts between equity contributed to the fund and earnings resulting from operations of the fund.

The most common examples of governmental enterprises are public utilities, notably water and sewer utilities. Electric and gas utilities, transportation systems, airports, ports, hospitals, toll bridges, produce markets, parking lots, parking garages, liquor stores, and public housing projects are other examples frequently found. Services of the kinds mentioned are generally accounted for by enterprise funds because they are intended to be largely self-supporting. However, they are properly accounted for by a general or special revenue fund by those governments that support the activities largely from general or special revenue sources other than user charges and are not concerned with measuring the costs of the activities.

Almost every kind of enterprise operated by a government has its counterpart in the private sector. In order to take advantage of the work done by regulatory agencies and trade associations to develop useful accounting information systems for investor-owned enterprises, **it is recommended that governmentally owned enterprises use the accounting structures developed for investor-owned enterprises of the same nature.** Budgetary accounts should be used only if required by law. Debt service and construction activities of a governmental enterprise are accounted for within an enterprise fund, rather than by a separate debt service and capital project funds. Thus, the reports of enterprise funds are self-contained; and creditors, legislators, or the general public can evaluate the performance of a governmental enterprise by the same criteria as they can the performance of investor-owned enterprises in the same industry.

By far the most numerous and important enterprise services rendered by local governments are public utilities. In this chapter, therefore, the example used is that of a water utility fund.

### Illustrative Case—Water Utility Fund

It is assumed that the Village of Elizabeth is located in a state that permits enterprise funds to operate without formal legal approval of their budgets. Accordingly, the budget is not recorded in enterprise accounts.

Assume that as of December 31, 19x5, the accountants for the Village of Elizabeth prepared the post-closing trial balance shown on the next page.

The item Accrued Utility Revenues in the trial balance represents

**VILLAGE OF ELIZABETH**
**Water Utility Fund**
**Post-Closing Trial Balance**
**December 31, 19x5**

|  | Debit | Credit |
|---|---|---|
| Utility Plant in Service | $4,125,140 | |
| Accumulated Provision for Depreciation of Utility Plant | | $ 886,500 |
| Utility Plant Acquisition Adjustment | 298,000 | |
| Accumulated Provision for Amortization of Plant Acquisition Adjustment | | 149,000 |
| Construction Work in Progress | 468,125 | |
| Restricted Assets | 55,000 | |
| Cash | 458,900 | |
| Customer Accounts Receivable | 72,500 | |
| Accumulated Provision for Uncollectible Accounts | | 2,175 |
| Accrued Utility Revenues | 25,300 | |
| Materials and Supplies | 37,500 | |
| Unamortized Debt Discount and Expense | 7,800 | |
| Revenue Bonds Payable | | 2,700,000 |
| Accounts Payable | | 73,700 |
| Customer Advances for Construction | | 25,000 |
| Customer Deposits | | 35,300 |
| Contribution from General Fund | | 1,100,000 |
| Contribution from Customers | | 169,000 |
| Retained Earnings—Appropriated | | 55,000 |
| Retained Earnings—Unappropriated | | 352,590 |
| Totals | $5,548,265 | $5,548,265 |

unbilled customer accounts receivable at year-end. Utilities that meter their service make extensive use of cycle billing, which, in substance, consists of billing part of their customers each day, instead of billing by calendar months. Cycle billing results in a sizable dollar amount of unbilled receivables on any given date, thus requiring accrual of unbilled receivables as of the financial statement date. When individual bills are prepared, it is not feasible to determine whether a portion of the bill has been accrued, and, if so, how much; therefore the simplest procedure is to reverse the accrual entry as of the start of the new fiscal year. Assuming that when Accrued Utility Revenues was debited by the Village of Elizabeth Water Utility Fund as a part of the December 31, 19x5 adjusting entries, the offsetting credit was to Sales of Water, the following entry is appropriate as of January 1, 19x6:

| 1. Sales of Water | 25,300 | |
|---|---|---|
| Accrued Utility Revenues | | 25,300 |

When utility customers are billed during the year, appropriate revenue accounts are credited. Assuming that during 19x6 the total bills to nongovernmental customers amounted to $875,300, bills to the Village of Elizabeth General Fund amounted to $40,000, and that all revenue was from sales of water, the following entry summarizes the results:

```
2. Customer Accounts Receivable . . . . . . . . . . . .  875,300
   Due from General Fund  . . . . . . . . . . . . . .   40,000
      Sales of Water   . . . . . . . . . . . . . . . . . .          915,300
```

If collections from nongovernmental customers totaled $868,500 for water billings, Entry 3 is needed:

```
3. Cash . . . . . . . . . . . . . . . . . . . . . . . .  868,500
      Customer Accounts Receivable . . . . . . . . . .          868,500
```

During 19x6, the Village of Elizabeth established a Supplies Fund and the Water Utility Fund advanced $200,000 to the Supplies Fund as a long-term loan. The entry by the Supplies Fund is illustrated in Entry 1 in the "Illustrative Case—Supplies Fund" section of this chapter. The following entry should be made by the Water Utility Fund:

```
4. Long-Term Advance to Supplies Fund . . . . . . . . .  200,000
      Cash . . . . . . . . . . . . . . . . . . . . . .          200,000
```

Materials and supplies in the amount of $231,500 were purchased during the year by the Water Utility Fund, and vouchers in that amount were recorded as a liability:

```
5. Materials and Supplies . . . . . . . . . . . . . . .  231,500
      Accounts Payable . . . . . . . . . . . . . . . .          231,500
```

When materials and supplies are issued to the functional departments of the Water Utility Fund the corresponding expense accounts are charged for the cost of materials and supplies (Source of Supply Expenses refers to the operating costs of reservoirs, and so on, from which untreated water is obtained).

Materials and supplies issued for use for construction projects are capitalized temporarily as Construction Work in Progress. (Entry 10 illustrates the entry required when a capital project is completed.)

```
6. Source of Supply Expenses . . . . . . . . . . . . . .    23,500
   Pumping Expenses  . . . . . . . . . . . . . . . . . .    19,800
   Water Treatment Expenses  . . . . . . . . . . . . . .    29,700
   Transmission and Distribution Expenses  . . . . . . .    37,400
   Construction Work in Progress  . . . . . . . . . . .   127,600
      Materials and Supplies . . . . . . . . . . . . . .          238,000
```

Payrolls for the year were chargeable to the accounts shown in the entry below. Tax Collections Payable is the account provided in utility accounting to report the liability for taxes collected from employees but not yet remitted to the taxing authority. Taxes Accrued is the liability account used to report the taxes that are the expense of the utility, such as the employer's share of social security taxes. In the entry below, it is assumed that checks have been issued for employees' net earnings.

```
 7. Source of Supply Expenses . . . . . . . . . . . . .      9,500
    Pumping Expenses   . . . . . . . . . . . . . . . .     19,300
    Water Treatment Expenses  . . . . . . . . . . . .      19,300
    Transmission and Distribution Expenses  . . . . . . .  92,300
    Customer Accounts Expenses . . . . . . . . . . . .    113,200
    Sales Expenses  . . . . . . . . . . . . . . . . .      17,200
    Administrative and General Expenses  . . . . . . . .   92,900
    Construction Work in Progress  . . . . . . . . . .     58,900
        Taxes Accrued  . . . . . . . . . . . . . . .                17,900
        Tax Collections Payable . . . . . . . . . . .               72,300
        Cash . . . . . . . . . . . . . . . . . . . .               332,400
```

Bond interest in the amount of $189,000 was paid. Amortization of Debt Discount and Expense amounted to $780.

```
 8. Interest on Long-Term Debt . . . . . . . . . . . . .  189,000
    Amortization of Debt Discount and Expense . . . . . .     780
        Unamortized Debt Discount and Expense  . . . . .              780
        Cash . . . . . . . . . . . . . . . . . . . . .           189,000
```

Bond interest in the amount of $17,800 was considered to be properly chargeable to construction (utility regulatory authorities provide the Allowance for Funds Used during Construction account which is deducted in the operating statement from Interest on Long-Term Debt, so that financial statement readers are informed of the amount of interest capitalized during the year):

```
 9. Construction Work in Progress  . . . . . . . . . . .   17,800
        Allowance for Funds Used during Construction . . .           17,800
```

Construction projects on which costs totaled $529,300 were completed and the assets placed in service. Utility Plant in Service summarizes the investment in fixed assets used for utility purposes. In an actual case detail would be presented to disclose the cost of fixed assets used for each of the principal functions of the utility.

```
10. Utility Plant in Service  . . . . . . . . . . . . . .  529,300
        Construction Work in Progress . . . . . . . . .             529,300
```

In order to receive service from a utility, potential customers ordinarily have to deposit with the utility an amount set by a regulatory commission, to be held by the utility as security against nonpayment of bills by the customer. Customers owing bills totaling $3,510 had left the Village of Elizabeth and could not be located. These customers had paid deposits to the water utility totaling $1,530; the deposits were applied to the bills, and the unpaid remainder was charged to the accumulated provision for uncollectible accounts.

```
11. Customer Deposits . . . . . . . . . . . . . . . .      1,530
    Accumulated Provision for Uncollectible Accounts  . .   1,980
        Customer Accounts Receivable  . . . . . . . . .              3,510
```

Customers' deposits amounting to $5,920 were refunded by check to customers discontinuing service (Entry 12a). Deposits totaling $6,350 were received from new customers (Entry 12b).

```
12a. Customer Deposits  . . . . . . . . . . . . . . . .     5,920
         Cash . . . . . . . . . . . . . . . . . . . . .              5,920
12b. Cash . . . . . . . . . . . . . . . . . . . . .         6,350
         Customer Deposits  . . . . . . . . . . . . .                6,350
```

Customers requesting services from the utility which necessitated additions to utility plant had advanced $25,000 to the Water Utility Fund as of December 31, 19x5. During 19x6 the construction was completed and service to these customers commenced. In accord with the agreement with the customers' advances in the amount of $12,500 were applied to their water bills; the remainder of the advances was transferred to Contributions from Customers, an equity account:

```
13. Customers Advances for Construction  . . . . . . . .    25,000
         Customer Accounts Receivable  . . . . . . . . .             12,500
         Contributions from Customers . . . . . . . . . .            12,500
```

Payments of accounts payable totaled $275,600. Payments of Taxes Accrued amounted to $13,700, and payments of Tax Collections Payable amounted to $67,500.

```
14. Accounts Payable  . . . . . . . . . . . . . . . .      275,600
        Taxes Accrued . . . . . . . . . . . . . . . . .     13,700
        Tax Collections Payable . . . . . . . . . . . . .    67,500
        Cash  . . . . . . . . . . . . . . . . . . . . .             356,800
```

The Water Utility Fund agreed to pay $30,000 to the Village General Fund as a contribution in lieu of property taxes. The entry in the General Fund is illustrated in Chapter 3 (see Chapter 3, Entry 18). The following entry records the event in the books of the Water Utility Fund:

```
15. Contribution in Lieu of Taxes  . . . . . . . . . . .    30,000
        Due to General Fund . . . . . . . . . . . . . .              30,000
```

Near the end of 19x6 the Water Utility fund received $10,000 cash from the Supplies Fund as part payment of the long-term advance (see Supplies Fund, Entry 8).

```
16. Cash  . . . . . . . . . . . . . . . . . . . . . . .    10,000
        Long-Term Advance to Supplies Fund . . . . . . .             10,000
```

The account, Utility Plant Acquisition Adjustment, represents the difference between the amount paid for assets acquired by the Water Utility Fund from another utility over the book value (the *original cost* less depreciation). Whereas in general commercial accounting, assets acquired are written up to market value when acquired, and any amount paid for a total business over the market value of the net assets would be recorded as Goodwill, utility accounting requires that fixed assets acquired from another utility be recorded in the accounts of the acquiring utility at the amount shown in the accounts of the selling utility. Any premium paid by the acquiring utility is debited to Plant Acquisition Adjustment. The latter account is amortized over the life of the fixed assets, unless a different period is specified by a regulatory authority. At year-end, entries to record depreciation expense, the Amortization of Plant Acquisition Adjustment, the Accumulated Provision for Uncollectible Accounts, and Unbilled Customer Accounts Receivable should be made as illustrated by Entry 17. Note that Customer Accounts Expenses is debited, in accord with regulatory authority manuals, instead of Bad Debts Expense, for the amount added to the Accumulated Provision for Uncollectible Accounts. Amounts are assumed:

| | | |
|---|---:|---:|
| 17. Amortization of Plant Acquisition Adjustment . . . . . | 29,800 | |
| Depreciation Expense . . . . . . . . . . . . . . . | 122,800 | |
| Customer Accounts Expenses . . . . . . . . . . . | 2,200 | |
| Accrued Utility Revenues . . . . . . . . . . . . . | 28,700 | |
| Accumulated Provision for Amortization of Plant Acquisition Adjustment . . . . . . . . . . . | | 29,800 |
| Accumulated Provision for Depreciation of Utility Plant . . . . . . . . . . . . . . . . | | 122,800 |
| Accumulated Provision for Uncollectible Accounts . | | 2,200 |
| Sales of Water . . . . . . . . . . . . . | | 28,700 |

In accord with the revenue bond indenture, $55,000 was transferred from operating cash to the Restricted Assets category. The transfer required an appropriation of retained earnings of an equal amount.

| | | |
|---|---:|---:|
| 18a. Restricted Assets . . . . . . . . . . . . . | 55,000 | |
| Cash . . . . . . . . . . . . . | | 55,000 |
| 18b. Unappropriated Retained Earnings . . . . . . . . | 55,000 | |
| Appropriated Retained Earnings . . . . . . . . . | | 55,000 |

Revenue and expense accounts for the year are closed to the Unappropriated Retained Earnings account.

| | | |
|---|---:|---:|
| 19. Sales of Water . . . . . . . . . . . . . . . . . | 918,700 | |
| Allowance for Funds Used During Construction . . . . | 17,800 | |
| Source of Supply Expenses . . . . . . . . . . | | 33,000 |
| Pumping Expenses . . . . . . . . . . . . . | | 39,100 |
| Water Treatment Expenses . . . . . . . . . . . | | 49,000 |
| Transmission and Distribution Expenses . . . . . . | | 129,700 |
| Customer Account Expenses . . . . . . . . . . | | 115,400 |
| Sales Expenses . . . . . . . . . . . . . | | 17,200 |
| Administrative and General Expenses . . . . . . . | | 92,900 |
| Depreciation Expense . . . . . . . . . . . . | | 122,800 |
| Interest on Long-Term Debt . . . . . . . . . . | | 189,000 |
| Amortization of Debt Discount and Expense . . . | | 780 |
| Contribution in Lieu of Taxes . . . . . . . . . | | 30,000 |
| Amortization of Plant Acquisition Adjustment . . . | | 29,800 |
| Unappropriated Retained Earnings . . . . . . . | | 87,820 |

## Illustrative Financial Statements—Water Utility Fund

The Balance Sheet for the Village of Elizabeth Water Utility Fund as of December 31, 19x6, would appear as shown in Illustration 8–4. Note that the fixed assets and long-term debt are listed ahead of the current assets and current liabilities, respectively. This is in accord with the regulatory format and highlights the fact that utilities are highly capital

## ILLUSTRATION 8–4

**VILLAGE OF ELIZABETH**
**Water Utility Fund**
**Balance Sheet**
**As of December 31, 19x6**

**Assets and Other Debits**

| | | | |
|---|---|--:|--:|
| Utility Plant: | | | |
| Utility plant in service . . . . . . . . . . . . . . | | $4,654,440 | |
| Less accumulated depreciation . . . . . . . . . . | | 1,009,300 | |
| Utility Plant—net . . . . . . . . . . . . | | | $3,645,140 |
| Utility plant acquisition adjustment . . . . . . . | | 298,000 | |
| Less accumulated amortization . . . . . . . . . | | 178,800 | |
| Plant Acquisition Adjustment—net . . . . . . . | | | 119,200 |
| Construction work in progress . . . . . . . . . | | | 143,125 |
| Net Utility Plant . . . . . . . . . . . . . | | | 3,907,465 |
| Other Property and Investments: | | | |
| Restricted Assets . . . . . . . . . . . . . | | 110,000 | |
| Long-term advance to supplies fund . . . . . . . . | | 190,000 | |
| Total Other Property and Investments . . . . . . | | | 300,000 |
| Current and Accrued Assets: | | | |
| Cash . . . . . . . . . . . . . . . . . . | | 204,630 | |
| Customer accounts receivable . . . . . . . . . | $ 63,290 | | |
| Less accumulated provision for uncollectibles . . . . | 2,395 | 60,895 | |
| Accrued utility revenues . . . . . . . . . . . . | | 28,700 | |
| Due from General Fund . . . . . . . . . . . . | | 10,000 | |
| Materials and supplies . . . . . . . . . . . . | | 31,000 | |
| Total Current and Accrued Assets . . . . . . . . | | | 335,225 |
| Deferred Debits: | | | |
| Unamortized debt discount and expense . . . . . . | | | 7,020 |
| Total Assets and Other Debits . . . . . . . . . . . | | | $4,549.710 |

**Liabilities and Other Credits**

| | | | |
|---|---|--:|--:|
| Long-Term Debt: | | | |
| Revenue bonds payable . . . . . . . . . . . . | | | $2,700,000 |
| Current Liabilities: | | | |
| Accounts payable . . . . . . . . . . . . . | | 29,600 | |
| Customer deposits . . . . . . . . . . . . . | | 34,200 | |
| Taxes accrued . . . . . . . . . . . . . . | | 4,200 | |
| Tax collections payable . . . . . . . . . . . | | 4,800 | |
| Total Current Liabilities . . . . . . . . . . . | | | 72,800 |
| Total Liabilities . . . . . . . . . . . . . . | | | 2,772,800 |
| Fund Equity: | | | |
| Contributions from general fund . . . . . . . . . | | 1,100,000 | |
| Contributions from customers . . . . . . . . . . | | 181,500 | |
| Retained earnings: | | | |
| Appropriated . . . . . . . . . . . . . . . | 110,000 | | |
| Unappropriated . . . . . . . . . . . . . . | 385,410 | 495,410 | |
| Total Fund Equity . . . . . . . . . . . . | | | 1,776,910 |
| Total Liabilities and Other Credits . . . . . . . . . | | | $4,549,710 |

**ILLUSTRATION 8–5**

**VILLAGE OF ELIZABETH**
Water Utility Fund
Statement of Revenues, Expenses, and
Changes in Retained Earnings
For the Year Ended December 31, 19x6

| | | |
|---|---:|---:|
| Utility Operating Revenue: | | |
| Sales of water | | $918,700 |
| Operating Expenses: | | |
| Source of supply expenses | $ 33,000 | |
| Pumping expenses | 39,100 | |
| Water treatment expenses | 49,000 | |
| Transmission and distribution expenses | 129,700 | |
| Customer account expenses | 115,400 | |
| Sales expenses | 17,200 | |
| Administrative and general expenses | 92,900 | |
| Depreciation expense | 122,800 | |
| Amortization of plant acquisition adjustment | 29,800 | |
| Contribution in lieu of taxes | 30,000 | |
| Total Operating Expenses | | 658,900 |
| Utility Operating Income | | 259,800 |
| Other Incomes and Deductions: | | |
| Interest on long-term debt | 189,000 | |
| Amortization of debt discount and expense | 780 | |
| Allowance for funds used during construction | (17,800) | |
| Total Interest Charges | | 171,980 |
| Net Income | | 87,820 |
| Unappropriated Retained Earnings, January 1, 19x6 | | 352,590 |
| Total | | 440,410 |
| Less: Appropriation of Retained Earnings | | (55,000) |
| Unappropriated Retained Earnings, December 1, 19x6 | | $385,410 |
| Appropriated Retained Earnings, January 1, 19x6 | | $ 55,000 |
| Add: Appropriated during Year | | 55,000 |
| Appropriated Retained Earnings, December 31, 19x6 | | $110,000 |

intensive and make extensive use of long-term debt. When statements are combined for state and local governmental units, the traditional format should be used, however. Notice also that the $30,000 due to the General Fund (Entry 15) is offset against the $40,000 due from the General Fund (Entry 2); the net receivable of $10,000 is reported as an asset in the Water Utility Fund Balance Sheet which agrees with the $10,000 liability shown in the General Fund Balance Sheet shown as Illustration 3–1 in Chapter 3.

Illustration 8–5 presents the Statement of Revenues, Expenses, and Changes in Retained Earnings for the year ended December 31, 19x6, and Illustration 8–6 shows the Statement of Cash Flows for the Village of Elizabeth Water Utility Fund.

## ILLUSTRATION 8–6

**VILLAGE OF ELIZABETH**
**Water Utility Fund**
**Statement of Cash Flows**
**For the Year Ended December 31, 19x6**

| | |
|---|---:|
| Cash flows from operating activities: | |
| Cash received from customers . . . . . . . . . . . . . . . . . . . | $ 868,500 |
| Cash provided by customer deposits . . . . . . . . . . . . . . . | 430 |
| Cash paid to suppliers and employees . . . . . . . . . . . . . . | (502,700) |
| Net cash provided by operating activities . . . . . . . . . . . | 366,230 |
| Cash flows from capital and related financing activities: . . . . . . . . | |
| Acquisition and construction of capital assets . . . . . . . . . . . | (204,300) |
| Interest paid on long-term debt . . . . . . . . . . . . . . . . | (171,200) |
| Transfer to restricted assets . . . . . . . . . . . . . . . . . . | (55,000) |
| Net cash used for capital and related financing activities . . . . . . | (430,500) |
| Cash flows from investing activities: | |
| Advance to Supplies Fund . . . . . . . . . . . . . . . . . . . . | (200,000) |
| Partial repayment of advance to Supplies Fund . . . . . . . . . . | 10,000 |
| Net cash used in investing activities . . . . . . . . . . . . . . | (190,000) |
| Net decrease in cash and cash equivalents . . . . . . . . . . . . . | (254,270) |
| Cash and cash equivalents, January 1, 19x6 . . . . . . . . . . . . | 458,900 |
| Cash and cash equivalents, December 31, 19x6 . . . . . . . . . . . | $ 204,630 |

### Reconciliation of Net Operating Income
### to Net Cash Provided by Operating Activities

| | | |
|---|---:|---:|
| Net operating income . . . . . . . . . . . . . . . . . . . | | $259,800 |
| Adjustments: | | |
| Depreciation expense . . . . . . . . . . . . . . . . . . . | $122,800 | |
| Amortization of plant acquisition adjustment . . . . . . . . | 29,800 | |
| Decrease in customer accounts receivable . . . . . . . . . | 9,430 | |
| Increase in interfund receivables . . . . . . . . . . . . . | (10,000) | |
| Increase in accrued receivables . . . . . . . . . . . . . . | (3,400) | |
| Decrease in inventory . . . . . . . . . . . . . . . . . . | 6,500 | |
| Decrease in accounts payable . . . . . . . . . . . . . . | (44,100) | |
| Customer advances applied to customer accounts receivable . | (12,500) | |
| Decrease in customer deposits . . . . . . . . . . . . . . | (1,100) | |
| Increase in acrued liabilities . . . . . . . . . . . . . . . | 9,000 | |
| Total Adjustments . . . . . . . . . . . . . . . . . . | | 106,430 |
| Net cash provided by operating activities . . . . . . . . . | | $366,230 |

## Accounting for Nonutility Enterprises

Early in this chapter it was stressed that each governmentally owned
enterprise should follow the accounting and financial reporting standards developed for investor-owned enterprises in the same industry.
Generally, the standards developed by the Financial Accounting Standards Board, and its predecessors, have been accepted by the Governmental Accounting Standards Board as applying to internal service
funds and to enterprise funds which account for activities whose accounting is not regulated by federal or state agencies. There is a trend

toward a belief that FASB Statements should apply to general purpose external financial reporting of regulated utilities also, and that the requirements of regulatory bodies should apply only to the reports submitted to the regulatory bodies. As of the present time, however, the material presented in this chapter in regard to accounting and financial reporting for governmentally owned utilities is considered authoritative.

## Required Segment Information

GASB standards require that general purpose financial statements include certain "segment information for major non-homogeneous enterprise funds." GASB Codification Sec. 2500 provides specific guidance as to the proper application of this requirement. The presentation of segment information in the "Notes to the Financial Statements" section of the annual report is considered to be preferable, although some of the information may be included in the body of the Combined Statements or in the Combining Statements if the latter are included with the Combined Statements as part of the General Purpose Financial Statements. Codification Sec. 2500 specifies that the information which should be presented for enterprise funds is that which is deemed essential to make the General Purpose Financial Statements not misleading. The following types of information are specified:

*a.* Material *inter*governmental operating subsidies to an enterprise fund.
*b.* Material *intra*governmental operating subsidies to or from an enterprise fund.
*c.* Material enterprise fund tax revenues.
*d.* A material enterprise fund *operating* income or loss.
*e.* A material enterprise fund *net* income or loss.

Materiality should be evaluated in terms of the individual enterprise funds, not in terms of the total enterprise fund type taken as a whole.

## SELECTED REFERENCES

American Institute of Certified Public Accountants. *Audits of State and Local Governmental Units.* Rev. ed. New York, 1986.

Governmental Accounting Standards Board. *Codification of Governmental Accounting and Financial Reporting Standards.* 2nd ed. Norwalk, Conn., 1987.

## QUESTIONS AND EXERCISES

**8–1.** Using the annual financial report obtained for Exercise 1–1, answer the following questions.

*a.* List the internal service funds. Do all the funds appear to be classified appropriately? Are all the funds providing service only within the reporting entity? Are all internal service funds operating at a breakeven? Accumulating retained earnings? Operating at a deficit?

*b.* Examine the financial statements for the internal service funds. Is only one column provided in the Combined Balance Sheet for internal service funds? Are internal service funds included in the Combined Statement of Revenues, Expenses, and Changes in Retained Earnings and in the Combined Statement of Changes in Financial Position? Are combining statements prepared if more than one internal service fund is operated by the reporting entity? Is full accrual accounting used? If fixed assets are used in fund operations, are they reported in the fund balance sheet, and is depreciation reported as an element of cost of goods or services produced by the fund? Do the statements report "expenses" rather than "expenditures"?

*c.* List the enterprise funds found in your report. Are all of these funds accounted for in the same manner as business organizations? Are enterprise funds included in the Combined Balance Sheet, the Combined Statement of Revenues, Expenses, and Changes in Retained Earnings/Fund Balances—All Proprietary Fund Types and Similar Trust Funds, and the Combined Statement of Changes in Financial Position—All Proprietary Fund Types and Similar Trust Funds? Do notes to the financial statements present segment information for enterprise funds? Are combining statements presented if more than one enterprise fund exists? Is full accrual accounting used, and are "expenses" reported rather than "expenditures"? Are fixed assets recorded and depreciated? If long-term debt is being serviced from enterprise fund revenues, is the debt reported in the Enterprise Fund Balance Sheet?

*d.* Review the financial condition and operating results of each of the enterprise funds. Are any of the funds operating at a deficit? If so, how is the deficit being financed? Look carefully at transfers to see if enterprise funds are transferring large amounts either in or out. If you find large transfers, carefully review the report to see if you can determine why the transfers were made (for example, to make up a General Fund deficit).

*e.* Read the disclosures relating to revenue bonds, if revenue bonds exist. Do the note disclosures provide information regarding payment schedules and the ability of the enterprise fund to pay the debt when due? Look at the statistical section to see if a schedule of revenue bond coverage is given. From your examination, can you tell if the revenue bonds are secondarily backed by the taxing power of the governmental unit? (Hint: Look at the schedule of legal debt margin.) In general, would you invest in the revenue bonds issued by enterprises of the reporting entity? Why or why not?

**8–2.** Write the numbers 1 through 10 on a sheet of paper. Beside each number, write the letter corresponding to the best answer to each of the following questions.

1. Which of the following funds of a governmental unit would account for depreciation in the accounts of the fund?
    *a.* General.
    *b.* Internal Service.
    *c.* Capital Projects.
    *d.* Special Assessment.

2. Fixed assets of an enterprise fund should be accounted for in the
   a. General Fixed Asset Account Group but **no** depreciation on the fixed assets should be recorded.
   b. General Fixed Asset Account Group and depreciation on the fixed assets should be recorded.
   c. Enterprise Fund but **no** depreciation on the fixed assets should be recorded.
   d. Enterprise Fund and depreciation on the fixed assets should be recorded.

3. Which of the following funds of a governmental unit would include contributed capital in its balance sheet?
   a. Expendable Pension Trust.
   b. Special Revenue.
   c. Capital Projects.
   d. Internal Service.

4. Lake City operates a centralized data processing center through an internal service fund, to provide data processing services to Lake's other governmental units. In 19x6, this internal service fund billed Lake's water and sewer fund $100,000 for data processing services. How should the internal service fund record this billing?

|  | Debit | Credit |
|---|---|---|
| a. Memorandum entry only | — | — |
| b. Due from Water and Sewer Fund | $100,000 | |
| Data Processing Department Expenses | | $100,000 |
| c. Intergovernmental Transfers | $100,000 | |
| Interfund Exchanges | | $100,000 |
| d. Due from Water and Sewer Fund | $100,000 | |
| Billings to Departments | | $100,000 |

5. During 19x7, Pine City recorded the following receipts from self-sustaining activities paid for by users of the services rendered:

| | |
|---|---|
| Municipal bus system | $1,000,000 |
| Operation of water supply and sewerage plant | 1,800,000 |

What amount should be accounted for in Pine's enterprise funds?
   a. $2,800,000.
   b. $1,800,000.
   c. $1,000,000.
   d. $0.

6. Customers' security deposits that cannot be spent for normal operating purposes were collected by a governmental unit and accounted for in the enterprise fund. A portion of the amount collected was invested in marketable securities. How would the portion in cash and the portion in marketable securities be classified in the balance sheet of the enterprise fund?

| | Portion in Cash | Portion in Marketable Securities |
|---|---|---|
| a. | Restricted asset | Restricted asset |
| b. | Restricted asset | Unrestricted asset |
| c. | Unrestricted asset | Unrestricted asset |
| d. | Unrestricted asset | Restricted asset |

7. The following funds are among those maintained by Arlon City:

Enterprise Funds . . . . . . . . . . . . . . . . . . . . . . . . . . . . $2,000,000
Internal Service Funds . . . . . . . . . . . . . . . . . . . . . . .       800,000

Arlon's proprietary funds amount to
a. $0.
b. $800,000.
c. $2,000,000.
d. $2,800,000.

Items 8 and 9 are based on the following information:
During the year ended December 31, 19x1, Leyland City received a state grant of $500,000 to finance the purchase of buses, and an additional grant of $100,000 to aid in the financing of bus operations in 19x1. Only $300,000 of the capital grant was used in 19x1 for the purchase of buses, but the entire operating grant of $100,000 was spent in 19x1.

8. If Leyland's bus transportation system is accounted for as part of the City's General Fund, how much should Leyland report as grant revenues for the year ended December 31, 19x1?
a. $100,000.
b. $300,000.
c. $400,000.
d. $500,000.

9. If Leyland's bus transportation system is accounted for as an Enterprise Fund, how much should Leyland report as grant revenues for the year ended December 31, 19x1?
a. $100,000.
b. $300,000.
c. $400,000.
d. $500,000.

10. The Town of Boyd Electric Utility Fund, which is an enterprise fund, had the following:

Prepaid insurance paid in December 19x5 . . . . . . . . . . . . . . . $ 43,000
Depreciation for 19x5 . . . . . . . . . . . . . . . . . . . . . . . .     129,000
Provision for doubtful accounts for 19x5 . . . . . . . . . . . . . . .     14,000

What amount should be reflected in the Statement of Revenues and Expenses (Income Statement) for the Town of Boyd Electric Utility Fund for the above items?
a. $(43,000).
b. $0.
c. $129,000.
d. $143,000.

(AICPA, adapted)

8–3.     The City of Davidson decided to open a motor pool to provide transportation service for all departments. During the first year, July 1, 19x0–June 30, 19x1, only passenger cars will be available, and a uniform mileage rate will be charged. A permanent contribution of $1,000,000 cash was received from the

General Fund and a $1,500,000 long-term loan was received from the Enterprise Fund. Interest at the rate of 7 percent per year is to be paid on the unpaid balance of the loan; principal in the amount of $250,000 is to be repaid each year.

At the beginning of the first year, the following were purchased for cash: land, $100,000; buildings (30-year life), $300,000; equipment (10-year life), $150,000; automobiles (4-year life), $1,600,000; and fuel and supplies, $100,000. Depreciation expense is to be computed by the straight-line method, assuming no salvage values.

During the first year, salaries are expected to amount to $250,000, and the cost of fuel and supplies used is expected to amount to $250,000.

*Required:*

Prepare an operating budget on the full accrual basis for the City of Davidson Motor Pool Fund. Compute the mileage charge needed to permit the Motor Pool to break even on operations and to make the required principal payment of $250,000, assuming the automobiles will travel 4,000,000 miles during the year. Round mileage charge to the nearest cent.

**8–4.** This exercise continues Exercise 8–3. Record the following transactions for the year 19x0–x1 for the City of Davidson Motor Pool Fund.
1. The cash transfer was received from the General Fund and cash in the full amount of the long-term loan was received from the Enterprise Fund.
2. The building, automobiles, equipment, and fuel and supplies were purchased for cash. (See Exercise 8–3 for amounts.)
3. A total of 3,050,000 miles were driven and charged to other funds during the year.
4. Fuel and supplies were purchased on account in the amount of $200,000.
5. $850,000 cash was received from other funds in payment of mileage charges.
6. Salaries were paid in the amount of $260,000.
7. During the year, fuel and supplies were consumed in the amount of $270,000.
8. Accounts payable at year-end amounted to $15,000.
9. Interest charges were paid to the Enterprise Fund. In addition, a $250,000 repayment was made on the long-term advance.
10. Depreciation charges were recorded for the year.
11. Closing entries were made.

*Required:*
*a.* Record the transactions listed above in the general journal of the City of Davidson Motor Pool Fund.
*b.* Prepare a Balance Sheet for the Motor Pool Fund as of June 30, 19x1.
*c.* Prepare a Statement of Revenues, Expenses, and Changes in Retained Earnings for the Motor Pool Fund for the Year Ended June 30, 19x1.
*d.* Prepare a Statement of Changes in Financial Position for the Motor Pool Fund for the Year Ended June 30, 19x1.

**8–5.** The Town of Wilson has a Water Utility Fund with the following trial balance as of July 1, 19y1, the first day of the fiscal year:

|                                                              | Debit       | Credit      |
|--------------------------------------------------------------|-------------|-------------|
| Utility Plant in Service . . . . . . . . . . . . . . . . .    | $7,100,000  |             |
| Accumulated Provision for Depreciation—Utility Plant . . .   |             | $2,600,000  |
| Construction Work in Progress . . . . . . . . . . . . .      | 100,000     |             |
| Restricted Assets . . . . . . . . . . . . . . . . . . .      | 300,000     |             |
| Cash . . . . . . . . . . . . . . . . . . . . . . . .         | 80,000      |             |
| Customer Accounts Receivable . . . . . . . . . . . .         | 300,000     |             |
| Accumulated Provision for Uncollectible Accounts . . . .     |             | 10,000      |
| Materials and Supplies . . . . . . . . . . . . . . . .       | 120,000     |             |
| Revenue Bonds Payable . . . . . . . . . . . . . . . .        |             | 3,500,000   |
| Vouchers Payable . . . . . . . . . . . . . . . . . .         |             | 130,000     |
| Accrued Expenses . . . . . . . . . . . . . . . . . .         |             | 80,000      |
| Contribution from General Fund . . . . . . . . . . . .       |             | 1,000,000   |
| Retained Earnings—Appropriated . . . . . . . . . .           |             | 300,000     |
| Retained Earnings—Unappropriated . . . . . . . . . .         |             | 380,000     |
| Totals . . . . . . . . . . . . . . . . . . . . . . .         | $8,000,000  | $8,000,000  |

During the year ended June 30, 19y2, the following transactions and events occurred in the Town of Wilson Water Utility Fund:

1. Accrued expenses at July 1, 19y1 were paid in cash.
2. Billings to nongovernmental customers for water usage for the year amounted to $1,310,000; billings to the General Fund amounted to $53,000.
3. Liabilities for the following were recorded during the year:

| | |
|---|---:|
| Materials and supplies . . . . . . . . . . . . . . . . . . . . . . . . . . . . | $215,000 |
| Source of supply expenses . . . . . . . . . . . . . . . . . . . . . . . . | 119,500 |
| Pumping expenses . . . . . . . . . . . . . . . . . . . . . . . . . . . | 88,300 |
| Water treatment expenses . . . . . . . . . . . . . . . . . . . . . . | 63,500 |
| Transmission and distribution expenses . . . . . . . . . . . . . . | 72,100 |
| Customer accounts expenses . . . . . . . . . . . . . . . . . . . . | 133,300 |
| Administrative and general expenses . . . . . . . . . . . . . . . . | 66,700 |
| Construction work in progress . . . . . . . . . . . . . . . . . . . | 212,200 |

4. Materials and supplies were used by the following departments in the following amounts: source of supply, $29,800; pumping, $43,900; water treatment, $114,100; transmission and distribution, $77,900.
5. $8,000 of old accounts receivable were written off.
6. Accounts receivable collections totaled $1,450,000 from nongovernmental customers and $48,400 from the General Fund.
7. $1,035,000 of vouchers payable were paid in cash.
8. One year's interest in the amount of $245,000 was paid.
9. Construction was completed on plant assets costing $135,000; that amount was transferred to Utility Plant in Service.
10. Depreciation was recorded in the amount of $235,000.
11. Interest in the amount of $25,000 was charged to Construction Work in Progress.
12. The Accumulated Provision for Uncollectible Accounts was increased by $13,100.
13. Cash in the amount of $100,000 was transferred to Restricted Assets for eventual redemption of the bonds. As required by the loan agreement, Retained Earnings in the amount of Restricted Assets was appropriated.

14. Accrued expenses, all related to water treatment, amounted to $15,600.
15. Nominal accounts for the year were closed.

**Required:**
a. Record the transactions for the year in general journal form.
b. Prepare a Balance Sheet as of June 30, 19y2.
c. Prepare a Statement of Revenues, Expenses, and Changes in Retained Earnings for the Year Ended June 30, 19y2.

8–6.   The City of Milton maintains a Computer Service Fund, an internal service fund, to handle its data processing operations. Charges are made to departments by charging a certain amount for each minute of computer time used. In effect, the charges are applied in such a way to make computer usage a completely variable cost to the departments, based on computer time used. On the other hand, most of the costs of the Computer Service Fund are fixed, as the equipment is owned and depreciated. Budget and actual data for the Computer Service Fund for 19x3 are as follows:

|  | Budgeted Costs | Actual Costs |
|---|---|---|
| Depreciation | $1,000,000 | $1,000,000 |
| Salaries | 200,000 | 170,000 |
| Supplies | 100,000 | 80,000 |
| Utilities, etc. | 40,000 | 32,000 |
| Totals | $1,340,000 | $1,282,000 |

A close examination of the records indicates that depreciation is a fixed cost and that all other costs are one-half fixed and one-half variable. Fixed costs were applied in accordance with predetermined amounts; actual variable costs per unit of service were exactly as budgeted.

In 19x3, the Computer Service Fund experienced a net loss for the year of $210,000, as shown below:

|  | Budgeted Revenues | Actual Revenues |
|---|---|---|
| Department 1 | $700,000 | $500,000 |
| Department 2 | 400,000 | 400,000 |
| Department 3 | 240,000 | 172,000 |
| Totals | $1,340,000 | $1,072,000 |

An inquiry to the managers of Departments 1 and 3 indicated that the computer was used less than budgeted because other items of their budget were running over. They incurred $100,000 in department clerical salary overtime costs but were able to save $268,000 in computer usage costs by incurring the additional salary and overtime costs.

**Required:**
a. Compute the fixed and variable portions of the budget for the Computer Service Fund.
b. Compute how much it cost the City, as a whole, for the departments to use extra departmental salary and overtime costs in order to save on computer costs.
c. Suggest solutions to the dysfunctional aspects of the charge system.

**8–7.**    The City of Benson issued tax-supported bonds in the amount of $1,000,000 in order to acquire the net assets of an investor-owned enterprise. From the proceeds of the bond issue, $900,000 was paid to the previous owners. Prior to acquisition, the following represented the book and fair values of the non-cash assets and liabilities:

|  | Book Value | Fair Value |
|---|---|---|
| Accounts receivable (net) . . . . . . . . . . . . | $140,000 debit | $100,000 debit |
| Inventories . . . . . . . . . . . . . . . . . . . | 100,000 debit | 150,000 debit |
| Fixed assets, net . . . . . . . . . . . . . . . . | 500,000 debit | 750,000 debit |
| Accounts payable . . . . . . . . . . . . . . . . | 100,000 credit | 100,000 credit |

*Required:*
  *a.* Assuming the enterprise was a swimming pool (not a regulated utility), prepare the Balance Sheet of the First Street Pool Fund as of January 1, 19y1, the first day of operations.
  *b.* Assuming the enterprise was a regulated water utility, prepare the Balance Sheet of the Water Utility Fund as of January 1, 19y1, the first day of operations.

## CONTINUOUS PROBLEM

**8–C.**    *Part 1.* The Stores and Service Fund of the City of Everlasting Sunshine had the following account balances as of January 1, 19y1:

|  | Debit | Credit |
|---|---|---|
| Cash . . . . . . . . . . . . . . . . . . . . . . . . . . . . . . . . . | $ 12,000 |  |
| Due from Other Funds . . . . . . . . . . . . . . . . . . . | 25,000 |  |
| Inventory of Supplies . . . . . . . . . . . . . . . . . . . . | 50,000 |  |
| Land . . . . . . . . . . . . . . . . . . . . . . . . . . . . . . . | 15,000 |  |
| Buildings . . . . . . . . . . . . . . . . . . . . . . . . . . . | 44,000 |  |
| Allowance for Depreciation—Buildings . . . . . . . . . . . . . |  | $ 11,000 |
| Equipment . . . . . . . . . . . . . . . . . . . . . . . . . . | 21,000 |  |
| Allowance for Depreciation—Equipment . . . . . . . . . . . |  | 10,500 |
| Vouchers Payable . . . . . . . . . . . . . . . . . . . . |  | 7,500 |
| Advance from Water Utility Fund . . . . . . . . . . . . . . |  | 30,000 |
| Contribution from General Fund . . . . . . . . . . . . . . |  | 70,000 |
| Retained Earnings . . . . . . . . . . . . . . . . . . . . |  | 38,000 |
| Totals . . . . . . . . . . . . . . . . . . . . . . . . . . . . . | $167,000 | $167,000 |

*Required:*
  *a.* Open a general journal for the City of Everlasting Sunshine Stores and Service Fund and record the following transactions. Use the account titles in requirement (*b*).
    (1) A budget was prepared for FY 19y1. It was estimated that supplies would be issued in the amount of $300,000, at cost. Operating expenses, including depreciation, were estimated to be $48,000. Issue prices of supplies were set to achieve a breakeven for the year. Assume a uniform markup percentage; compute the markup on cost.
    (2) The amount due from other funds as of January 1, 19y1, was collected in full.

(3) During the year, supplies were ordered and received in the amount of $285,000. This amount was vouchered.

(4) $10,000 of the advance from the Water Utility Fund was repaid.

(5) During the year, supplies costing $270,000 were issued to the General Fund and supplies costing $50,000 were issued to the Water Utility Fund.

(6) Operating expenses, exclusive of depreciation, were vouchered as follows: Purchasing, $10,100; Warehousing, $15,300; Delivery, $13,200; and Administrative, $7,300.

(7) Cash was received from the General Fund in the amount of $300,000 and from the Water Utility Fund in the amount of $50,000.

(8) Vouchers were paid in the amount of $330,000.

(9) Depreciation in the amount of $2,200 was recorded for buildings and $2,100 for equipment. Allocation of depreciation charges was as follows: Purchasing, 30 percent; Warehousing, 40 percent; Delivery, 20 percent, and Administrative, 10 percent.

(10) Closing entries were made.

b. Open a general ledger and enter January 1, 19y1 balances given in the problem. Post the entries for requirement (a) to the general ledger. Use five lines each for the following accounts:

> Cash
> Due from Other Funds
> Inventory of Supplies
> Land
> Buildings
> Allowance for Depreciation—Buildings
> Equipment
> Allowance for Depreciation—Equipment
> Vouchers Payable
> Advance from Water Utility Fund
> Contribution from General Fund
> Retained Earnings
> Billings to Departments
> Cost of Supplies Issued
> Purchasing Expenses
> Warehousing Expenses
> Delivery Expenses
> Administrative Expenses
> Excess of Net Billings to Departments over Costs

c. Prepare the following financial statements:

(1) A Balance Sheet as of December 31, 19y1.

(2) A Statement of Revenues, Expenses, and Changes in Retained Earnings for the Year Ended December 31, 19y1.

(3) A Statement of Changes in Financial Position for the Year Ended December 31, 19y1.

Part 2. The City of Everlasting Sunshine maintains a Water and Sewer Fund in order to provide utility services to its citizens. As of January 1, 19y1, the City of Everlasting Sunshine Water and Sewer Fund had the following account balances:

|                                                              | Debit       | Credit      |
|--------------------------------------------------------------|-------------|-------------|
| Utility Plant in Service . . . . . . . . . . . . . . . . .    | $4,135,200  |             |
| Construction Work in Progress . . . . . . . . . . . . .      | 215,000     |             |
| Accumulated Provision for Depreciation of Utility Plant . .  |             | $ 692,600   |
| Advance to Stores and Services Fund . . . . . . . . . .      | 30,000      |             |
| Restricted Assets . . . . . . . . . . . . . . . . . . . .    | 135,000     |             |
| Cash . . . . . . . . . . . . . . . . . . . . . . . . . .     | 98,000      |             |
| Customer Accounts Receivable . . . . . . . . . . . .         | 113,000     |             |
| Accumulated Provision for Uncollectible Accounts . . . .     |             | 2,260       |
| Accrued Utility Revenues . . . . . . . . . . . . . . . .     | 25,100      |             |
| Materials and Supplies . . . . . . . . . . . . . . . .       | 72,400      |             |
| Unamortized Debt Discount and Expense . . . . . . . . .      | 13,200      |             |
| Revenue Bonds Payable . . . . . . . . . . . . . . . . .      |             | 2,300,000   |
| Customer Advances for Construction . . . . . . . . . . .     |             | 15,000      |
| Accounts Payable . . . . . . . . . . . . . . . . . . .       |             | 116,000     |
| Customer Deposits . . . . . . . . . . . . . . . . . . .      |             | 61,100      |
| Contributions from City . . . . . . . . . . . . . . . .      |             | 1,000,000   |
| Contributions from Customers . . . . . . . . . . . . .       |             | 310,000     |
| Appropriated Retained Earnings . . . . . . . . . . . .       |             | 135,000     |
| Unappropriated Retained Earnings . . . . . . . . . . . .     |             | 204,940     |
| Totals . . . . . . . . . . . . . . . . . . . . . . . .       | $4,836,900  | $4,836,900  |

## Required:
a. Open a general journal for the City of Everlasting Sunshine Water and Sewer Utility Fund and record the following transactions. Use the account titles in requirement (b).

(1) The entry establishing Accrued Utility Revenues was reversed by debiting Sales of Water.

(2) During the year sales of water to nonmunicipal customers amounted to $910,600, and sales of water to the General Fund amounted to $45,000.

(3) Collections from nonmunicipal customers amounted to $875,000.

(4) The Stores and Services Fund repaid $10,000 of the long-term advance to the Water and Sewer Fund.

(5) Materials and supplies in the amount of $235,000 were received. A liability in that amount was recorded.

(6) Materials and supplies were issued and were charged to the following accounts: Source of Supply Expenses, $22,000; Pumping Expenses, $41,000; Water Treatment Expenses, $71,000; Transmission and Distribution Expenses, $45,000; and Construction Work in Progress, $59,000.

(7) Payroll expense for the year totaled $416,200. Of that amount, $351,900 was paid in cash, and the remainder was withheld for taxes. In addition, taxes that are expenses of the utility amounted to $34,200. The $450,400 was distributed as follows: Source of Supply Expenses, $15,100; Pumping Expenses, $31,400; Water Treatment Expenses, $32,400; Transmission and Distribution Expenses, $72,300; Customer Accounts Expenses, $89,600; Sales Expenses, $24,900; Administrative and General Expenses, $91,400; and Construction Work in Progress, $93,300.

(8) Bond interest in the amount of $184,000 was paid. Amortization of debt discount and expense amounted to $880.

(9) Interest in the amount of $13,100 was charged to Construction Work in Progress.

(10) Construction projects were completed in the amount of $250,000, and the assets were placed in service.

(11) The Water and Sewer Fund agreed to pay $35,000 to the General Fund as a contribution in lieu of taxes.

(12) Collection efforts were discontinued on bills totaling $5,820. The customers owing the bills had paid deposits totaling $4,260 to the utility; the deposits were applied to the bills, and the unpaid remainder was charged to the Accumulated Provision for Uncollectible Accounts.

(13) Customers' deposits amounting to $3,590 were refunded by check to customers discontinuing service. Deposits totaling $4,140 were received from new customers.

(14) Payment of accounts payable amounted to $225,000. Payments of taxes accrued totaled $31,200, and payments of tax collections payable amounted to $64,000.

(15) Customers' advances for construction in the amount of $5,000 were applied to their water bills.

(16) Supplies transferred from the Stores and Services Fund amounted to $58,000. Cash in the amount of $50,000 was paid to the Stores and Services Fund for supplies.

(17) Depreciation expense for 19y1 was computed to be $210,000.

(18) The provision for uncollectible accounts for 19y1 amounted to $4,160.

(19) Unbilled customer accounts receivable at year-end amounted to $31,300

(20) In accord with the revenue bond indenture, $35,000 cash was transferred from operating cash to the Restricted Assets. The transfer requires an appropriation of Retained Earnings in an equal amount.

(21) Closing entries were made.

b. Open a ledger and enter the balances as of January 1, 19y1. Post the entries made for requirement (a). Allow six lines for each of the following accounts except Cash, which requires 11 lines:

> Utility Plant in Service
> Construction Work in Progress
> Accumulated Provision for Depreciation of Utility Plant
> Advance to Stores and Services Fund
> Restricted Assets
> Cash (11 lines)
> Customer Accounts Receivable
> Accumulated Provision for Uncollectible Accounts
> Due from General Fund
> Accrued Utility Revenues
> Materials and Supplies
> Unamortized Debt Discount and Expense
> Revenue Bonds Payable
> Customer Advances for Construction
> Accounts Payable
> Customer Deposits
> Taxes Accrued
> Tax Collections Payable
> Due to General Fund

Due to Stores and Service Fund
Contributions from City
Contributions from Customers
Appropriated Retained Earnings
Unappropriated Retained Earnings
Sales of Water
Allowance for Funds Used during Construction
Source of Supply Expenses
Pumping Expenses
Water Treatment Expenses
Transmission and Distribution Expenses
Customer Accounts Expenses
Sales Expenses
Administrative and General Expenses
Interest on Long-term Debt
Amortization of Debt Discount and Expense
Contribution in Lieu of Taxes
Depreciation Expense

c. Prepare, in good form, the following:
   (1) A Balance Sheet for the Water and Sewer Fund as of December 31, 19y1.
   (2) A Statement of Revenues, Expenses, and Changes in Retained Earnings for the Year Ended December 31, 19y1.
   (3) A Statement of Changes in Financial Position for the Year Ended December 31, 19y1.

# Chapter 9

# FIDUCIARY FUNDS

Fiduciary funds are used to account for assets held by a governmental unit acting as a trustee or agent for individuals, organizations, other governmental units, or other funds of the same governmental unit. For that reason fiduciary funds are often identified in governmental financial reports as Trust and Agency Funds. In law there is a clear distinction between an agency relationship and a trust relationship. In practice the legalistic distinctions between trust funds and agency funds are not of major significance.

Authoritative pronouncements distinguish four types of fiduciary funds: (1) agency funds, (2) nonexpendable trust funds, (3) expendable trust funds, and (4) pension trust funds. An **agency** fund accounts for assets held by a governmental unit temporarily as agent for individuals, organizations, other funds, or other governmental units. A **nonexpendable trust** fund accounts for situations in which the trust agreement requires that the assets be held intact in perpetuity, or for a specified length of time, or until a specified event occurs. An **expendable trust** fund accounts for assets and resources that may be expended for the purposes set forth in the document creating the trust. Finally, a **pension trust** fund is a separate category of trust fund because of the importance of disclosure of pension funds and because both the assets contributed to the trust fund and the earnings thereon may be expended for the purposes and in the amounts set forth in the pension agreement.

Agency funds and expendable trust funds use the same basis of accounting as do governmental funds. Nonexpendable trust and pension trust funds use the same basis of accounting as do proprietary funds. For financial reporting purposes, expendable trust funds are often grouped with the governmental funds in the operating statements while the nonexpendable and pension trust funds are often grouped with the proprietary funds. Agency funds are reported only in the Combined Balance Sheet, not in any combined operating statement, as the agency relationship creates no revenues, expenditures, or expenses of the reporting entity.

## AGENCY FUNDS

Agency funds are used to account for assets held by a governmental unit acting as agent for one or more other governmental units, or for individuals or private organizations. Similarly, if a fund of a governmental unit regularly receives assets that are to be transmitted to other funds of that unit, an agency relationship exists. Assets accounted for in an agency fund belong to the party or parties for which the governmental unit acts as agent. Therefore, **agency fund assets are offset by liabilities equal in amount; no fund equity exists.** Agency fund assets and liabilities are to be recognized at the time the government becomes responsible for the assets. In the typical case, revenues, expenditures, and expenses are not recognized in the accounts of agency funds.

Unless use of an agency fund is mandated by law, by GASB standards, or by decision of the governing board of a governmental unit, an agency relationship may be accounted for within governmental and/or proprietary funds. For example, local governmental units must act as agent of the federal and state governments in the collection of employees' withholding taxes, retirement contributions, and (in many instances) social security taxes. In the absence of contrary requirements or administrative decisions, it is perfectly acceptable to account for the withholdings, and the remittance to federal and state governments, within the funds that account for the gross pay of the employees.

Only rarely is the use of a certain fund type mandated by GASB standards, rather than by law or by decision of the governing board of a government. However, GASB *Statement No. 2, Financial Reporting of Deferred Compensation Plans Adopted under the Provisions of Internal Revenue Code Section 457* (now codified as Section D25 of the GASB codification), requires governmental units which provide deferred compensation plans for their employees to "display" in an agency fund the amount of IRC Section 457 deferred compensation plan asset balances. Total plan assets are, of course, offset by the liability to employees for deferred compensation and accumulated net earnings thereon. (Deferred compensation plans offer employees the opportunity to defer receipt of a portion of their salary, and, consequently to defer the related liability for federal income taxes. IRC Section 457 authorizes state and local governments to establish eligible deferred compensation plans for their employees, if the plans meet requirements set forth in Section 457.)

Readers of Chapters 1 through 8 of this text would assume that the agency fund structure would be used to account for deferred compensation plan assets and liabilities pertaining to employees of governmental activities accounted for by funds classified as "governmental funds." However, GASB Codification Sec. D25 specifies that if employees of activities accounted for by proprietary funds are not covered by a separate deferred compensation plan, a single agency fund should be used to account for IRC Section 457 plan assets and liabilities.[1] GASB standards require the use of an agency fund whether the assets are held by the employer, a public employee retirement system, a "nongovernmental third party" (such as an insurance company), or another governmental unit under a multiple-jurisdiction plan.

GASB standards also mandate that a governmental unit which has **no** obligation to assume debt service on special assessment debt in the event of property owners' default, but which does perform the functions of billing property owners for the assessments, collecting installments of assessments and interest on the assessments and **from the collections** paying interest and principal on the special assessment debt, account for those activities in an agency fund.

## Tax Agency Funds

An agency relationship that usually results in the creation of an agency fund is the collection of taxes, and other revenues, by an official of one governmental unit for the funds that government operates and/or for other governmental units. State governments commonly collect sales taxes, gasoline taxes, and many other taxes that are apportioned to state agencies and to local governmental units within the state. At the local government level, it is common for an elected county official to serve as collector for all property taxes owed by persons or corporations owning property within the county. Taxes levied by all funds and units within the County are certified to the County Collector for collection. The County Collector is required by law to make periodic distributions of tax collections for each year to each fund or unit in the proportion the levy for that fund or unit bears to the total levy for the year.

## Accounting for Tax Agency Funds

Assume that, for a given year, a county government levies for its General Fund the amount of $2,000,000 in property taxes, from which it expects to realize $1,960,000. For the same year, there is certified to it the amount of $3,000,000 in property taxes for the Consolidated School District and $1,000,000 in property taxes for a village within the County.

---

[1]GASB Codification Sec. D25.110 provides that if employees of "separately constituted governmental public utilities and public authorities" are covered by a separate plan, balance sheets of those entities should display the deferred compensation liability with a corresponding asset identified as "designated for deferred compensation benefits." (This disclosure is consistent with the disclosure of restricted assets of utilities, illustrated in Chapter 8.)

The County General Fund levy would be recorded in the accounts of the **County General Fund** in the same manner as in Chapter 3.

```
Taxes Receivable—Current . . . . . . . . . . . . .  2,000,000
    Estimated Uncollectible Current Taxes  . . . . . .            40,000
    Revenues  . . . . . . . . . . . . . . . . . . .          1,960,000
```

Each unit using the Tax Agency Fund would record its own levy in the manner illustrated above.

The **Tax Agency Fund** entry for recording all levies certified to it, in this example totaling $6,000,000, would be:

```
1. Taxes Receivable for Other Funds and Units—
    Current . . . . . . . . . . . . . . . . . . . .  6,000,000
        Due to Other Funds and Units  . . . . . . . .          6,000,000
```

Note that the *gross* amount of the tax levy for all funds and units should be recorded in the Tax Agency Fund as a receivable, not the net amount expected to be collected, because the County Collector is responsible for attempting to collect all taxes as billed. Note also that the receivable is offset in total by the liability.

If collections of taxes during a certain portion of the year amounted to $2,400,000, the **Tax Agency Fund** entry would be:

```
2. Cash . . . . . . . . . . . . . . . . . . . . . .  2,400,000
        Taxes Receivable for Other Funds and Units—
        Current . . . . . . . . . . . . . . . . . .          2,400,000
```

The tax collections must in an actual case be identified with the parcels of property against which the taxes are levied, because the location of each parcel determines the governmental units and funds that should receive the tax collections. Assuming for the sake of simplicity that the collections for the period represent collections of 40 percent of the taxes levied against each parcel in the County, and that the County General Fund is given 1 percent of all collections for units other than the County as reimbursement for the cost of operating the Tax Agency Fund, the distribution of the $2,400,000 collections would be:

|  | Taxes Collected (40 Percent of Levy) | Collection Fee (Charged) Received | Cash to Be Distributed |
|---|---|---|---|
| County  . . . . . . . . . . . . | $  800,000 | $16,000 | $  816,000 |
| Village . . . . . . . . . . . . | 400,000 | (4,000) | 396,000 |
| School District  . . . . . . . . | 1,200,000 | (12,000) | 1,188,000 |
|  | $2,400,000 | $ –0– | $2,400,000 |

If cash is not distributed as soon as the above computation is made, the entry by the **Tax Agency Fund** to record the liability would be:

```
3. Due to Other Funds and Units  . . . . . . . . . .  2,400,000
        Due to County General Fund . . . . . . . . .            816,000
        Due to Village . . . . . . . . . . . . . . .            396,000
        Due to Consolidated School District . . . . . .        1,188,000
```

The entry made by the **County General Fund** for this transaction would be:

| | | |
|---|---|---|
| Due from County Tax Agency Fund . . . . . . . . . . | 816,000 | |
| Taxes Receivable—Current . . . . . . . . . . . . . | | 800,000 |
| Revenues   . . . . . . . . . . . . . . . . . . . | | 16,000 |

At the same time, the entry made by the **Village General Fund** would be:

| | | |
|---|---|---|
| Due from County Tax Agency Fund . . . . . . . . . . | 396,000 | |
| Expenditures . . . . . . . . . . . . . . . . . . . | 4,000 | |
| Taxes Receivable—Current . . . . . . . . . . . . | | 400,000 |

A similar entry would be made by the General Fund of the Consolidated School District. When cash is transferred the assets and liabilities to and from the specific funds would be extinguished.

If, as is likely, collections during a current year include collections of taxes that were levied for preceding years, computations must be made to determine the appropriate distribution of collections for each tax year to each fund and unit that levied taxes against the property for which collections have been received. It may also be necessary for a Tax Agency Fund to account for interest and penalties on delinquent taxes and advance collections.

### Financial Reporting for Agency Funds

The assets and liabilities of agency funds should be included in the Combined Balance Sheet. However, since agency relationships do not generate revenues, expenditures, or expenses for the reporting entity, the operations of agency funds are not included in the combined operating statements. The Comprehensive Annual Financial Report should include a "Combining Statement of Changes in Assets and Liabilities—All Agency Funds." This statement is shown as Illustration 9–1.

## TRUST FUNDS

Trust funds differ from agency funds principally in degree. Frequently a trust fund is in existence over a longer period of time than an agency fund; it represents and develops vested interests to a greater extent; and it involves more complex administrative and financial problems. In both trust and agency funds, the governmental unit has a fiduciary relationship with the creditors and beneficiaries of the trust or agency. A historically important reason for the creation of a trust fund is the acceptance by a governmental unit of trusteeship over assets to be invested to produce income to be used for specified purposes (generally cultural or educational). The fair value of the assets placed in trust under such an agreement is referred to as the principal, or corpus, of the trust. Since the principal of this form of trust must be held intact in

**ILLUSTRATION 9–1**

## NAME OF GOVERNMENTAL UNIT
### Combining Statement of Changes in Assets and Liabilities—All Agency Funds
### For Fiscal Year Ended December 31, 19x2

| | Balance January 1, 19x2 | Additions | Deductions | Balance December 31, 19x2 |
|---|---|---|---|---|
| **SPECIAL PAYROLL FUND:** | | | | |
| **Assets** | | | | |
| Cash . . . . . . . . . . | $ 6,000 | $ 40,900 | $ 43,550 | $ 3,350 |
| **Liabilities** | | | | |
| Vouchers payable . . . . . | $ 6,000 | $ 40,900 | $ 43,550 | $ 3,350 |
| **PROPERTY TAX FUND:** | | | | |
| **Assets** | | | | |
| Cash . . . . . . . . . . | $ 25,800 | $ 800,000 | $ 725,000 | $100,800 |
| Taxes receivable . . . . . | 174,200 | 1,205,800 | 800,000 | 580,000 |
| Total Assets . . . . . . . | $200,000 | $2,005,800 | $1,525,000 | $680,800 |
| **Liabilities** | | | | |
| Due to Other Taxing Units: | | | | |
| County . . . . . . . . | $180,000 | $1,085,220 | $ 652,500 | $612,720 |
| Special District . . . . . . | 20,000 | 120,580 | 72,500 | 68,080 |
| Total Liabilities . . . . . . | $200,000 | $1,205,800 | $ 725,000 | $680,800 |
| **STUDENT ACTIVITY FUND:** | | | | |
| **Assets** | | | | |
| Cash . . . . . . . . . . | $ 1,600 | $ 1,900 | $ 1,650 | $ 1,850 |
| **Liabilities** | | | | |
| Due to student groups . . . | $ 1,600 | $ 1,900 | $ 1,650 | $ 1,850 |
| **TOTALS—ALL AGENCY FUNDS:** | | | | |
| **Assets** | | | | |
| Cash . . . . . . . . . . | $ 33,400 | $ 842,800 | $ 770,200 | $106,000 |
| Taxes receivable . . . . . | 174,200 | 1,205,800 | 800,000 | 580,000 |
| Total Assets . . . . . . . | $207,600 | $2,048,600 | $1,570,200 | $686,000 |
| **Liabilities** | | | | |
| Vouchers payable . . . . . | $ 6,000 | $ 40,900 | $ 43,550 | $ 3,350 |
| Due to other taxing units . . | 200,000 | 1,205,800 | 725,000 | 680,800 |
| Due to student groups . . . | 1,600 | 1,900 | 1,650 | 1,850 |
| Total Liabilities . . . . . . | $207,600 | $1,248,600 | $ 770,200 | $686,000 |

Source: GASB Codification Sec. 2200.610.

order to produce income, the trust is **nonexpendable.** Nonexpendable trust funds are often called endowment funds. The income from the assets of a nonexpendable trust may be used for only the purposes specified by the trustor; in some instances the terms of the trust require income to be added to the corpus for a specified time, but generally the income is **expendable.** Separate funds should be established to account for expendable and nonexpendable assets. Nonexpendable trust funds should be accounted for in essentially the same manner as proprietary funds (Internal Service and Enterprise Funds, discussed in Chapter 8). Expendable trust funds should be accounted for in essentially the same manner as the governmental funds discussed in Chapters 2, 3, 4, and 6.

Not all trust funds require the distinction between corpus and income; public employee retirement systems are an example of funds whose principal and income are both expendable for specified purposes. Accounting for public employee retirement systems follows the general pattern of accounting for proprietary funds, but there are many accounting and financial reporting problems not yet settled, as discussed in the final section of this chapter.

## Illustrative Case—Nonexpendable Trust Funds and Expendable Trust Funds

As an illustration of the nature of accounting for nonexpendable trust principal and expendable trust revenue, assume that on May 1, 19x6, Richard Lee died, having made a valid will that provided for the gift of various securities to the Village of Elizabeth to be held as a nonexpendable trust; the net income from the securities is to be computed on the full accrual basis. Income received in cash, less any amount needed to amortize bond premium or discount on a straight-line basis, is to be transferred to the Village's Library Book Fund. In this jurisdiction, the latter fund is classified as an expendable trust fund and is operated as a budgetary fund in the manner described in Chapter 3. The gift was accepted by the Village of Elizabeth and two funds were established: (1) a Library Endowment Fund to account for the nonexpendable trust, and (2) a Library Book Fund to account for the purchase of the library books under the trust agreement. The following securities were received by the Library Endowment Fund:

|  | Interest Rate per Year | Maturity Date | Face Value | Fair Value as of 5/1/x6 | Fair Value over (under) Face |
|---|---|---|---|---|---|
| Bonds: |  |  |  |  |  |
| AB Company . . . . | 10% | 7/1/y0 | $240,000 | $250,000 | $10,000 |
| C and D Co. . . . . | 9 | 1/1/x8 | 120,000 | 124,000 | 4,000 |
| Total . . . . . . . |  |  | $360,000 | $374,000 | $14,000 |

|  | Number of Shares | Fair Value as of 5/1/x6 |
|---|---|---|
| Stocks: |  |  |
| M Company, common . . . . . . . . . . . | 5,000 | $250,000 |
| S Company, common . . . . . . . . . . | 10,000 | 170,000 |
| Total . . . . . . . . . . . . . . . . . | 15,000 | $420,000 |

## Illustrative Entries—Nonexpendable Trust Fund

The receipt of the securities by the Library Endowment Fund is properly recorded at the fair value of the securities as of the date of the gift because this is the amount for which the trustees are responsible. Inasmuch as the trustees will receive the face value of the bonds upon maturity (if the bonds are held until maturity), accrual accounting theory dictates that the difference between fair value of the bonds and their face value be amortized over the period from date of receipt by the fund to date of maturity of the bonds. Thus, the entry in the Library Endowment Fund to record the receipt of the securities must disclose both the par of the bonds held as investments and the difference between the fair market value and par. The interest accrued on the bonds as of the date of their transfer to the Endowment Fund, $11,600, is a part of the trust corpus. Assuming semiannual interest payments on 1/1 and 7/1 on both bond issues, the entry in the **Library Endowment Fund** as of May 1, 19x6 is:

```
1. Bonds, at par  . . . . . . . . . . . . . . . . . . .   360,000
   Unamortized Bond Premium  . . . . . . . . . . . .    14,000
   Stocks  . . . . . . . . . . . . . . . . . . . . .   420,000
   Accrued Interest Receivable . . . . . . . . . . . .    11,600
      Fund Balance . . . . . . . . . . . . . . . . . .            805,600
      (Interest accrued is AB $240,000 × 10% × ⁴⁄₁₂ =
      $8,000; C and D $120,000 × 9% × ⁴⁄₁₂ =
      $3,600)
```

As of July 1, 19x6, interest is received on both bonds—$12,000 from AB Company, and $5,400 from C and D Company. The AB Company bonds were worth $250,000 when received by the Library Endowment Fund; when they mature, they will be worth $240,000. Therefore, the $10,000 difference between value on May 1, 19x6 and on July 1, 19y0, should be amortized over the 50 months intervening. Customarily, amortization is recorded as an adjustment of interest earnings when the earnings are received or accrued. As of July 1, 19x6, 2 of the 50 months between receipt of the bonds and their maturity have expired; therefore, amortization of premium is $400 [($10,000 / 50) × 2]. Similarly, C and D Company bonds were worth $124,000 when received but will be worth $120,000 20 months later; therefore, on July 1, 19x6, amortization should be $400 [($4,000 / 20) × 2]. The total bond premium to be amortized as of July 1, 19x6, therefore, is $800; this amount is treated as an adjustment of interest earnings, and results in retention in the Library Endowment Fund of cash in the amount of premium amortized as well as cash in the amount of accrued interest recorded in Entry 1. Thus, only interest for the two months since the Library Endowment Fund was established, less premium amortized, is to be transferred to the Library Book Fund. The receipt of bond interest on July 1, 19x6, the amortization of premium, and the revenue earned for transfer to the Library Book Fund are recorded in the **Library Endowment Fund** as:

```
2. Cash  . . . . . . . . . . . . . . . . . . . . . .   17,400
       Unamortized Bond Premium  . . . . . . . . . .            800
       Accrued Interest Receivable . . . . . . . . . . .      11,600
       Revenues—Bond Interest  . . . . . . . . . . . .        5,000
```

Stock does not mature; therefore, its fair value at date of receipt need not be adjusted, and the stock may be carried at fair value on date of receipt until sold, unless it suffers a market decline which is judged to be "other than temporary."[2]

Dividends on stock do not accrue. They become a receivable only when declared by the corporation issuing the stock. Ordinarily the receivable is not recorded because it is followed in a reasonably short time by issuance of a dividend check. Assuming that dividends on the stock held by the Library Endowment Fund were received on July 2, 19x6, in the amount of $18,000, Entry 3 is appropriate:

```
3. Cash  . . . . . . . . . . . . . . . . . . . . . .   18,000
       Revenues—Dividends  . . . . . . . . . . . . .          18,000
```

The Library Endowment Fund has sufficient cash to pay the amount owed to the Library Book Fund for bond interest during the two months since the bonds were received (Entry 2) and for dividends received (Entry 3). Assuming that cash is transferred as of July 3, 19x6, Entry 4 is:

```
4. Operating Transfers Out . . . . . . . . . . . . . .   23,000
       Cash  . . . . . . . . . . . . . . . . . . . . .        23,000
```

On the advice of an investment manager, 1,000 shares of M Company stock were sold for $55,000. The M Company stock sold was one fifth the number of shares received when the trust was established; therefore, it was recorded at its fair value then of $50,000; the difference between its book value and the proceeds is generally considered to belong to the corpus and must be retained in the nonexpendable trust fund; it is **not** an element in the computation of net income to be transferred to the Library Book Fund. Therefore, the sale of M Company stock should be recorded in the **Library Endowment Fund** as:

---

[2]FASB Accounting Standards—Current Text, Sec. l89.115, is considered to apply to the valuation of equity securities of nonexpendable trust funds.

```
5. Cash . . . . . . . . . . . . . . . . . . . . . . .    55,000
     Stocks  . . . . . . . . . . . . . . . . . . . . .              50,000
     Fund Balance—Gain on Sale of Stocks . . . . . .               5,000
```

The amount received for the sale of the M Company stock, plus an additional $5,000 in cash on hand, was invested in 2,000 shares of X Company common stock:

```
6. Stocks  . . . . . . . . . . . . . . . . . . . . .    60,000
     Cash . . . . . . . . . . . . . . . . . . . . . .              60,000
```

Assuming that there were no further purchases or sales of stock and that dividends received late in 19x6 amounted to $20,000, Entry 7 records the receipt of dividends in cash. Entry 8 records the transfer of cash to the Library Book Fund:

```
7. Cash . . . . . . . . . . . . . . . . . . . . . .    20,000
     Revenues—Dividends  . . . . . . . . . . . . .                20,000
8. Operating Transfers Out . . . . . . . . . . . . .   20,000
     Cash  . . . . . . . . . . . . . . . . . . . . .              20,000
```

As of December 31, 19x6, accrued interest on the bonds amounted to $17,400, the same amount as received in cash on July 1. Inasmuch as all bonds had been held for six months, the amortization of premium on AB Company bonds is $1,200 [($10,000 / 50) × 6], and the amortization of premium on C and D Company bonds is $1,200 [($4,000 / 20) × 6]. Therefore the total amortization of premium, $2,400, is treated as an adjustment of interest earnings and is retained by the Library Endowment Fund. Entry 9 records the accrual of interest, the amortization of premium, and the revenue earned for the Library Book Fund. Entry 10 records the liability to the Library Book Fund.

```
 9. Accrued Interest Receivable . . . . . . . . . . .   17,400
      Unamortized Bond Premium  . . . . . . . . . .                2,400
      Revenues—Bond Interest . . . . . . . . . . .                15,000
10. Operating Transfers Out . . . . . . . . . . . . .   15,000
      Due to Library Book Fund . . . . . . . . . . .              15,000
```

### Illustrative Financial Statements—Nonexpendable Trust Fund

At December 31, the end of the Village of Elizabeth's fiscal year, the Library Endowment Fund should prepare statements for inclusion in the Village's annual report, even though the fund was created on May 1 and has been in operation only 8 months. The financial statements required for this nonexpendable trust fund for inclusion in the Village's report for the period ended December 31, 19x6 are shown in Illustrations 9–2, 9–3, and 9–4.

ILLUSTRATION 9–2

**VILLAGE OF ELIZABETH**
**Library Endowment Fund**
**Balance Sheet**
**As of December 31, 19x6**

**Assets**

| | | |
|---|---:|---:|
| Cash . . . . . . . . . . . . . . . . . . . . . . . . . . . . . | | $ 7,400 |
| Accrued interest receivable . . . . . . . . . . . . . . . . . | | 17,400 |
| Investments: | | |
| Bonds, at par . . . . . . . . . . . . . . . . . . . . . | $360,000 | |
| Unamortized bond premium . . . . . . . . . . . . . . | 10,800 | 370,800 |
| Stocks . . . . . . . . . . . . . . . . . . . . . . . . | | 430,000 |
| Total Assets . . . . . . . . . . . . . . . . . . . . . . . | | $825,600 |

**Liabilities and Fund Equity**

| | |
|---|---:|
| Liabilities | |
| Due to Library Book Fund . . . . . . . . . . . . . . . . | $ 15,000 |
| Fund Equity: | |
| Fund Balance . . . . . . . . . . . . . . . . . . . . . | 810,600 |
| Total Liabilities and Fund Equity . . . . . . . . . . . . . . | $825,600 |

ILLUSTRATION 9–3

**VILLAGE OF ELIZABETH**
**Library Endowment Fund**
**Statement of Revenues, Expenses, and**
**Changes In Fund Balance**
**Eight Months Ended December 31, 19x6**

| | |
|---|---:|
| Revenues earned for transfer to Library Book Fund: | |
| Interest on bonds, net of amortization of bond premium . . . . . . . . | $ 20,000 |
| Dividends on stock . . . . . . . . . . . . . . . . . . . . . . . . | 38,000 |
| Total Revenue . . . . . . . . . . . . . . . . . . . . . . . . | 58,000 |
| Expenses . . . . . . . . . . . . . . . . . . . . . . . . . . . . | –0– |
| Income before Operating Transfers . . . . . . . . . . . . . . . . . | 58,000 |
| Other Financing Sources (Uses): | |
| Operating transfers to Library Book Fund . . . . . . . . . . . . . | (58,000) |
| Increase in Fund Balance . . . . . . . . . . . . . . . . . . . . | –0– |
| Fund Balance Received from Executor, May 1, 19x6 . . . . . . . . . . . | 805,600 |
| Realized Gain from Sale of Stock . . . . . . . . . . . . . . . . . | 5,000 |
| Fund Balance, December 31, 19x6 . . . . . . . . . . . . . . . . . | $810,600 |

## Illustrative Entries—Expendable Trust Fund

In the case of the gift of Richard Lee to the Village of Elizabeth, the trust corpus, or principal, was nonexpendable. Accounting and financial reporting for the nonexpendable trust fund, the Library Endowment Fund, which was established to account for the gift, is illustrated in the preceding section of this chapter. By the terms of Richard Lee's will, the net income from the nonexpendable trust, after amortization of bond premium, is to be transferred to the Village's Library Book Fund,

**ILLUSTRATION 9–4**

**VILLAGE OF ELIZABETH**
**Library Endowment Fund**
**Statement of Cash Flows**
**For Eight Months Ended December 31, 19x6**

Cash flows from investing activities:

| | |
|---|---:|
| Interest and dividends on investments . . . . . . . . . . . . . . . | $55,400 |
| Proceeds of sale of investments . . . . . . . . . . . . . . . . . . | 55,000 |
| Purchase of investments . . . . . . . . . . . . . . . . . . . . . | (60,000) |
| Operating transfers to expendable trust . . . . . . . . . . . . . . | (43,000) |
| Net cash provided by investing activities . . . . . . . . . . . . | $ 7,400 |

**Reconciliation of Net Income to Net Cash**
**Provided by Investing Activities**

| | | |
|---|---:|---:|
| Net income . . . . . . . . . . . . . . . . . . . . . . . . . . . . | | $    -0- |
| Adjustments: | | |
| Amortization of bond premium . . . . . . . . . . . . | $ 3,200 | |
| Increase in accrued receivables . . . . . . . . . . . . . | (5,800) | |
| Increase in interfund liabilities . . . . . . . . . . . . . | 15,000 | |
| Increase in investments . . . . . . . . . . . . . . . . . | (5,000) | |
| Total adjustments . . . . . . . . . . . . . . . . . | | 7,400 |
| Net cash provided by investing activities . . . . . . . . . | | $ 7,400 |

which was also created at the time of the establishment of the trust. The Library Book Fund, created to provide a mechanism through which to purchase books with endowment income, is similar in nature to the general and special revenue funds described in Chapters 2 and 3 and should be accounted for on the accrual basis used for governmental funds.

After the securities were transferred to the Library Endowment Fund and an estimate could be made of the revenues to be made available to the Library Book Fund, the Library Board approved a budget to record the Estimated Other Financing Sources of $50,000 and to appropriate that amount for subscriptions to periodicals ($7,000) and purchases of books ($43,000). Entry 1 is required to record the budget of the Library Book Fund:

```
1. Estimated Other Financing Sources  . . . . . . . . . . .  50,000
       Appropriations  . . . . . . . . . . . . . . . . . . . .         50,000
```

The Library Book Fund received $23,000 from the Library Endowment Fund (see Library Endowment Fund Entry 4):

```
2. Cash . . . . . . . . . . . . . . . . . . . . . . . . . . .  23,000
       Operating Transfers In  . . . . . . . . . . . . . . . .         23,000
```

The Library Book Fund ordered subscriptions for periodicals expected to cost $7,000 and ordered books expected to cost $14,000:

```
3. Encumbrances—19x6  . . . . . . . . . . . . . . . . . .  21,000
       Reserve for Encumbrances—19x6 . . . . . . . . . . .         21,000
```

The Library Book Fund received $20,000 from the Library Endowment Fund (see Library Endowment Fund, Entry 8). It also received and approved for payment invoices from magazine publishers ($7,020) and book publishers ($14,130), fulfilling all purchase orders recorded in Entry 3.

```
4. Cash  . . . . . . . . . . . . . . . . . . . . . . .   20,000
      Operating Transfers In  . . . . . . . . . . . . .              20,000
5. Reserve for Encumbrances—19x6  . . . . . . . . . . .   21,000
   Expenditures—19x6  . . . . . . . . . . . . . . . . .   21,150
      Encumbrances—19x6  . . . . . . . . . . . . . . .               21,000
      Vouchers Payable  . . . . . . . . . . . . . . . .               21,150
```

The Library ordered books expected to cost $28,000 in anticipation of receiving further distributions from the Library Endowment Fund:

```
6. Encumbrances—19x6  . . . . . . . . . . . . . . . . .   28,000
      Reserve for Encumbrances—19x6  . . . . . . . . . .              28,000
```

The Library Book Fund was notified that it would receive $15,000 from the Library Endowment Fund on the first working day in January, 19x7 (see Library Endowment Fund, Entry 10).

```
7. Due from Library Endowment Fund  . . . . . . . . . .   15,000
      Operating Transfers In  . . . . . . . . . . . . .              15,000
```

Closing entries would be as follows:

```
8. Appropriations  . . . . . . . . . . . . . . . . . .   50,000
   Operating Transfers In  . . . . . . . . . . . . . . .   58,000
      Estimated Other Financing Sources  . . . . . . . .              50,000
      Expenditures—19x6  . . . . . . . . . . . . . . . .              21,150
      Encumbrances—19x6  . . . . . . . . . . . . . . . .              28,000
      Fund Balance . . . . . . . . . . . . . . . . . . .               8,850
```

## Illustrative Financial Statements—Expendable Trust Fund

Financial statements prepared for the Library Book Fund for inclusion in the Village of Elizabeth's annual report for the period ending December 31, 19x6, would be similar in content and format to those illustrated in Chapter 3 and are shown as Illustrations 9–5 and 9–6.

## PUBLIC EMPLOYEE RETIREMENT SYSTEMS (PENSION TRUST FUNDS)

Assets held by pension plans were estimated recently to amount to over $800 billion and are growing at a rate of almost 20 percent each year. Fifteen of the 25 largest pension plans are public employee retirement systems (PERS), sometimes called *pension trust funds*. When a PERS is considered to be a part of a governmental reporting entity, its financial data are included in the combined financial statements, and in

**ILLUSTRATION 9–5**

### VILLAGE OF ELIZABETH
Library Book Fund
Balance Sheet
As of December 31, 19x6

**Assets**

| | |
|---|---|
| Cash . . . . . . . . . . . . . . . . . . . . . . . . . . . . . . . | $43,000 |
| Due from Library Endowment Fund . . . . . . . . . . . . . . | 15,000 |
| Total Assets . . . . . . . . . . . . . . . . . . . . . . . . . | $58,000 |

**Liabilities and Fund Equity**

| | | |
|---|---|---|
| Liabilities: | | |
| Vouchers payable . . . . . . . . . . . . . . . . . . . | | $21,150 |
| Fund Equity: | | |
| Reserve for encumbrances—19x6 . . . . . . . . . . . | $28,000 | |
| Fund Balance . . . . . . . . . . . . . . . . . . . . . | 8,850 | |
| Total Fund Equity . . . . . . . . . . . . . . . . . . | | 36,850 |
| Total Liabilities and Fund Equity . . . . . . . . . . . . . | | $58,000 |

**ILLUSTRATION 9–6**

### VILLAGE OF ELIZABETH
Library Book Fund
Statement of Revenues, Expenditures, and
Changes in Fund Balance
For the Eight Months Ended December 31, 19x6

| | |
|---|---|
| Other Financing Sources: | |
| Operating Transfers In from Library Endowment Fund . . . . . . . . . . . | $58,000 |
| Expenditures: | |
| Purchase of library books and periodicals . . . . . . . . . . . . . . . . | 21,150 |
| Excess of Other Financing Sources over Expenditures . . . . . . . . . . . | 36,850 |
| Fund Balance, May 1, 19x6 . . . . . . . . . . . . . . . . . . . . . . . . | — |
| (Increase) in Reserve for Encumbrances . . . . . . . . . . . . . . . . . . | (28,000) |
| Fund Balance, December 31, 19x6 . . . . . . . . . . . . . . . . . . . . . | $ 8,850 |

the combining financial statements prepared for fiduciary funds accounted for on the full accrual basis.

Accounting for pension trust funds should be distinguished from the governmental unit's responsibility as an employer to account for expenditures, expenses, and liabilities related to pension plans, and to disclose in the notes to the financial statements a long list of items specified in GASB statements. Reporting requirements are complex, and are in a process of change. Further, reporting requirements vary depending on whether the plan is administered by a unit of the reporting entity or by another entity. Full treatment of accounting and reporting requirements for both governmental employers and PERS is considerably beyond the scope of this book. This section is intended to introduce the topic and present a general overview of current standards.

The GASB Codification notes that pension accounting and reporting standards set forth in NCGA *Statement 1*, NCGA *Statement 6*, or in

FASB *Statement No. 35* may be used pending the issuance by the GASB of a Statement or Statements on pension accounting and financial reporting. Indications are that the standards set forth in GASB Codification Sec. Pe5 (largely based on NCGA *Statement 6*) and Sec. Pe6 (the codification of GASB *Statement No. 5*) are a good guide to future standards, therefore Secs. Pe5 and Pe6 standards are used as a basis for the following sections of this chapter; major differences from FASB standards are noted in the following discussion.

### Objectives of PERS and Government Employer Financial Reporting

GASB Codification Sec. Pe6.106 states that the primary objective of PERS financial statements and pension disclosures contained in financial statements of state and local government employers is to provide persons familiar with financial matters with information useful in:

*a.* Assessing the funding status of PERS on a going-concern basis.
*b.* Ascertaining the progress made in accumulating assets to pay benefits when due.
*c.* Assessing the extent to which employers are making contributions to PERS at actuarially determined rates.

### Required Balance Sheet Disclosures—Retirement Plans

The implication of the phrase "going-concern basis" in item *(a)*, above, is to distinguish the position taken in this standard from the position taken by the FASB in *Statement of Financial Accounting Standards No. 35,* which has been criticized as a liquidation viewpoint. *SFAS No. 35* requires defined benefit pension plans of business organizations to disclose the actuarial present value of **accumulated plan benefits.** Accumulated plan benefits arc defined as future benefit payments attributable under the plan's provisions to employees' service rendered to the benefit information date. In contrast, PERS following the requirements of GASB standards set forth in GASB Codification Sec. Pe6 disclose the actuarial present value of **credited projected benefits.** Projected benefits take into account the effect of anticipated future compensation and service credits (as well as benefits attributable to service rendered to the benefit information date). The actuarial present value of plan benefits represents the interests of persons covered by the plan in the net assets of the PERS. Consequently, the actuarial present value of projected benefits of each class of person covered by the plan is shown in a PERS balance sheet as an element of the fund equity, or Fund Balance, as shown in Illustration 9–7. Although the FASB and the GASB have different standards for reporting assets and for reporting actuarial present values of benefits, both agree that it is desirable for the balance sheet of a retirement plan to show liabilities as a deduction from total

**ILLUSTRATION 9–7**

## VILLAGE OF ELIZABETH
### Public Employees Retirement Fund
### Balance Sheet
### January 1, 19x6

### Assets

| | |
|---|---:|
| Cash . . . . . . . . . . . . . . . . . . . . . . . . . . . . . . . . . . . | $      30,500 |
| Accrued interest receivable . . . . . . . . . . . . . . . . . . . . . . | 2,400,000 |
| Investments: | |
| Bonds at amortized cost | |
| (market value $76,500,000) . . . . . . . . . . . . . . . . . | 80,000,000 |
| Common stocks at cost | |
| (market value $39,000,000) . . . . . . . . . . . . . . . . . | 40,500,000 |
| Commercial paper and repurchase agreements, at cost (market value | |
| $15,698,500) . . . . . . . . . . . . . . . . . . . . . . . . . | 11,300,000 |
| Equipment and fixtures, net of accumulated depreciation of $15,000 . . | 70,000 |
| Total Assets . . . . . . . . . . . . . . . . . . . . . . . . . | 134,300,500 |

### Liabilities

| | |
|---|---:|
| Accounts payable and accrued expenses . . . . . . . . . . . . . . | 600,000 |
| Net Assets Available for Benefits . . . . . . . . . . . . . . . . . | $133,700,500 |

### Fund Balance

| | |
|---|---:|
| Actuarial present value of projected benefits: | |
| Payable to current retirants and beneficiaries . . . . . . . . . . . | $ 27,600,000 |
| Payable to terminated vested participants . . . . . . . . . . . . | 2,350,000 |
| Actuarial present value of credited projected benefits for active | |
| employees: | |
| Member contributions . . . . . . . . . . . . . . . . . . . . | 32,100,000 |
| Employer financed portion . . . . . . . . . . . . . . . . . . | 81,500,000 |
| Total Actuarial Present Value of Credited Projected Benefits . . . . . | 143,550,000 |
| Unfunded actuarial present value of credited projected benefits . . . . | (9,849,500) |
| Total Fund Balance . . . . . . . . . . . . . . . . . . . . . . | $133,700,500 |

assets, and to label the difference as "Net Assets Available for Benefits," as is done in Illustration 9–7. Net Assets Available for Benefits is simply another name for Fund Balance.

If the total actuarial present value of projected benefits exceeds the net assets available for benefits, the excess is captioned as shown in Illustration 9–7. The caption "Unfunded Actuarial Present Value of Credited Projected Benefits" signifies that contributions to the plan, and earnings on plan investments, have not been as large as assumed in actuarial computations. As shown in Illustration 9–7, Unfunded Actuarial Present Value of Credited Projected Benefits is subtracted from the total Actuarial Present Value of Credited Projected Benefits in determining Total Fund Balance. In the event that net assets available for benefits exceeds the total actuarial present value of projected benefits, the excess should be captioned "Net Assets Available for Future Benefit Credits" and added to the total actuarial present value of credited projected benefits in arriving at the Total Fund Balance.

*SFAS No. 35* requires defined benefit retirement plans of businesses to report investments at market value as of balance sheet date, which critics claim is a liquidation view. In contrast, GASB Codification Secs.

Pe5.108–.109 require the investments of a PERS to be reported at cost, or amortized cost, with market value at balance sheet date disclosed parenthetically, which is thought to be consistent with the going-concern viewpoint. Both the FASB and the GASB require depreciable assets of a retirement plan to be reported at cost less accumulated depreciation. In addition to investments and depreciable assets, retirement plans generally have some uninvested cash and accrued interest on investments as of balance sheet date. The assets section of a retirement plan does not classify assets as current and fixed. Liabilities of the plan are usually short term (benefits due but not yet paid, other vouchers payable, and accrued expenses).

### Additional Financial Statements and Note Disclosures Required for PERS

In addition to a balance sheet, presented in conformity with the standards discussed above, the GASB Codification Sec. Pe5 states that the annual financial statements (GPFS) for a PERS should include a Statement of Revenues, Expenses, and Changes in Fund Balance (Illustration 9–9). Notes to the financial statements should include all disclosures needed to make the financial statements not misleading. GASB Codification Sec. Pe6.130 specifies a series of items that must be disclosed in the notes to PERS annual financial statements under the following captions:

a. Plan Description.
b. Summary of Significant Accounting Policies and Plan Asset Matters.
c. Funding Status and Progress.
d. Contribution Required and Contribution Made.
e. Location of Required 10-Year Historical Trend Information.

Items a, b, c, and d above are reasonably self-explanatory; item e refers to historical trend information, which is required to be presented as supplementary information. (The distinction between display on the face of financial statements or disclosure in the notes to the financial statements and disclosure as supplementary information is that the statements and notes are covered by the auditor's report, whereas supplementary information is ordinarily unaudited.)

### PERS—Illustrative Case

As of the beginning of 19x6 the Public Employee Retirement Fund of the Village of Elizabeth had the assets and liabilities shown in Illustration 9–7.

During the year ended December 31, 19x6, the following events and transactions which affected the Village of Elizabeth's Public Employees Retirement Fund are assumed to have taken place:

Accrued interest receivable as of January 1, 19x6, was collected:

```
1. Cash . . . . . . . . . . . . . . . . . . . . . . .    2,400,000
      Accrued Interest Receivable  . . . . . . . .                      2,400,000
```

Member contributions in the amount of $7,850,000 and employer contributions in the amount of $15,300,000 were received in cash:

```
2. Cash . . . . . . . . . . . . . . . . . . . . . . .   23,150,000
      Revenues—Member Contributions . . . . . . .                       7,850,000
      Revenues—Employer Contributions  . . . . . .                     15,300,000
```

Annuity benefits in the amount of $3,100,000 and disability benefits in the amount of $312,500 were recorded as liabilities:

```
3. Annuity Benefits . . . . . . . . . . . . . . . .     3,100,000
   Disability Benefits  . . . . . . . . . . . . . . .      312,500
      Accounts Payable and Accrued Expenses . . . .                     3,412,500
```

Accounts payable and accrued expenses paid in cash amounted to $3,650,000:

```
4. Accounts Payable and Accrued Expenses . . . . . .    3,650,000
      Cash . . . . . . . . . . . . . . . . . . . . .                    3,650,000
```

Terminated employees whose benefits were not vested were refunded $2,130,000 in cash:

```
5. Refunds to Terminated Employees . . . . . . . . .    2,130,000
      Cash . . . . . . . . . . . . . . . . . . . . .                    2,130,000
```

Investment income received in cash amounted to $9,350,000; additionally, $3,916,000 interest income was accrued at year-end:

```
6. Cash . . . . . . . . . . . . . . . . . . . . . . .    9,350,000
   Accrued Interest Receivable  . . . . . . . . . .     3,916,000
      Investment Income . . . . . . . . . . . . . .                    13,266,000
```

Commercial paper and repurchase agreements carried at a cost of $1,958,000 matured, and cash in that amount was received:

```
7. Cash . . . . . . . . . . . . . . . . . . . . . . .    1,958,000
      Commercial Paper and Repurchase Agreements .                      1,958,000
```

Common stocks carried at a cost of $7,250,000 were sold for that amount; $1,900,000 was reinvested in common stocks and the remainder in bonds. An additional amount of $30,500,000 was also invested in bonds.

```
8a. Cash . . . . . . . . . . . . . . . . . . . . . . .   7,250,000
       Common Stocks . . . . . . . . . . . . . . . .                    7,250,000
8b. Bonds  . . . . . . . . . . . . . . . . . . . . .   35,850,000
    Common Stocks . . . . . . . . . . . . . . . . .     1,900,000
       Cash . . . . . . . . . . . . . . . . . . . . .                  37,750,000
```

Administrative expenses for the year totaled $600,000, all paid in cash:

```
 9. Administrative Expenses  . . . . . . . . . . . .        600,000
      Cash . . . . . . . . . . . . . . . . . . . .                     600,000
```

Equipment costing $12,500, on which depreciation in the amount of $5,000 had accumulated, was sold for $7,500 cash:

```
10. Accumulated Depreciation—Equipment  . . . . . .          5,000
      Cash . . . . . . . . . . . . . . . . . . . .           7,500
      Equipment  . . . . . . . . . . . . . . . .                      12,500
```

Equipment costing $15,000 was purchased:

```
11. Equipment  . . . . . . . . . . . . . . . . . .          15,000
      Cash . . . . . . . . . . . . . . . . . . . .                    15,000
```

Depreciation expense for the year amounted to $8,000 (charge to Administrative Expenses):

```
12. Administrative Expenses  . . . . . . . . . . . .          8,000
      Accumulated Depreciation—Equipment  . . . .                      8,000
```

No amortization of bond premium or discount was necessary during the year. Nominal accounts for the year were closed:

```
13. Revenues—Member Contributions . . . . . . . . .      7,850,000
    Revenues—Employer Contributions  . . . . . . . .    15,300,000
    Investment Income . . . . . . . . . . . . . . .     13,266,000
      Annuity Benefits . . . . . . . . . . . . . .                   3,100,000
      Disability Benefits  . . . . . . . . . . . .                     312,500
      Refunds to Terminated Employees  . . . . . .                   2,130,000
      Administrative Expenses  . . . . . . . . . .                     608,000
      Net Operating Income . . . . . . . . . . . .                  30,265,500
```

In order that the accounts of the Retirement Fund may contain the information which GASB standards require to be shown in a balance sheet, it is necessary to distribute the Net Operating Income to the various accounts which are components of the Fund Balance (see the second portion of Illustration 9–7 or Illustration 9–8). Entry 14 records the distribution of Net Operating Income for 19x6:

```
14. Net Operating Income  . . . . . . . . . . . . .     30,265,500
      Actuarial Present Value of Projected Benefits
        Payable to:
          Current Retirants and Beneficiaries  . . . . .             5,600,000
          Terminated Vested Participants  . . . . . . .                650,000
      Actuarial Present Value of Credited Projected
        Benefits for Active Employees:
          Member Contributions . . . . . . . . . . . .               6,900,000
          Employer Financed Portion . . . . . . . . .               16,800,000
      Unfunded Actuarial Present Value of Credited
        Projected Benefits . . . . . . . . . . . . . .                 315,500
```

The financial position of the Village of Elizabeth Public Employee Retirement Fund as of December 31, 19x6, and the results of its opera-

**ILLUSTRATION 9–8**

**VILLAGE OF ELIZABETH**
**Public Employee Retirement Fund**
**Balance Sheet**
**December 31, 19x6**

**Assets**

| | | |
|---|---:|---:|
| Cash | | $        1,000 |
| Accrued interest receivable | | 3,916,000 |
| Investments: | | |
| Bonds, at amortized cost (market value, $112,300,000) | $115,850,000 | |
| Common stocks, at cost (market value, $36,100,000) | 35,150,000 | |
| Commercial paper and repurchase agreements, at cost (market value, $9,816,000) | 9,342,000 | |
| Total Investments | | 160,342,000 |
| Equipment and fixtures, net of accumulated depreciation of $18,000 | | 69,500 |
| Total Assets | | 164,328,500 |

**Liabilities**

| | |
|---|---:|
| Accounts payable and accrued expenses | 362,500 |
| Net Assets Available for Benefits | $163,966,000 |

**Fund Balance**

| | |
|---|---:|
| Actuarial present value of projected benefits payable to current retirants and beneficiaries | $ 33,200,000 |
| Actuarial present value of projected benefits payable to terminated vested participants | 3,000,000 |
| Actuarial present value of credited projected benefits for active employees: | |
| Member contributions | 39,000,000 |
| Employer-financed portion | 98,300,000 |
| Total Actuarial Present Value of Credited Projected Benefits | 173,500,000 |
| Unfunded actuarial present value of credited projected benefits | (9,534,000) |
| Total Fund Balance | $163,966,000 |

**ILLUSTRATION 9–9**

**VILLAGE OF ELIZABETH**
**Public Employee Retirement Fund**
**Statement of Revenues, Expenses, and Changes in Fund Balance**
**For the Fiscal Year Ended December 31, 19x6**

Operating Revenues:

| | |
|---|---:|
| Member Contributions | $  7,850,000 |
| Employer Contributions | 15,300,000 |
| Investment Income | 13,266,000 |
| Total Operating Revenues | 36,416,000 |

Operating Expenses:

| | |
|---|---:|
| Annuity benefits | 3,100,000 |
| Disability benefits | 312,500 |
| Refunds to terminated employees | 2,130,000 |
| Administrative expenses | 608,000 |
| Total Operating Expenses | 6,150,500 |
| Net Operating Income | 30,265,500 |
| Fund Balance, January 1, 19x6 | 133,700,500 |
| Fund Balance, December 31, 19x6 | $163,966,000 |

tions for the year then ended, are presented in Illustrations 9–8 and 9–9.[4]

## Summary of Requirements for Government Employers' Financial Reporting

**Requirements if PERS is component of employer reporting entity**
Government employer entities must incorporate in their annual financial statements the financial statements of a PERS if a PERS is considered to be part of the reporting entity. The nature and extent of the employer's obligation to provide resources for PERS contributions may have a

---

[4]GASB Statement No. 9 specifically exempts PERS and pension trust funds that report in the manner illustrated in this chapter from presenting either a Statement of Changes in Financial Position or a Statement of Cash Flows.

significant impact on the employer's financial position. The note disclosures and required supplementary information enumerated in the section preceding the "Illustrative Case" are also applicable to employer reporting, except that note disclosure may be somewhat less detailed.

When PERS financial statements are incorporated in the employer's combined statements, PERS balance sheets should be formatted in the same manner as those of the other funds and component units. In a combined balance sheet, the PERS Fund Balance is to be shown as a single figure (captioned "Reserved for Employees' Retirement System"). Details required to be shown in the Fund Balance section of a PERS balance sheet are to be shown in the notes to the employer's GPFS (and in the PERS statements included in the employer's CAFR).

**Requirements if PERS is not component of employer reporting entity** State and local government employers liable for making contributions to a single-employer PERS that is not considered to be a part of the employer reporting entity are required to report in their GPFS all the note disclosures previously described and to report in their CAFRs all the statistical data previously itemized. State and local government employers which participate in a multiple-employer PERS are required to report all information required by GASB Codification Sec. Pe6 if separate actuarial valuations are made for each participating employer; if separate actuarial valuations are not made, disclosures specified in GASB Codification Sec. Pe6 should be made in the notes to the employer financial statements.

**Employer reporting of contributions** Employers are required to report as an expenditure of governmental funds and as an expense of proprietary funds the employer contribution amount developed by one of the actuarial cost methods specified in GASB Codification Sec. Pe6, regardless of whether such amount has actually been contributed. To the extent that the amount has not been or will not be funded by a governmental fund, current GASB standards provide that the unfunded amount must be reported in the General Long-Term Debt Account Group; amounts that have not been or will not be funded by proprietary funds or nonexpendable trust funds shall be shown as liabilities of those funds.

## SELECTED REFERENCES

Financial Accounting Standards Board. *Statement of Financial Accounting Standards No. 35: Accounting and Reporting by Defined Benefit Pension Plans.* Norwalk, Conn., 1980, as amended by *SFAS No. 59* (1982) and *SFAS No. 75* (1983).

Governmental Accounting Standards Board. *Codification of Governmental Accounting and Financial Reporting Standards.* 2nd ed. Norwalk, Conn., 1987.

## QUESTIONS AND EXERCISES

9–1.    Using the annual financial report obtained for Exercise 1–1, answer the following questions:

      *a.* Does the annual report include a Combining Statement of Changes in Assets and Liabilities—All Agency Funds? If so, list the agency funds for which data are presented. Can you determine the reason for the use of each agency fund? Can you trace total agency fund assets and liabilities from the Combining Statement to the Fiduciary Funds column of the Combined Balance Sheet?

            In the absence of legal requirements, do all agency funds seem necessary, or could some of the activities have been handled in liability accounts of other funds? Do the agency funds have only assets and liability accounts, or are fund equity accounts also used? If so, is the fund properly classified as an agency fund or should it be classified as a trust fund or some other type of fund?

      *b.* List the nonexpendable trust funds included in the report. Does the report describe the funds sufficiently so you can tell the nature and purpose of each nonexpendable trust fund? Are the funds classified correctly? Does the report present financial data of the nonexpendable trust funds in the Combined Statement of Revenues, Expenses, and Changes in Fund Balances/Retained Earnings and in the Combined Statement of Changes in Financial Position along with the proprietary funds? Are all account titles the same as illustrated in this book? Are transfers to expendable trust and other funds handled as illustrated in this book? If not, describe how transfers are handled.

      *c.* List the expendable trust funds included in the report. Do any of these relate to nonexpendable trust funds as in the Village of Elizabeth example, or are they independent of other funds? Do the classifications seem appropriate? Are expendable trust funds reported in the Combined Statement of Revenues, Expenditures, and Changes in Fund Balances along with the governmental funds? Can you tell if annual budgets are legally required for the expendable trust funds? If budgets appear to be required, are the funds included in the Combined Statement of Revenues, Expenditures, and Changes in Fund Balances—Budget and Actual along with governmental funds which have legally adopted annual budgets?

      *d.* List the pension funds included in the financial statements. From the notes, list the other pension plans that are available to employees of your governmental unit. Are required disclosures made in the notes for all pension plans, whether or not the plans are included as trust funds? Is the "required supplementary information" presented for pension activities? Does the report have expendable trust or special revenue funds that serve as conduits through which the governmental entity sends funds to statewide plans? Does note disclosure reflect the criteria used to determine if pension plans should be included in the reporting entity? When included, do the pension trust funds use full accrual accounting? Are pension trust funds reported in the Combined Statement of Revenues, Expenses, and Changes in Fund Balances/Retained Earnings and in the Combined Statement of Changes in Financial Position along with the proprietary and nonexpendable trust funds?

9–2.    Write the numbers 1 through 10 on a sheet of paper. Beside each number, write the letter corresponding with the best answer to each of the following:

1. The fund types referred to as *fiduciary funds* in GASB standards are:
   a. General, Special Revenue, Expendable Trust, and Nonexpendable Trust.
   b. Expendable Trust, Nonexpendable Trust, Agency, and Endowment.
   c. Agency, Nonexpendable Trust, Pension Trust, and Internal Service.
   d. Agency, Expendable Trust, Nonexpendable Trust, and Pension Trust.

2. Grove County collects property taxes levied within its boundaries and receives a 1 percent fee for administering these collections on behalf of the municipalities located in the county. In 19x7, Grove collected $1,000,000 for its municipalities and remitted $990,000 to them after deducting fees of $10,000. In the initial recording of the 1 percent fee, Grove's Agency Fund should credit:
   a. Fund Balance—Agency Fund, $10,000.
   b. Fees Earned—Agency Fund, $10,000.
   c. Due to Grove County General Fund, $10,000.
   d. Revenues Control, $10,000.

3. Agency Funds should be included in the GPFS in:
   a. The same combined statements as the governmental funds.
   b. The same combined statements as the proprietary funds.
   c. The Combined Balance Sheet and the Combined Statement of Changes in Financial Position.
   d. The Combined Balance Sheet only.

4. Expendable Trust Funds should be included in the GPFS in:
   a. The same combined statements as the governmental funds.
   b. The same combined statements as the proprietary funds.
   c. The Combined Balance Sheet and the Combined Statement of Changes in Financial Position.
   d. The Combined Balance Sheet only.

5. Nonexpendable Trust Funds should be included in the GPFS in:
   a. The same combined statements as the governmental funds.
   b. The same combined statements as the proprietary funds.
   c. The Combined Balance Sheet and the Combined Statement of Changes in Financial Position.
   d. The Combined Balance Sheet only.

6. Pension Trust Funds (PERS) should be included in the GPFS in:
   a. The same combined statements as the governmental funds.
   b. The same combined statements as the proprietary funds.
   c. The Combined Balance Sheet and the Combined Statement of Changes in Financial Position.
   d. The Combined Balance Sheet only.

7. Which of the following funds of a governmental unit often includes contributed capital in its balance sheet?
   a. Expendable Trust.
   b. Nonexpendable Trust.
   c. Pension Trust.
   d. None of the above.

8. GASB standards mandate the presentation of *required supplementary information* for:

a. All fiduciary funds.

b. All trust funds.

c. Nonexpendable Trust Funds only.

d. Pension Trust Funds (PERS) only.

9. State and local governmental units should use the agency fund type to record agency transactions:

a. If required by law.

b. If required by GASB standards.

c. If needed to enhance financial management.

d. All of the above.

10. Fiduciary funds which should be accounted for in a manner similar to proprietary funds are:

a. Agency Funds and Nonexpendable Trust Funds.

b. Agency Funds and Expendable Trust Funds.

c. Expendable Trust Funds and Nonexpendable Trust Funds.

d. Nonexpendable Trust Funds and Pension Trust Funds.

(Item 2, AICPA, adapted)

9–3.     Benton County maintains a tax agency fund for use by the County Treasurer to record receivables, collections, and disbursements of all property tax collections to all units of government in the County. For FY 19x5–x6, the following taxes were assessed:

| | |
|---|---:|
| Benton County General Fund | $10,500,000 |
| City of Thomas | 7,400,000 |
| City of Hart | 3,200,000 |
| Benton County School District | 23,900,000 |
| Various Special Districts | 6,300,000 |
| Total | $51,300,000 |

During the first six months of the fiscal year, the following transactions took place:

1. The tax levy became effective. All units of government provided for an estimated 3 percent in uncollectible taxes.

2. Cash collections of the first installment of taxes amounted to $24,624,000.

3. It was determined that the cash collections pertained to the funds and governmental units in the following amounts. Record the liability to the County General Fund and to the other governmental units, assuming that the County General Fund charges other governments 1 percent of all tax collected, because the County General Fund incurs all costs of billing, recording, and collecting taxes.

| | |
|---|---:|
| Benton County General Fund | $ 5,080,000 |
| City of Thomas | 4,070,000 |
| City of Hart | 1,018,000 |
| Benton County School District | 11,472,000 |
| Various Special Districts | 2,984,000 |
| Total | $24,624,000 |

4. Cash was transferred to the various governmental units.

**Required:**

Record the above transactions on the books of the:

a. Benton County Tax Agency Fund.

   b. Benton County General Fund.
   c. Benton County School District.

**9–4.**    On July 1, 19x0, the City of Belvedere accepted a gift of securities from a
nonprofit foundation to be held as a nonexpendable trust; the net income from
the trust is to be computed on a full accrual basis. Income received in cash,
less any amount needed to amortize premiums on fixed-income securities, is
to be transferred to an expendable trust fund operated on the budgetary basis
for the purchase of works of art for display in public buildings. The nonexpendable trust fund, to be known as the Art Endowment Fund, received the
following as trust principal on July 1, 19x0: (1) EF Company bonds, face value
$2,600,000 (fair value $2,650,000), annual interest rate 8 percent payable on
March 1 and September 1, 50 months until maturity; (2) 10,000 shares GH
Company common stock, fair value $500,000. Accrued interest on the bonds
amounted to $69,333 as of July 1, 19x0.

*Required:*
   a. The following events and transactions occurred during the fiscal year
      ended June 30, 19x1. Record them, as appropriate, in the (1) Art Endow-
      ment Fund, and/or (2) Artworks Expendable Trust Fund:
      (1) On July 1, 19x0, the gift was recorded.
      (2) A budget was passed for the Artworks Expendable Trust Fund, pro-
          viding for one year's interest in the EF bonds, less one year's amor-
          tization of the premium, plus anticipated dividends of $25,000. It was
          decided that appropriations for the period should be $200,000.
      (3) On September 1, six months' interest was received on the EF bonds.
          The portion accrued at July 1 and the amortized interest were re-
          tained by the Endowment Fund. The remainder was transferred to
          the Expendable Trust Fund.
      (4) Based on the appropriation, paintings and other artworks were or-
          dered and commissioned at an estimated cost of $180,000.
      (5) On January 1, 19x1, dividends were received in the amount of $28,000
          by the Endowment Fund and transferred to the Expendable Trust
          Fund.
      (6) On March 1, 19x1, a six-month interest payment was received by the
          Endowment Fund. That amount, less amortization of premium, was
          transferred to the Expendable Trust Fund.
      (7) On June 15, 5,000 of the shares of stock of GH Company were sold
          for $275,000. The $275,000 and an additional $25,000 were used to
          purchase 10,000 shares of ST Company stock.
      (8) Artwork, ordered at a cost of $80,000, was received and displayed at
          a cost of $81,500 which was paid in cash.
      (9) As of June 30, 19x1, interest was accrued on EF Company bonds.
          The four months' interest, less the amortization of premium, was re-
          corded by the Endowment Fund as Due to Artworks Expendable
          Trust Fund. The Artworks Expendable Trust Fund recorded the re-
          ceivable from the Endowment Fund and credited Operating Transfers
          In.
      (10) Closing entries were made.

> b. For the Art Endowment Fund, prepare: (1) a Balance Sheet as of June 30, 19x1, and (2) a Statement of Revenues, Expenses, and Changes in Fund Balance for the year then ended.
>
> c. For the Artworks Expendable Trust Fund, prepare: (1) a Balance Sheet as of June 30, 19x1, and (2) a Statement of Revenues, Expenditures, and Changes in Fund Balance for the year then ended.

9–5.    The City of Pigeon Forge maintains an Employees' Retirement Fund. The fund is financed by actuarially determined contributions from the City's General Fund and by contributions from employees. Administration of the retirement fund is handled by General Fund employees, and the retirement fund does not bear any administrative expense. The Balance Sheet of the Employees' Retirement Fund as of July 1, 19x6 is shown below.

**CITY OF PIGEON FORGE**
**Employees' Retirement Fund**
**Balance Sheet**
**As of July 1, 19x6**

**Assets**

| | |
|---|---:|
| Cash . . . . . . . . . . . . . . . . . . . . . . . . . . . . . . . . . . . | $    35,100 |
| Accrued interest receivable . . . . . . . . . . . . . . . . . . . . . | 60,000 |
| Investments, at cost (market value $2,600,000) . . . . . . . . . . . | 2,400,000 |
| Total assets . . . . . . . . . . . . . . . . . . . . . . . . . . . . . . | 2,495,100 |

**Liabilities**

| | |
|---|---:|
| Accounts payable and accrued expenses . . . . . . . . . . . . . . | 33,000 |
| Net Assets Available for Benefits . . . . . . . . . . . . . . . . | $2,462,100 |

**Fund Balance**

| | |
|---|---:|
| Actuarial present value of projected benefits to current retirants and beneficiaries . . . . . . . . . . . . . . . . . . . . . . . . . . . . . . | $   323,000 |
| Actuarial present value of credited projected benefits for active employees: | |
|     Member contribution . . . . . . . . . . . . . . . . . . . . . . . . | 1,075,000 |
|     Employer financed portion . . . . . . . . . . . . . . . . . . . . | 1,075,000 |
|     Total Actuarial Present Value of Credited Projected Benefits . . . | 2,473,000 |
| Unfunded Actuarial Present Value of Credited Projected Benefits . . . | (10,900) |
| Total Fund Balance . . . . . . . . . . . . . . . . . . . . . . . . . . | $2,462,100 |

During the year ended June 30, 19x7, the following transactions occurred:

1. The interest receivable on investments as of the beginning of the year was collected in cash.
2. Member contributions in the amount of $350,000 were received in cash. The city contributed $250,000, also in cash.
3. Annuity benefits in the amount of $80,000 were recorded as liabilities.
4. Accounts payable and accrued expenses paid in cash amounted to $86,000.
5. Investment income received in cash amounted to $180,000. In addition, $65,000 interest was accrued at year-end.
6. Additional investments were purchased in the amount of $700,000.
7. Nominal accounts for the year were closed. Information from the actuary indicated that the actuarial present value of projected benefits to current

retirees and beneficiaries increased by $212,000 and the actuarial present value of credited projected benefits for active employees increased by $200,000 (employees' portion) and $200,000 (employer's portion).

**Required:**
*a.* Prepare journal entries to record the above transactions of the Employees' Retirement Fund.
*b.* Prepare a Balance Sheet as of June 30, 19x7.
*c.* Prepare a Statement of Revenues, Expenses, and Changes in Fund Balance for the Year Ended June 30, 19x7.

**9–6.** Assume that a local government unit maintains a pension trust fund for its police and fire department employees and participates in a statewide plan for all of its other employees. Individual accounts are maintained for all local governments in the statewide plan. Discuss the financial reporting requirements related to pensions for *(a)* police and fire department employees and *(b)* all other employees.

## CONTINUOUS PROBLEM

**9–C.** On January 1, 19y1, Henry J. Moneybag gave $1,500,000 par value, 10 percent XYZ Company bonds to the City of Everlasting Sunshine with the provision that the endowment be made permanent and that all income be used to buy flowers for the city parks. The bonds were dated 4/1/y0, are due on 4/1/z0 (10-year bonds), and were quoted at par on the date of the gift. Bond interest payment dates are 4/1 and 10/1. The City Council decided to create two funds: (1) the Moneybag Park Flower Endowment Fund (nonexpendable) to account for the principal and (2) the Park Flower Operating Fund (expendable) to account for the purchase and maintaining of the flowers.

*a.* You are required to open two general journals, one for each fund, and record the following transactions. Use the account titles in requirement *(b):*

   (1) Record the gift, as of 1/1/y1.
   (2) A budget was passed for the Park Flower Operating Fund, providing Estimated Other Financing Sources in the amount of one year's bond interest and providing Appropriations equal to the cash that will be transferred by the Park Flower Endowment Fund during 19y1.
   (3) On 4/1/y1, the first interest payment was received, and cash in the appropriate amount was transferred to the Operating Fund.
   (4) Flowers were ordered (including planting) in the amount of $110,000. Flowers amounting to $100,000 of the purchase orders were received and planted, along with invoices amounting to $99,500. The invoices were approved for payment.
   (5) On 10/1/y1, the second interest payment was received, and cash in that amount was transferred to the Operating Fund.
   (6) Vouchers in the amount of $95,000 were paid for the flowers.
   (7) On 12/31/y1, the accrued interest receivable and the liability to the Park Flower Operating Fund were recorded in the Endowment Fund. The receivable was recorded in the Park Flower Operating Fund.
   (8) Any necessary adjusting and closing entries were made.

*b.* Open two general ledgers, one for each fund, and post the transactions listed in requirement *(a)*. Use five lines for each of the following accounts:

**Moneybag Park Flower Endowment Fund**
Cash
Accrued Interest Receivable
Bonds, at par
Due to Park Flower Operating Fund
Revenues—Bond Interest
Operating Transfers Out
Fund Balance

**Park Flower Operating Fund**
Cash
Due from Moneybag Park Flower Endowment Fund
Estimated Other Financing Sources
Operating Transfers In
Vouchers Payable
Appropriations
Expenditures—19y1
Encumbrances—19y1
Reserve for Encumbrances—19y1
Fund Balance

*c.* Prepare the following financial statements:
   (1) A Combining Balance Sheet for the two trust funds as of December 31, 19y1.
   (2) A Statement of Revenues, Expenses, and Changes in Fund Balance for the Moneybag Park Flower Endowment Fund for the year ended December 31, 19y1.
   (3) A Statement of Changes in Financial Position for the Park Flower Endowment Fund for the year ended December 31, 19y1.
   (4) A Statement of Revenues, Expenditures, and Changes in Fund Balance for the Park Flower Operating Fund for the year ended December 31, 19y1.
   (5) A Statement of Revenues, Expenditures, and Changes in Fund Balance—Budget and Actual for the Park Flower Operating Fund for the year ended December 31, 19y1.

# Chapter 10

# INTERFUND TRANSACTIONS; FINANCIAL REPORTING FOR STATE AND LOCAL GOVERNMENTAL UNITS; AUDITING

Chapters 2 through 9 present extended discussion of the nature of fund types and account groups which are to be used by state and local governmental units as needed for legal compliance, to enhance financial management, or, in a few instances, conformity with GASB standards. In the first section of this chapter, interfund transactions are reviewed. The second section presents a brief discussion of the complexities of defining the governmental reporting entity. The third section reviews and illustrates general purpose financial statements and comprehensive annual financial reports. The fourth section presents a discussion of the unique aspects of governmental auditing.

## SUMMARY OF INTERFUND TRANSACTIONS

Transactions, or events, that affect the accounts of more than one fund or account group of a single governmental unit have been noted in the discussions and illustrative entries of preceding chapters. A brief review of interfund transactions and events at this point should aid the understanding of the relationships that exist among the funds and groups.

Events and transactions that must be recognized in more than one accounting entity of a single governmental unit may be classified in the following manner:

1. Interfund loans and advances.
2. Quasi-external transactions.
3. Reimbursements.
4. Operating transfers.
5. Equity transfers.
6. Acquisition of general fixed assets.
7. Creation, or repayment, of general long-term debt.

Examples of each of the seven classes of interfund events or transactions, and entries which record them in each affected fund or group, are illustrated in the following paragraphs.

## Interfund Loans and Advances

The terms **loans** and **advances** are used to indicate amounts that are temporarily transferred from one fund to another but that will have to be repaid in due time. For example, assume that the Water Utility Fund, an enterprise fund, made a long-term advance to a Stores and Services Fund in the amount of $200,000. The effect of the advance on each fund is:

**Water Utility Fund**

| | | |
|---|---|---|
| Long-Term Advance to Stores and Services Fund . . . . . . | 200,000 | |
| Cash . . . . . . . . . . . . . . . . . . . . . . . . | | 200,000 |

**Stores and Services Fund**

| | | |
|---|---|---|
| Cash . . . . . . . . . . . . . . . . . . . . . . . . | 200,000 | |
| Advance from Water Utility Fund . . . . . . . . . | | 200,000 |

Partial repayment of the advance was made at year-end:

**Water Utility Fund**

| | | |
|---|---|---|
| Cash . . . . . . . . . . . . . . . . . . . . . . . . | 40,000 | |
| Long-Term Advance to Stores and Services Fund . . . . | | 40,000 |

**Stores and Services Fund**

| | | |
|---|---|---|
| Advance from Water Utility Fund . . . . . . . . . . . | 40,000 | |
| Cash . . . . . . . . . . . . . . . . . . . . . . . . | | 40,000 |

Since each fund is a fiscal entity the interfund receivables and payables resulting from loans and advances must be disclosed in a combined balance sheet. They may not be eliminated, as would be proper in the preparation of consolidated statements for parent and subsidiary profit-seeking corporations. However, if one fund has a receivable from another fund and a related payable to the same fund it is considered proper to report in the year-end balance sheet only the net receivable or net payable.

## Quasi-External Transactions

Interfund transactions which would result in the recognition of revenues, expenditures, or expenses if one of the parties were external to

the governmental unit are called **quasi-external** transactions. One of the
most common examples of this type of interfund transaction which
properly results in the recognition of revenue by one fund and the recording of an expenditure by another fund is the provision of fire hydrants and water for fire protection by a governmentally owned water
utility; illustrative entries are given in Chapters 3 and 8 for this type of
interfund transaction. The effect upon the general ledger accounts of the
Village of Elizabeth's General Fund and the Water Utility Fund for fire
protection service provided by the utility is:

### General Fund

| | | |
|---|---|---|
| Expenditures | 40,000 | |
| Due to Water Utility Fund | | 40,000 |

### Water Utility Fund

| | | |
|---|---|---|
| Due from General Fund | 40,000 | |
| Sales of Water | | 40,000 |

The Water Utility Fund of the Village of Elizabeth made a contribution to the General Fund in consideration for having received police and
fire protection services during the year. The entries to record the resulting expense and revenues, as given in Chapters 3 and 8, are:

### General Fund

| | | |
|---|---|---|
| Due from Water Utility Fund | 30,000 | |
| Revenues | | 30,000 |

### Water Utility Fund

| | | |
|---|---|---|
| Contribution in Lieu of Taxes | 30,000 | |
| Due to General Fund | | 30,000 |

## Reimbursements

If one fund performs services for another fund on an incidental,
rather than recurring basis, administrators and accountants may consider it to result in better disclosure for the fund receiving the services
to reimburse the fund rendering the services for its expenditures rather
than to treat the transaction as a quasi-external transaction. Similarly,
it is not uncommon for an amount to be recorded as an expenditure, or
expense, of one fund which, in fact, should have been recorded as an
expenditure, or expense, of another fund. Errors of this nature usually
result from clerical errors when data are input into the accounting system; at other times there is simply a lack of sufficient information at
time of data input to determine the correct account code. For example,
assume that an invoice for supplies in the amount of $20,500 was ini-
tially charged to the General Fund but later information disclosed that
$3,500 of the supplies were actually for the Library Fund, a special rev-
enue fund. The entries would be (assuming a transfer of cash):

**General Fund**

Cash . . . . . . . . . . . . . . . . . . . . . . . . . . . . 3,500
    Expenditures . . . . . . . . . . . . . . . . . . . . .         3,500

**Library Fund**

Expenditures . . . . . . . . . . . . . . . . . . . . . . . 3,500
    Cash . . . . . . . . . . . . . . . . . . . . . . . . . .         3,500

## Operating Transfers

An example of a transfer of resources which would occur at regular periodic intervals, but which would not result in a true expenditure to the fund raising the revenue or a true revenue to the fund receiving the transfer appears in Chapters 3 and 6. Revenue to be used for debt service activities of the Village of Elizabeth is raised by the General Fund and transferred to the Debt Service Fund. Assume the 19x7 transfer of $168,000 illustrated in Chapter 6 (Entry 7):

**General Fund**

Operating Transfers Out . . . . . . . . . . . . . . . . . 168,000
    Cash . . . . . . . . . . . . . . . . . . . . . . . . . .     168,000

**Debt Service Fund**

Cash . . . . . . . . . . . . . . . . . . . . . . . . . . . 168,000
    Operating Transfers In . . . . . . . . . . . . . . . .     168,000

The transfer illustrated above also has an effect upon the General Long-Term Debt Account Group of the Village of Elizabeth: $120,000 of the $168,000 transferred from the General Fund to the Debt Service Fund is for the payment of principal. As illustrated in Chapter 7 (Entry 2) the entry in the GLTDAG is:

**General Long-Term Debt Account Group**

Amount Available in Debt Service Fund for Payment of
   Regular Serial Bonds . . . . . . . . . . . . . . . . . . . 120,000
    Amount to Be Provided for Payment of Regular Serial
      Bonds . . . . . . . . . . . . . . . . . . . . . . . . .     120,000

Amounts transferred to Debt Service Funds for payment of interest on long-term debt are not recorded in the GLTDAG.

## Equity Transfers

In Chapter 8, the first entry in the illustrative case of the Village of Elizabeth's Supplies Fund reflects the transfer of cash from the General Fund as a contribution of working capital which is not expected to be repaid. This transfer would have to have been authorized by appropriate legal action and therefore is an example of a nonrecurring transfer made in compliance with special statutes or ordinances that does not result in revenues or expenditures to the receiving or disbursing fund. Equity transfers are reported in the Changes in Fund Balance section of governmental fund operating statements and are recorded as follows:

**General Fund**

| | | |
|---|---|---|
| Equity Transfers Out . . . . . . . . . . . . . . . . . . . . | 100,000 | |
| Cash . . . . . . . . . . . . . . . . . . . . . . . . . . . . | | 100,000 |

**Supplies Fund**

| | | |
|---|---|---|
| Cash . . . . . . . . . . . . . . . . . . . . . . . . . . . . | 100,000 | |
| Equity Transfers In . . . . . . . . . . . . . . . . . . . | | 100,000 |

An example similar to the one discussed above is the contribution of equity by a general fund to a utility fund. The return of part or all of such contributions would also be a transfer of the nature comprehended in this category. A further example would be the transfer of residual equity balances of discontinued funds to the General Fund, or to a debt service fund if required by statute.

## Events Requiring Recognition in More than One Accounting Entity

Previous chapters of this book illustrate the impact of transactions on more than one fund, especially the interaction of the capital projects and debt service funds and the two account groups. Two important examples of this type of interfund transactions are (a) the acquisition of general fixed assets and (b) the creation or repayment of general long-term debt.

**Acquisition of general fixed assets**  Preceding discussions of the General Fixed Assets Account Group have emphasized that the group was created to place under accounting control assets acquired through expenditures of the General Fund, special revenue funds, and capital projects funds, none of which accounts for fixed assets. For example, if a motor vehicle is purchased with General Fund resources, the entries would be:

**General Fund**

| | | |
|---|---|---|
| Expenditures . . . . . . . . . . . . . . . . . . . . . . . . . . . | 12,500 | |
| Vouchers Payable . . . . . . . . . . . . . . . . . . . . . . . | | 12,500 |

**General Fixed Assets Account Group**

| | | |
|---|---|---|
| Motor Vehicles (or Equipment) . . . . . . . . . . . . . . . . . | 12,500 | |
| Investment in General Fixed Assets—General Fund | | |
| Revenues . . . . . . . . . . . . . . . . . . . . . . . . . . | | 12,500 |

The acquisition of general fixed assets by use of a capital lease arrangement results in three sets of entries at the inception of the lease: The asset must be recorded in the General Fixed Assets Account Group, the related liability must be recorded in the General Long-Term Debt Account Group, and an expenditure and an Other Financing Source must be recorded in a governmental fund (ordinarily a capital projects fund).

**Creation or repayment of general long-term debt**  One event that must be recorded in a fund and, also, in the General Long-Term Debt Account Group is the issuance of tax-supported bonds or special assessment bonds in order to finance the acquisition of capital facilities. In the Village of Elizabeth case presented in Chapters 4, 6, and 7, the Village sold $1,200,000 of serial bonds at a premium of $12,000. The premium is to be used for the payment of interest on the bonds. The following entries are necessary.

**Capital Projects Fund**

| | | |
|---|---|---|
| Cash | 1,212,000 | |
| Proceeds of Bonds | | 1,200,000 |
| Due to Debt Service Fund | | 12,000 |

**Debt Service Fund**

| | | |
|---|---|---|
| Due from Capital Projects Fund | 12,000 | |
| Revenues | | 12,000 |

**General Long-Term Debt Account Group**

| | | |
|---|---|---|
| Amount to Be Provided for Payment of Regular Serial Bonds | 1,200,000 | |
| 8% Regular Serial Bonds Payable | | 1,200,000 |

Similarly, as amounts are made available to the Debt Service Fund for the payment of principal, the General Long-Term Debt Account Group must record an increase in the "Amount Available in Debt Service Fund for Payment of Regular Serial Bonds" and a corresponding decrease in the "Amount to Be Provided" account. When bonds mature and are to be repaid from resources accumulated in the Debt Service Fund, the liability for the matured bonds is recorded in the Debt Service Fund, and is removed from the GLTDAG. In the Village of Elizabeth example the following entries are made (Entry 8, Chapter 6, and Entry 3, Chapter 7):

**Debt Service Fund**

| | | |
|---|---|---|
| Expenditures | 120,000 | |
| Matured Bonds Payable | | 120,000 |

**General Long-Term Debt Account Group**

| | | |
|---|---|---|
| 8% Regular Serial Bonds Payable | 120,000 | |
| Amount Available in Debt Service Fund for Payment of Regular Serial Bonds | | 120,000 |

General long-term debt arising from a capital lease arrangement is recorded at the inception of the lease. The payment of rentals during the term of the lease requires entries in a governmental fund (ordinarily a debt service fund) for both the portion of the lease rental regarded as interest and the portion of the lease rental regarded as partial payment of the capital lease obligation. Only the latter is recorded in the General Long-Term Debt Account Group.

## THE GOVERNMENTAL REPORTING ENTITY

General purpose governments such as states, counties, and large cities typically are complex organizations that include semiautonomous boards, commissions, and agencies created to accomplish projects or activities that for one reason or another (generally restrictive clauses in state constitutions or statutes) may not be carried out by a government as originally constituted. Until recently separate annual reports were issued for each legal entity. The entity was usually consistent with governments as defined by the U.S. Bureau of the Census, which takes a census of governments every five years.

Currently effective GASB pronouncements, however, require state and local governments to follow the standards set forth in GASB Codification Sec. 2100, *Defining the Reporting Entity,* and in Sec. 2600, *Reporting Entity and Component Unit Presentation and Disclosure,* as well as all other financial reporting standards relating to the presentation of the general purpose financial statements (GPFS) and the comprehensive annual financial report (CAFR). Underlying GASB standards are the assumptions that all functions of government are responsible to elected officials at the federal, state, or local level, and that the financial activities and condition of each governmental function should be reported at the lowest level of legislative authority consistent with the criteria set forth in the Codification.

For the purposes of this section the following definitions are useful:

**Reporting Entity**—The oversight unit and all related component units, if any, combined in accordance with GASB Codification Sec. 2100 to constitute the governmental reporting entity.

**Oversight Unit**—The component unit that has the ability to exercise the basic criterion of oversight responsibility, as defined in GASB Codification Sec. 2100, over other component units. Typically, an oversight unit is the primary unit of government directly responsible to the chief executive and the elected legislative body.

**Component Unit**—A separate governmental unit, agency, or nonprofit corporation that, pursuant to the criteria in Codification Sec. 2100, is combined with other component units and the oversight unit to constitute the reporting entity.

The basic criterion for determining that one governmental body is dependent upon another and should be included in the latter's general purpose financial statements is **the exercise of oversight responsibility** over such agencies by the governmental unit's elected officials. In addition to oversight responsibility, two other criteria are considered in the inclusion/exclusion decision: **scope of public service** and **special financing relationships.** Each of these criteria is discussed below.

**Oversight responsibility**   Responsibility on the part of elected officials of one governmental unit for oversight over an agency, authority, board, commission, and so on, may be explicit in legislation establishing either the oversight unit or the (potential) component unit. If not, oversight responsibility may be deduced from the existence of such factors as financial interdependency; appointment of the person or persons who possess final decision-making authority for the component unit; designation of the managers of the component unit; the ability to influence operations of the component unit to a significant extent; and accountability for fiscal matters. The foregoing list should not be considered as all-inclusive; other relationships may exist that would persuade report preparers and auditors that one entity is, in fact, dependent on another and should be included in the reporting entity's GPFS and CAFR. The application of professional judgment is of greatest importance in the inclusion/exclusion decision.

**Scope of public service**   If application of the basic criterion of oversight responsibility indicates that there is partial oversight, but does not lead to a clear-cut decision as to whether a certain governmental organization is a component unit of a reporting entity, two additional aspects should be considered:

a. Whether the activity is for the benefit of the reporting entity and/or its residents.
b. Whether the activity is conducted within the geographic boundaries of the reporting entity and is generally available to the citizens of that entity.

**Special financing relationships**   Special financing relationships may exist that are so significant that exclusion of an organization from the reporting entity's statements would be misleading. Examples of such special financing relationships are: serving as a financing conduit, or serving as a device for asset ownership. Mere provision of support services such as tax billing and collection and maintenance of accounting records by one entity for another is **not** evidence of a "special financing relationship" which would indicate that one entity is a component unit of the other.

## FINANCIAL REPORTING

Chapter 1 contains a summary of the content of the CAFR of a state or local governmental reporting entity. This section discusses interim financial reporting and provides more extensive discussion of standards

established for CAFR presentation and disclosures, including illustrations of the five basic statements (GPFS) required for conformity with
GAAP.

## Interim Financial Reports

Interim financial reports are useful for administrators, legislators,
news media, and interested residents of a governmental unit. A complete
interim financial report should include at least the following statements
and schedules:

1. Statement of Actual and Estimated Revenue (for each fund for which
   revenue budgets are prepared).
2. Statement of Actual Expenditures and Outstanding Encumbrances
   and Appropriations (for each fund for which appropriations budgets
   are prepared).
3. Comparative Statement of Revenue and Expense (for each enterprise,
   internal service fund, nonexpendable trust funds, and PERS).
4. Combined Statement of Cash Receipts, Disbursements, and Balances—All Funds.
5. Forecast of Cash Position—All Funds.

## Comprehensive Annual Financial Report

A CAFR should be prepared by each state and local governmental
reporting entity as a matter of public record. In addition to the GPFS,
a CAFR should contain introductory material, combining and individual
fund financial statements, schedules necessary to demonstrate legal
compliance, and statistical tables.

The **introductory section** includes the title page, a table of contents,
an organization chart, the letter of transmittal, and other material
deemed appropriate by management. The letter of transmittal may be a
letter from the chief finance officer addressed to the chief executive officer and governing body of the governmental unit, or it may be a narrative over the signature of the chief executive. Contents might include
a discussion of the accounting system and budgetary control, the reporting entity and its services, a comparative summary of revenues and
expenditures, debt administration, cash management, a disclosure of the
independent audit, prospects for the future, and acknowledgments to
staff. Note that the introductory material is not covered by the auditor's
report, but care should be taken to ensure its accuracy.

The **financial section** of the CAFR includes the (1) auditor's report,
(2) General Purpose Financial Statements, and (3) combining and individual fund and account group statements and schedules.

Governmental auditing is discussed in the final section of this chapter. Briefly, the federal Single Audit Act of 1984 and related federal cir-
culars establish auditing requirements for state and local governments

and other organizations which receive specified amounts of federal financial assistance. State laws, however, establish requirements which are effective within the state. State laws vary markedly. In some, all state agencies and all governmental units created pursuant to state law are required to be audited by an audit agency of the state government. In others, local governmental units are audited by independent certified public accountants. In still others, some governmental units are audited by the state audit agency and some by independent certified public accountants. In any event, the auditor's report should accompany the financial statements reproduced in the CAFR. The American Institute of CPAs establishes auditing standards and suggests the wording of auditor's reports which should be presented in certain cases discussed in the final section of this chapter.

## General Purpose Financial Statements

The GPFS, shown as Illustrations 10–1 through 10–5, are a required part of the CAFR. In addition, the GPFS may be issued separately for widespread distribution to users requiring less detailed information than is contained in the complete CAFR. The required statements for the GPFS are:

1. Combined Balance Sheet—All Fund Types and Account Groups. (Illustration 10–1.)
2. Combined Statement of Revenues, Expenditures, and Changes in Fund Balances—All Governmental Fund Types and Expendable Trust Funds. (Illustration 10–2.)
3. Combined Statement of Revenues, Expenditures, and Changes in Fund Balances—Budget and Actual—General and Special Revenue Fund Types. (Illustration 10–3.)
4. Combined Statement of Revenues, Expenses, and Changes in Retained Earnings/Fund Balances—All Proprietary Fund Types and Similar Trust Funds. (Illustration 10–4.)
5. Combined Statement of Changes in Financial Position—All Proprietary Fund Types and Similar Trust Funds. (Illustration 10–5.)[1]

Notes to the Financial Statements are considered to be an integral part of the GPFS and **must accompany** the five Combined Statements listed above. Additionally, entities with pension activities must include supplementary information specified in GASB standards.

It is important for the reader to understand that the term *GPFS* properly refers to the governmental *reporting entity*—the oversight unit and all component units. Separately issued financial statements of a component unit are referred to as CUFS (component unit financial state-

---

[1]For years beginning after December 15, 1989, this statement will be replaced by a Combined Statement of Cash Flows.

**ILLUSTRATION 10–1**

## NAME OF GOVERNMENTAL UNIT
## Combined Balance Sheet—All Fund Types and Account Groups
### December 31, 19X2

| | Governmental Fund Types | | | | Proprietary Fund Types | | Fiduciary Fund Types | Account Groups | | Totals (Memorandum Only) | |
| --- | --- | --- | --- | --- | --- | --- | --- | --- | --- | --- | --- |
| ASSETS | General | Special Revenue | Debt Service | Capital Projects | Enterprise | Internal Service | Trust and Agency | General Fixed Assets | General Long-Term Debt | December 31, 19X2 | December 31, 19X1 |
| Cash | $258,500 | $101,385 | $185,624 | $ 659,100 | $ 257,036 | $ 29,700 | $ 216,701 | $ — | $ — | $ 1,708,046 | $ 1,300,944 |
| Cash with fiscal agent | | | 102,000 | | | | | | | 102,000 | — |
| Investments, at cost or amortized cost | 65,000 | 37,200 | 160,990 | | | | 1,239,260 | | | 1,502,450 | 1,974,354 |
| Receivables (net of allowances for uncollectibles): | | | | | | | | | | | |
| Taxes | 58,300 | 2,500 | 3,829 | | | | 580,000 | | | 644,629 | 255,400 |
| Accounts | 8,300 | 3,300 | | 100 | 29,130 | | | | | 40,830 | 32,600 |
| Special assessments | | | 458,930 | | | | | | | 458,930 | 420,000 |
| Notes | | | | | 2,350 | | | | | 2,350 | 1,250 |
| Loans | | | | | | | 35,000 | | | 35,000 | 40,000 |
| Accrued interest | 50 | 25 | 1,907 | | 650 | | 2,666 | | | 5,298 | 3,340 |
| Due from other funds | 2,000 | | | | 2,000 | 12,000 | 11,189 | | | 27,189 | 17,499 |
| Due from other governments | 30,000 | 75,260 | | 640,000 | | | | | | 745,260 | 101,400 |
| Advances to internal service funds | 65,000 | | | | | | | | | 65,000 | 75,000 |

| | | | | | | | | | | | |
|---|---|---|---|---|---|---|---|---|---|---|---|
| Inventory of supplies, at cost | 7,200 | 5,190 | — | — | 23,030 | 40,000 | — | — | — | 75,420 | 70,900 |
| Prepaid expenses | — | — | — | — | 200 | — | — | — | — | 1,200 | 900 |
| Restricted assets: | | | | | | | | | | | |
| Cash | — | — | — | — | 113,559 | — | — | — | — | 113,559 | 272,968 |
| Investments, at cost or amortized cost | — | — | — | — | 176,800 | — | — | — | — | 176,800 | 143,800 |
| Land | — | — | — | — | 211,100 | 20,000 | — | 1,259,500 | — | 1,490,600 | 1,456,100 |
| Buildings | — | — | — | — | 447,700 | 60,000 | — | 2,855,500 | — | 3,363,200 | 2,836,700 |
| Accumulated depreciation | — | — | — | — | (90,718) | (4,500) | — | — | — | (95,218) | (83,500) |
| Improvements other than buildings | — | — | — | — | 3,887,901 | 15,000 | — | 1,036,750 | — | 4,939,651 | 3,922,200 |
| Accumulated depreciation | — | — | — | — | (348,944) | (3,000) | — | — | — | (351,944) | (283,750) |
| Machinery and equipment | — | — | — | — | 1,841,145 | 25,000 | — | 452,500 | — | 2,318,645 | 1,924,100 |
| Accumulated depreciation | — | — | — | — | (201,138) | (9,400) | — | — | — | (210,538) | (141,900) |
| Construction in progress | — | — | — | — | 22,713 | — | — | 1,722,250 | — | 1,744,963 | 1,359,606 |
| Amount available in debt service funds | — | — | — | — | — | — | — | — | 256,280 | 256,280 | 284,813 |
| Amount to be provided for retirement of general long-term debt | — | — | — | — | — | — | — | — | 1,939,790 | 1,939,790 | 1,075,187 |
| Amount to be provided from special assessments | — | — | — | — | — | — | — | — | 458,930 | 458,930 | 420,000 |
| Total Assets | $494,350 | $224,860 | $913,280 | $1,299,200 | $6,375,514 | $184,800 | $2,084,816 | $7,326,500 | $2,655,000 | $21,558,320 | $17,479,911 |

## ILLUSTRATION 10–1 (concluded)

| LIABILITIES AND FUND EQUITY | Governmental Fund Types — General | Special Revenue | Debt Service | Capital Projects | Proprietary Fund Types — Enterprise | Internal Service | Fiduciary Fund Types — Trust and Agency | Account Groups — General Fixed Assets | General Long-Term Debt | Totals (Memorandum Only) — December 31, 19X2 | December 31, 19X1 |
|---|---|---|---|---|---|---|---|---|---|---|---|
| **Liabilities:** | | | | | | | | | | | |
| Vouchers payable | $118,261 | $33,850 | $ — | $ 49,600 | $131,071 | $15,000 | $ 3,350 | $ — | $ — | $ 351,132 | $ 223,412 |
| Contracts payable | 57,600 | 18,300 | — | 119,000 | 8,347 | — | — | — | — | 203,247 | 1,326,511 |
| Judgments payable | — | 2,000 | — | 33,800 | — | — | — | — | — | 35,800 | 32,400 |
| Accrued liabilities | — | — | — | 10,700 | 16,870 | — | 4,700 | — | — | 32,270 | 27,417 |
| Payable from restricted assets: | | | | | | | | | | | |
|   Construction contracts | — | — | — | — | 17,760 | — | — | — | — | 17,760 | — |
|   Fiscal agent | — | — | — | — | 139 | — | — | — | — | 139 | — |
|   Accrued interest | — | — | — | — | 32,305 | — | — | — | — | 32,305 | 67,150 |
|   Revenue bonds | — | — | — | — | 48,000 | — | — | — | — | 48,000 | 52,000 |
|   Deposits | — | — | — | — | 63,000 | — | — | — | — | 63,000 | 55,000 |
| Due to other taxing units | — | — | — | — | — | — | 680,800 | — | — | 680,800 | 200,000 |
| Due to other funds | 24,189 | 2,000 | — | 1,000 | — | — | — | — | — | 27,189 | 17,499 |
| Due to student groups | — | — | — | — | — | — | 1,850 | — | — | 1,850 | 1,600 |
| Deferred revenue | 15,000 | — | 555,000 | — | — | — | — | — | — | 570,000 | 423,000 |
| Advance from general fund | — | — | — | — | — | 65,000 | — | — | — | 65,000 | 75,000 |
| Matured bonds payable | — | — | 100,000 | — | — | — | — | — | — | 100,000 | — |
| Matured interest payable | — | — | 2,000 | — | — | — | — | — | — | 2,000 | — |
| General obligation bonds payable | — | — | — | — | 700,000 | — | — | — | 2,100,000 | 2,800,000 | 2,110,000 |
| Special assessment debt with governmental commitment | — | — | — | — | — | — | — | — | 555,000 | 555,000 | 420,000 |
| Revenue bonds payable | — | — | — | — | 1,798,000 | — | — | — | — | 1,798,000 | 1,846,000 |
| Total Liabilities | 215,050 | 56,150 | 657,000 | 214,100 | 2,815,492 | 80,000 | 690,700 | — | 2,655,000 | 7,383,492 | 6,876,989 |

| | | | | | | | | | | | |
|---|---|---|---|---|---|---|---|---|---|---|---|
| **Fund Equity:** | | | | | | | | | | | |
| Contributed capital | — | — | — | — | 1,392,666 | 95,000 | — | — | — | 1,487,666 | 815,000 |
| Investment in general fixed assets | — | — | — | — | — | — | — | 7,326,500 | — | 7,326,500 | 5,299,600 |
| Retained earnings: | | | | | | | | | | | |
|   Reserved for revenue bond retirement | — | — | — | — | 129,155 | — | — | — | — | 129,155 | 96,975 |
|   Unreserved | — | — | — | — | 2,038,201 | 9,800 | — | — | — | 2,048,001 | 1,998,119 |
| **Fund Balances:** | | | | | | | | | | | |
|   Reserved for encumbrances | 38,000 | 46,500 | — | 1,076,500 | — | — | — | — | — | 1,161,000 | 410,050 |
|   Reserved for inventory of supplies | 7,200 | 5,190 | — | — | — | — | — | — | — | 12,390 | 10,890 |
|   Reserved for advance to internal service funds | 65,000 | — | — | — | — | — | — | — | — | 65,000 | 75,000 |
|   Reserved for loans | — | — | — | — | — | — | 50,050 | — | — | 50,050 | 45,100 |
|   Reserved for endowments | — | — | — | — | — | — | 134,000 | — | — | 134,000 | 94,000 |
|   Reserved for employees' retirement system | — | — | — | — | — | — | 1,426,201 | — | — | 1,426,201 | 1,276,150 |
|   Unreserved: | | | | | | | | | | | |
|     Designated for debt service | — | — | 256,280 | — | — | — | — | — | — | 256,280 | 325,888 |
|     Designated for subsequent years' expenditures | 50,000 | — | — | — | — | — | — | — | — | 50,000 | 50,000 |
|     Undesignated | 119,100 | 117,020 | — | 8,600 | — | — | (216,135) | — | — | 28,585 | 106,150 |
| Total Fund Equity | 279,300 | 168,710 | 256,280 | 1,085,100 | 3,560,022 | 104,800 | 1,394,116 | 7,326,500 | — | 14,174,828 | 10,602,922 |
| Total Liabilities and Fund Equity | $494,350 | $224,860 | $913,280 | $1,299,200 | $6,375,514 | $184,800 | $2,084,816 | $7,326,500 | $2,655,000 | $21,558,320 | $17,479,911 |

The notes to the financial statements are an integral part of this statement.
Source: GASB Codification Sec. 2200.503.

# ILLUSTRATION 10–2

## NAME OF GOVERNMENTAL UNIT
### Combined Statement of Revenues, Expenditures, and Changes in Fund Balances—
### All Governmental Fund Types and Expendable Trust Funds
### For the Fiscal Year Ended December 31, 19X2

| | Governmental Fund Types | | | | Fiduciary Fund Type | Totals (Memorandum Only) Year Ended | |
|---|---|---|---|---|---|---|---|
| | General | Special Revenue | Debt Service | Capital Projects | Expendable Trust | December 31, 19X2 | December 31, 19X1 |
| **Revenues:** | | | | | | | |
| Taxes | $ 881,300 | $ 189,300 | $ 79,177 | $ — | $ — | $1,149,777 | $1,137,900 |
| Special assessments | | — | 55,500 | — | — | 55,500 | 250,400 |
| Licenses and permits | 103,000 | | — | — | — | 103,000 | 96,500 |
| Intergovernmental revenues | 186,500 | 831,100 | 41,500 | 1,250,000 | — | 2,309,100 | 1,258,800 |
| Charges for services | 91,000 | 79,100 | — | — | — | 170,100 | 160,400 |
| Fines and forfeits | 33,200 | | — | — | — | 33,200 | 26,300 |
| Miscellaneous revenues | 19,500 | 71,625 | 36,235 | 3,750 | 200 | 131,310 | 111,500 |
| Total Revenues | 1,314,500 | 1,171,125 | 212,412 | 1,253,750 | 200 | 3,951,987 | 3,041,800 |
| **Expenditures:** | | | | | | | |
| Current: | | | | | | | |
| General government | 121,805 | | — | — | — | 121,805 | 134,200 |
| Public safety | 258,395 | 480,000 | — | — | — | 738,395 | 671,300 |
| Highways and streets | 85,400 | 417,000 | — | — | — | 502,400 | 408,700 |
| Sanitation | 56,250 | | — | — | — | 56,250 | 44,100 |
| Health | 44,500 | | — | — | — | 44,500 | 36,600 |
| Welfare | 46,800 | | — | — | — | 46,800 | 41,400 |
| Culture and recreation | 40,900 | 256,450 | — | — | — | 297,350 | 286,400 |
| Education | 509,150 | | — | — | 2,420 | 511,570 | 512,000 |
| Capital outlay | | | — | 1,939,100 | — | 1,939,100 | 803,000 |
| Debt service: | | | | | | | |
| Principal retirement | | — | 115,500 | — | — | 115,500 | 52,100 |
| Interest and fiscal charges | | — | 68,420 | — | — | 68,420 | 50,000 |
| Total Expenditures | 1,163,200 | 1,153,450 | 183,920 | 1,939,100 | 2,420 | 4,442,090 | 3,039,800 |

| | | | | | | |
|---|---:|---:|---:|---:|---:|---:|
| Excess of Revenues over (under) Expenditures | 151,300 | 17,675 | 28,492 | (685,350) | (2,220) | (490,103) | 2,000 |
| Other Financing Sources (Uses): | | | | | | | |
| Proceeds of general obligation bonds | — | — | — | 900,000 | — | 900,000 | — |
| Proceeds of special assessment debt | — | — | — | 190,500 | — | 190,500 | — |
| Operating transfers in | — | — | — | 74,500 | 2,530 | 77,030 | 89,120 |
| Operating transfers out | (74,500) | — | — | — | — | (74,500) | (87,000) |
| Total Other Financing Sources (Uses) | (74,500) | — | — | 1,165,000 | 2,530 | 1,093,030 | 2,120 |
| Excess of Revenues and Other Sources over (under) Expenditures and Other Uses | 76,800 | 17,675 | 28,492 | 479,650 | 310 | 602,927 | 4,120 |
| Fund Balances—January 1 | 202,500 | 151,035 | 227,788 | 605,450 | 26,555 | 1,213,328 | 1,209,208 |
| Fund Balances—December 31 | $ 279,300 | $ 168,710 | $ 256,280 | $1,085,100 | $26,865 | $1,816,255 | $1,213,328 |

The notes to the financial statements are an integral part of this statement.
Source: GASB Codification Sec. 2200.604.

ILLUSTRATION 10–3

**NAME OF GOVERNMENTAL UNIT**
**Combined Statement of Revenues, Expenditures, and Changes in Fund Balances—**
**Budget and Actual—General and Special Revenue Fund Types**
**For the Fiscal Year Ended December 31, 19X2**

| | General Fund | | | Special Revenue Funds | | | Totals (Memorandum Only) | | |
|---|---|---|---|---|---|---|---|---|---|
| | Budget | Actual | Variance— Favorable (Unfavorable) | Budget | Actual | Variance— Favorable (Unfavorable) | Budget | Actual | Variance— Favorable (Unfavorable) |
| **Revenues:** | | | | | | | | | |
| Taxes | $ 882,500 | $ 881,300 | $ (1,200) | $ 189,500 | $ 189,300 | $ (200) | $1,072,000 | $1,070,600 | $ (1,400) |
| Licenses and permits | 125,500 | 103,000 | (22,500) | — | — | — | 125,500 | 103,000 | (22,500) |
| Intergovernmental revenues | 200,000 | 186,500 | (13,500) | 837,600 | 831,100 | (6,500) | 1,037,600 | 1,017,600 | (20,000) |
| Charges for services | 90,000 | 91,000 | 1,000 | 78,000 | 79,100 | 1,100 | 168,000 | 170,100 | 2,100 |
| Fines and forfeits | 32,500 | 33,200 | 700 | — | — | — | 32,500 | 33,200 | 700 |
| Miscellaneous revenues | 19,500 | 19,500 | — | 81,475 | 71,625 | (9,850) | 100,975 | 91,125 | (9,850) |
| Total Revenues | 1,350,000 | 1,314,500 | (35,500) | 1,186,575 | 1,171,125 | (15,450) | 2,536,575 | 2,485,625 | (50,950) |
| **Expenditures:** | | | | | | | | | |
| **Current:** | | | | | | | | | |
| General government | 129,000 | 121,805 | 7,195 | | | | 129,000 | 121,805 | 7,195 |
| Public safety | 277,300 | 258,395 | 18,905 | 494,500 | 480,000 | 14,500 | 771,800 | 738,395 | 33,405 |
| Highways and streets | 84,500 | 85,400 | (900) | 436,000 | 417,000 | 19,000 | 520,500 | 502,400 | 18,100 |
| Sanitation | 50,000 | 56,250 | (6,250) | | | | 50,000 | 56,250 | (6,250) |
| Health | 47,750 | 44,500 | 3,250 | | | | 47,750 | 44,500 | 3,250 |
| Welfare | 51,000 | 46,800 | 4,200 | | | | 51,000 | 46,800 | 4,200 |
| Culture and recreation | 44,500 | 40,900 | 3,600 | 272,000 | 256,450 | 15,550 | 316,500 | 297,350 | 19,150 |
| Education | 541,450 | 509,150 | 32,300 | | | | 541,450 | 509,150 | 32,300 |
| Total Expenditures | 1,225,500 | 1,163,200 | 62,300 | 1,202,500 | 1,153,450 | 49,050 | 2,428,000 | 2,316,650 | 111,350 |
| Excess of Revenues over (under) Expenditures | 124,500 | 151,300 | 26,800 | (15,925) | 17,675 | 33,600 | 108,575 | 168,975 | 60,400 |
| **Other Financing Sources (Uses):** | | | | | | | | | |
| Operating transfers out | (74,500) | (74,500) | — | — | — | — | (74,500) | (74,500) | — |
| Excess of Revenues over (under) Expenditures and Other Uses | 50,000 | 76,800 | 26,800 | (15,925) | 17,675 | 33,600 | 34,075 | 94,475 | 60,400 |
| Fund Balances—January 1 | 202,500 | 202,500 | — | 151,035 | 151,035 | — | 353,535 | 353,535 | — |
| Fund Balances—December 31 | $ 252,500 | $ 279,300 | $26,800 | $ 135,110 | $ 168,710 | $33,600 | $ 387,610 | $ 448,010 | $ 60,400 |

The notes to the financial statements are an integral part of this statement.
Source: GASB Codification Sec. 2200.605.

ILLUSTRATION 10–4

# NAME OF GOVERNMENTAL UNIT
## Combined Statement of Revenues, Expenses, and Changes in Retained Earnings/Fund Balances—All Proprietary Fund Types and Similar Trust Funds
### For the Fiscal Year Ended December 31, 19X2

| | Proprietary Fund Types | | Fiduciary Fund Types | | Totals (Memorandum Only) Year Ended | |
|---|---|---|---|---|---|---|
| | Enterprise | Internal Service | Nonexpendable Trust | Pension Trust | December 31, 19X2 | December 31, 19X1 |
| Operating Revenues: | | | | | | |
| Charges for services | $ 672,150 | $88,000 | $ — | $ — | $ 760,150 | $ 686,563 |
| Interest | — | — | 2,480 | 28,460 | 30,940 | 26,118 |
| Contributions | — | — | — | 160,636 | 160,686 | 144,670 |
| Gifts | — | — | 45,000 | — | 45,000 | |
| Total Operating Revenues | 672,150 | 88,000 | 47,480 | 189,146 | 996,776 | 857,351 |
| Operating expenses: | | | | | | |
| Personal services | 247,450 | 32,500 | — | — | 279,950 | 250,418 |
| Contractual services | 75,330 | 400 | — | — | 75,730 | 68,214 |
| Supplies | 20,310 | 1,900 | — | — | 22,210 | 17,329 |
| Materials | 50,940 | 44,000 | — | — | 94,940 | 87,644 |
| Heat, light, and power | 26,050 | 1,500 | — | — | 27,550 | 22,975 |
| Depreciation | 144,100 | 4,450 | — | — | 148,550 | 133,210 |
| Benefit payments | — | — | — | 21,000 | 21,000 | 12,000 |
| Refunds | — | — | — | 25,745 | 25,745 | 13,243 |
| Total Operating Expenses | 564,180 | 84,750 | — | 46,745 | 695,675 | 605,033 |
| Operating Income | 107,970 | 3,250 | 47,480 | 142,401 | 301,101 | 252,318 |
| Nonoperating Revenues (Expenses): | | | | | | |
| Operating grants | 55,000 | — | — | — | 55,000 | 50,000 |
| Interest revenue | 3,830 | — | — | — | 3,830 | 3,200 |
| Rent | 5,000 | — | — | — | 5,000 | 5,000 |
| Interest expense and fiscal charges | (92,988) | — | — | — | (92,988) | (102,408) |
| Total Nonoperating Revenues (Expenses) | (29,158) | — | — | — | (29,158) | (44,208) |
| Income before Operating Transfers | 78,812 | 3,250 | 47,480 | 142,401 | 271,943 | 208,110 |
| Operating Transfers In (Out) | — | — | (2,530) | — | (2,530) | (2,120) |
| Net Income | 78,812 | 3,250 | 44,950 | 142,401 | 269,413 | 205,990 |
| Retained Earnings/Fund Balances—January 1 | 2,088,544 | 6,550 | 139,100 | 1,040,800 | 3,274,994 | 3,069,004 |
| Retained Earnings/Fund Balances—December 31 | $2,167,356 | $ 9,800 | $184,050 | $1,183,201 | $3,544,407 | $3,274,994 |

The notes to the financial statements are an integral part of this statement.
Source: GASB Codification Sec. 2200.506.

ILLUSTRATION 10–5

## NAME OF GOVERNMENTAL UNIT
### Combined Statement of Changes in Financial Position—
### All Proprietary Fund Types and Similar Trust Funds
### For the Fiscal Year Ended December 31, 19X2*

| | Proprietary Fund Types | | Fiduciary Fund Types | | Totals (Memorandum Only) Year Ended | |
| --- | --- | --- | --- | --- | --- | --- |
| | Enterprise | Internal Service | Nonexpendable Trust | Pension Trust | December 31, 19X2 | December 31, 19X1 |
| Sources of Working Capital: | | | | | | |
| Operations: | | | | | | |
| Net income | $ 78,812 | $ 3,250 | $44,950 | $142,401 | $ 269,413 | $ 205,990 |
| Items not requiring (providing) working capital: | | | | | | |
| Depreciation | 144,100 | 4,450 | — | — | 148,550 | 133,210 |
| Working Capital Provided by Operations | 222,912 | 7,700 | 44,950 | 142,401 | 417,963 | 339,200 |
| Cash from revenue bond construction account | 127,883 | — | — | — | 127,883 | 743,800 |
| Contributions | 672,666 | — | — | — | 672,666 | — |
| Total Sources of Working Capital | 1,023,461 | 7,700 | 44,950 | 142,401 | 1,218,512 | 1,083,000 |
| Uses of Working Capital: | | | | | | |
| Acquisition of property, plant, and equipment | 324,453 | 7,000 | — | — | 331,453 | 842,812 |
| Retirement of general obligation bonds | 50,000 | — | — | — | 50,000 | 50,000 |
| Retirement of revenue bonds payable | 52,000 | — | — | — | 52,000 | 48,000 |
| Repayment of advance from general fund | — | 10,000 | — | — | 10,000 | 10,000 |

| | | | | | | |
|---|---:|---:|---:|---:|---:|---:|
| Net decrease in other current liabilities payable from restricted assets | 8,946 | — | — | — | 8,946 | 4,318 |
| Net increase in other restricted assets | 1,624 | — | — | — | 1,624 | 414 |
| Total Uses of Working Capital | 437,023 | 17,000 | — | — | 454,023 | 955,544 |
| Net Increase (Decrease) in Working Capital | $ 586,438 | $ (9,300) | $44,950 | $142,401 | $ 764,489 | $ 127,456 |
| **Elements of Net Increase (Decrease) in Working Capital:** | | | | | | |
| Cash | $ 119,276 | $(20,300) | $ 4,310 | $ 20,121 | $ 123,407 | $ 796,412 |
| Investments | — | — | 45,640 | 118,341 | 163,981 | (84,286) |
| Receivables (net of allowances for uncollectibles) | (5,570) | — | (5,000) | — | (10,570) | 2,396 |
| Due from other funds | (6,000) | (8,000) | — | 2,189 | (11,811) | (4,923) |
| Inventory of supplies | 11,250 | 14,000 | — | — | 25,250 | (3,414) |
| Prepaid expenses | 460 | — | — | — | 460 | 520 |
| Vouchers payable | (72,471) | 5,000 | — | — | (67,471) | (42,427) |
| Contracts payable | 551,653 | — | — | 1,750 | 553,403 | (525,400) |
| Accrued liabilities | (12,160) | — | — | — | (12,160) | (11,422) |
| Net Increase (Decrease) in Working Capital | $ 586,438 | $ (9,300) | $44,950 | $142,401 | $ 764,489 | $ 127,456 |

The notes to the financial statements are an integral part of this statement.

*Note: For years beginning after December 15, 1989, a Combined Statement of Cash Flows will be required in place of this statement. Pension trust fund cash flows will not be reported.

Source: GASB Codification Sec. 2200.607.

ments). Similarly, a CAFR is the comprehensive annual financial report of a governmental reporting entity; the annual report of a component unit is a CUFR—component unit financial report. In the GPFS only the General Fund of the oversight unit is reported as the General Fund of the reporting entity. The General Funds of component units are considered to be **special revenue funds** of the reporting entity and are combined with all special revenue funds of the oversight unit and all special revenue funds of all component units for presentation in the Special Revenue Funds column of the GPFS. All other fund types and account groups of component units are combined with the related fund type or account group of the oversight unit for presentation in the GPFS.

In those instances in which a component unit has adopted accounting principles that are not in conformity with governmental accounting and reporting standards but which are considered to be generally accepted for the type of organization represented by the component unit (for example, a college or university which conforms with standards discussed in Chapter 11), financial data for that component unit may be presented in a separate column in the GPFS as a **discrete presentation.** The accompanying notes to the financial statements should clearly disclose the accounting policies of the component unit and the relationship of the component unit to the oversight unit. The GASB Codification Sec. 2600 provides that a **discrete presentation** should also be used if inclusion of financial data for a component unit would distort a fund type of the reporting entity.

## Combining Statements

The five statements shown as Illustrations 10–1 through 10–5 are all *combined* statements. In order to support each fund-type column in the combined statements, *combining* statements are necessary if more than one fund exists of a given fund type. For example, if a governmental unit had five special revenue funds, it would be necessary to include in the CAFR a Combining Balance Sheet; a Combining Statement of Revenues, Expenditures, and Changes in Fund Balances; and a Combining Statement of Revenues, Expenditures, and Changes in Fund Balances— Budget and Actual for the special revenue funds. An example of a combining balance sheet for debt service funds is presented as Illustration 6–3.

## Individual Fund and Account Groups Statements

Individual fund statements should be included in a CAFR if the reporting entity has only one fund of a given type (always true of the General Fund), and when detail to assure disclosure sufficient to meet

GASB standards is not presented in the combining statements. Individual fund statements are also used to present budgetary data and prior year comparative data.

## Statistical Tables

Statistical tables must be presented in each CAFR. This section, which is normally not audited, includes information said to be desired by creditors, potential creditors, and others interested in the financial affairs of a governmental reporting entity. Statistical tables specified in GASB standards include:

a. General Governmental Expenditures by Function—Last 10 Fiscal Years

b. General Revenues by Source—Last 10 Fiscal Years

c. Property Tax Levies and Collections—Last 10 Fiscal Years

d. Assessed and Estimated Actual Value of Taxable Property—Last 10 Fiscal Years

e. Property Tax Rates—All Overlapping Governments—Last 10 Fiscal Years

f. Special Assessment Billings and Collections—Last 10 Fiscal Years (if the government is obligated in some manner for related special assessment debt)

g. Ratio of Net General Bonded Debt to Assessed Value and Net Bonded Debt per Capita—Last 10 Fiscal Years

h. Computation of Legal Debt Margin, if not presented in the General Purpose Financial Statements (GPFS)

i. Computation of Overlapping Debt (if not presented in the GPFS)

j. Ratio of Annual Debt Service for General Bonded Debt to Total General Expenditures—Last 10 Fiscal Years

k. Revenue Bond Coverage—Last 10 Fiscal Years

l. Demographic Statistics

m. Property Value, Construction, and Bank Deposits—Last 10 Fiscal Years

n. Principal Taxpayers

o. Miscellaneous Statistics

## AUDITS OF STATE AND LOCAL GOVERNMENTS

Federal financial assistance has been an important source of financing operations and capital expenditures of state and local governments for over 40 years. Federal grants-in-aid, and federal contracts, have been subject to accounting, reporting, and auditing requirements which varied depending on which agency of the federal government administered the grant program, or contract. Efforts were made during the 1960s and 1970s to standardize requirements, but with only moderate success. In order to provide statutory authority for uniform requirements for audits of organizations receiving federal financial assistance, the Single Audit Act of 1984 was enacted. The Office of Management and Budget, a part of the Executive Office of the President, issued Circular A–128 as guidance for federal agencies to comply with the provisions of the Single Audit Act. States and large local governments are assigned a "cognizant agency" of the federal government, which has authority to represent the government in all matters relating to the audit. Smaller local governments are under the oversight of the agency that provides them the most federal funds. Guidance for independent CPAs who have need to know requirements of the Single Audit Act, and other federal audit requirements, is incorporated in the revised edition of the AICPA's accounting and audit guide, *Audits of State and Local Governmental Units*. Additional guidance is provided to independent auditors in *Statement on Auditing Standards No. 63: Compliance Auditing Applicable to Governmental Entities and Other Recipients of Governmental Financial Assistance* (New York: AICPA, 1989).

The Single Audit Act provides that each state and local government that receives a total amount of federal financial assistance equal to or in excess of $100,000 in any fiscal year shall have a financial and compliance audit of its entire operations for that fiscal year made by an independent auditor in accordance with generally accepted government auditing standards. A state or local government receiving federal assistance equal to or in excess of $25,000, but less than $100,000, has the option of having a single audit or complying with any applicable requirements concerning financial or financial and compliance audits contained in the federal statutes and regulations under which financial assistance is provided to that government. Recipients receiving less than $25,000 are exempt from federal audit requirements, but must maintain records concerning federal financial assistance and permit grantor federal agencies and the U.S. Comptroller General access to the records.

Single audits may be performed by state or local government auditors or by public accountants who meet the independence standards specified in the statement of GAGAS promulgated by the U.S. Comptroller General. GAGAS (generally accepted **government** auditing standards), evolved from GAAS (generally accepted auditing standards) established by the American Institute of CPAs for the guidance of independent CPAs engaged to express their professional opinion on the fairness of presentation of clients' financial statements and the conformity of those statements "with generally accepted accounting principles." Audits conducted with the purpose of expressing such an opinion are referred to in AICPA pronouncements as **financial** audits. Even in financial audits of businesses, auditors must be aware of statutes and regulations that constrain the financial activities of business organizations, because failure of a business to comply with relevant laws could lead to material liabilities not disclosed in the financial statements. Governmental units typically are subject to legal constraints to a much greater extent than businesses; therefore, the AICPA's *Audits of State and Local Governmental Units, Revised Edition,* emphasizes that independent CPAs should be aware that when auditing governmental units they are accepting responsibility for determining compliance with relevant laws, regulations, and agreements, as well as determining conformity with GAAP. GAAP are, of course, defined as GASB standards, and applicable FASB standards.

The Comptroller General's *Government Auditing Standards,* usually known as the "yellow book," uses the term **financial statement** audit in place of the AICPA term financial audit, and introduces the term **financial related** audit to describe audits which have the objective of determining whether *(a)* financial reports and related items such as elements, accounts, or funds are fairly presented, *(b)* whether financial information is presented in accordance with "established or stated criteria," and *(c)* whether the entity has adhered to specific financial compliance requirements. As shown in Illustration 10–6, *Government Auditing Standards* classifies both financial statement audits and financial related audits as **financial** audits. Illustration 10–6 also shows that performance audits are also subject to GAGAS. The term **performance audits** includes **economy and efficiency** audits and **program** audits.

Economy and efficiency audits are concerned with the degree to which a program is achieving its objectives in a cost-efficient manner. Program audits are designed to determine whether or not a program is

**ILLUSTRATION 10–6   Types of Government Audits**

**Financial Audits**
1. Financial statement audits determine (a) whether the financial statements of an audited entity present fairly the financial position, results of operations, and cash flows or changes in financial position in accordance with generally accepted accounting principles, and (b) whether the entity has complied with laws and regulations for those transactions and events that may have a material effect on the financial statements.
2. Financial related audits include determining (a) whether financial reports and related items, such as elements, accounts, or funds are fairly presented, (b) whether financial information is presented in accordance with established or stated criteria, and (c) whether the entity has adhered to specific financial compliance requirements.

**Performance Audits**
1. Economy and efficiency audits include determining (a) whether the entity is acquiring, protecting, and using its resources (such as personnel, property, and space) economically and efficiently, (b) the causes of inefficiencies or uneconomical practices, and (c) whether the entity has complied with laws and regulations concerning matters of economy and efficiency.
2. Program audits include determining (a) the extent to which the desired results or benefits established by the legislature or other authorizing body are being achieved, (b) the effectiveness of organizations, programs, activities, or functions, and (c) whether the entity has complied with laws and regulations applicable to the program.

Source: Comptroller General of the United States, *Government Auditing Standards, 1988 Revision* (Washington, D.C.: U.S. General Accounting Office, 1988), p. A–1.

achieving the results intended in the legislation. For example, an auditor performing an economy and efficiency audit of a Head Start program might observe purchasing procedures, and evaluate transportation routes, classroom sizes, and general office procedures. An auditor performing a program audit would look to the original legislation to determine explicit or implicit objectives, develop criteria to determine whether or not the objectives were being met, compare actual results with the criteria, and report the results. The audit team would often include social scientists or educators employed to compare achievements of children, over time, who were in the program with similar children who were not in the program. Performance audits are not intended to be done on an annual basis but are expected to be performed periodically as a means of holding government accountable for carrying out its legislative mandates. Note that the Comptroller General's definitions of the types of government audits specify that both types of financial audits and both types of performance audits require the auditor to determine the entity's compliance with applicable laws and regulations.

## Auditor's Reports

The AICPA has developed standard wording for auditor's reports to make clear the responsibility the auditor is accepting. If the financial statements are prepared in conformity with generally accepted accounting principles, the auditor expresses an "unqualified" opinion. An example of an independent auditor's report expressing an unqualified opinion is shown in Illustration 10–7. Note that the title of the report stresses that the auditor is independent. The report contains four paragraphs. The first paragraph, the introductory paragraph, states that the GPFS were audited, that the GPFS are the responsibility of the City's management, and that the auditor's responsibility is to express an opinion on the financial statements based on the audit.

The second paragraph, the scope paragraph, describes the nature of an audit; the scope paragraph includes:

- A statement that the audit was conducted in accordance with generally accepted auditing standards.
- A statement that generally accepted auditing standards require that the auditor plan and perform the audit to obtain reasonable assurance about whether the financial statements are free of material misstatement.
- A statement that an audit includes—
  (1) Examining, on a test basis, evidence supporting the amounts and disclosures in the financial statements.
  (2) Assessing the accounting principles used and significant estimates made by management.
  (3) Evaluating the overall financial statement presentation.

• A statement that the auditor believes that his audit provides a reasonable basis for his opinion.[1]

The third paragraph, the opinion paragraph, presents the auditor's opinion as to whether the financial statements present fairly, in all material respects, the financial position of the City as of the balance sheet date and the results of its operations and changes in financial position of its proprietary and similar trust funds for the period then ended in conformity with generally accepted accounting principles.

The introductory, scope, and opinion paragraphs would be sufficient if the independent auditor's report accompanied separately issued GPFS. If the auditor's report is associated with the GPFS in the financial section of a CAFR, however, as is customary, a fourth paragraph, known as an explanatory paragraph, is added. The purpose of the explanatory paragraph is to make clear that the combining, individual fund, and individual account group financial statements and schedules are not a required part of the GPFS, but that such information has been subjected to auditing procedures applied in the audit of the GPFS, and,

### ILLUSTRATION 10–7    Independent Auditor's Report

We have audited the general purpose financial statements of the City of Example, Any State, as of and for the year ended June 30, 198x, as listed in the accompanying table of contents. These general purpose financial statements are the responsibility of the City's management. Our responsibility is to express an opinion on these general purpose financial statements based on our audit.

We conducted our audit in accordance with generally accepted auditing standards. Those standards require that we plan and perform the audit to obtain reasonable assurance about whether the general purpose financial statements are free of material misstatement. An audit includes examining, on a test basis, evidence supporting the amounts and disclosures in the general purpose financial statements. An audit also includes assessing the accounting principles used and significant estimates made by management, as well as evaluating the overall financial statement presentation. We believe that our audit provides a reasonable basis for our opinion.

In our opinion, the general purpose financial statements referred to above present fairly, in all material respects, the financial position of the City of Example, Any State, at June 30, 198x, and the results of its operations and the changes in financial position of its proprietary and similar trust fund types for the year then ended in conformity with generally accepted accounting principles.

Our audit was made for the purpose of forming an opinion on the general purpose financial statements taken as a whole. The combining, individual fund, and individual account group financial statements and schedules listed in the accompanying table of contents are presented for purposes of additional analysis and are not a required part of the general purpose financial statements of the City of Example, Any State. Such information has been subjected to the auditing procedures applied in the audit of the general purpose financial statements and, in our opinion, is fairly presented in all material respects in relation to the general purpose financial statements taken as a whole.

(Date)                                    (Signature)

Source: KPMG Peat Marwick, *Government Services Newsletter,* June 1988, p. 4.

---

[1]American Institute of Certified Public Accountants, Inc., *Statement on Auditing Standards No. 58,* par. 8 (New York: AICPA, 1988).

in the auditor's opinion, is fairly presented in all material respects in relation to the GPFS taken as a whole.

In addition to the unqualified opinion shown in Illustration 10–7, independent auditors also issue **qualified** opinions, **adverse** opinions, and, if circumstances warrant, may **disclaim** an opinion. The AICPA's *Statement on Auditing Standards No. 58* defines these terms in the following manner:

- *Qualified opinion.* A qualified opinion states that, except for the effects of the matter(s) to which the qualification relates, the financial statements present fairly, in all material respects, the financial position, results of operations, and cash flows of the entity in conformity with generally accepted accounting principles.
- *Adverse opinion.* An adverse opinion states that the financial statements do not present fairly the financial position, results of operations, or cash flows of the entity in conformity with generally accepted accounting principles.
- *Disclaimer of opinion.* A disclaimer of opinion states that the auditor does not express an opinion on the financial statements.[2]

## SELECTED REFERENCES

American Institute of Certified Public Accountants. *Audits of State and Local Governmental Units.* Rev. ed. New York, 1986.

————. *Statement on Auditing Standards,* No. 1, et seq. New York, 1973 to date.

Broadus, W. A., Jr., and Comtois, Joseph R. "The Single Audit Act: A Needed Reform." *The Journal of Accountancy,* April 1985, pp. 62–66, 68, 70.

Comptroller General of the United States. *Government Auditing Standards, 1988 Revision.* Washington, D.C.: U.S. General Accounting Office.

Governmental Accounting Standards Board. *Codification of Governmental Accounting and Financial Reporting Standards.* 2nd ed. Norwalk, Conn., 1987.

Office of Management and Budget. *Circular A–128.* April 12, 1985.

————. *Compliance Supplement for Single Audits of State and Local Government.*

U.S. General Accounting Office. *Guidelines for Financial and Compliance Audits of Federally Assisted Programs.* Washington, D.C.: U.S. General Accounting Office, 1980.

## QUESTIONS AND EXERCISES

**10–1.**   Using the annual financial report obtained for Exercise 1–1, answer the following questions.

---

[2]Ibid., par. 10.

a. Examine the introductory material. Does the report include a title page, table of contents, organization chart, and letter of transmittal? List the topics covered in the letter of transmittal. Can you think of any other topics that might have been included, based on your reading of this chapter? If the letter of transmittal includes a summary of revenues and expenditures, compare material amounts reported in the transmittal letter with related amounts in the combined statements. Do the amounts agree? If not, can you reconcile the differences?

b. Examine the financial section. Are all five required combined statements presented? Are these statements in the same format as the statements illustrated in this chapter? Specify any exceptions. Do the notes follow the combined statements, as they should? List the topics covered by the notes. Can you think of any other disclosures that should have been made in the notes or in the body of a combined statement? Read the "Summary of Significant Accounting Policies." Do the accounting policies agree with the standards discussed in this book? Specify any exceptions. Are combining statements included for each fund type that has more than one fund? Are the nature and purpose identified for each fund? Are separate individual fund statements or schedules provided for any of the funds? If so, list any additional information provided that is not in the combined or combining statements.

c. Do the notes contain disclosures relating the definition of the accounting entity for reporting purposes? Is information presented in the letter of transmittal relating to the reporting entity? Do these disclosures reveal criteria used for inclusion or exclusion of potential component units? Are the criteria the same as those set forth in this chapter? List any units specifically listed as excluded or included. If reasons are given for exclusion or inclusion, do the reasons seem persuasive?

d. Look at the statistical section of the report. Do you find this information useful in analyzing the financial condition of your governmental unit? If so, list several useful items of information in the statistical section and how you would use them.

e. Examine the auditor's report. Is the auditor's report placed immediately in front of the Combined Balance Sheet? Is the auditor identified as an independent CPA firm? A state audit agency? Other? Is the wording of the auditor's report the same as illustrated in this chapter? Does the scope paragraph indicate exactly which statements are covered by the auditor's opinion? If the auditor is expressing an opinion only on the combined statements, what responsibility is taken for the combining and individual fund statements? Is the opinion unqualified or qualified? If qualified, what are the reasons given?

f. Look at the general report format. Is the report easy to read? Does the report have an excessive number of foldout pages? Is the printing large enough to read legibly? Are the sections separated by divider pages and tabs? Does the report lie flat when opened? Do you have any suggestions to improve the readability of the report?

g. Report the following ratios (some of the ratios may be found in statistical tables; compute all ratios not given in the report, using, as needed, data from the financial statements, notes to the statements, schedules, and statistical tables):

1. Expenditures (general, special revenue, and debt service funds) per capita.
2. Expenditures (general, special revenue, and debt service funds) per dollar of assessed value of property.
3. Intergovernmental revenue as a percentage of total revenue of the General Fund, special revenue funds, and debt service funds. Ignore transfers.
4. Capital outlay as a percentage of total expenditures (general, special revenue, debt service, and capital projects funds).
5. Net income or loss—each enterprise fund.
6. General obligation debt per capita.
7. General obligation debt as a percentage of assessed value of property. Unfunded pension liability as a percentage of assessed value of property.
8. Unfunded pension liability per capita.
9. Population of the current year divided by the population the previous year. Population of the current year divided by the population 10 years ago.

Comment on the impact each of these ratios have on your evaluation of the financial report you have obtained.

10–2.  Write the numbers 1 through 10 on a sheet of paper. Beside each number, write the letter corresponding to the best answer to each of the following questions:

1. The comprehensive annual financial report (CAFR) of a governmental unit should contain a Combined Balance Sheet reporting:

|    | Govermental Funds | Proprietary Funds | Account Groups |
|----|-------------------|-------------------|----------------|
| a. | Yes | Yes | No |
| b. | Yes | Yes | Yes |
| c. | Yes | No | Yes |
| d. | No | Yes | No |

2. The comprehensive annual financial report (CAFR) of a governmental unit should contain a Combined Statement of Revenues, Expenditures, and Changes in Fund Balances for

|    | Governmental Funds | Expendable Trust Funds | Pension Trust Funds |
|----|--------------------|------------------------|---------------------|
| a. | Yes | Yes | No |
| b. | Yes | No | Yes |
| c. | No | No | Yes |
| d. | No | Yes | No |

3. The comprehensive annual financial report (CAFR) of a governmental unit should contain a Combined Statement of Revenues, Expenses, and Changes in Retained Earnings for

|    | Governmental Funds | Proprietary Funds | Nonexpendable Trust Funds |
|----|--------------------|-------------------|---------------------------|
| a. | No | Yes | Yes |
| b. | No | No | No |
| c. | Yes | No | Yes |
| d. | Yes | Yes | No |

4. The comprehensive annual financial report (CAFR) of a governmental unit should contain a Combined Statement of Revenues, Expenses, and Changes in Retained Earnings for

| | Account Groups | Expendable Trust Funds | Agency Funds |
|---|---|---|---|
| a. | Yes | Yes | Yes |
| b. | Yes | No | Yes |
| c. | No | No | No |
| d. | No | Yes | No |

5. In the comprehensive annual financial report (CAFR) of a governmental unit, the account groups are included in:
   a. Both the Combined Balance Sheet and the Combined Statement of Revenues, Expenditures, and Changes in Fund Balances.
   b. The Combined Statement of Revenues, Expenditures, and Changes in Fund Balances, but **not** the Combined Balance Sheet.
   c. The Combined Balance Sheet but **not** the Combined Statement of Revenues, Expenditures, and Changes in Fund Balances.
   d. Neither the Combined Balance Sheet nor the Combined Statement of Revenues, Expenditures, and Changes in Fund Balances.
6. Which of the following funds of a governmental unit uses the same basis of accounting as a special revenue fund?
   a. Expendable Trust Funds.
   b. Nonexpendable Trust Funds.
   c. Enterprise Funds.
   d. Internal Service Funds.

   Items 7 through 9 are based on the following data relating to Lely Township:

| | |
|---|---|
| Printing and binding equipment used for servicing all of Lely's departments and agencies, on a cost-reimbursement basis | $100,000 |
| Equipment used for supplying water to Lely residents | 900,000 |
| Receivable for completed sidewalks to be paid for in installments by affected property owners | 950,000 |
| Cash received from federal government, dedicated to highway maintenance, which must be accounted for in a separate fund | 995,000 |

7. How much should be accounted for in a special revenue fund or funds?
   a. $995,000.
   b. $1,050,000.
   c. $1,095,000.
   d. $2,045,000.
8. How much should be accounted for in an internal service fund?
   a. $100,000.
   b. $900,000.
   c. $950,000.
   d. $995,000.
9. How much should be accounted for in an enterprise fund?
   a. $100,000.
   b. $900,000.
   c. $950,000.
   d. $995,000.

10. Which of the following accounts would be included in the asset section of the Combined Balance Sheet of a governmental unit for the General Long-Term Debt Account Group?

|  | *Amount Available in Debt Service Funds* | *Amount to Be Provided for Retirement of General Long-Term Debt* |
|---|---|---|
| *a.* | Yes | Yes |
| *b.* | Yes | No |
| *c.* | No | Yes |
| *d.* | No | No |

(Items 1, 7–10, AICPA, adapted)

**10–3.** Answer the following review questions:
   *a.* Which fund types should use the full accrual basis of accounting?
   *b.* Which fund types should use an accrual basis of accounting which differs from the full accrual basis?
   *c.* Which fund types generally use encumbrance accounting?
   *d.* Which fund types should be included in the Combined Statement of Changes in Financial Position?
   *e.* Which statements are required in order for financial reports to be in conformity with GAAP?
   *f.* Which fund type normally has no fund equity?
   *g.* What sections should the Comprehensive Annual Financial Report of a state or local governmental unit contain in addition to the GPFS?
   *h.* Identify and describe briefly the four types of government audits.

**10–4.** Record in general journal form the following transactions of the City of Cocoa. Indicate the fund(s) and/or group(s) in which each transaction should be entered. The fiscal year is July 1, 19x5–June 30, 19x6.
   1. The City General Fund received $970,000 in cash from Baker County Tax Agency Fund. The County had deducted 3 percent in collections fees from the total amount of property taxes collected prior to making this payment. The taxes receivable had been recorded properly by the General Fund at the time they were billed.
   2. On July 1, 19x5, the City was given $800,000 par value DEF Corporation bonds with the provision that the endowment be made permanent and that all income be used to buy artwork for public buildings. The bonds were dated April 1, 19x5, were due April 1, 19y5, and were quoted at par on the date of the gift. Bond interest payment dates are 4/1 and 10/1, and the bonds carried a nominal interest rate of 8 percent. Record the gift.
   3. On October 1, 19x5, the first interest payment was received on the bonds described in transaction 2. The liability to the expendable trust fund was recorded.
   4. The City Water Department sold water to General Fund departments; the amount of $30,000 was charged to the General Fund. The Water Department also made a payment of $20,000 in lieu of taxes to the City.
   5. The General Fund transferred $100,000 cash to the Water Utility Fund as a permanent contribution and made a long-term advance of $50,000 to the Stores and Services Fund.

6. The Community Development Fund (a special revenue fund) reimbursed the General Fund for $20,000 in supplies which were purchased by the General Fund (which had previously debited Expenditures) for use by the Community Development Fund.
7. The General Fund purchased a police car for $21,500, paying cash.
8. On July 1, 19x5, the City sold $10,000,000 of 8 percent tax-supported bonds at 101 to finance the construction of a new police station. The premium was transferred to a debt service fund for the future payment of principal. Record the sale of the bonds.
9. On July 1, 19x5, the City sold $8,000,000 in utility revenue bonds at par for the purpose of purchasing a utility plant. The entire proceeds of the bond issue were given to the former owners of the utility. The utility plant was carried at cost, $10,000,000 less accumulated depreciation of $3,000,000, on the books of the former owners. The City-owned utility will be subject to regulation by the State Public Service Commission.

10–5.   The City of Rogers sold tax-supported bonds in the face amount of $5,000,000 on January 1, 19x1, in order to finance the construction of a fire station. The bonds bore interest at the annual rate of 8 percent, payable on January 1 and July 1; the first principal payment, in the amount of $500,000, was due on January 1, 19x2.

*Required:*
Record each transaction below in the accounts of the Capital Projects Fund, the Debt Service Fund, the General Fixed Assets Account Group, and the General Long-Term Debt Account Group, as appropriate. Indicate the name of the fund or account group in which each entry is made.
1. Record the sale of the bonds at par.
2. A contract was signed with the Benthammer Construction Company in the amount of $4,900,000.
3. A budget was prepared for the Debt Service Fund, providing for transfer from the General Fund for the amount needed for disbursement in 19x1.
4. The General Fund transferred to the Debt Service Fund the amount budgeted in transaction 3.
5. The first interest payment was made on July 1, 19x1.
6. The construction was completed and the contractor was paid all but a 5 percent retainage.
7. The contractor was paid the retainage. Any remaining balance in the Capital Projects Fund was paid to the Debt Service Fund for the eventual payment of principal.
8. The accounts related to this project were closed.

10–6.   The City of Hyde Park has only three governmental funds: The General Fund, a Debt Service Fund, and a Capital Projects Fund. The following data relate to the operations of the three funds for the year ending December 31, 19y1:
1. The beginning Fund Balances were: General, $1,110,000; Debt Service, $14,000; and Capital Projects, $0.
2. Revenues for the year were: General Fund, $10,532,000.
3. Expenditures for the year were: General Fund, $8,649,000; Debt Service Fund, $580,000; Capital Projects Fund, $985,000.

4. The General Fund made an operating transfer to the Debt Service Fund in the amount of $600,000.

5. The Capital Projects Fund received $1,000,000 from the sale of bonds at par.

6. In addition to the above, the Capital Projects Fund reimbursed the General Fund $10,000 for expenditures previously recorded by the General Fund and included in the General Fund expenditures reported in (3).

7. An equity transfer of $5,000 was made from the Capital Projects Fund to the Debt Service Fund.

8. The General Fund made a contribution to a newly created Water Fund (an enterprise fund) in the amount of $500,000.

9. The General Fund also made a long-term advance to the Water Fund in the amount of $200,000.

**Required:**

Prepare, in good form, a Combined Statement of Revenues, Expenditures, and Changes in Fund Balances—All Governmental Fund Types for the Year Ended December 31, 19y1.

10–7.  The City of Pulaski was recently incorporated and began financial operations on January 1, 19y0, the beginning of its fiscal year. The following transactions occurred during this first fiscal year.

1. The City Council adopted a budget for the General Fund: Revenues were estimated at $2,000,000, Appropriations totaled $1,970,000.

2. Property taxes were levied in the amount of $1,530,000; it was estimated that taxes in the amount of $30,000 would prove to be uncollectible.

3. During the year a resident of the City donated marketable securities valued at $100,000 to the Village under the terms of a trust agreement. The terms of the trust agreement stipulated that the principal amount is to be kept intact; use of revenue generated by the securities is restricted to providing financial aid for families of police and fire fighters who are killed in the line of duty. Revenue earned on these marketable securities amounted to $6,000 in 19y0; this amount was deposited directly in the Expendable Trust Fund.

4. The General Fund transferred $50,000 to establish an Internal Service Fund. The amount is considered to be a contribution, and is not to be repaid.

5. A sidewalk project in the amount of $250,000 was authorized. The project is to be financed by a special assessment levied against property deemed to be particularly benefited by the project. Property owners paid their assessments in full on July 1, 19y0.

6. A contract for $245,000 was let for the construction of the sidewalks (transaction 5). On August 1, 19y0, the contract was completed. The contractor was paid in full on August 15.

7. During the year the Internal Service Fund purchased various supplies at a cost of $38,000.

8. Cash collections recorded by the General Fund during 19y0 were as follows:

| | |
|---|---:|
| Property taxes | $1,300,000 |
| Licenses and permits | 200,000 |
| Intergovernmental revenues | 500,000 |

9. On December 31, 19y0, all uncollected property taxes became delinquent. The original estimate of $30,000 uncollectible still appears realistic.

***Required:***

Prepare journal entries to record each of the above transactions in the appropriate fund(s) or account groups of the City of Pulaski for the year ended December 31, 19y0. (The City of Pulaski utilizes all fund types and account groups provided in GASB standards and discussed in Chapters 2 through 9 of this book.) Number each journal entry to correspond with the numbers of the transactions described above. Identify the fund type or account group in which each entry should be made. Closing entries are not required.

## CONTINUOUS PROBLEM

**10–C.** *a.* Assemble all statements prepared for your solutions to Problems 1–C through 9–C.

*b.* From your solutions to Continuous Problems 1–C through 9–C, prepare (using the formats illustrated in this chapter):

(1) A Combined Balance Sheet for All Funds and Account Groups of the City of Everlasting Sunshine as of December 31, 19y1.

(2) A Combined Statement of Revenues, Expenditures, and Changes in Fund Balances—All Governmental Fund Types and Expendable Trust Funds for the Year Ending December 31, 19y1.

(3) A Combined Statement of Revenues, Expenditures, and Changes in Fund Balances—Budget and Actual—General, Special Revenue, Debt Service Fund Types, and Expendable Trust Fund for the Year Ended December 31, 19y1.

(4) A Combined Statement of Revenues, Expenses, and Changes in Retained Earnings/Fund Balances—All Proprietary Fund Types and Similar Fiduciary Funds for the Year Ended December 31, 19y1.

(5) A Combined Statement of Changes in Financial Position—All Proprietary Fund Types and Similar Fiduciary Funds for the Year Ended December 31, 19y1.

*c.* Review the combined statements you prepared for part (*b*). Assume that you, as a Certified Public Accountant, wish to issue an unqualified opinion on the general purpose financial statements. Write the auditor's report.

*d.* List the additional information that should be presented in the Comprehensive Annual Financial Report of the City of Everlasting Sunshine in conformity with GASB standards discussed in this chapter.

# Chapter 11

# COLLEGE AND UNIVERSITY ACCOUNTING

Chapters 2 through 10 discuss accounting for state and local governmental units. Chapters 11, 12, 13, and 14 discuss accounting and financial reporting for not-for-profit organizations which may be owned and operated by entities in the private sector, or by governmental entities: colleges and universities (Chapter 11), hospitals (Chapter 12), voluntary health and welfare organizations (Chapter 13), and other not-for-profit organizations (Chapter 14). Currently, the **Financial Accounting Standards Board (FASB)** has jurisdiction over accounting and financial reporting standards for nongovernmental, not-for-profit organizations (for example, the University of Chicago), and the **Governmental Accounting Standards Board (GASB)** has the authority to issue standards for separately issued financial reports of governmental not-for-profit organizations (for example, the University of Illinois) as well as principles of incorporating these organizations as component units in the governmental financial reports. The Financial Accounting Foundation has approved for exposure a proposal that each governmentally owned college or university be subject to FASB jurisdiction unless its governing body makes an irrevocable election to be subject to GASB's jurisdiction.

To date, few standards have been issued by either the FASB or the GASB relating to these organizations; most guidance is found in *Audit Guides* and *Statements of Position* of the American Institute of Certified Public Accountants (AICPA) and in publications of industry associations. In 1979, the FASB incorporated the prior AICPA publications in *Statement 32* by declaring that the material in those *Audit Guides* and *Statements of Position* constituted preferred accounting practices. Since that time both the FASB and GASB have issued standards, sometimes different, that affect these organizations; most notably for pensions and depreciation. The potential exists, and is beginning to be realized, that the same "industry" (for example colleges and universities) may have different accounting standards for privately and governmentally owned units.

FASB *Statement 93* required that all not-for-profit organizations record depreciation. The GASB followed with its *Statement 8,* which stated that governmental not-for-profit organizations need not record depreciation, pending further study. More recently, FASB *Statement 99* deferred the effective date of its *Statement 93* until January 1, 1990. Presumably, the effective date will be extended until the date by which governmentally owned colleges and universities must make an irrevocable election to be under the FASB's jurisdiction or the GASB's jurisdiction.

## Summary—College and University Accounting

In the United States, colleges and universities may be classified as public or private. Public universities generally are part of state government, although some have a great deal of autonomy. Some public community colleges are separate local governments, with elected governing boards. Other public institutions may have governing boards for one or more campuses and are subject to varying degrees of state involvement in operating decisions. Financial reports of public institutions may be issued for one campus, for several campuses in a university "system," or may not be separately issued, if a given state determines that external reporting should be only as a part of a state report. On the other hand, private institutions nearly always issue separately audited financial reports, which are used for debt analysis and other purposes in a manner similar to business enterprises.

In the college and university accounting field the most comprehensive authoritative publication is *College and University Business Administration,* published by the National Association of College and University Business Officers (NACUBO). The current edition of *College and University Business Administration (CUBA)* was developed in close communication with the AICPA committee which wrote the audit guide, *Audits of Colleges and Universities* (1973). The audit guide was amended by AICPA *Statement of Position 74-8.* The accounting and financial reporting recommended in CUBA and the audit guide, as amended, are virtually the same.

A few summary comments may help the reader understand the sometimes complex accounting and financial reporting used by colleges and universities:

- Fund accounting is used. Funds are grouped together into "fund groups." With the exception of agency funds, each fund group may be unrestricted or restricted.
- Full accrual accounting is used by colleges and universities. However, depreciation is not normally recorded as a charge against operations.

Those colleges choosing to depreciate fixed assets do so in the plant funds.
- The three required financial statements are the Balance Sheet, the Statement of Current Funds Revenues, Expenditures, and Other Changes, and the Statement of Changes in Fund Balances. (See Illustrations 11–1, 11–2, and 11–3, which are shown later in this chapter.)
- Revenues and expenditures are recorded only in the current funds (unrestricted and restricted). All increases and decreases in the other funds are recorded by credits and debits to Fund Balance.
- Current restricted fund revenues are equal to current restricted fund expenditures (see Illustration 11–2). Additions to the Current Funds— Restricted before expenditures are recognized are recorded as direct additions to Fund Balance (compare with governmental accounting where similar receipts are recorded as Deferred Revenues).
- Transfers, as reported in the current funds, are reported as either mandatory or nonmandatory, in order to help disclose the funds available to the governing board of the institutions.
- Auxiliary enterprise operations, such as bookstores and food service operations, are reported in the current funds, rather than in a separate fund group as is the case with state and local governments. Auxiliary enterprise plant is recorded in the plant funds, and the same depreciation policy applied to other plant applies to auxiliary enterprise plant.

## The Fund Structure for Colleges and Universities

CUBA defines a fund as "an accounting entity with a self-balancing set of accounts consisting of assets, liabilities and a fund balance." Separate funds are grouped together into **fund groups.** The fund groups generally used by colleges and universities are:
Current funds
Loan funds
Endowment and similar funds
Annuity and life income funds
Plant funds
Agency funds
With the exception of agency funds, each of the fund groups may contain restricted as well as unrestricted balances.

**Current funds**   Current resources available for use in carrying out operations directly related to the institution's education objectives are accounted for in the current funds category. "Directly related" operations include residence halls, food service operations, intercollegiate athletics, student stores, and other auxiliary enterprises, as well as the instruction, research, and public service activities of the college or university. *Assets that are available for all purposes of the institution at the discre-*

*tion of the governing board are* **unrestricted.** *Assets that are available for current operating purposes subject to limitations placed on them by persons or organizations outside the institution are* **restricted.** For financial reporting purposes, unrestricted assets and related liabilities and fund balances should be reported separately from restricted assets, liabilities, and fund balances, as shown in Illustration 11–1. Revenues, expenditures, and transfers also must be classified as being related to restricted or unrestricted current funds as shown by Illustration 11–2. Combined Balance Sheets of fund groups may be presented in a columnar format as shown by Illustration 10–1, or in a vertical or "layered" format as shown in Illustration 11–1. Note that the Statement of Changes in Fund Balances (Illustration 11–3) contains separate columns for the current unrestricted and current restricted fund groups and a single column for each other fund group.

Current funds **revenues** should be reported on the full accrual basis. *Revenues of current restricted funds are not considered to be earned until all of the terms of the agreement under which they were given to the institution have been met;* authoritative bodies agree that the *terms are met only when the expenditures are recognized in accordance with the donor's restrictions.* Thus, restricted assets are initially reported as **additions** in the Statement of Changes in Fund Balances when received and are recognized as revenues in the periods when required expenditures are made and in amounts equal to the expenditures.

The term **Revenues** is properly used only in relation to the current funds and not in relation to any of the other fund groups, as shown by Illustrations 11–2 and 11–3. Items shown in Illustration 11–3 which increase funds other than current funds are reported under the "Revenues and Other Additions" caption and are considered to be "additions."

Gross tuition and fees should be recorded as a revenue even though some will be offset by fee remissions, scholarships, and fellowships. Fee remissions, or waivers, scholarships, and fellowships should be recorded as Expenditures. Actual refunds of tuition or fees, however, should be treated as a reduction of Revenues.

Since college fiscal years and academic years often do not coincide, it is common for tuition and fees collected near the end of a fiscal year to relate in large part to services to be rendered by the institution during the ensuing fiscal year. Revenues and related expenditures which apply to an academic term that encompasses two fiscal years should be recognized totally within the fiscal year in which the term is predominantly conducted. Amounts received in one year which will not be recognized as revenue until the following year are reported in the year-end balance sheet as "Deferred Credits," a NACUBO phrase equivalent to Deferred Revenues.

Current funds **expenditures** should also be recognized on the full accrual basis. The term **expenditures** applies only to the current funds group. Expenditure accounts are identified as to function, organizational unit, and object. Functional expenditures are to be the primary basis of reporting and are shown in Illustration 11–2.

In state and local governmental reporting a distinction is made between operating and equity transfers. In college and university financial reporting a distinction is made between Mandatory and Nonmandatory Transfers. **Mandatory Transfers** are transfers made from one fund to another in order to comply with legally enforceable agreements, such as bond indentures and grant agreements. **Nonmandatory Transfers** are made at the discretion of the governing board to serve whatever purpose the board agrees is desirable. Note that Mandatory Transfers are reported with Expenditures in the Statement of Current Funds Revenues, Expenditures, and Other Changes (Illustration 11–2) and that the two types of transfers are reported separately in the Statement of Changes in Fund Balances (Illustration 11–3).

**Loan funds**   Loan funds account for the resources available for loans to students, faculty, and staff. Individuals, foundations, and governmental agencies provide these resources. Loan funds generally are operated as "revolving" funds in that repayments of loan principal plus interest are returned to the loan fund and made available for future loans.

Assets may be given to the institution under very specific restrictions as to who may receive loans; other assets may be used in accord with policies set by the governing board of the institution. Loan funds of the first kind are restricted; loan funds of the second kind are unrestricted. See Illustration 11–1 for typical loan fund asset, liability, and Fund Balance accounts. See Illustration 11–3 for additions to and deductions from the Fund Balance of the loan funds for a given period.

**Endowment and similar funds**   Funds whose principal is to be maintained intact are classified as endowment and similar funds. Income from investments of this fund group which may be expended at the discretion of the governing board of the institution is recognized on the accrual basis as revenue of the Current Funds—Unrestricted. Income that may be expended only for purposes specified by donors or grantors is reported initially as an addition to Current Funds—Restricted in the Statement of Changes in Fund Balances. Investments may be carried at market; present standards allow recognition of unrealized appreciation in market value of investments, but if unrealized appreciation is recorded it should be reported as a transfer to, not a revenue of, the current funds.

Endowment and similar funds are of three types: (1) **endowment funds,** those in which a donor or external agency has specified that the principal remain intact in perpetuity; (2) **term endowment funds,** in which all or part of the principal may be expended after a specified period of time or the occurrence of a certain event; and (3) **quasi-endowment funds,** which are funds set aside by the governing board to function as endowments. Quasi-endowment funds are unrestricted unless the assets are taken from restricted funds.

Balance Sheet accounts of endowment and similar funds are shown in Illustration 11–1. Typical additions to and deductions from Fund Balance are shown in Illustration 11–3.

**Annuity and life income funds**  **Annuity** funds account for resources given to an institution under agreements which bind the institution to pay stipulated amounts periodically to the donors or other designated individuals for a period of time specified in the agreements. After that time, the resources are transferred to the fund group specified in the agreement. The assets (cash and investments) of an annuity fund are offset by liabilities which include indebtedness against the assets and, also, the present value of future annuity payments, based on actuarial calculations. **Life income** funds provide that all the income from fund investments be paid to the donor, or designated individual, usually until that person's death. Accounting for life income funds is simpler than for annuity funds, as no actuarial calculations are possible since the amount to be paid periodically will vary from period to period as the income earned varies. The assets, liabilities, and fund balances of annuity and life income funds are shown in Illustration 11–1. The changes in fund balances of these funds are shown in Illustration 11–3.

**Plant funds**  The plant funds group includes four subgroups. **Unexpended plant funds** account for assets set aside for the acquisition of fixed assets. These funds differ from capital projects funds of local government in that they account for debt issued to finance the asset acquisition. Construction activities may be accounted for within this subgroup, or within the investment in plant subgroup. **Funds for the retirement of indebtedness** is a subgroup which is similar to debt service funds of local government. **Funds for renewals and replacements,** used largely by private colleges, consist of resources set aside by external requirements or by governing board action. Resources in this category are often accumulated over a number of years. The **investment in plant** subgroup accounts for the cost of institutional fixed assets, including those used by auxiliary enterprises (except those held as investments by endowment and similar funds), as well as long-term debt associated with those assets. Donated assets are carried at fair value at date of acquisition. The difference between the asset carrying value and debt is reported in the Fund Balance account (called Net Investment in Plant).

Asset, liability, and Fund Balance accounts for plant funds are shown in Illustration 11–1. Changes in fund balances are shown in Illustration 11–3.

**Agency funds** As is true of governmental units, colleges and universities often act as agents of others for the collection, custodianship, and disbursement of assets. Colleges may act as fiscal agents for student or faculty organizations as well as for individuals. The Balance Sheet accounts for agency funds are shown in Illustration 11–1. Note that no Fund Balance account is used; instead, a liability account, "Deposits Held in Custody for Others," reflects the fact that the college does not "own" the assets. No changes in fund balances are shown for agency funds in Illustration 11–3, as Fund Balance accounts do not exist. Of course, individual statements of activity should be sent to the organizations or individuals for whom the college is acting as agent.

## ILLUSTRATIVE TRANSACTIONS

The following section presents illustrative transactions of all the fund groups. In each case, a beginning trial balance is presented. Those balances and transactions lead into the statements presented in Illustrations 11–1, 11–2, and 11–3.

### Current Funds—Unrestricted

Assume the following trial balance for the Current Funds—Unrestricted for Razorback University as of July 1, 19y0:

|  | Debit | Credit |
|---|---|---|
| Cash | $135,000 | |
| Accounts Receivable | 200,000 | |
| Inventories | 55,000 | |
| Prepaid Expenses and Deferred Charges | 45,000 | |
| Accounts Payable | | $ 80,000 |
| Deferred Credits | | 300,000 |
| Fund Balance | | 55,000 |
| Totals | $435,000 | $435,000 |

Current standards do not require that colleges and universities record their budgets in their accounting systems, but allow this to be done if desired. If Razorback University's Board of Trustees desired that the budget providing for $8,000,000 in anticipated revenues and $7,800,000 in anticipated expenditures and other charges be recorded, the entry would be:

| | | | |
|---|---|---|---|
| 1. Unrealized Revenues | | 8,000,000 | |
|     Budget Allocations for Expenditures | | | |
|       and Other Changes | | | 7,800,000 |
|     Unallocated Budget Balance | | | 200,000 |

The account "Unallocated Budget Balance" is credited, rather than the Fund Balance account, in order to keep Fund Balance unaffected by the budget entry. All budgetary accounts would be closed at year-end, as is true of state and local governmental units.

In the beginning trial balance, the amount of $300,000 is shown on the Deferred Credits line (Deferred Credits is another name for Deferred Revenues). This amount represents tuition and fees received in cash near the end of the prior year for classes offered predominantly in the current year. Entry 2 removes $300,000 from the liability account, Deferred Credits, and records the recognition of revenue in the current year.

| | | |
|---|---|---|
| 2. Deferred Credits . . . . . . . . . . . . . . . . . | 300,000 | |
| Revenues—Tuition and Fees . . . . . . . . . | | 300,000 |

Entry 3a records the recognition of revenues from the sources and in the amounts shown in the Current Funds—Unrestricted column of Illustration 11–2 (recall that Entry 2 reported the recognition of $300,000 revenues from tuition and fees; Entry 3a records the recognition of the remaining $2,580,000 from that source). Separate general ledger accounts for each revenue source are used in Entry 3a:

| | | |
|---|---|---|
| 3a. Accounts Receivable . . . . . . . . . . . . . . | 7,680,000 | |
| Revenues—Tuition and Fees . . . . . . . . . | | 2,580,000 |
| Revenues—Federal Appropriations . . . . . . | | 450,000 |
| Revenues—State Appropriations . . . . . . . | | 1,200,000 |
| Revenues—Local Appropriations . . . . . . . | | 50,000 |
| Revenues—Federal Grants and Contracts . . . | | 30,000 |
| Revenues—State Grants and Contracts . . . . | | 20,000 |
| Revenues—Local Grants and Contracts . . . . | | 15,000 |
| Revenues—Private Gifts, Grants, and Contracts | | 600,000 |
| Revenues—Endowment Income . . . . . . . . | | 250,000 |
| Revenues—Sales and Services of Educational Activities . . . . . . . . . . . . . . . . . | | 180,000 |
| Revenues—Sales and Services of Auxiliary Enterprises . . . . . . . . . . . . . . . . | | 2,275,000 |
| Revenues—Expired Term Endowment . . . . . | | 30,000 |

The source, "Expired Term Endowment," represents an expired endowment for which the agreement provided that the principal would become unrestricted at the expiration of the term of the endowment.

Entry 3b records the collection of cash from students and others who owed money to the university.

| | | |
|---|---|---|
| 3b. Cash . . . . . . . . . . . . . . . . . . . . . . | 7,630,000 | |
| Accounts Receivable . . . . . . . . . . . . | | 7,630,000 |

Entry 4 records the incurring of expenditures of current funds—unrestricted. Disbursements were made for the bulk of expenditures, but Accounts Payable increased in the amount shown.

| | |
|---|---|
| 4. Expenditures—Educational and General—Instruction | 2,995,000 |
| Expenditures—Educational and General—Research . | 150,000 |
| Expenditures—Educational and General—Public Service . . . . . . . . . . . . . . . . . . . . | 210,000 |
| Expenditures—Educational and General—Academic Support . . . . . . . . . . . . . . . . . . . . | 225,000 |

Expenditures—Educational and General—Student
　　Services . . . . . . . . . . . . . . . . . . . . . .    340,000
Expenditures—Educational and General—Institutional
　　Support . . . . . . . . . . . . . . . . . . . . .    370,000
Expenditures—Educational and General—Operation
　　and Maintenance of Physical Plant . . . . . . .    440,000
Expenditures—Educational and General—
　　Scholarships and Fellowships . . . . . . . . . .    80,000
Expenditures—Auxiliary Enterprises . . . . . . . . 2,050,000
　　Cash . . . . . . . . . . . . . . . . . . . .                                          6,820,000
　　Accounts Payable . . . . . . . . . . . . . .                                             40,000

Mandatory Transfers from current funds—unrestricted to other funds
are recorded by Entry 5a. Nonmandatory Transfers from current
funds—unrestricted are recorded by Entry 5b. Entry 5c records the accompanying transfer of cash from current funds—unrestricted to other
funds of Razorback University.

5a. Mandatory Transfer for Principal and Interest—
　　　Educational and General . . . . . . . . . . .    100,000
　　Mandatory Transfer for Principal and Interest—
　　　Auxiliary Enterprises . . . . . . . . . . . . .    225,000
　　Mandatory Transfer for Renewals and
　　　Replacements—Educational and General . . . .    80,000
　　Mandatory Transfer for Renewals and
　　　Replacements—Auxiliary Enterprises . . . . . .    50,000
　　Mandatory Transfer for Loan Fund Matching Grant .    2,000
　　　Due to Funds for the Retirement of
　　　　Indebtedness . . . . . . . . . . . . . . . .                                        325,000
　　　Due to Funds for Renewals and Replacements .                                          130,000
　　　Due to Loan Funds . . . . . . . . . . . . .                                              2,000

5b. Nonmandatory Transfer for Unrestricted Gifts
　　　Allocated to Other Funds . . . . . . . . . . .    580,000
　　　Due to Loan Funds . . . . . . . . . . . . . .                                        100,000
　　　Due to Endowment and Similar Funds . . . .                                          450,000
　　　Due to Unexpended Plant Funds . . . . . . .                                           30,000

5c. Due to Funds for the Retirement of Indebtedness . .    325,000
　　Due to Funds for Renewals and Replacements . . .    130,000
　　Due to Loan Funds . . . . . . . . . . . . . . .    102,000
　　Due to Endowment and Similar Funds . . . . . .    450,000
　　Due to Unexpended Plant Funds . . . . . . . . .    30,000
　　　Cash . . . . . . . . . . . . . . . . . . . .                                        1,037,000

During the year, inventories increased by $3,000. The increase was
paid in cash. Prepaid expenses and deferred charges remained the same.

6. Inventories . . . . . . . . . . . . . . . . . . . .    3,000
　　Cash . . . . . . . . . . . . . . . . . . . . . . .                                        3,000

Near the end of the current year the university collected tuition and
fees in the amount of $325,000 for classes to be offered in a term to be
held predominantly in the following year. In conformity with current
standards the university recognizes a liability of $325,000 and will rec-
ognize the entire amount as revenue in the following year.

7. Cash . . . . . . . . . . . . . . . . . . . . . . .    325,000
　　Deferred Credits . . . . . . . . . . . . . . . .                                        325,000

At year-end the budget entry must be reversed (See Entry 8*a*) and Revenues, Expenditures, and Transfers accounts closed (see Entries 8*b* and 8*c*).

| | | |
|---|---:|---:|
| 8*a*. Budget Allocations for Expenditures and Other Changes . . . . . . . . . . . . . . . . . . | 7,800,000 | |
| Unallocated Budget Balance . . . . . . . . . . . | 200,000 | |
| Unrealized Revenues . . . . . . . . . . . . | | 8,000,000 |
| | | |
| 8*b*. Revenues—Tuition and Fees . . . . . . . . . . | 2,880,000 | |
| Revenues—Federal Appropriations . . . . . . . . | 450,000 | |
| Revenues—State Appropriations . . . . . . . . | 1,200,000 | |
| Revenues—Local Appropriations . . . . . . . . | 50,000 | |
| Revenues—Federal Grants and Contracts . . . . . | 30,000 | |
| Revenues—State Grants and Contracts . . . . . . | 20,000 | |
| Revenues—Local Grants and Contracts . . . . . . | 15,000 | |
| Revenues—Private Gifts, Grants, and Contracts . . | 600,000 | |
| Revenues—Endowment Income . . . . . . . . . | 250,000 | |
| Revenues—Sales and Services of Educational Activities . . . . . . . . . . . . . . . . . | 180,000 | |
| Revenues—Sales and Services of Auxiliary Enterprises . . . . . . . . . . . . . . . . | 2,275,000 | |
| Revenues—Expired Term Endowment . . . . . . . | 30,000 | |
| Fund Balance . . . . . . . . . . . . . . | | 7,980,000 |
| | | |
| 8*c*. Fund Balance . . . . . . . . . . . . . . . | 7,897,000 | |
| Expenditures—Educational and General— Instruction . . . . . . . . . . . . . . . | | 2,995,000 |
| Expenditures—Educational and General— Research . . . . . . . . . . . . . . . . | | 150,000 |
| Expenditures—Educational and General— Public Service . . . . . . . . . . . . . . | | 210,000 |
| Expenditures—Educational and General— Academic Support . . . . . . . . . . . . | | 225,000 |
| Expenditures—Educational and General— Student Services . . . . . . . . . . . . . | | 340,000 |
| Expenditures—Educational and General— Institutional Support . . . . . . . . . . . | | 370,000 |
| Expenditures—Educational and General— Operation and Maintenance of Physical Plant . . . . . . . . . . . . . . . . . | | 440,000 |
| Expenditures—Educational and General— Scholarships and Fellowships . . . . . . . | | 80,000 |
| Expenditures—Auxiliary Enterprises . . . . . . | | 2,050,000 |
| Mandatory Transfer for Principal and Interest— Educational and General . . . . . . . . | | 100,000 |
| Mandatory Transfer for Principal and Interest— Auxiliary Enterprises . . . . . . . . . . | | 225,000 |
| Mandatory Transfer for Renewals and Replacements—Educational and General . . | | 80,000 |
| Mandatory Transfer for Renewals and Replacements—Auxiliary Enterprises . . . . | | 50,000 |
| Mandatory Transfer for Loan Fund Matching Grant . . . . . . . . . . . . . . . . . | | 2,000 |
| Nonmandatory Transfer for Unrestricted Gifts Allocated to Other Funds . . . . . . . . | | 580,000 |

Note that the net increase in the Fund Balance account in Entries 8*b* and 8*c* is $83,000, which agrees with the amounts shown in Illustrations 11–2 and 11–3.

## Current Funds—Restricted

Assume the beginning balances for the current funds—restricted are as follows:

|  | Debit | Credit |
|---|---|---|
| Cash . . . . . . . . . . . . . . . . . . . . . . . . . . . . | $ 80,000 |  |
| Investments . . . . . . . . . . . . . . . . . . . . . . . | 225,000 |  |
| Accounts receivable . . . . . . . . . . . . . . . . . . . | 50,000 |  |
| Accounts payable . . . . . . . . . . . . . . . . . . . . |  | $ 30,000 |
| Fund balances . . . . . . . . . . . . . . . . . . . . . . |  | 325,000 |
| Totals . . . . . . . . . . . . . . . . . . . . . . . . . . . | $355,000 | $355,000 |

Since current restricted revenues are not considered to be earned until authorized expenditures take place, increases in assets of current funds—restricted are recorded as additions to the Fund Balances accounts. Illustration 11–3 shows the sources of additions for the period totaling $1,025,000. Entry 9 records the additions.

| 9. Cash . . . . . . . . . . . . . . . . . . . . . . | 980,000 |  |
|---|---|---|
| Accounts Receivable . . . . . . . . . . . . . . . | 45,000 |  |
| Fund Balances—Federal Grants and Contracts— |  |  |
| Restricted . . . . . . . . . . . . . . . . |  | 370,000 |
| Fund Balances—Private Gifts, Grants, and |  |  |
| Contracts—Restricted . . . . . . . . . . . |  | 335,000 |
| Fund Balances—Investment Income—Restricted . |  | 320,000 |

Expenditures for the period amounted to $965,000 in total; the detail shown in Illustration 11–2 is omitted for the sake of brevity:

| 10. Expenditures—Educational and General . . . . . . | 965,000 |  |
|---|---|---|
| Accounts Payable . . . . . . . . . . . . . . . |  | 2,000 |
| Cash . . . . . . . . . . . . . . . . . . . . . . |  | 963,000 |

As noted previously when current funds—restricted incur expenditures specified by donors and grantors, revenue is considered to be earned in an equal amount. The amount debited to Fund Balances in Entry 11 equals the amounts shown as Revenues for the various sources as shown in the "Restricted" column in Illustration 11–2.

| 11. Fund Balances . . . . . . . . . . . . . . . . . . | 965,000 |  |
|---|---|---|
| Revenues—Federal Grants and Contracts . . . |  | 320,000 |
| Revenues—Private Gifts, Grants, and Contracts |  | 330,000 |
| Revenues—Endowment Income . . . . . . . |  | 315,000 |

Many granting agencies, including the federal government, allow colleges to include overhead charges, including depreciation, as part of grant expenditures. In this example, $25,000 has been allowed as indirect cost recoveries. Since that amount is now available for unrestricted purposes the entry in the current restricted funds would be as follows (this amount is included in the $30,000 unrestricted revenues from Federal Grants and Contracts in Entry 3a):

```
12. Fund Balances—Indirect Costs Recovered . . . . .    25,000
        Cash  . . . . . . . . . . . . . . . . . . .                25,000
```

Both Illustrations 11–2 and 11–3 report that the institution refunded $10,000 to grantors, apparently because the governing board determined that actions required by the grantors would not be undertaken.

```
13. Fund Balances—Refunded to Grantors  . . . . . . .    10,000
        Cash  . . . . . . . . . . . . . . . . . .                10,000
```

Cash was received in the amount of $48,000 from various grantors who had been billed in the previous year:

```
14. Cash  . . . . . . . . . . . . . . . . . . . .    48,000
        Accounts Receivable  . . . . . . . . . . .            48,000
```

Investments were purchased in the amount of $30,000:

```
15. Investments  . . . . . . . . . . . . . . . . .    30,000
        Cash  . . . . . . . . . . . . . . . . . . .            30,000
```

The Statement of Changes in Fund Balances during the year reports a net increase in Current Funds—Restricted in the amount of $25,000. The revenues and expenditures are offsetting, as they should be, and are closed with the following entry:

```
16. Revenues—Federal Grants and Contracts  . . . . .   320,000
    Revenues—Private Gifts, Grants, and Contracts  . .   330,000
    Revenues—Endowment Income  . . . . . . . . . .   315,000
        Expenditures—Educational and General . . . .          965,000
```

## Loan Funds

Loan Funds assets consist primarily of cash, investments, and receivables resulting from loans to students, faculty, and staff. Illustration 11–1 indicates that the Fund Balances relate to the federal government, and to university funds, both unrestricted and restricted. Assume the following balances for the Loan Funds for Razorback University as of July 1, 19y0:

| | Debit | Credit |
|---|---|---|
| Cash . . . . . . . . . . . . . . . . . . . . . . . . . . . . | $ 15,000 | |
| Investments . . . . . . . . . . . . . . . . . . . . . . . . | 87,000 | |
| Loans to students, faculty, and staff . . . . . . . . . . . . | 459,000 | |
| Allowance for uncollectible loans . . . . . . . . . . . . . . | | $ 9,000 |
| Fund balances: | | |
|   U.S. government grants refundable . . . . . . . . . . . . | | 35,000 |
|   University funds—restricted . . . . . . . . . . . . . . | | 320,000 |
|   University funds—unrestricted . . . . . . . . . . . . . | | 197,000 |
|     Totals . . . . . . . . . . . . . . . . . . . . . . . . | $561,000 | $561,000 |

The following entry summarizes the additions and transfers to the loan fund Fund Balances accounts. Each credit account is self-explanatory:

| | | |
|---|---|---|
| 17. Cash . . . . . . . . . . . . . . . . . . . . . . . | 221,000 | |
|     Fund Balances—University Funds—Restricted— | | |
|       Private Gifts and Contracts . . . . . . . . . | | 80,000 |
|     Fund Balances—University Funds—Restricted— | | |
|       Investment Income . . . . . . . . . . . . | | 8,000 |
|     Fund Balances—University Funds—Restricted— | | |
|       Realized Gains on Investments . . . . . . | | 2,000 |
|     Fund Balances—University Funds—Restricted— | | |
|       Interest on Loans Receivable . . . . . . . | | 12,000 |
|     Fund Balances—U.S. Government Grants . . . | | 17,000 |
|     Fund Balances—University Funds—Restricted— | | |
|       Mandatory Transfer from Unrestricted Funds | | |
|       for Matching Grant . . . . . . . . . . . . | | 2,000 |
|     Fund Balances—University Funds— | | |
|       Unrestricted—Nonmandatory Transfer of | | |
|       Unrestricted Gifts . . . . . . . . . . . . . | | 100,000 |

Separate Fund Balance accounts should be kept for the individual restricted loan funds in order to facilitate the preparation of periodic reports to the grantors, and to provide for appropriate compliance audits.

Deductions from the Fund Balances accounts of the loan funds as shown in Illustration 11–3 are summarized in the following entry:

| | | |
|---|---|---|
| 18. Fund Balances—University Funds—Restricted— | | |
|     Refunded to Grantors . . . . . . . . . . . . . | 6,000 | |
|     Fund Balances—University Funds—Restricted— | | |
|     Administrative and Collection Costs . . . . . . | 2,000 | |
|       Cash . . . . . . . . . . . . . . . . . . . | | 8,000 |

Assume that loans were made in the amount of $301,000 and that other loans were repaid in the amount of $90,000. Assume, also, that a year-end adjusting entry was made to increase the Allowance for Uncollectible Loans for estimated write-offs:

| | | |
|---|---|---|
| 19a. Loans to Students, Faculty, and Staff . . . . . . . | 301,000 | |
|       Cash . . . . . . . . . . . . . . . . . . . . | | 301,000 |
| | | |
| 19b. Cash . . . . . . . . . . . . . . . . . . . . . . | 90,000 | |
|       Loans to Students, Faculty, and Staff . . . . . | | 90,000 |
| | | |
| 19c. Fund Balances—U.S. Government Grants | | |
|     Refundable—Loan Cancellations and Write-Offs | 2,000 | |
|     Allowance for Uncollectible Loans . . . . . | | 2,000 |

## Endowment and Similar Funds

An examination of Illustration 11–1 indicates that Razorback University has fund balances for endowment, term endowment, and quasi-endowment funds. The quasi-endowment funds are further classified as restricted and unrestricted. Each category of Fund Balance should, of course, be supported by subsidiary records to show the balance for each individual endowment. Assume that Razorback University's endowment and similar funds had the following balances as of July 1, 19y0:

|  | Debit | Credit |
|---|---|---|
| Cash . . . . . . . . . . . . . . . . . . . . . . . . . . . | $ 50,000 |  |
| Investments . . . . . . . . . . . . . . . . . . . . . . | 8,050,000 |  |
| Fund balances—endowment . . . . . . . . . . . . . . . |  | $6,100,000 |
| Fund balances—term endowment . . . . . . . . . . . |  | 1,050,000 |
| Fund balances—quasi-endowment—unrestricted . . . . . . |  | 605,000 |
| Fund balances—quasi-endowment—restricted . . . . . . . |  | 345,000 |
| Totals . . . . . . . . . . . . . . . . . . . . . . . . | $8,100,000 | $8,100,000 |

The additions to the Fund Balances of this fund group and transfers to the group result from entries during the year which are summarized as:

```
20. Cash  . . . . . . . . . . . . . . . . . .   1,500,000
        Fund Balances—Endowment—Private Gifts,
            Grants, and Contracts . . . . . . . . . .           800,000
        Fund Balances—Term Endowment—Private
            Gifts, Grants, and Contracts . . . . . . . .        200,000
        Fund Balances—Term Endowment—Investment
            Income  . . . . . . . . . . . . . . . . .            50,000
        Fund Balances—Quasi-Endowment—
            Unrestricted—Nonmandatory Transfer from
            Current Funds . . . . . . . . . . . . . .           450,000
```

During the year, $60,000 in term endowments expired. $30,000 was unrestricted and was recorded as a revenue in the current funds—unrestricted (see Entries 3a and 3b). $30,000 was restricted to plant purposes and is also recorded in Entry 30:

```
21. Fund Balances—Term Endowments—Expired Term
        Endowments . . . . . . . . . . . . . . . . .    60,000
            Cash  . . . . . . . . . . . . . . . . . . .           60,000
```

Investments in the amount of $3,000,000 were sold for $3,105,000. Investments costing $4,500,000 were purchased:

```
22. Cash  . . . . . . . . . . . . . . . . . . .   3,105,000
        Fund Balances—Quasi-Endowment—
            Unrestricted—Realized Gains on Investments           55,000
        Fund Balances—Quasi-Endowment—
            Restricted—Realized Gains on Investments  .           50,000
            Investments  . . . . . . . . . . . . . . .          3,000,000

23. Investments  . . . . . . . . . . . . . . . . .   4,500,000
            Cash  . . . . . . . . . . . . . . . . . . .          4,500,000
```

It should be noted that many public universities maintain separate Foundations where endowments and many restricted accounts are kept. In those cases, note disclosure should disclose the existence of those Foundations.

## Annuity and Life Income Funds

The annuity and life income funds of Razorback University had the following balances as of July 1, 19y0:

|                          | Debit       | Credit      |
|--------------------------|-------------|-------------|
| Annuity funds:           |             |             |
| Cash                     | $   30,000  |             |
| Investments              | 2,500,000   |             |
| Annuities payable        |             | $1,600,000  |
| Fund balances            |             | 930,000     |
| Life income funds:       |             |             |
| Cash                     | 20,000      |             |
| Investments              | 2,050,000   |             |
| Income payable           |             | 10,000      |
| Fund balances            |             | 2,060,000   |
| Totals                   | $4,600,000  | $4,600,000  |

Note that annuity funds have a large balance in the account Annuities Payable. That amount represents the present value of future payments due under the annuity agreements. The liability in the **life income** funds reflects only the currently unpaid portion of income due contributors, as explained in a previous section of this chapter. The following entries summarize the transactions in **annuity** funds:

| 24. Cash—Annuity Funds | 410,000 | |
|---|---|---|
| Fund Balances—Private Gifts and Contracts— | | |
| Annuity Funds | | 410,000 |
| | | |
| 25. Fund Balances—Adjustment of Actuarial Liability for | | |
| Annuities Payable | 300,000 | |
| Annuities Payable | | 300,000 |
| | | |
| 26. Annuities Payable | 250,000 | |
| Cash—Annuity Funds | | 250,000 |
| | | |
| 27. Investments | 180,000 | |
| Cash—Annuity Funds | | 180,000 |

Summary entries for the **life income** funds are:

| 28. Cash—Life Income Funds | 295,000 | |
|---|---|---|
| Fund Balances—Private Gifts and Contracts | | 295,000 |
| | | |
| 29. Investments | 305,000 | |
| Cash—Life Income Funds | | 305,000 |

Additional entries would be required for the receipt of investment income and the simultaneous recording of liabilities to the life income recipients. These transactions do not flow through the Statement of Changes in Fund Balances as the income is a liability, not a resource of the fund.

## Plant Funds

Remember that the plant fund group consists of four distinct subgroups: (1) unexpended plant funds, (2) funds for renewals and replacements, (3) funds for retirement of indebtedness, and (4) investment in plant. Transactions related to Illustration 11–3 are illustrated for each subgroup in turn.

**Unexpended plant funds** account for assets held for the acquisition or construction of property, plant, and equipment of colleges and universities. This subgroup is similar to the capital projects funds of state and local governmental units except that the debt associated with uncompleted projects is included within the fund structure and that the Construction in Progress account may be maintained (or in the Investment in Plant subgroup). The beginning balances for the unexpended plant funds are as follows:

|  | Debit | Credit |
|---|---|---|
| Cash . . . . . . . . . . . . . . . . . . . . . . . . . | $ 250,000 | |
| Investments . . . . . . . . . . . . . . . . . . . . | 1,300,000 | |
| Fund balances—restricted . . . . . . . . . . . . . . : . . | | $1,200,000 |
| Fund balances—unrestricted . . . . . . . . . . . . . . . | | 350,000 |
| Totals . . . . . . . . . . . . . . . . . . . . . | $1,550,000 | $1,550,000 |

The entries for the fiscal year are presented below. Receipts, all received in cash, represented borrowed funds and additions to Fund Balances—Restricted and Fund Balances—Unrestricted, as indicated by the descriptive account titles:

```
30. Cash  . . . . . . . . . . . . . . . . . . . . .  1,180,000
        Notes Payable  . . . . . . . . . . . . . . .              100,000
        Bonds Payable  . . . . . . . . . . . . . . .              540,000
        Fund Balances  Restricted—Expired Term
          Endowment  . . . . . . . . . . . . . . . .               30,000
        Fund Balances—Restricted—State
          Appropriations . . . . . . . . . . . . . .              300,000
        Fund Balances—Restricted—Private Gifts,
          Grants, and Contracts . . . . . . . . . . .              50,000
        Fund Balances—Restricted—Investment
          Income  . . . . . . . . . . . . . . . . . .             130,000
        Fund Balances—Unrestricted—Nonmandatory
          Transfer from Current Funds for Allocation of
          Unrestricted Gifts . . . . . . . . . . . . .             30,000
```

During the year, construction amounted to $1,390,000:

```
31. Construction in Progress . . . . . . . . . . . .  1,390,000
        Cash  . . . . . . . . . . . . . . . . . . . .            1,390,000
```

All projects were completed. Fund Balances accounts and debt were closed out, to be recorded in the investment in plant subgroup (see Entry 40). Note that the net effect of Entries 30 and 32 is that Restricted Fund Balances were increased by $10,000 and that the Unrestricted Fund Balances were decreased by $220,000:

```
32. Fund Balances—Restricted—Expended for Plant
      Facilities . . . . . . . . . . . . . . . . . . .   500,000
    Fund Balances—Unrestricted—Expended for Plant
      Facilities . . . . . . . . . . . . . . . . . . .   250,000
    Notes Payable  . . . . . . . . . . . . . . . . . .   100,000
    Bonds Payable  . . . . . . . . . . . . . . . . . .   540,000
        Construction in Progress . . . . . . . . . . .            1,390,000
```

The **funds for renewals and replacements** exist to provide a mechanism to accumulate resources for rehabilitation and replacements of existing facilities. Often, in practice, this subgroup is used to account for construction (really, remodeling) activities, as is the case for Razorback University. The balances, as of July 1, 19y0, were as follows:

|  | Debit | Credit |
|---|---|---|
| Cash | $ 5,000 | |
| Investments | 200,000 | |
| Deposits with trustees | 80,000 | |
| Fund balances—restricted | | $250,000 |
| Fund balances—unrestricted | | 35,000 |
| Totals | $285,000 | $285,000 |

Investment income and a required transfer from the Current Funds—Unrestricted was received, some of which was deposited with trustees:

```
33. Cash                                      135,000
       Deposits with Trustees                  15,000
          Fund Balances—Restricted—Investment
             Income                                        20,000
          Fund Balances—Restricted—Mandatory Transfer
             for Renewals and Replacements                130,000
```

Some investments were sold at a gain:

```
34. Cash                                      130,000
       Investments                                        125,000
       Fund Balances—Restricted—Realized Gains on
          Investments                                       5,000
```

Funds were used for renovations and replacements:

```
35. Fund Balances—Restricted—Expended for Plant
       Facilities                             260,000
       Cash                                               260,000
```

The **funds for retirement of indebtedness** are accounted for in a manner similar to debt service funds of state and local governmental units. As Illustration 11–1 shows, the investments of this subgroup are deposited with trustees. The beginning balances for this subgroup are as follows:

|  | Debit | Credit |
|---|---|---|
| Cash | $ 30,000 | |
| Deposits with trustees | 330,000 | |
| Fund balances—restricted | | $280,000 |
| Fund balances—unrestricted | | 80,000 |
| Totals | $360,000 | $360,000 |

Cash was received from a private gift, investment earnings, and a mandatory transfer from the unrestricted funds:

| 36. Cash . . . . . . . . . . . . . . . . . . . . | 385,000 | |
| Fund Balances—Restricted—Private Gifts, | | |
| Grants and Contracts . . . . . . . . . . . | | 30,000 |
| Fund Balances—Restricted—Investment | | |
| Income . . . . . . . . . . . . . . . . . | | 30,000 |
| Fund Balances—Restricted—Mandatory | | |
| Transfer from Current Funds for Principal | | |
| and Interest . . . . . . . . . . . . . . . | | 325,000 |

Interest and principal payments were made; $50,000 was from previously accumulated unrestricted funds. Some administrative costs were also paid:

| 37. Fund Balances—Restricted—Retirement of | | |
| Indebtedness . . . . . . . . . . . . . . . | 150,000 | |
| Fund Balances—Restricted—Interest on | | |
| Indebtedness . . . . . . . . . . . . . . . | 140,000 | |
| Fund Balances—Unrestricted—Interest on | | |
| Indebtedness . . . . . . . . . . . . . . . | 50,000 | |
| Fund Balances—Restricted—Administrative Costs . | 2,000 | |
| Cash . . . . . . . . . . . . . . . . . . . | | 342,000 |

Investments in the amount of $3,000 were converted into cash:

| 38. Cash . . . . . . . . . . . . . . . . . . . . | 3,000 | |
| Deposits with Trustees . . . . . . . . . . . . | | 3,000 |

The **investment in plant** section of the plant funds consists of fixed asset accounts, debt related to the fixed assets, and an equity account, "Net Investment in Plant."

As mentioned earlier in the chapter, colleges and universities may choose either to record, or not to record, depreciation. While FASB guidance is not specific regarding procedures, most colleges recording depreciation will make the entry in the investment in plant subgroup. The entry would be:

| Fund Balances—Depreciation Charges . . . . . . . . | xx | |
| Allowance for Depreciation . . . . . . . . . . . | | xx |

The debit to Fund Balances would reduce the Net Investment in Plant account (the equity account) at year-end.

Assume that Razorback University chooses not to record depreciation at this time. The beginning balances for the investment in plant subgroup are as follows:

|  | Debit | Credit |
| --- | --- | --- |
| Land . . . . . . . . . . . . . . . . . . . . . . . . . | $    600,000 | |
| Land improvements . . . . . . . . . . . . . . . . . . | 1,200,000 | |
| Buildings . . . . . . . . . . . . . . . . . . . . . . | 35,000,000 | |
| Equipment . . . . . . . . . . . . . . . . . . . . . . | 10,800,000 | |
| Library books . . . . . . . . . . . . . . . . . . . . | 1,800,000 | |
| Notes payable . . . . . . . . . . . . . . . . . . . . | | $    500,000 |
| Bonds payable . . . . . . . . . . . . . . . . . . . . | | 20,000,000 |
| Net investment in plant . . . . . . . . . . . . . . . | | 28,900,000 |
| Totals . . . . . . . . . . . . . . . . . . . . . . | $49,400,000 | $49,400,000 |

## ILLUSTRATION 11–1

### RAZORBACK UNIVERSITY
### Balance Sheet
### June 30, 19y1
#### (with comparative figures at June 30, 19y0)

**Assets**

| | Current Year | Prior Year |
|---|---|---|
| **Current Funds:** | | |
| Unrestricted: | | |
| Cash | $ 230,000 | $ 135,000 |
| Accounts receivable | 250,000 | 200,000 |
| Inventories | 58,000 | 55,000 |
| Prepaid expenses and deferred charges | 45,000 | 45,000 |
| Total Unrestricted | 583,000 | 435,000 |
| Restricted: | | |
| Cash | 80,000 | 80,000 |
| Accounts receivable | 47,000 | 50,000 |
| Investments | 255,000 | 225,000 |
| Total Restricted | 382,000 | 355,000 |
| Total Current Funds | $ 965,000 | $ 790,000 |
| **Loan Funds:** | | |
| Cash | $ 17,000 | $ 15,000 |
| Investments | 87,000 | 87,000 |
| Loans to students, faculty, and staff, less allowance of $11,000 current year and $9,000 prior year | 659,000 | 450,000 |
| Total Loan Funds | $ 763,000 | $ 552,000 |
| **Endowment and Similar Funds:** | | |
| Cash | $ 95,000 | $ 50,000 |
| Investments | 9,550,000 | 8,050,000 |
| Total Endowment and Similar Funds | $ 9,645,000 | $ 8,100,000 |

**Liabilities and Fund Balances**

| | Current Year | Prior Year |
|---|---|---|
| **Current Funds:** | | |
| Unrestricted: | | |
| Accounts payable | $ 120,000 | $ 80,000 |
| Deferred credits | 325,000 | 300,000 |
| Fund balance | 138,000 | 55,000 |
| Total Unrestricted | 583,000 | 435,000 |
| Restricted: | | |
| Accounts payable | 32,000 | 30,000 |
| Fund balances | 350,000 | 325,000 |
| Total Restricted | 382,000 | 355,000 |
| Total Current Funds | $ 965,000 | $ 790,000 |
| **Loan Funds:** | | |
| Fund balances: | | |
| U.S. government grants refundable | $ 50,000 | $ 35,000 |
| University funds: | | |
| Restricted | 416,000 | 320,000 |
| Unrestricted | 297,000 | 197,000 |
| Total Loan Funds | $ 763,000 | $ 552,000 |
| **Endowment and Similar Funds:** | | |
| Fund balances: | | |
| Endowment | $ 6,900,000 | $ 6,100,000 |
| Term endowment | 1,240,000 | 1,050,000 |
| Quasi-endowment—unrestricted | 1,110,000 | 605,000 |
| Quasi-endowment—restricted | 395,000 | 345,000 |
| Total Endowment and Similar Funds | $ 9,645,000 | $ 8,100,000 |

**Assets**

| Annuity and Life Income Funds: | | |
|---|---:|---:|
| Annuity Funds: | | |
| Cash | $ 10,000 | $ 30,000 |
| Investments | 2,680,000 | 2,500,000 |
| Total Annuity Funds | 2,690,000 | 2,530,000 |
| Life Income Funds: | | |
| Cash | 10,000 | 20,000 |
| Investments | 2,355,000 | 2,050,000 |
| Total Life Income Funds | 2,365,000 | 2,070,000 |
| Total Annuity and Life Income Funds | $ 5,055,000 | $ 4,600,000 |
| **Plant Funds:** | | |
| Unexpended: | | |
| Cash | $ 40,000 | $ 250,000 |
| Investments | 1,300,000 | 1,300,000 |
| Total Unexpended | 1,340,000 | 1,550,000 |
| Renewals and Replacements: | | |
| Cash | 10,000 | 5,000 |
| Investments | 75,000 | 200,000 |
| Deposits with trustees | 95,000 | 80,000 |
| Total Renewals and Replacements | 180,000 | 285,000 |
| Retirement of Indebtedness: | | |
| Cash | 76,000 | 30,000 |
| Deposits with trustees | 327,000 | 330,000 |
| Total Retirement of Indebtedness | 403,000 | 360,000 |
| Investment in Plant: | | |
| Land | 600,000 | 600,000 |
| Land improvements | 1,090,000 | 1,200,000 |
| Buildings | 37,040,000 | 35,000,000 |
| Equipment | 10,935,000 | 10,800,000 |
| Library books | 1,835,000 | 1,800,000 |
| Total Investment in Plant | 51,500,000 | 49,400,000 |
| Total Plant Funds | $53,423,000 | $51,595,000 |
| **Agency Funds:** | | |
| Cash | $ 40,000 | $ 80,000 |
| Investments | 280,000 | 220,000 |
| Total Agency Funds | $ 320,000 | $ 300,000 |

**Liabilities and Fund Balances**

| Annuity and Life Income Funds: | | |
|---|---:|---:|
| Annuity Funds: | | |
| Annuities payable | $ 1,650,000 | $ 1,600,000 |
| Fund balances | 1,040,000 | 930,000 |
| Total Annuity Funds | 2,690,000 | 2,530,000 |
| Life Income Funds: | | |
| Income payable | 10,000 | 10,000 |
| Fund balances | 2,355,000 | 2,060,000 |
| Total Life Income Funds | 2,365,000 | 2,070,000 |
| Total Annuity and Life Income Funds | $ 5,055,000 | $ 4,600,000 |
| **Plant Funds:** | | |
| Unexpended: | | |
| Fund balances | | |
| Restricted | $ 1,210,000 | $ 1,200,000 |
| Unrestricted | 130,000 | 350,000 |
| Total Unexpended | 1,340,000 | 1,550,000 |
| Renewals and Replacements: | | |
| Fund balances | | |
| Restricted | 145,000 | 250,000 |
| Unrestricted | 35,000 | 35,000 |
| Total Renewals and Replacements | 180,000 | 285,000 |
| Retirement of Indebtedness: | | |
| Fund balances | | |
| Restricted | 373,000 | 280,000 |
| Unrestricted | 30,000 | 80,000 |
| Total Retirement of Indebtedness | 403,000 | 360,000 |
| Investment in Plant: | | |
| Notes payable | 550,000 | 500,000 |
| Bonds payable | 20,390,000 | 20,000,000 |
| Net investment in plant | 30,560,000 | 28,900,000 |
| Total Investment in Plant | 51,500,000 | 49,400,000 |
| Total Plant Funds | $53,423,000 | $51,595,000 |
| **Agency Funds:** | | |
| Deposits held in custody for others | $ 320,000 | $ 300,000 |
| Total Agency Funds | $ 320,000 | $ 300,000 |

Source: Reprinted from College and University Business Administration, Administrative Service, Part 5:7, pp. 2–3. Copyright 1974, by permission of the National Association of College and University Business Officers.

253

# ILLUSTRATION 11–2

## RAZORBACK UNIVERSITY
### Statement of Current Funds Revenues, Expenditures, and Other Changes
### Year Ended June 30, 19y1

| | Current Year | | | Prior Year |
| | Unrestricted | Restricted | Total | Total |
|---|---|---|---|---|
| **Revenues:** | | | | |
| Tuition and fees . . . . . . . . . | $2,880,000 | | $2,880,000 | $2,560,000 |
| Federal appropriations . . . . . . | 450,000 | | 450,000 | 425,000 |
| State appropriations . . . . . . . | 1,200,000 | | 1,200,000 | 1,150,000 |
| Local appropriations . . . . . . | 50,000 | | 50,000 | 65,000 |
| Federal grants and contracts . . . . . | 30,000 | $320,000 | 350,000 | 335,000 |
| State grants and contracts . . . . . . | 20,000 | | 20,000 | 25,000 |
| Local grants and contracts . . . . . | 15,000 | | 15,000 | 25,000 |
| Private gifts, grants, and contracts . . | 600,000 | 330,000 | 930,000 | 905,000 |
| Endowment income . . . . . . . | 250,000 | 315,000 | 565,000 | 550,000 |
| Sales and services of educational | | | | |
| activities . . . . . . . . . . . | 180,000 | | 180,000 | 190,000 |
| Sales and services of auxiliary | | | | |
| enterprises . . . . . . . . . . | 2,275,000 | | 2,275,000 | 2,200,000 |
| Expired term endowment . . . . . | 30,000 | | 30,000 | |
| Total Current Revenues . . . . . | 7,980,000 | 965,000 | 8,945,000 | 8,430,000 |
| **Expenditures and mandatory transfers:** | | | | |
| **Educational and general:** | | | | |
| Instruction . . . . . . . . . . . | 2,995,000 | 415,000 | 3,410,000 | 3,300,000 |
| Research . . . . . . . . . . . | 150,000 | 330,000 | 480,000 | 500,000 |
| Public service . . . . . . . . | 210,000 | 15,000 | 225,000 | 240,000 |
| Academic support . . . . . . . | 225,000 | | 225,000 | 205,000 |
| Student services . . . . . . . | 340,000 | | 340,000 | 330,000 |
| Institutional support . . . . . . | 370,000 | | 370,000 | 365,000 |
| Operation and maintenance | | | | |
| of plant . . . . . . . . . . . | 440,000 | | 440,000 | 405,000 |
| Scholarships and fellowships . . . . | 80,000 | 205,000 | 285,000 | 260,000 |
| Educational and General | | | | |
| Expenditures . . . . . . . . | 4,810,000 | 965,000 | 5,775,000 | 5,605,000 |
| Mandatory transfers for: | | | | |
| Principal and interest . . . . . . | 100,000 | | 100,000 | 90,000 |
| Renewals and replacements . . . | 80,000 | | 80,000 | 80,000 |
| Loan fund matching grant . . . . | 2,000 | | 2,000 | |
| Total Educational and General . | 4,992,000 | 965,000 | 5,957,000 | 5,775,000 |
| **Auxiliary enterprises:** | | | | |
| Expenditures . . . . . . . . . | 2,050,000 | | 2,050,000 | 1,980,000 |
| Mandatory transfers for: | | | | |
| Principal and interest . . . . . . | 225,000 | | 225,000 | 220,000 |
| Renewals and replacements . . . | 50,000 | | 50,000 | 50,000 |
| Total Auxiliary Enterprises . . . | 2,325,000 | | 2,325,000 | 2,250,000 |
| Total Expenditures and | | | | |
| Mandatory Transfers . . . . . | 7,317,000 | 965,000 | 8,282,000 | 8,025,000 |
| Other transfers and additions | | | | |
| (deductions) | | | | |
| Excess of restricted receipts over | | | | |
| transfers to revenues . . . . . . . | | 35,000 | 35,000 | 40,000 |
| Refunded to grantors . . . . . . . | | (10,000) | (10,000) | |
| Unrestricted gifts allocated to | | | | |
| other funds . . . . . . . . . . | (580,000) | | (580,000) | (530,000) |
| Net Increase in Fund Balances . | $  83,000 | $ 25,000 | $ 108,000 | $ (85,000) |

Source: Reprinted from *College and University Business Administration, Administrative Service,* Part 5:7, pp. 6–7.
Copyright 1974, by permission of the National Association of College and University Business Officers.

Assume that equipment with a market value of $15,000 was given to the university:

```
39. Equipment . . . . . . . . . . . . . . . . . . .      15,000
        Net Investment in Plant—Private Gifts, Grants
        and Contracts  . . . . . . . . . . . . . . .              15,000
```

During the year, the following plant acquisitions were made from all funds, including current funds acquisition of equipment, library books, and so on. Note the addition of bonds and notes payable from completion of the project in Entry 32:

```
40. Buildings  . . . . . . . . . . . . . . . . . .  2,040,000
    Equipment . . . . . . . . . . . . . . . . . . .   220,000
    Library Books  . . . . . . . . . . . . . . . .     35,000
        Notes Payable . . . . . . . . . . . . . .                100,000
        Bonds Payable . . . . . . . . . . . . . .                540,000
        Net Investment in Plant—Expended for Plant
        Facilities . . . . . . . . . . . . . . . .              1,655,000
```

Principal was paid on notes and bonds. This action increases the equity account:

```
41. Notes Payable . . . . . . . . . . . . . . . .      50,000
    Bonds Payable . . . . . . . . . . . . . . . .     150,000
        Net Investment in Plant—Retirement of
        Indebtedness . . . . . . . . . . . . . . .              200,000
```

Certain facilities were scrapped or sold:

```
42. Net Investment in Plant—Disposal of Facilities . . .  210,000
        Land Improvements . . . . . . . . . . . .                110,000
        Equipment . . . . . . . . . . . . . . . .                100,000
```

It should be remembered that the investment in plant subgroup accounts for fixed assets and for related debt of auxiliary enterprise activities in the same manner as the fixed assets (and related debt) used for educational and general activities.

## Agency Funds

Agency funds do not have Fund Balance accounts, therefore additions to and deductions from agency funds should not be reported in the Statement of Changes in Fund Balances. A Statement of Changes in Assets and Liabilities of agency funds could be reported as illustrated in Chapter 9 (Illustration 9-1), but this is not generally done by colleges and universities. Assets and offsetting liabilities of agency funds are reported in the Balance Sheet (Illustration 11–1) to disclose the existence of the agency relationship.

Assume the beginning balances for the agency funds for Razorback University were as follows:

ILLUSTRATION 11–3

**RAZORBACK UNIVERSITY**
**Statement of Changes in Fund Balances**
**Year Ended June 30, 19y1**

| | Current Funds | | Loan Funds | Endowment and Similar Funds | Annuity and Life Income Funds | Plant Funds | | | |
|---|---|---|---|---|---|---|---|---|---|
| | Unrestricted | Restricted | | | | Unexpended | Renewals and Replacements | Retirement of Indebtedness | Investment in Plant |
| Revenues and other additions: | | | | | | | | | |
| Unrestricted current fund revenues | $7,980,000 | | | | | | | | |
| Expired term endowment—restricted | | | | | | $ 30,000 | | | |
| State appropriations—restricted | | | | | | 300,000 | | | |
| Federal grants and contracts—restricted | | $ 370,000 | | | | | | | |
| Private gifts, grants, and contracts—restricted | | 335,000 | $ 80,000 | $1,000,000 | $ 705,000 | 50,000 | $ 20,000 | $ 30,000 | $ 15,000 |
| Investment income—restricted | | 320,000 | 8,000 | 50,000 | | 130,000 | | 30,000 | |
| Realized gains on investments—unrestricted | | | | 55,000 | | | | | |
| Realized gains on investments—restricted | | | 2,000 | 50,000 | | | 5,000 | | |
| Interest on loans receivable | | | 12,000 | | | | | | |
| U.S. government advances | | | 17,000 | | | | | | |
| Expended for plant facilities | | | | | | | | | 1,655,000 |
| Retirement of indebtedness | | | | | | | | | 200,000 |
| Total Revenues and Other Additions | $7,980,000 | $1,025,000 | $119,000 | $1,155,000 | $ 705,000 | $ 510,000 | $ 25,000 | $ 60,000 | $ 1,870,000 |

Expenditures and other deductions:

| | | | | | | | | |
|---|--:|--:|--:|--:|--:|--:|--:|--:|--:|
| Educational and general expenditures | $4,810,000 | $ 965,000 | | | | | | | |
| Auxiliary enterprises expenditures | 2,050,000 | | | | | | | | |
| Indirect costs recovered | | 25,000 | | | | | | | |
| Refunded to grantors | | 10,000 | $ 6,000 | | | | | | |
| Loan cancellations and writeoffs | | | 2,000 | | | | | | |
| Administrative and collection costs | | | 2,000 | | | | | $ 2,000 | |
| Adjustment of actuarial liability for annuities payable | | | | | $ 300,000 | | | | |
| Expended for plant facilities | | | | | | $ 750,000 | $260,000 | | |
| Retirement of indebtedness | | | | | | | | 150,000 | |
| Interest on indebtedness | | | | | | | | 190,000 | |
| Disposal of plant facilities | | | | | | | | | $ 210,000 |
| Expired term endowments ($30,000 unrestricted, $30,000 restricted to plant) | | | | $ 60,000 | | | | | |
| Total Expenditures and Other Deductions | $6,860,000 | $1,030,000 | $ 10,000 | $ 60,000 | $ 300,000 | $ 750,000 | $260,000 | $342,000 | $ 210,000 |
| Transfers among funds—additions (deductions) | | | | | | | | | |
| Mandatory: | | | | | | | | | |
| Principal and interest | (325,000) | | | | | | | 325,000 | |
| Renewals and replacements | (130,000) | | | | | | 130,000 | | |
| Loan fund matching grant | (2,000) | | 2,000 | | | | | | |
| Unrestricted gifts allocated | (580,000) | | 100,000 | 450,000 | 30,000 | | | | |
| Total Transfers | (1,037,000) | | 102,000 | 450,000 | 30,000 | | 130,000 | 325,000 | |
| Net increase (decrease) for the year | 83,000 | | 25,000 | 1,545,000 | 405,000 | (210,000) | (105,000) | 43,000 | 1,660,000 |
| Fund Balance at Beginning of Year | 55,000 | | 325,000 | 8,100,000 | 2,990,000 | 1,550,000 | 285,000 | 360,000 | 28,900,000 |
| Fund Balance at End of Year | $ 138,000 | | $ 350,000 | $9,645,000 | $3,395,000 | $1,340,000 | $180,000 | $403,000 | $30,560,000 |

Source: Reprinted from College and University Business Administration, Administrative Service, Part 5:7, pp. 4–5. Copyright 1974, by permission of the National Association of College and University Business Officers.

|                                              | Debit      | Credit     |
| -------------------------------------------- | ---------- | ---------- |
| Cash  . . . . . . . . . . . . . . . . . . . . . . . . . . . | $ 80,000   |            |
| Investments  . . . . . . . . . . . . . . . . . . . . . . | 220,000    |            |
| Deposits held in custody for others . . . . . . . . . . . . . . |            | $300,000   |
| Totals . . . . . . . . . . . . . . . . . . . . . . . | $300,000   | $300,000   |

Assume student groups and others deposited $130,000, $110,000 in withdrawals were made, and $60,000 in cash was invested:

| 43. | Cash  . . . . . . . . . . . . . . . . . . . . | 130,000 |         |
|     | Deposits Held in Custody for Others  . . . . . |         | 130,000 |

| 44. | Deposits Held in Custody for Others . . . . . . . | 110,000 |         |
|     | Cash  . . . . . . . . . . . . . . . . . . . . |         | 110,000 |

| 45. | Investments  . . . . . . . . . . . . . . . . . | 60,000 |        |
|     | Cash  . . . . . . . . . . . . . . . . . . . . |        | 60,000 |

Detailed records should be kept for each student group and for others for which the agency is acting as agent.

## ILLUSTRATIVE FINANCIAL STATEMENTS

Illustrations 11–1, 11–2, and 11–3 presented the three required financial statements for colleges and universities.

The **Balance Sheet** (Illustration 11–1) is presented in a "pancake" format, although a columnar approach may be used. Note that, in all cases, restricted and unrestricted fund balance accounts are disclosed separately. Some universities choose to present combined information for the plant funds group, with separate disclosure of the Fund Balance amounts for the four subgroups.

The **Statement of Current Funds Revenues, Expenditures, and Other Changes** (Illustration 11–2) presents those revenues and expenditures that have been recognized, as well as other Fund Balance changes, separately, for the unrestricted and restricted portions. Note that the revenues equal the expenditures for the Current Funds—Restricted; remember that revenues are recognized only after the expenditures are recognized. The $35,000 "Excess of Restricted Receipts over Transfers to Revenues" represents the total additions to Fund Balance (see Illustration 11–3) of $1,025,000 less the indirect cost recoveries of $25,000 less the revenues recognized of $965,000. Note also that Mandatory Transfers are reported together with Expenditures, while other changes are reported separately.

The **Statement of Changes in Fund Balances** (Illustration 11–3) presents **all** of the changes in the Fund Balance accounts of all except the agency funds. The only "Revenues" in this statement are reported in the Current Funds—Unrestricted. All other amounts represent direct credits to the Fund Balance accounts. Similarly, the only "Expenditures" in this statement are reported in the Current Funds, both Unrestricted and

Restricted. All other amounts represent direct credits to Fund Balances, as described in this chapter. Students should compare how the net increases in Fund Balance for the current funds are presented in Illustrations 11–2 and 11–3.

## SELECTED REFERENCES

American Institute of Certified Public Accountants, *Audits of Colleges and Universities.* 2nd ed. New York, 1975.

_____: *Statement of Position 74-8.* New York, 1974.

Financial Accounting Standards Board. *Statement of Financial Accounting Standards No. 32: Specialized Accounting and Reporting Principles and Practices in AICPA Statements of Position and Guides on Accounting and Auditing Matters.* Norwalk, Conn., 1979.

_____. *Statement of Financial Accounting Standards No. 93: Recognition of Depreciation by Not-for-Profit Organizations.* Norwalk, Conn., 1988.

_____. *Statement of Financial Accounting Standards No. 99: Deferral of the Effective Date of Recognition of Depreciation by Not-for-Profit Organizations: An Amendment of FASB Statement No. 93.* Norwalk, Conn., 1988.

Governmental Accounting Standards Board. *Statement No. 8: Applicability of FASB Statement No. 93, "Recognition of Depreciation by Not-for-Profit Organizations," to Certain State and Local Governmental Entities.* Norwalk, Conn., 1988.

National Association of College and University Business Officers. *College and University Business Administration: Administrative Service.* Washington, D.C. In looseleaf form with periodic changes and supplements.

## QUESTIONS AND EXERCISES

11–1.  Write the numbers 1 through 10 on a sheet of paper. Beside each number, write the letter corresponding to the **best** answer to each of the following questions:

1. During the years ended June 30, 19x1 and 19x2, Sonata University conducted a cancer research project financed by a $2,000,000 gift from an alumnus. This entire amount was pledged by the donor on July 10, 19x0, although he paid only $500,000 at that date. The gift was restricted to the financing of this particular research project. During the two-year research period, Sonata's related gift receipts and research expenditures were as follows:

| | Year Ended June 30 | |
| --- | --- | --- |
| | *19x1* | *19x2* |
| Gift receipts . . . . . . . . . . . . . . . . . . . . . . | $1,200,000 | $ 800,000 |
| Cancer research expenditures . . . . . . . . . . . . | 900,000 | 1,100,000 |

How much gift revenue should Sonata report in the Restricted column of its Statement of Current Funds Revenues, Expenditures, and Other Changes for the Year Ended June 30, 19x2?

 *a.* $0.
 *b.* $800,000.
 *c.* $1,100,000.
 *d.* $2,000,000.

2. On January 2, 19x2, John Reynolds established a $500,000 trust, the income from which is to be paid to Mansfield University for general operating purposes. The Wyndham National Bank was appointed by Reynolds as trustee of the fund. What journal entry is required on Mansfield's books?

|  | Debit | Credit |
|---|---|---|
| *a.* Memorandum entry only . . . . . . . . . . . . . . . . |  |  |
| *b.* Cash . . . . . . . . . . . . . . . . . . . . . . | 500,000 |  |
|     Endowment Fund Balance . . . . . . . . . . . . |  | 500,000 |
| *c.* Nonexpendable Endowment Fund . . . . . . . . . . | 500,000 |  |
|     Endowment Fund Balance . . . . . . . . . . . . |  | 500,000 |
| *d.* Expendable Funds . . . . . . . . . . . . . . . . . . | 500,000 |  |
|     Endowment Fund Balance . . . . . . . . . . . . |  | 500,000 |

3. For the summer session of 1987, Ariba University assessed its students $1,700,000 (net of refunds), covering tuition and fees for education and general purposes. However, only $1,500,000 was expected to be realized because scholarships totaling $150,000 were granted to students, and tuition remissions of $50,000 were allowed to faculty members' children attending Ariba. What amount should Ariba include in the unrestricted current funds as revenues from student tuition and fees?
 *a.* $1,500,000.
 *b.* $1,550,000.
 *c.* $1,650,000.
 *d.* $1,700,000.

4. The following information was available from Forest College's accounting records for its current funds for the year ended March 31, 1988:

Restricted gifts received:
   Expended . . . . . . . . . . . . . . . . . . . . . . . . . . . $100,000
   Not expended . . . . . . . . . . . . . . . . . . . . . . . . . 300,000
Unrestricted gifts received:
   Expended . . . . . . . . . . . . . . . . . . . . . . . . . . . 600,000
   Not expended . . . . . . . . . . . . . . . . . . . . . . . . . 75,000

What amount should be included in current funds revenues for the year ended March 31, 1988:
 *a.* $600,000.
 *b.* $700,000.
 *c.* $775,000.
 *d.* $1,000,000.

5. Which of the following is utilized for current expenditures by a not-for-profit university?

|  | Unrestricted Current Funds | Restricted Current Funds |
|---|---|---|
| *a.* | No | No |
| *b.* | No | Yes |
| *c.* | Yes | No |
| *d.* | Yes | Yes |

6. Which of the following receipts is properly recorded as restricted current revenue on the books of a university?
   *a.* Tuition.
   *b.* Student laboratory fees.
   *c.* Housing fees.
   *d.* Research grants.

7. The following receipts were among those recorded by Kery College during 1986:

   | | |
   |---|---|
   | Unrestricted gifts | $500,000 |
   | Restricted current funds (expended for current operating purposes) | 200,000 |
   | Restricted current funds (not yet expended) | 100,000 |

   The amount that should be included in current funds revenues is:
   *a.* $800,000.
   *b.* $700,000.
   *c.* $600,000.
   *d.* $500,000.

8. Tuition waivers for which there is **no** intention of collection from the student should be classified by a not-for-profit university as:

   | | Revenues | Expenditures |
   |---|---|---|
   | *a.* | No | No |
   | *b.* | No | Yes |
   | *c.* | Yes | Yes |
   | *d.* | Yes | No |

9. Abbey University's current funds—unrestricted comprised the following:

   | | |
   |---|---|
   | Assets | $5,000,000 |
   | Liabilities (including deferred revenues of $100,000) | 3,000,000 |

   The fund balance of Abbey's unrestricted current fund was:
   *a.* $1,900,000.
   *b.* $2,000,000.
   *c.* $2,100,000.
   *d.* $5,000,000.

10. Which of the following should be included in the current funds revenues of a not-for-profit private university?

    | | Tuition Waivers | Unrestricted Bequests |
    |---|---|---|
    | *a.* | Yes | No |
    | *b.* | Yes | Yes |
    | *c.* | No | Yes |
    | *d.* | No | No |

    (AICPA, adapted)

11–2. A partial Balance Sheet of Rapapo State University as of the end of its fiscal year ended July 31, 19y0, is presented below.

**RAPAPO STATE UNIVERSITY**
**Current Funds Balance Sheet**
**July 31, 19y0**

| Assets | | Liabilities and Fund Balances | |
|---|---|---|---|
| Unrestricted: | | Unrestricted: | |
| Cash . . . . . . . . . . . | $200,000 | Accounts payable . . . . . | $100,000 |
| Accounts receivable—tuition | | Due to other funds . . . . | 40,000 |
| and fees, less allowance | | Deferred credits—tuition | |
| for doubtful accounts of | | and fees . . . . . . . . | 25,000 |
| $15,000 . . . . . . . . | 370,000 | Fund balance . . . . . . . | 445,000 |
| Prepaid expenses . . . . . | 40,000 | | |
| Total Unrestricted . . . . | 610,000 | Total Unrestricted . . . . | 610,000 |
| Restricted: | | Restricted: | |
| Cash . . . . . . . . . . . | 10,000 | Accounts payable . . . . . | 5,000 |
| Investments . . . . . . . . | 210,000 | Fund balance . . . . . . . | 215,000 |
| Total Restricted . . . . . | 220,000 | Total Restricted . . . . . | 220,000 |
| Total Current Funds . . . . . | $830,000 | Total Current Funds . . . . . | $830,000 |

The following information pertains to the year ended July 31, 19y1:

1. Cash collected from students' tuition totaled $3,000,000. Of this $3,000,000, $362,000 represented accounts receivable outstanding at July 31, 19y0; $2,500,000 was for current year tuition; and $138,000 was for tuition applicable to the semester beginning in August 19y1.
2. Deferred credits at July 31, 19y0 was recorded as earned during the year ended July 31, 19y1.
3. Accounts receivable in the amount of $13,000 was determined to be uncollectible and were written off against the allowance account. At July 31, 19y1, the allowance account was estimated at $10,000.
4. During the year, an unrestricted appropriation of $60,000 was made by the state. This state appropriation was to be paid to Rapapo sometime in August 19y1.
5. During the year, unrestricted cash gifts of $80,000 were received from alumni. Rapapo's board of trustees allocated $30,000 of these gifts to the student loan fund.
6. During the year, investments costing $25,000 were sold for $31,000. Additional restricted fund investments were purchased at a cost of $40,000. Investment income of $18,000 was earned and collected during the year.
7. Educational and general expenditures totaling $1,500,000, and auxiliary enterprise expenditures totaling $1,000,000 were recorded as accounts payable in Current Funds—Unrestricted. At July 31, 19y1, the unrestricted accounts payable balance was $75,000.
8. The restricted accounts payable balance at July 31, 19y0 was paid.
9. The $40,000 due to other funds at July 31, 19y0, was paid to the plant fund as required.
10. One quarter of the prepaid expenses at July 31, 19y0, expired during the current year, and pertained to general education expense. There was no addition to prepaid expenses during the year.

*Required:*
a. Prepare journal entries to record the foregoing transactions for the year ended July 31, 19y1. Number each entry to correspond with the number

indicated in the description of its respective transaction. Indicate whether each entry is made in the Current Funds—Unrestricted or in the Current Funds—Restricted.

b. Prepare a Statement of Changes in Fund Balances for the Current Funds for the year ended July 31, 19y1.

(AICPA, adapted)

11–3.  Show entries in general journal form for the following transactions and events which affect the accounts of a certain university. For each entry, indicate the name of the fund group affected by the entry. Assume that the account, Construction in Progress, is maintained in the Investment in Plant section of the plant funds group.

1. Unrestricted current funds cash in the amount of $180,000 was transferred to the appropriate plant fund for the payment of bonds. The transfer was required by the bond indenture. During the year bonds with a face value of $170,000 were retired by use of that cash.

2. A federal grant to the university was made in the amount of $2,000,000 to be used for a specified research project. During the year the entire $2,000,000 was received, and expenditures for the specified project totaled $900,000.

3. A grant of $800,000 was made to the university by the X Foundation, to be used for the acquisition of laboratory equipment for a new chemistry building. The grant was to be paid to the university in equal installments over a two-year period; the sum for the current year was received in cash.

4. Invoices and payrolls amounting to $30,000 for construction in progress were recorded as accounts payable.

5. Liabilities totaling $758,000 were incurred during the year for construction in progress. Construction projects were completed during the year; total costs incurred on these projects amounted to $3,500,000 for buildings, and $500,000 for improvements other than buildings.

11–4.  The following transactions took place on the books of Plato University for the fiscal year ended June 30, 19y1.

1. Unrestricted student fees amounted to $12,000,000, of which $11,000,000 was received in cash.

2. The Allowance for Doubtful Accounts for student fees was increased by $50,000. Accounts in the amount of $30,000 were written off as uncollectible.

3. Educational and general expenditures, in addition to (2) above, amounted to $11,800,000, of which $10,900,000 was paid in cash.

4. Summer fees in the amount of $200,000 were on hand as of the prior June 30 and are to be recognized as revenues in the current year. In June of the current year, $150,000 was collected in summer fees and are to be recognized as revenues in the following year.

5. Plato University received in cash a federal grant in the amount of $300,000 to conduct accounting research. Of that amount, $200,000 was expended and paid during the current year.

6. Henry J. Moneybags contributed $1,000,000 to Plato with the stipulation that the amount be permanently invested with the proceeds to be used as salary supplements for the accounting faculty. All the cash was invested in bonds. During the year, $40,000 was earned and received in cash from these investments, but none of the $40,000 was expended.

**Required:**

a. Prepare journal entries to record the foregoing transactions. Indicate the fund in which each entry is recorded.

b. Prepare, in good form, a Statement of Changes in Fund Balances for the Year Ended June 19y1. As of July 1, the Fund Balances were $100,000 for each of the funds in the problem.

**11–5.** Northern State University and Northland County both had fiscal years ending December 31.

a. Assume the following transactions were transactions of Northern State University. Prepare entries in general journal form to record each transaction in conformity with current accounting standards for colleges and universities. For each entry indicate the name of the fund, or funds, affected. You may ignore bond interest payments.

   1. On January 1, 19y1, bonds were sold at par in the amount of $3,000,000 to finance the construction of a building.

   2. On January 2, 19y1, a contract for the building construction was signed in the amount of $3,000,000.

   3. On December 31, 19y1, the building was completed, and the contractor was paid the full amount.

   4. On January 1, 19y2, a $500,000 research grant was received in cash from the federal government.

   5. On December 31, 19y2, the grant research was completed at a cost of $500,000.

   6. On December 31, 19y2, you note that the building constructed in transaction (3) is expected to last 30 years with no salvage value. Unrestricted cash in the amount of $100,000 is designated by the governing board to be held for eventual replacement or expansion of the building.

b. Assume the above transactions were transactions of Northland County. Prepare entries in general journal form to record each transaction in conformity with current accounting standards for state and local governments. For each entry, indicate the name of the fund, or funds, affected. You may ignore interest payments on the bonds.

c. Comment on the differences in accounting for colleges and universities compared with accounting for state and local government that are brought out by this problem.

**11–6.** Compare and contrast present college and university accounting and financial reporting standards with those for state and local governments in regard to: (a) current unrestricted revenues, (b) revenues restricted for certain current purposes, (c) endowments and endowment income, and (d) plant acquisition and depreciation.

Exercises 11–7 through 11–12 require entries in all of the fund groups used in college and university accounting with the exception of Funds for Renewals and Replacements. Each exercise may be assigned separately, or all of the exercises may be assigned, and combined (rather than individual fund group) statements required.

**11–7. Current Funds.** As of July 1, 19y0, the trial balance for the Current Funds for Huskie University was as follows:

|                                                    | Debit     | Credit    |
|----------------------------------------------------|-----------|-----------|
| *Current Funds—Unrestricted:*                      |           |           |
| Cash | $112,000 | |
| Accounts receivable | 232,000 | |
| Inventories | 35,000 | |
| Prepaid expenses and deferred charges | 47,000 | |
| Accounts payable | | $ 79,000 |
| Deferred credits | | 325,000 |
| Fund Balances | | 22,000 |
| Subtotals | $426,000 | $426,000 |
| *Current Funds—Restricted:*                        |           |           |
| Cash | $178,000 | |
| Investments | 125,000 | |
| Accounts receivable | 100,000 | |
| Accounts payable | | $ 77,000 |
| Fund Balances | | 326,000 |
| Subtotals | $403,000 | $403,000 |
| Totals | $829,000 | $829,000 |

During the fiscal year ended June 30, 19y1, the following transactions occurred:

**Current Funds—Unrestricted**

1. The budget was approved by the Board of Trustees, providing for anticipated revenues of $6,500,000 and planned expenditures and other charges of $6,300,000.
2. Revenues earned during the year included $850,000 in tuition and fees, $1,100,000 in state appropriations, $115,000 in federal grants and contracts (indirect cost recoveries), $600,000 in private gifts, grants, and contracts, $735,000 in endowment income, $2,560,000 in sales and services of auxiliary enterprises, and $80,000 as an expired term endowment. All but $125,000 of the student fees were collected in cash.
3. Summer school revenues of the previous year (recorded as Deferred Credits) are recognized as revenue of the current year. An additional $341,200 collected in this fiscal year will be recognized as revenue next year.
4. Educational and general expenditures amounted to $2,530,000, and expenditures for auxiliary enterprises totaled $1,980,000. All but $80,000 of these expenditures were paid in cash.
5. Mandatory transfers out included $750,000 to the funds for the retirement of indebtedness for payment of principal and interest on educational and general property and $730,000 for principal and interest on auxiliary enterprise property, and $6,000 for a loan fund matching grant. Nonmandatory transfers of unrestricted gifts were made as follows: $50,000 to the loan funds, $75,000 to the endowment and similar funds, and $80,000 to unexpended plant funds. All these transfers were made in cash. (Hint: Record the payables first to facilitate preparation of the statements in proper detail.)
6. Prepaid expenses and deferred charges increased by $3,000 during the year; the increase was paid in cash. Inventory levels remained the same.
7. The ending balance of accounts receivable at year-end was $79,000; the ending balance of accounts payable was $92,000.

8. Investments were purchased in the amount of $300,000.
9. Closing entries were prepared at year-end.

**Current Funds—Restricted**

10. Additions to Fund Balance for the year were: federal grants and contracts, $755,000; private gifts, grants, and contracts, $429,000; and investment income, $75,000. All were received in cash.
11. Expenditures for the period amounted to $1,188,000. The funding sources for these expenditures were: federal grants and contracts, $646,000; private gifts, grants, and contracts, $453,000, and endowment income, $89,000. The expenditures were all paid in cash.
12. Indirect cost recoveries amounted to $115,000. That balance was recognized as a revenue in the current unrestricted fund in transaction (2).
13. The institution refunded $15,000 to grantors.
14. The ending balance of accounts receivable was $87,000. The year-end balance of accounts payable was $75,000.

*Required:*

*a.* Prepare journal entries to record the transactions listed above.
*b.* Prepare, in good form, a Statement of Current Funds Revenues, Expenditures, and Other Changes for the Year Ended June 30, 19y1.
*c.* Prepare, in good form, a Statement of Changes in Fund Balances for the Current Funds for Huskie University for the Year Ended June 30, 19y1.
*d.* Prepare, in good form, a Balance Sheet for the Current Funds for Huskie University as of June 30, 19y1.

11–8.   **Loan Funds.** As of July 1, 19y0, the trial balance for the Loan Funds for Huskie University was as follows:

|  | Debit | Credit |
|---|---|---|
| Cash | $    32,500 | |
| Investments | 325,400 | |
| Loans to students, faculty and staff | 742,300 | |
| Allowance for uncollectible loans | | $    72,300 |
| Fund Balances—U.S. Government Grants Refundable | | 350,000 |
| Fund Balances—University Funds—Restricted | | 325,200 |
| Fund Balances—University Funds—Unrestricted | | 352,700 |
| Totals | $1,100,200 | $1,100,200 |

During the fiscal year ended June 30, 19y1, the following transactions occurred:

1. Additions to the fund balance accounts included restricted private gifts of $135,000, restricted investment income of $25,000, restricted interest on loans receivable of $21,000 and $28,000 refundable grants from the U.S. government. The entire amount was received in cash.
2. Investments costing $116,000 were sold for $119,000 (credit Fund Balances—University Funds—Restricted for the realized gain). Investments in the amount of $70,000 were purchased from university funds.
3. A mandatory transfer in the amount of $6,000 was received in cash from the Current Unrestricted Funds for a matching grant. In addition, a nonmandatory transfer was received from the same fund in the amount of $50,000.
4. Cash amounting to $13,000 was refunded from restricted university funds

to grantors. Additionally, $16,000 in restricted university loan funds cash was used for administrative and collection costs.

5. New loans were made in the amount of $350,000. Other loans were repaid in the amount of $73,000. The Allowance for Uncollectible Loans was increased by $3,000, all relating to university restricted funds.

**Required:**

a. Prepare journal entries to record the transactions listed above.

b. Prepare, in good form, a Statement of Changes in Fund Balances for the Loan Funds for Huskie University for the Year Ended June 30, 19y1.

c. Prepare, in good form, a Balance Sheet for the Loan Funds for Huskie University as of June 30, 19y1.

**11–9. Endowment and Similar Funds.** As of July 1, 19y0, the trial balance of the Endowment and Similar Funds for Huskie University was as follows:

| | Debit | Credit |
|---|---|---|
| Cash | $ 32,500 | |
| Investments | 17,650,000 | |
| Fund Balances—Endowment | | $10,350,000 |
| Fund Balances—Term Endowment | | 3,200,000 |
| Fund Balances—Quasi-Endowment Unrestricted | | 4,132,500 |
| Totals | $17,682,500 | $17,682,500 |

During the fiscal year ended June 30, 19y1, the following transactions occurred:

1. Private gifts were received in the amount of $450,000 for the endowment funds and in the amount of $125,000 for the term endowment funds.

2. Endowment investments, the income from which is restricted, were sold for $755,000. The investments originally cost $745,000. New investments were purchased in the amount of $1,050,000.

3. A nonmandatory transfer of unrestricted funds in the amount of $75,000 was received.

4. An expired term endowment was transferred to the current unrestricted fund in the amount of $80,000.

**Required:**

a. Prepare journal entries to record the transactions listed above.

b. Prepare, in good form, a Statement of Changes in Fund Balances for the Endowment and Similar Funds for Huskie University for the Year Ended June 30, 19y1.

c. Prepare, in good form, a Balance Sheet for the Endowment and Similar Funds for Huskie University as of June 30, 19y1,

**11–10. Annuity and Life Income Funds.** As of July 1, 19y0, the trial balances of the Annuity Funds and of the Life Income Funds for Huskie University were as follows:

| | Debit | Credit |
|---|---|---|
| Annuity Funds: | | |
| Cash | $ 13,200 | |
| Investments | 5,490,000 | |
| Annuities payable | | $3,865,000 |
| Fund Balances | | 1,638,200 |
| Totals | $5,503,200 | $5,503,200 |

|                              | Debit | Credit |
|------------------------------|------:|-------:|
| Life Income Funds:           |       |        |
| Cash . . . . . . . . . . . . . . . . . . . . . . . . . . . | $ 32,300 |  |
| Investments . . . . . . . . . . . . . . . . . . . . . | 2,190,000 |  |
| Income payable . . . . . . . . . . . . . . . . . . . |  | $ 17,500 |
| Fund Balances . . . . . . . . . . . . . . . . . . . |  | 2,204,800 |
| Totals . . . . . . . . . . . . . . . . . . . . . . . . | $2,222,300 | $2,222,300 |

During the fiscal year ended June 30, 19y1, the following transactions occurred:

**Annuity Funds**

1. Cash in the amount of $963,000 was received from individuals establishing annuities. The present value of annuities payable to these individuals was ascertained to be $475,000.
2. Annuitants were paid $416,000 in cash.
3. The actuary reported that the present value of the liability to the annuitants should be increased by $25,000.
4. Investments were purchased in the amount of $500,000.

**Life Income Funds**

5. An additional $562,000 was provided by persons establishing life income agreements. That amount was invested.
6. Income on investments was received in the amount of $170,000. $175,000 was paid to life income recipients.

*Required:*

a. Prepare journal entries to record the transactions listed above.
b. Prepare, in good form, a Statement of Changes in Fund Balances for the Annuity and Life Income Funds (one column) for Huskie University as of June 30, 19y1.
c. Prepare, in good form, Balance Sheets for the Annuity Funds and for the Life Income Funds for Huskie University as of June 30, 19y1.

11–11. **Plant Funds.** As of July 1, 19y0, the trial balance for the Unexpended Plant Funds, Funds for the Retirement of Indebtedness, and the Investment in Plant subgroups for Huskie University were as follows:

|                              | Debit | Credit |
|------------------------------|------:|-------:|
| Unexpended Plant Funds:      |       |        |
| Cash . . . . . . . . . . . . . . . . . . . . . . . | $ 385,000 |  |
| Investments . . . . . . . . . . . . . . . . . . . | 1,650,000 |  |
| Accounts Payable . . . . . . . . . . . . . . . . . |  | $ 35,000 |
| Fund Balances—Restricted . . . . . . . . . . . . . |  | 1,250,000 |
| Fund Balances—Unrestricted . . . . . . . . . . . . |  | 750,000 |
| Totals . . . . . . . . . . . . . . . . . . . . . | $ 2,035,000 | $ 2,035,000 |
| Funds for Retirement of Indebtedness: |  |  |
| Cash . . . . . . . . . . . . . . . . . . . . . . . | $ 72,000 |  |
| Investments . . . . . . . . . . . . . . . . . . . | 586,000 |  |
| Fund Balances—Restricted . . . . . . . . . . . . . |  | $ 435,000 |
| Fund Balances—Unrestricted . . . . . . . . . . . . |  | 223,000 |
| Totals . . . . . . . . . . . . . . . . . . . . . | $ 658,000 | $ 658,000 |

|  | Debit | Credit |
|---|---|---|
| Investment in Plant: | | |
| Land . . . . . . . . . . . . . . . . . . . . . . | $ 325,000 | |
| Land improvements . . . . . . . . . . . . . . | 1,100,000 | |
| Buildings . . . . . . . . . . . . . . . . . . . | 23,200,000 | |
| Equipment . . . . . . . . . . . . . . . . . . . | 13,250,000 | |
| Library books . . . . . . . . . . . . . . . . . | 875,000 | |
| Bonds payable . . . . . . . . . . . . . . . . . | | $18,750,000 |
| Net investment in plant . . . . . . . . . . . . | | 20,000,000 |
| Totals . . . . . . . . . . . . . . . . . . . . | $38,750,000 | $38,750,000 |

During the year ended June 30, 19y1, the following transactions occurred:

**Unexpended Plant Funds**

1. During the year, state appropriations in the amount of $125,000, private gifts of $340,000, and investment income of $140,000 were received, all in cash. These funds were all restricted.
2. A nonmandatory transfer of $80,000 was received in cash from the current unrestricted fund as a part of the allocation of unrestricted gifts.
3. $850,000 in cash was expended for university facilities. Of that amount, $750,000 was restricted and $100,000 was unrestricted.

**Funds for Retirement of Indebtedness**

4. Additions to fund balances for the year included $58,000 in restricted private gifts, $43,000 in investment income (restricted), and a mandatory transfer of $1,480,000 from the current unrestricted fund.
5. Reductions in fund balances for the year included restricted fund payments of $1,100,000 for interest and $535,000 for the payment of bonds.

**Investment in Plant**

6. The $850,000 expended for plant facilities consisted of: land, $125,000; buildings, $352,000; equipment, $241,000; library books, $132,000. No additional debt was issued in connection with the plant acquisitions.
7. $535,000 was paid on the principal of university bonds by the Funds for Retirement of Indebtedness.
8. Buildings in the amount of $1,250,000 were retired during the year as well as equipment in the amount of $543,000.

*Required:*

a. Prepare journal entries to record the transactions listed above.
b. Prepare, in good form, a Statement of Changes in Fund Balances (three separate columns) for the Plant Funds for Huskie University for the Year Ended June 30, 19y1.
c. Prepare, in good form, Balance Sheets for the Plant Funds for Huskie University as of June 30, 19y1.

11–12. **Agency Funds.** As of July 1, 19y0, the trial balance of the Agency Funds for Huskie University was as follows:

|  | Debit | Credit |
|---|---|---|
| Cash . . . . . . . . . . . . . . . . . . . . . . . . . . . . . . | $ 38,500 | |
| Investments . . . . . . . . . . . . . . . . . . . . . . . . . . | 129,600 | |
| Deposits held in custody for others . . . . . . . . . . . . . . . | | $168,100 |
| Totals . . . . . . . . . . . . . . . . . . . . . . . . . . . | $168,100 | $168,100 |

During the fiscal year ended June 30, 19y1, the following transaction occurred:

Receipts of funds to be held in custody for others during the year amounted to $75,000; disbursements amounted to $83,200.

No investment activity took place.

### Required:

a. Prepare journal entries to record the transaction listed above.

b. Prepare, in good form, a Balance Sheet for the Agency Funds for Huskie University as of June 30, 19y1.

# Chapter 12

# ACCOUNTING FOR HOSPITALS AND OTHER HEALTH CARE PROVIDERS

**M**edical care expenditures now exceed 10 percent of the gross national product in the United States. In many cases, payments for health care expenditures are made by Medicare, Medicaid, commercial insurance companies, and by state and local assistance programs. Health care entities may be owned and operated by governments, by not-for-profit corporations, or by profit-seeking corporations. Health care providers include hospitals, clinics and other ambulatory care organizations, continuing care retirement communities, health maintenance and similar organizations, home health agencies, and nursing homes. All of these organizations are subject to various forms of regulation by federal, state, and local governments and must meet the reporting needs for that regulation as well as for the various third-party payors.

Generally accepted accounting principles for health care providers have evolved through the efforts of the American Hospital Association (AHA), the Healthcare Financial Management Association (HFMA), and the American Institute of Certified Public Accountants (AICPA). Governmentally owned and operated providers which are financed largely by user charges should be accounted for as enterprise funds (see Chapter 8), and, for separately issued reports are expected to adhere to the same standards as other not-for-profit providers. The Financial Accounting Foundation has approved for exposure a proposal that each governmentally owned health care provider will be subject to FASB jurisdiction unless its governing body makes an irrevocable election to be subject to the GASB's jurisdiction.

As yet, neither the GASB nor the FASB has issued statements to supersede accounting and financial reporting standards found in the AICPA *Hospital Audit Guide,* as amended by *Statements of Position (SOP) 78–1, 78–7, 81–2,* and *85–1,* although certain standards do apply, such as for pensions and compensated absences. Accordingly, this chapter is based on currently effective AICPA pronouncements. The AICPA is presently preparing a new accounting and audit guide, *Audits of Providers of Health Care Services,* which, in its present version, incorporates some changes in terminology, requires the issuance of a cash flow statement in lieu of a Statement of Changes in Financial Position, and provides an additional restricted fund category (student loan funds).

## Summary—Accounting for Health Care Providers

A few comments about accounting and reporting for health care providers should be helpful:

- Fund accounting is used. The general funds are unrestricted and account for all the activities of hospitals. The restricted funds (specific purpose, student loan, plant replacement and expansion, and endowment) are "holding funds" for restricted assets until expended.
- Full accrual accounting is employed in the general funds. Depreciation is charged, revenues are accrued, expenses are charged as incurred, and debt premiums and discounts are amortized.
- The four basic statements are the Balance Sheet, the Statement of Revenues and Expenses, the Statement of Changes in Fund Balances, and the Statement of Changes in Financial Position (the latter is expected to be replaced by the Statement of Cash Flows).
- Patient service revenues are recognized at the total amount that would be charged if each patient were paying the full charges. Contractual adjustments, estimated bad debts, employee discounts, and charity allowances are all accrued and shown as revenue deductions.
- Revenues are classified as patient service revenues, other operating revenues, and nonoperating revenues. Other operating revenues include grants for operating purposes, when recognized, cafeteria and parking lot revenue, donated materials, and so on. Nonoperating revenues include donations, unrestricted endowment income, and donated services.
- Investments are recorded in the same manner as for businesses. Marketable equity securities should be carried at the lower of cost or market.

## The Fund Structure for Health Care Providers

Like other nonbusiness organizations health care providers use a fund structure to facilitate reporting on the use of assets held under external restrictions versus assets available for use at the discretion of the governing board. However, unlike local governments and colleges, all unrestricted resources and obligations, including long-term assets and liabilities, are accounted for in hospital general funds. The current AICPA *Hospital Audit Guide* provides the following fund structure:

A. General funds
B. Restricted funds
   1. Specific purpose funds
   2. Endowment funds
   3. Plant replacement and expansion fund

Student loan funds and agency funds are also used as needed.

## General Funds

The AICPA's *Statement of Position 85–1* provides the following definition:

> *General Funds*. Funds not restricted for identified purposes by donors or grantors, including resources that the governing board may use for any designated purpose and resources whose use is limited by agreement between the health care entity and an outside party other than a donor or grantor.

Property, plant, and equipment used in rendering services are accounted for in the general funds, and depreciation is recognized as a general funds expense. Long-term debt, except that related to assets of endowment funds, is accounted for in the general funds. **All** revenues and expenses (not expenditures) are reported in the general funds. As is true of colleges and universities, health care providers report additions to and deductions from restricted funds in the Statement of Changes in Fund Balances rather than in the Statement of Revenues and Expenses.

AICPA *Statement of Position 85–1* states that assets set aside by the **governing board** for identified purposes, and assets whose use is limited under terms of debt indentures, trust agreements, third-party reimbursement arrangements, or other similar agreements should be reported in the general funds section of the balance sheet as **Assets Whose Use Is Limited.** If liabilities exist which are to be paid from "Assets Whose Use Is Limited" it is proper to segregate those liabilities from liabilities to be paid from other assets of the general funds; captions should be provided to explain the reason for segregation.

## Restricted Funds

According to AICPA *Statement of Position 85–1,* "Only assets restricted by a **donor** or by a **grantor** should be reported in the donor-restricted funds section of the balance sheet." (Emphasis added.) The restricted funds essentially act as "holding funds" for restricted assets until used.

**Specific purpose funds**   Assets restricted for current uses, and not for endowment or plant replacement or expansion, are recorded in the specific purpose funds. Often these funds are restricted for use in research or education. Expenses incurred for purposes specified by donors or grantors should be recorded in the general funds; specific purpose fund assets in amounts equal to such expenses should then be transferred to the general funds as Other Operating Revenues.

**Endowment funds**   Endowment funds of health care providers are similar to those of colleges and universities. They are created to account for resources which external donors require to be set aside permanently, or for a specified term, or until a specified event occurs. The use of income from endowment funds may be restricted by the donor, or may be available for use at the discretion of the governing board. Restricted income from endowments should be transferred to a specific purpose fund or to the plant replacement and expansion fund as an addition to Fund Balance. Unrestricted income should be transferred to the general funds as Nonoperating Revenue. When the term of an endowment ends, the assets should be transferred to the specific purpose, plant replacement and expansion, or general funds, as specified by the donor.

**Plant replacement and expansion fund**   This fund is used to account for restricted resources given to a health care provider for the acquisition of property, plant, or equipment. Unrestricted resources designated by the governing board for plant acquisition purposes are accounted for in the general funds. When expenditures are made for the purposes specified by donors, the plant replacement and expansion fund fund balance is decreased in the amount of the cash decrease; the cost of the fixed assets acquired is recorded by debits to the appropriate general funds accounts, offset by a credit to Transfers from Plant Replacement and Expansion Fund for Capital Outlays—an account which is closed to the general funds Fund Balance at year-end.

## ILLUSTRATIVE TRANSACTIONS

### General Funds

Typical general funds transactions are illustrated below as they are assumed to occur in a hypothetical not-for-profit hospital. They are designed to generate the statements shown in Illustrations 12–1 through 12–4 later in this chapter.

During the year, revenue from nursing services and other professional services amounted to $8,500,000. These are recorded as "Patient Service Revenue" at the gross amount, the amount that would have been collected if all services rendered patients were paid for as billed.

    1. Accounts and Notes Receivable . . . . . . . . .  8,500,000
          Patient Service Revenue . . . . . . . . . . .              8,500,000

In accord with long-standing practices, the estimated provision for bad debts, and actual credits to patients' accounts made because of contracts with various third-party payors, and other actual credits to patients' accounts because of hospital policies, are recognized as "Deductions from Revenue," rather than as operating expenses.

    2. Provision for Bad Debts . . . . . . . . . . . .    450,000
       Contractual and Other Adjustments . . . . . . . 1,382,000
          Allowance for Uncollectible Receivables . . .               450,000
          Accounts and Notes Receivable . . . . . . .              1,382,000

Some recovery of adjustments to patients' accounts was received by this hypothetical hospital, as often happens in actual cases. Assume that a not-for-profit organization contributed $47,000 to this hospital in consideration for services rendered by this hospital to certain charity patients. For the same reason an additional $8,000 was transferred from Specific Purpose Funds. The total of these amounts is treated as a partial offset to the Contractual and Other Adjustments account:

    3. Cash  . . . . . . . . . . . . . . . . . . . . .     55,000
          Contractual and Other Adjustments . . . . . .               55,000

In addition to revenues from patient services, general funds may receive **other operating revenues,** such as: transfers from restricted funds in the amount of expenses incurred for research, education, or other operating activities eligible for support by a restricted fund; tuition from nursing students, interns, or residents; cafeteria revenues; parking fees; fees for copies of medical records; gift shop revenues; and other activities somewhat related to the provision of patient services. If $84,000 was received in cash, and an additional $100,000 is to be transferred from specific purpose funds, the entry would be (note Entry 23):

    4. Due from Restricted Funds . . . . . . . . . . . .   100,000
       Cash  . . . . . . . . . . . . . . . . . . . . .     84,000
          Other Operating Revenues . . . . . . . . . .               184,000

Health care providers may receive unrestricted donations of money or services. Under the current *Hospital Audit Guide* such donations are considered to be **nonoperating revenues** as are income and gains from general investments and unrestricted income from endowment funds. When the principal of an endowment fund is transferred to general funds because of the occurrence of an event or the expiration of the term specified in the endowment agreement, the transfer is reported as nonoperating revenue. (Transfers from other funds, if material, should be identified separately in the operating statements.) Assume that total nonoperating revenues amounted to $452,000 from sources shown in the following entry; $398,000 is available for current use and $54,000 is, by direction of the hospital governing board, added to assets set aside for expansion of facilities:

```
5. Cash  . . . . . . . . . . . . . . . . . . .        398,000
      Assets Whose Use Is Limited—Cash  . . . . . . .      54,000
      Nonoperating Revenue—Unrestricted Gifts and
        Bequests . . . . . . . . . . . . . . . . .                      228,000
      Nonoperating Revenue—Unrestricted Income
        from Endowment Funds . . . . . . . . . .                       224,000
```

Assume that equipment costing $25,000 with accumulated depreciation of $15,000 was scrapped. The loss of $10,000 is shown in Illustration 12–2 as an operating expense. The entry would be:

```
6. Accumulated Depreciation—Equipment . . . . . .       15,000
   Loss on Disposal of Equipment . . . . . . . . . .      10,000
      Equipment . . . . . . . . . . . . . . . . . .                     25,000
```

Buildings costing $315,000 and equipment costing $313,000 were purchased during the year by the plant replacement and expansion fund. Entries in that fund are illustrated in Entry 26. The entry made by the general funds should be:

```
7. Buildings  . . . . . . . . . . . . . . . . . . .     315,000
   Equipment . . . . . . . . . . . . . . . . . . . .    313,000
      Transfers from Plant Replacement and
        Expansion Fund for Capital Outlays . . . . .                    628,000
```

New equipment was purchased with cash set aside for that purpose within the general funds in the amount of $50,000:

```
8. Equipment . . . . . . . . . . . . . . . . . . .      50,000
      Assets Whose Use Is Limited—Cash  . . . . .                       50,000
```

Cash in the amount of $20,000 was designated by the governing board to be held for use for fixed asset replacement in accord with an agreement with third-party payors.

```
9. Assets Whose Use Is Limited—Cash  . . . . . . .      20,000
      Cash  . . . . . . . . . . . . . . . . . . . .                     20,000
```

During the year, the following items were recorded as Accounts Payable: $147,000 accrued expenses payable at the beginning of the year; nursing services expenses, $2,000,000; other professional services expenses, $1,750,000; general services expenses of $1,930,000; fiscal services expenses of $325,000; administrative services expenses of $360,000; supplies added to inventory, $277,000; and prepaid expenses of $161,000:

```
10. Accrued Expenses Payable . . . . . . . . . . . .      147,000
    Nursing Services Expenses . . . . . . . . . . . .   2,000,000
    Other Professional Services Expenses . . . . . . .  1,750,000
    General Services Expenses . . . . . . . . . . . .   1,930,000
    Fiscal Services Expenses . . . . . . . . . . . .      325,000
    Administrative Services Expenses . . . . . . . . .     360,000
    Inventory  . . . . . . . . . . . . . . . . . . .      277,000
    Prepaid Expenses . . . . . . . . . . . . . . . .      161,000
        Accounts Payable . . . . . . . . . . . . . .                6,950,000
```

Collections on accounts and notes receivable during the year amounted to $6,710,000; accounts and notes receivable totaling $395,000 were written off:

```
11. Cash  . . . . . . . . . . . . . . . . . . . . .    6,710,000
    Allowance for Uncollectible Receivables  . . . . .    395,000
        Accounts and Notes Receivable  . . . . . . .                7,105,000
```

Current liabilities and long-term debt were paid in the amounts shown in Entry 12:

```
12. Accounts Payable . . . . . . . . . . . . . . . .    6,963,000
    Notes Payable to Banks—Current . . . . . . . . .       73,000
    Current Installment of Mortgage Bonds . . . . . .      90,000
        Cash  . . . . . . . . . . . . . . . . . . .                 7,126,000
```

General Funds cash in the amount of $15,000 was used for purposes specified by donors; the General Funds will be reimbursed by the Specific Purpose Funds:

```
13a. Other Professional Services Expenses  . . . . . .     15,000
         Cash . . . . . . . . . . . . . . . . . . .                    15,000
13b. Due from Restricted Funds . . . . . . . . . . .      15,000
         Other Operating Revenues  . . . . . . . . .                   15,000
```

Supplies costing $284,000 were used during the year. Requisitions indicated that the following functional expense accounts should be charged:

```
14. Nursing Services Expenses . . . . . . . . . . . .     102,000
    Other Professional Services Expenses . . . . . . .      80,000
    General Services Expenses . . . . . . . . . . . .       80,000
    Fiscal Services Expenses . . . . . . . . . . . .        20,000
    Administrative Services Expenses . . . . . . . . .       2,000
        Inventory  . . . . . . . . . . . . . . . . .                  284,000
```

Prepaid expenses expiring during the year amounted to $166,000; this amount was allocated to the functional expense accounts:

```
15. Nursing Services Expenses . . . . . . . . . . . .      48,000
    Other Professional Services Expenses . . . . . . .      30,000
    General Services Expenses . . . . . . . . . . . .       40,000
    Fiscal Services Expenses . . . . . . . . . . . .        20,000
    Administrative Services Expenses . . . . . . . . .      28,000
        Prepaid Expenses . . . . . . . . . . . . . .                  166,000
```

Accrued expenses at year-end amounted to $150,000:

```
16. Nursing Services Expenses . . . . . . . . . . .          50,000
    Other Professional Services Expenses . . . . . . .       40,000
    General Services Expenses . . . . . . . . . . . .        40,000
    Fiscal Services Expenses . . . . . . . . . . . .         10,000
    Administrative Services Expenses . . . . . . . .         10,000
        Accrued Expenses Payable . . . . . . . . . .                      150,000
```

Depreciation of plant and equipment for the year was recorded in the amounts shown in Entry 17:

```
17. Provision for Depreciation . . . . . . . . . . .        300,000
        Accumulated Depreciation—Buildings  . . . .                      120,000
        Accumulated Depreciation—Equipment . . . .                       180,000
```

Investments set aside by the hospital governing board to be held until needed to finance expansion of facilities were sold at carrying value, $83,000.

```
18. Assets Whose Use Is Limited—Cash  . . . . . . .         83,000
        Assets Whose Use Is Limited—Investments  . .                      83,000
```

Mortgage bonds in the amount of $90,000 will mature within the coming year; Entry 19a reclassifies that amount as a current liability.

```
19a. Mortgage Bonds . . . . . . . . . . . . . . .           90,000
        Current Installments of Mortgage Bonds  . . .                     90,000
```

Entry 19b records the closing of revenue and expense accounts at year-end.

```
19b. Patient Service Revenue  . . . . . . . . . . . .     8,500,000
     Other Operating Revenues . . . . . . . . . . .        199,000
     Nonoperating Revenue—Unrestricted Gifts and
        Bequests  . . . . . . . . . . . . . . . . .         228,000
     Nonoperating Revenue—Unrestricted Income from
        Endowment Funds . . . . . . . . . . . . .           224,000
     Transfers from Plant Replacement and Expansion
        Fund for Capital Outlays . . . . . . . . . .         628,000
        Provision for Bad Debts  . . . . . . . . . .                      450,000
        Contractual and Other Adjustments . . . . .                     1,327,000
        Nursing Services Expenses  . . . . . . . . .                     2,200,000
        Other Professional Services Expenses  . . . .                    1,915,000
        General Services Expenses  . . . . . . . . .                     2,090,000
        Fiscal Services Expenses  . . . . . . . . . .                      375,000
        Administrative Services Expenses  . . . . . .                      400,000
        Provision for Depreciation  . . . . . . . . .                      300,000
        Loss on Disposal of Equipment  . . . . . . .                       10,000
        Fund Balance—Undesignated . . . . . . . .                         712,000
```

Entry 19c records the transfer of $24,000 from Fund Balance—Undesignated to Fund Balance—Designated for Expansion of Facilities. This transfer is necessitated by the net increase during the year of $24,000 in Assets Whose Use Is Limited.

```
19c. Fund Balance—Undesignated . . . . . . . . .            24,000
        Fund Balance—Designated for Expansion of
        Facilities  . . . . . . . . . . . . . . . .                        24,000
```

## Restricted Funds

Increases and decreases in the three restricted fund types are recorded as additions to and deductions from the appropriate Fund Balance accounts inasmuch as present standards define revenues and expenses as affecting only the general funds. Illustrative transactions for the specific purpose, plant replacement and expansion, and endowment funds are illustrated below.

## Specific Purpose Funds

Specific purpose funds of the hospital in this example were established to record assets given to the hospital under grantor- or donor-imposed restrictions. Entry 20 records the receipt of $70,260 in Cash and the receivable for a research grant:

```
20. Cash  . . . . . . . . . . . . . . . . . . . .    70,260
       Grants Receivable  . . . . . . . . . . . . . . . .    40,000
          Fund Balance—Other—Restricted Gifts and
             Bequests . . . . . . . . . . . . . . . . .                 35,000
          Fund Balance—Research Grants  . . . . . . .                 40,000
          Fund Balance—Other—Income from
             Investments  . . . . . . . . . . . . . . .                 35,260
```

Investments, costing $20,000, held for donor-specified purposes were sold for $28,000; additional investments were purchased for $35,000.

```
21. Cash  . . . . . . . . . . . . . . . . . . . .    28,000
       Investments  . . . . . . . . . . . . . . . . . .                 20,000
       Fund Balance—Other—Gain on Sale of
          Investments  . . . . . . . . . . . . . . . . .                  8,000

22. Investments  . . . . . . . . . . . . . . . . . .    35,000
       Cash  . . . . . . . . . . . . . . . . . . . .                     35,000
```

As noted in the discussion of General Funds Entries 3 and 4, specific purpose funds cash in the amount of $8,000 was transferred to general funds and an additional $100,000 is to be transferred. The reasons for these transfers are indicated by the debits to the Fund Balance accounts of the specific purpose funds. The $8,000 item is included in the credit to Contractual and Other Adjustments in Entry 3; the $100,000 item is included in the credit to Other Operating Revenues in Entry 4.

```
23. Fund Balance—Research Grants—Transferred to
       General Funds . . . . . . . . . . . . . . . .    50,000
    Fund Balance—Other—Transferred to General
       Funds—Other Operating Revenue  . . . . . . .    50,000
    Fund Balance—Other—Transferred to General
       Funds—Charity Services . . . . . . . . . . . .     8,000
          Cash  . . . . . . . . . . . . . . . . . . .                     8,000
          Due to General Funds . . . . . . . . . . . .                  100,000
```

The hospital was informed that a research grant in the amount of $50,000 had been awarded by a private foundation.

24. Grants Receivable . . . . . . . . . . . . . . .          50,000
        Fund Balance—Research Grants . . . . . . .                          50,000

The hospital was required to return $55,000 to the federal government because expenditures required by a grant had not been made by the date specified; specific purpose funds also records the liability to reimburse general funds for $15,000 expenses (see Entries 13a and 13b).

25. Fund Balance—Other—Transfer to General Funds  .       15,000
        Fund Balance—Research Grants . . . . . . . . .         55,000
        Cash  . . . . . . . . . . . . . . . . . . .                            55,000
        Due to General Funds . . . . . . . . . . . .                          15,000

## Plant Replacement and Expansion Funds

Plant replacement and expansion funds account for assets restricted by donors or grantors to the acquisition of property, plant, and equipment. When fixed assets are acquired, the restricted fund is decreased, and general funds, which accounts for the fixed assets, is increased. Entry 7 illustrates the effect on general funds of the purchase of buildings and equipment from plant replacement and expansion funds cash. Entry 26 records the effect of that transaction on the plant replacement and expansion funds.

26. Fund Balance—Purchase of Buildings and
        Equipment . . . . . . . . . . . . . . . . . . . .       628,000
        Cash  . . . . . . . . . . . . . . . . . . . . . .                        628,000

During the year plant replacement and expansion funds cash is increased by $468,000 due to the collection of Pledges Receivable in the amount of $340,000; gifts and bequests totaling $113,000; and interest on investments, $15,000:

27. Cash  . . . . . . . . . . . . . . . . . . . . . .       468,000
        Pledges Receivable . . . . . . . . . . . . . .                        340,000
        Fund Balance—Restricted Gifts and Bequests  .                      113,000
        Fund Balance—Income from Investments  . . .                        15,000

Cash in the amount of $280,000 was invested:

28. Investments  . . . . . . . . . . . . . . . . . . .       280,000
        Cash  . . . . . . . . . . . . . . . . . . . . . .                        280,000

## Endowment Funds

Endowment funds account for assets held for the generation of income in compliance with donors' requirements. If the donors specify that the income is to be used for a specific objective, the income will be recognized as an addition to Fund Balance of the specific purpose funds, or plant replacement and expansion funds, as appropriate. On the other hand, if the donors specify that the income be used at the discretion of the governing board, the income will be recognized as Nonoperating Revenue in the general funds (see Entry 5). Fund Balances of endowment funds are classified as either (1) term endowment or (2) permanent endowment. The receipt of gifts and bequests restricted for endowments is recorded as an addition to appropriate Fund Balance accounts:

```
29. Cash  . . . . . . . . . . . . . . . . . . . .  2,000,000
        Fund Balance—Permanent Endowment—
          Restricted Gifts and Bequests  . . . . . .          2,000,000
```

The sale of investments costing $1,000,000 for $1,175,000 and the purchase of additional investments costing $3,158,000 would be recorded as follows:

```
30. Cash  . . . . . . . . . . . . . . . . . . . .  1,175,000
        Investments  . . . . . . . . . . . . . . .          1,000,000
        Fund Balance—Permanent Endowment—Net
          Gain on Sale of Investments . . . . . . . .            175,000

31. Investments  . . . . . . . . . . . . . . . . .  3,158,000
        Cash  . . . . . . . . . . . . . . . . . . .          3,158,000
```

## ILLUSTRATIVE FINANCIAL STATEMENTS FOR HOSPITALS

The AICPA *Hospital Audit Guide* states that the four basic financial statements for hospitals are: (1) Balance Sheet, (2) Statement of Revenues and Expenses, (3) Statement of Changes in Fund Balances, and (4) Statement of Changes in Financial Position of General Funds.

### Balance Sheet

Assuming that the hospital for which journal entries are illustrated in the preceding section had the assets, liabilities, and fund balance sheet shown in the "Prior Year" column of the balance sheet shown as Illustration 12–1, the journal entries would produce the amounts reported in the "Current Year" column of that statement, and also the results shown in the "Current Year" column of Illustrations 12–2, 12–3, and 12–4. The balance sheet (Illustration 12–1) is shown in a layer format, with each fund reported separately with no grand total of all funds. Since all unrestricted assets and all liabilities to be paid from unrestricted assets are reported in the general funds, the total Fund Balance represents the net equity available for use at the discretion of the hospital governing board. The fact that the board has designated that certain assets will be held for expansion of facilities is shown on the asset side by the caption "Assets Whose Use Is Limited," and by segregation of Fund Balance in

# ILLUSTRATION 12–1

**HYPOTHETICAL HOSPITAL**
**Balance Sheet**
**December 31, 19—**
(with comparative figures for 19—)

## General Funds

| Assets | Current Year | Prior Year |
|---|---|---|
| Current: | | |
| Cash | $ 119,000 | $ 33,000 |
| Receivables | 1,282,000 | 1,269,000 |
| Less estimated uncollectibles and allowances | (160,000) | (105,000) |
| Net | 1,122,000 | 1,164,000 |
| Due from restricted funds | 115,000 | — |
| Inventories at cost | 176,000 | 183,000 |
| Prepaid expenses | 68,000 | 73,000 |
| Total Current Assets | 1,600,000 | 1,453,000 |
| Assets Whose Use Is Limited: | | |
| Cash | 147,000 | 40,000 |
| Investments | 1,807,000 | 1,890,000 |
| Total | 1,954,000 | 1,930,000 |
| Property, plant, and equipment | 11,028,000 | 10,375,000 |
| Less accumulated depreciation | (3,885,000) | (3,600,000) |
| Net | 7,143,000 | 6,775,000 |
| Total | $10,697,000 | $10,158,000 |

| Liabilities and Fund Balances | Current Year | Prior Year |
|---|---|---|
| Current: | | |
| Notes payable to banks | $ 227,000 | $ 300,000 |
| Current installments of mortgage bonds | 90,000 | 90,000 |
| Accounts payable | 450,000 | 463,000 |
| Accrued expenses | 150,000 | 147,000 |
| Total Current Liabilities | 917,000 | 1,000,000 |
| Long-term debt: | | |
| Mortgage bonds | 520,000 | 610,000 |
| Tax exempt bonds | 1,500,000 | 1,500,000 |
| Total Long-Term Debt | 2,020,000 | 2,110,000 |
| Fund Balance: | | |
| Designated for expansion of facilities | 1,954,000 | 1,930,000 |
| Undesignated | 5,806,000 | 5,118,000 |
| Total Fund Balance | 7,760,000 | 7,048,000 |
| Total | $10,697,000 | $10,158,000 |

**Assets**

| | | |
|---|---:|---:|
| Specific purpose funds: | | |
| Cash | $ 1,260 | $ 1,000 |
| Investments | 85,000 | 70,000 |
| Grants receivable | 90,000 | — |
| Total Specific Purpose Funds | $ 176,260 | $ 71,000 |
| Plant replacement and expansion funds: | | |
| Cash | $ 10,000 | $ 450,000 |
| Investments | 420,000 | 140,000 |
| Pledges receivable, net of estimated uncollectible | 20,000 | 360,000 |
| Total Plant Replacement and Expansion Funds | $ 450,000 | $ 950,000 |
| Endowment funds: | | |
| Cash | $ 50,000 | $ 33,000 |
| Investments | 6,100,000 | 3,942,000 |
| Total Endowment Funds | $ 6,150,000 | $ 3,975,000 |

**Liabilities and Fund Balances**

| | | |
|---|---:|---:|
| Specific purpose funds: | | |
| Due to general funds | $ 115,000 | $ — |
| Fund balances: | | |
| Research grants | 15,000 | 30,000 |
| Other | 46,260 | 41,000 |
| Total Fund Balances | 61,260 | 71,000 |
| Total Specific Purpose Funds | $ 176,260 | $ 71,000 |
| Plant replacement and expansion funds: | | |
| Fund balances | 450,000 | 950,000 |
| Total Plant Replacement and Expansion Funds | $ 450,000 | $ 950,000 |
| Endowment funds: | | |
| Fund balances: | | |
| Permanent endowment | $ 4,850,000 | $ 2,675,000 |
| Term endowment | 1,300,000 | 1,300,000 |
| Total Endowment Funds | $ 6,150,000 | $ 3,975,000 |

Source: AICPA *Hospital Audit Guide*, pp. 40–41 (amended to conform with SOP 85–1).

a corresponding amount. The three restricted fund categories reflect only the assets restricted by grantors and donors, and the corresponding Fund Balance accounts.

## Statement of Revenues and Expenses

All revenues and expenses of health care entities are recognized in the general funds. As a result, this statement (Illustration 12–2) reflects all revenues and expenses of the hospital, on the full accrual basis. Note that revenues are identified in this statement as Patient Service Revenue, Other Operating Revenue, and Nonoperating Revenue. Patient service revenues are reported on the first line of Illustration 12–2 at gross. The next line reports as deductions from patient service revenue the amounts by which charges to patients were reduced because of agreements with third-party payors and because of policies established by the hospital governing board. The provision for bad debts, an estimate, is also reported as a deduction from patient service revenue. The AICPA *Hospital Audit Guide* defines **Other Operating Revenues** as including amounts transferred from restricted funds; tuition from nursing students; cafeteria, gift shop, and parking lot revenues; and the fair value of donated medicines and other supplies. The *Audit Guide* defines **Nonoperating Revenues** as including gifts, bequests, and investment income available for unrestricted purposes. The fair value of donated services of individuals may be recorded as a nonoperating revenue if there is the equivalent of an employer-employee relationship and an objective basis for valuing such services.

Operating expenses are reported by function, as noted in the discussion of illustrative entries for the General Funds. Depreciation, although reported as an operating expense, is not allocated to the functional categories in the AICPA *Hospital Audit Guide*.

## Statement of Changes in Fund Balances

The Statement of Changes in Fund Balances (Illustration 12–3) reflects the major factors that caused the changes in the Fund Balance accounts of each of the four fund types. Note that the general funds section of the statement reflects transfers as well as the excess of revenues over expenses. The specific purpose and plant replacement and expansion funds statements reflect the beginning Fund Balances, additions to Fund Balances (not revenues), and transfers to other funds. The disclosure for endowment funds reflects the beginning balance plus additions. If principal amounts were distributed to general funds, a "Transfer to" account would be included. If endowment fund assets were sold at a loss, a deduction from Fund Balances would be reported. Income from

**ILLUSTRATION 12–2**

**HYPOTHETICAL HOSPITAL**
**Statement of Revenues and Expenses**
**Year Ended December 31, 19—**
**(with comparative figures for 19—)**

|  | Current Year | Prior Year |
|---|---|---|
| Patient service revenue | $8,500,000 | $8,000,000 |
| Allowances and uncollectible accounts (after deduction of related gifts, grants, subsidies, and other income—$55,000 and $40,000) | (1,777,000) | (1,700,000) |
| Net Patient Service Revenue | 6,723,000 | 6,300,000 |
| Other operating revenue (including $115,000 and $80,000 from Specific Purpose Funds) | 199,000 | 173,000 |
| Total Operating Revenue | 6,922,000 | 6,473,000 |
| Operating expenses: |  |  |
| Nursing services | 2,200,000 | 2,000,000 |
| Other professional services | 1,915,000 | 1,700,000 |
| General services | 2,090,000 | 2,000,000 |
| Fiscal services | 375,000 | 360,000 |
| Administrative services (including interest expense of $50,000 and $40,000) | 400,000 | 375,000 |
| Provision for depreciation | 300,000 | 250,000 |
| Loss on disposal of equipment | 10,000 | — |
| Total Operating Expenses | 7,290,000 | 6,685,000 |
| Loss from Operations | (368,000) | (212,000) |
| Nonoperating revenue: |  |  |
| Unrestricted gifts and bequests | 228,000 | 205,000 |
| Unrestricted income from endowment funds | 224,000 | 121,000 |
| Total Nonoperating Revenue | 452,000 | 326,000 |
| Excess of Revenues over Expenses | $    84,000 | $  114,000 |

Source: AICPA *Hospital Audit Guide*, p. 42.

endowment fund investments should be shown as a nonoperating revenue of the general funds (if available for use at the discretion of the
governing board), or as an addition to the Fund Balances account of one
of the restricted funds (if subject to donor or grantor restrictions).

## Statement of Changes in Financial Position of General Funds

This statement (Illustration 12–4) is similar to the statements prepared by businesses prior to the issuance of FASB *Statement 95: Statement of Cash Flows*. That Statement specifically excluded not-for-profit
organizations, pending FASB action on financial display issues for not-
for-profits. As of this writing, both the GASB and FASB are considering
whether health care providers should change from the Statement of
Changes in Financial Position to the Statement of Cash Flows.

## ILLUSTRATION 12–3

### HYPOTHETICAL HOSPITAL
Statement of Changes in Fund Balances
Year Ended December 31, 19—
(with comparative figures for 19—)

|  | Current Year | Prior Year |
|---|---|---|
| **General Funds:** | | |
| Balance at beginning of year . . . . . . . . . . . . | $7,048,000 | $6,172,000 |
| Excess of revenues over expenses . . . . . . . . . . | 84,000 | 114,000 |
| Fixed assets purchased from Plant Replacement and Expansion Fund cash . . . . . . . . . . . . . . | 628,000 | 762,000 |
| Balance at End of Year . . . . . . . . . . . . . | $7,760,000 | $7,048,000 |
| **Restricted Funds:** | | |
| Specific Purpose Funds: | | |
| Balance at beginning of year . . . . . . . . . . . | $ 71,000 | $ 50,000 |
| Restricted gifts and bequests . . . . . . . . . . . . | 35,000 | 20,000 |
| Research grants . . . . . . . . . . . . . . . . | 90,000 | 45,000 |
| Income from investments . . . . . . . . . . . . . | 35,260 | 39,000 |
| Gain on sale of investments . . . . . . . . . . . . | 8,000 | — |
| Transferred to General Funds for: | | |
| Other operating revenue . . . . . . . . . . . . . | (115,000) | (80,000) |
| Charity services . . . . . . . . . . . . . . . . | (8,000) | (3,000) |
| Returned to grantor . . . . . . . . . . . . . . . | (55,000) | — |
| Balance at End of Year . . . . . . . . . . . . . | $ 61,260 | $ 71,000 |
| Plant Replacement and Expansion Funds: | | |
| Balance at beginning of year . . . . . . . . . . . | $ 950,000 | $1,544,000 |
| Restricted gifts and bequests . . . . . . . . . . . . | 113,000 | 150,000 |
| Income from investments . . . . . . . . . . . . . | 15,000 | 18,000 |
| Transferred to General Funds (described above) . . . . | (628,000) | (762,000) |
| Balance at End of Year . . . . . . . . . . . . . | $ 450,000 | $ 950,000 |
| Endowment Funds: | | |
| Balance at beginning of year . . . . . . . . . . . | $3,975,000 | $2,875,000 |
| Restricted gifts and bequests . . . . . . . . . . . . | 2,000,000 | 1,000,000 |
| Net gain on sale of investments . . . . . . . . . . | 175,000 | 100,000 |
| Balance at End of Year . . . . . . . . . . . . . | $6,150,000 | $3,975,000 |

Source: AICPA *Hospital Audit Guide*, p. 43.

## SELECTED REFERENCES

American Institute of Certified Public Accountants. *Exposure Draft: Proposed Audit and Accounting Guide: Audits of Providers of Health Care Services.* New York, 1988.

―――――. *Hospital Audit Guide.* 4th ed. New York, 1982.

―――――. *Statement of Position 78–1: Accounting by Hospitals for Certain Marketable Equity Securities.* New York, 1978.

―――――. *Statement of Position 78–7: Financial Accounting and Reporting by Hospitals Operated by a Governmental Unit.* New York, 1978.

**ILLUSTRATION 12–4**

**HYPOTHETICAL HOSPITAL**
**Statement of Changes in Financial Position of General Funds**
**Year Ended December 31, 19—**
**(with comparative figures for 19—)**

| | Current Year | Prior Year |
|---|---|---|
| Funds provided: | | |
| Loss from operations . . . . . . . . . . . . . . . . . . | $ (368,000) | $ (212,000) |
| Deduct (add) items included in operations not requiring (providing) funds: | | |
| Provision for depreciation . . . . . . . . . . . . . | 300,000 | 250,000 |
| Loss on disposal of equipment . . . . . . . . . . . | 10,000 | — |
| Funds provided by operations . . . . . . . . . | (58,000) | 38,000 |
| Nonoperating revenue . . . . . . . . . . . . . . | 452,000 | 326,000 |
| Funds derived from operations and nonoperating revenues . . . . . . . . . . . . . . . . . . . | 394,000 | 364,000 |
| Property, plant, and equipment purchased from Plant Replacement and Expansion funds . . . . . . . . . | 628,000 | 762,000 |
| Decrease in working capital . . . . . . . . . . . . . | — | 46,000 |
| | 1,022,000 | 1,172,000 |
| Funds applied: | | |
| Additions to property, plant, and equipment . . . . . . | 678,000 | 762,000 |
| Reductions of long-term debt . . . . . . . . . . . . | 90,000 | 90,000 |
| Increase in assets whose use is limited . . . . . . . . | 24,000 | 320,000 |
| Increase in working capital . . . . . . . . . . . . . | 230,000 | — |
| | 1,022,000 | 1,172,000 |
| Changes in working capital: | | |
| Increase (decrease) in current assets: | | |
| Cash . . . . . . . . . . . . . . . . . . . . . . | $ 86,000 | $ (50,000) |
| Receivables . . . . . . . . . . . . . . . . . . . | (42,000) | 75,000 |
| Due from restricted funds . . . . . . . . . . . . . | 115,000 | (100,000) |
| Inventories . . . . . . . . . . . . . . . . . . . | (7,000) | 16,000 |
| Prepaid expenses . . . . . . . . . . . . . . . . . | (5,000) | 1,000 |
| | 147,000 | (58,000) |
| Increase (decrease) in current liabilities: | | |
| Note payable to banks . . . . . . . . . . . . . . . | (73,000) | (50,000) |
| Accounts payable . . . . . . . . . . . . . . . . | (13,000) | (10,000) |
| Accrued expenses . . . . . . . . . . . . . . . . | 3,000 | 48,000 |
| | (83,000) | (12,000) |
| Increase (Decrease) in Working Capital . . . . . . . . . | $ 230,000 | $ (46,000) |

Source: *Hospital Audit Guide*, pp. 46–47, as amended by *SOP 85–1*.

_____. *Statement of Position 81–2: Reporting Practices Concerning Hospital-Related Organizations.* New York, 1981.

_____. *Statement of Position 85–1: Financial Reporting by Not-for-Profit Health Care Entities for Tax-Exempt Debt and Certain Funds Whose Use Is Limited.* New York, 1985.

Financial Accounting Standards Board. *Statement of Financial Accounting Standards No. 95: Statement of Cash Flows.* Norwalk, Conn., 1987.

## QUESTIONS AND EXERCISES

**12–1.** Write the numbers 1 through 10 on a sheet of paper. Beside each number write the letter corresponding with the best answer to each of the following questions:

  1. Revenue from the gift shop of a hospital would normally be included in:
     a. Other nonoperating revenue.
     b. Other operating revenue.
     c. Patient service revenue.
     d. Professional services revenue.
  2. Glenmore Hospital's property, plant, and equipment (net of depreciation) consists of the following:

Land . . . . . . . . . . . . . . . . . . . . . . . . . . . . . . . $    500,000
Buildings . . . . . . . . . . . . . . . . . . . . . . . . . . . .  10,000,000
Movable equipment . . . . . . . . . . . . . . . . . . . . . . . .   2,000,000

What amount should be included in the Restricted Fund grouping?
     a. $0.
     b. $2,000,000.
     c. $10,500,000.
     d. $12,500.000.
  3. Which of the following would be included in the General Funds of a not-for-profit hospital?
     a. Permanent endowments.
     b. Term endowments.
     c. Assets Whose Use is Limited by decision of the governing board.
     d. Plant Replacement and Expansion funds.
  4. During 19x6, Shaw Hospital purchased medicines for hospital use totaling $800,000. Included in this $800,000 was an invoice of $10,000 that was canceled in 19x6 by the vendor because the vendor wished to donate this medicine to Shaw. This donation of medicine should be recorded as:
     a. A $10,000 reduction of medicine expense.
     b. An increase in other operating revenue of $10,000.
     c. A direct $10,000 credit to the general (unrestricted) funds balance.
     d. A $10,000 credit to the restricted funds balance.
  5. On July 1, 19x1, Lilydale Hospital's Board of Trustees designated $200,000 for expansion of outpatient facilities. The $200,000 is expected to be expended in the fiscal year ending June 30, 19x4. In Lilydale's Balance Sheet at June 30, 19x2, this cash should be classified as a $200,000:
     a. Restricted current asset.
     b. Restricted noncurrent asset.
     c. Unrestricted current asset.
     d. Assets whose use is limited.
  6. Which of the following would normally be included in Other Operating Revenues of a voluntary not-for-profit hospital?
     a. Unrestricted interest income from an endowment fund.
     b. An unrestricted gift.
     c. Donated services.
     d. Tuition received from an educational program.

7. Payne Hospital received an unrestricted bequest of $100,000 in 19x6. This bequest should be recorded as:
   a. A memorandum entry only.
   b. Other operating revenue of $100,000.
   c. Nonoperating revenue of $100,000.
   d. A direct credit of $100,000 to the fund balance.

8. Ross Hospital's accounting records disclosed the following information:

Net resources invested in plant assets . . . . . . . . . . . . . . . $10,000,000
Board designated funds  . . . . . . . . . . . . . . . . . . . . .   2,000,000

What amount should be included as part of unrestricted funds?
   a. $12,000,000.
   b. $10,000,000.
   c. $2,000,000.
   d. $0.

9. Depreciation should be recognized in the financial statements of:
   a. Proprietary (for-profit) hospitals only.
   b. Both proprietary (for-profit) and not-for-profit hospitals.
   c. Both proprietary (for-profit) and not-for-profit hospitals, only when they are affiliated with a college or university.
   d. All hospitals, as a memorandum entry not affecting the statement of revenues and expenses.

10. On March 1, 1988, Allan Rowe established a $100,000 endowment fund, the income from which is to be paid to Elm Hospital for general operating purposes. Elm does not control the fund's principal. Rowe appointed West National Bank as trustee of this fund. What journal entry is required by Elm to record the establishment of this endowment?

|  | Debit | Credit |
|---|---|---|
| a. Cash . . . . . . . . . . . . . . . . . . . . . . . . . . . . | 100,000 | |
| Nonexpendable Endowment Fund . . . . . . . . . . | | 100,000 |
| b. Cash . . . . . . . . . . . . . . . . . . . . . . . . . . . . | 100,000 | |
| Endowment Fund Balance . . . . . . . . . . . . . | | 100,000 |
| c. Nonexpendable Endowment Fund . . . . . . . . . . . . | 100,000 | |
| Endowment Fund Balance . . . . . . . . . . . . . | | 100,000 |
| d. Memorandum entry only . . . . . . . . . . . . . . . . . | — | — |

(AICPA, adapted)

12-2. During 19y1, the following events and transactions were recorded by Dexter Hospital. Show in general journal form the entries that should be made for each of the 12 transactions in accord with the standards discussed in Chapter 12. Number your entries to correspond with the transactions described below and indicate the fund in which each transaction takes place.

1. Gross charges for hospital services, all charged to accounts and notes receivable, were as follows:

Revenue from nursing services  . . . . . . . . . . . . . . . . . . . $780,000
Revenue from other professional services . . . . . . . . . . . . . .  321,000

2. Deductions from revenues were as follows:

Provision for bad debts (estimated) . . . . . . . . . . . . . . . . . $30,000
Charity services (actual) . . . . . . . . . . . . . . . . . . . . . .  15,000

3. The General Funds paid $18,000 to retire mortgage bonds payable with an equivalent face value.
4. During the year, the General Funds received in cash unrestricted contributions of $50,000 and unrestricted income from Endowment Fund investments of $6,500.
5. New equipment costing $26,000 was acquired from donor-restricted cash. An X-ray machine that originally cost $24,000 and that had an undepreciated cost of $2,400 was sold for $500 cash.
6. Vouchers totaling $1,191,000 were issued for the following items:

Fiscal and administrative services expenses . . . . . . . . . . . . . $215,000
General services expenses . . . . . . . . . . . . . . . . . . . . . .  225,000
Nursing services expenses . . . . . . . . . . . . . . . . . . . . . .  520,000
Other professional services expenses . . . . . . . . . . . . . . . .  165,000
Inventory . . . . . . . . . . . . . . . . . . . . . . . . . . . . . .   60,000
Expenses accrued at December 31, 19y0 . . . . . . . . . . . . . . .     6,000

7. Collections of accounts receivable totaled $985,000. Accounts written off as uncollectible amounted to $11,000.
8. Cash payments on vouchers payable during the year were $825,000.
9. Supplies of $37,000 were issued to nursing services.
10. On December 31, 19x6, accrued interest income on Plant Replacement and Expansion Fund investments was $800.
11. Depreciation of buildings and equipment was as follows:

Buildings . . . . . . . . . . . . . . . . . . . . . . . . . . . . . . $44,000
Equipment . . . , . . . . . . . . . . . . . . . . . . . . . . . . . .  73,000

12. On December 31, 19y1, an accrual of $6,100 was made for interest on mortgage bonds payable.

(AICPA, adapted)

12–3.   The following selected information was taken from the books and records of Glendora Hospital (a voluntary hospital) as of and for the year ended June 30, 19y1:

1. Patient service revenue totaled $16,000,000, with allowances and uncollectible accounts amounting to $3,400,000. Other operating revenue aggregated $346,000 and included $160,000 from Specific Purpose Funds. Revenue of $6,000,000 recognized under cost reimbursement agreements is subject to audit and retroactive adjustment by third-party payors. Estimated retroactive adjustments under these agreements have been included in allowances.
2. Unrestricted gifts and bequests of $410,000 were received.
3. Unrestricted income from endowment funds totaled $160,000.
4. Income from assets whose use is limited aggregated $82,000.
5. Operating expenses totaled $13,370,000 and included $500,000 for depreciation computed on the straight-line basis. However, accelerated depreciation is used to determine reimbursable costs under certain third-party

reimbursement agreements. Net cost reimbursement revenue amounting to $220,000, resulting from the difference in depreciation methods, was deferred to future years.

6. Also included in operating expenses are pension costs of $100,000, in connection with a noncontributory pension plan covering substantially all of Glendora's employees. Accrued pension costs are funded currently. Prior service cost is being amortized over a period of 20 years. The actuarially computed value of vested and nonvested benefits at year-end amounted to $3,000,000 and $350,000, respectively. The assumed rate of return used in determining the actuarial present value of accumulated plan benefits was 8 percent. The plan's net assets available for benefits at year-end was $3,050,000.

7. Gifts and bequests are recorded at fair market values when received.

8. Patient service revenue is accounted for at established rates on the accrual basis.

### Required:

a. Prepare a formal statement of revenues and expenses for Glendora Hospital for the year ended June 30, 19y1.

b. Draft the appropriate disclosures in separate notes accompanying the statement of revenues and expenses, referencing each note to its respective item in the statement.

(AICPA)

12–4. St. Luke's Hospital uses the fund structure and account titles recommended by the American Institute of Certified Public Accountants. During the fiscal year ended December 31, 19y1, the following transactions occurred.

1. Gross charges for hospital services amounted to $1,000,000, of which $900,000 was received in cash.

2. The bad debt estimate was $10,000; contractual and other adjustments to patients' accounts totaled $25,000.

3. Vouchers were issued for the following items: fiscal and administrative expenses, $80,000; general service expenses, $100,000; nursing services expenses, $500,000; other professional services expenses, $300,000; and supplies inventory, $50,000. Vouchers in the amount of $800,000 were paid.

4. A building fund drive collected $800,000 in cash and $400,000 in pledges, all of which are expected to be collected.

5. A building addition was constructed for $700,000, which was paid in cash from the Plant Replacement and Expansion Funds.

6. A federal grant was received in cash in the amount of $300,000 for the purpose of conducting cancer research. Of that amount, $200,000 was expended and paid during the current period. Research expense was charged.

7. The hospital received $1,000,000 from a wealthy donor with the stipulation that the amount be invested permanently. One half of the interest earnings are to be used for equipment purchases, and one half may be used at the board's discretion. During the year, $40,000 was earned and recorded in the appropriate funds, but not expended.

8. Depreciation was recorded on hospital plant in the amount of $100,000.

**Required:**

    *a.* Record the above transactions in the general journal of St. Luke's Hospital. Indicate the fund in which each entry is to be made. Number each entry to correspond with the appropriate transaction.

    *b.* Prepare a Statement of Revenues and Expenses for St. Luke's Hospital for the Year Ended December 31, 19y1.

**12–5.**    Northland County Hospital and Northland County both had fiscal years ending December 31.

    *a.* Assume the following transactions were transactions of Northland County Hospital. Prepare entries in general journal form to record each transaction in conformity with current accounting standards for hospitals. For each entry indicate the name of the fund, or funds, affected. You may ignore bond interest payments.

        1. On January 1, 19y1, bonds were sold at par in the amount of $3,000,000 to finance the construction of a building.

        2. On January 2, 19y1, a contract for the construction of the building was signed in the amount of $3,000,000.

        3. On December 31, 19y1, the building was completed, and the contractor was paid the full amount.

        4. On January 1, 19y2, a $500,000 research grant was received in cash from the federal government.

        5. On December 31, 19y2, the grant work was completed at a cost of $500,000.

        6. On December 31, 19y2, you note that the building constructed in transaction (3) is expected to last 30 years, with no salvage value. Unrestricted cash in the amount of $100,000 is designated by the governing board to be held for eventual replacement or expansion of the building.

    *b.* If you did not solve Exercise 11–5, part (*b*), assume the above transactions were transactions of Northland County and prepare entries in general journal form to record each transaction in conformity with current accounting standards for state and local governments. For each entry indicate the name of the fund, or funds, affected. You may ignore bond interest payments. (If you did solve Exercise 11–5, Part (*b*), review that solution before answering Part (*c*) below.)

    *c.* Comment on the differences between accounting for hospitals compared with accounting for state and local governments that are brought out by this problem.

**12–6.**    Compare and contrast accounting for health care providers with state and local government accounting for:

    *a.* Current unrestricted resources.

    *b.* Assets restricted by donors or grantors to certain current purposes.

    *c.* Endowments and endowment income.

    *d.* Plant acquisition and depreciation.

Exercises 12–7 through 12–10 require entries in the General Funds, the Specific Purpose Funds, the Plant Replacement and Expansion Funds, and the Endowment Funds for hospitals. Each exercise can be done separately, or all of the exercises may be assigned, as some of the transactions are interrelated.

**12–7.** **General Funds.** As of January 1, 19y1, the trial balance for the General Funds for DeKalb Hospital was as follows:

|  | Debit | Credit |
|---|---:|---:|
| Cash | $ 125,000 | |
| Accounts and notes receivable | 1,535,000 | |
| Allowance for uncollectible receivables | | $ 132,000 |
| Inventories | 116,000 | |
| Prepaid expenses | 35,000 | |
| Assets whose use is limited—cash | 17,000 | |
| Assets whose use is limited—investments | 1,505,000 | |
| Property, plant, and equipment | 12,529,000 | |
| Accumulated depreciation—property, plant, and equipment | | 3,543,000 |
| Notes payable to banks | | 275,000 |
| Current installments of long-term debt | | 170,000 |
| Accounts payable | | 398,000 |
| Accrued expenses | | 79,000 |
| Bonds payable | | 3,900,000 |
| Fund balance | | 7,365,000 |
| Totals | $15,862,000 | $15,862,000 |

During the fiscal year ended December 31, 19y1, the following transactions occurred:

1. During the year, patient service revenue, at gross amount, was $9,325,000. This amount was charged to patients' accounts and notes receivable.

2. The bad debt estimate was $491,000; actual contractual and other adjustments amounted to $1,311,000.

3. A total of $432,000 was transferred from Specific Purpose Funds for research expenses incurred this period. In addition, $1,211,000 was earned in various other operating revenues. All was received in cash.

4. During the year, the hospital received $325,000 in unrestricted gifts and bequests and $240,000 in unrestricted income from Endowment Fund investments. All was received in cash.

5. Collections on accounts and notes receivable during the year amounted to $7,539,000; accounts and notes totaling $512,000 were written off.

6. During the year, the following items were recorded as accounts payable: $79,000, accrued expenses payable as of January 1; nursing services expenses of $2,900,000; other professional services expenses of $2,365,000; general services expenses of $2,342,000; fiscal services expenses of $348,000; administrative services expenses of $358,000; research expenses of $432,000; inventory of $345,000; and prepaid expenses of $17,000.

7. Cash disbursements made by the General Funds were as follows: accounts payable, $9,204,000; notes payable to banks, $200,000; and the current installment of long-term debt, $170,000.

8. Supplies were issued during the year for: nursing services, $225,000; other professional services, $75,000; general services, $63,000; fiscal services, $17,000; and administrative services, $14,000.

9. Prepaid expenses expired during the year were charged to: nursing services, $5,300; other professional services, $1,700; general services, $5,800; fiscal services, $2,300; and administrative services, $1,400.

10. Accrued expenses at year-end were: nursing services, $42,000; other professional services, $38,000; general services, $35,000; fiscal services, $5,800, and administrative services, $15,300.

11. Property, plant, and equipment costing $590,000 was purchased by the Plant Replacement and Expansion Fund.

12. Property, plant, and equipment originally costing $120,000, on which $80,000 depreciation had accumulated, was sold for $35,000 cash.

13. In accord with third-party agreements, cash in the amount of $300,000 was transferred to Assets Whose Use is Limited—Cash to provide for future plant expansion. Investments costing $300,000 were purchased with that cash.

14. The provision for depreciation for the year amounted to $650,000.

15. Closing entries were prepared.

***Required:***

*a.* Prepare journal entries to record the transactions listed above.

*b.* Prepare, in good form, a Statement of Revenues and Expenses for the General Funds for DeKalb Hospital for the Year Ended December 31, 19y1.

*c.* Prepare, in good form, a Statement of Changes in Fund Balances for the General Funds for DeKalb Hospital for the Year Ended December 31, 19y1.

*d.* Prepare, in good form, a Balance Sheet for the General Funds for DeKalb Hospital for the Year Ended December 31, 19y1.

*e.* Prepare, in good form, a Statement of Changes in Financial Position for the General Funds for DeKalb Hospital for the Year Ended December 31, 19y1.

12–8. **Specific Purpose Funds.**   As of January 1, 19y1, the trial balance for the Specific Purpose Funds for DeKalb Hospital was as follows:

| | | |
|---|---:|---:|
| Cash | $ 3,500 | |
| Investments | 535,000 | |
| Grants receivable | 40,000 | |
| Fund balances—research grants | | $ 75,000 |
| Fund balances—other | | 503,500 |
| Totals | $578,500 | $578,500 |

During the fiscal year ended December 31, 19y1, the following transactions occurred:

1. The Specific Purpose Funds received $175,000 in restricted gifts and bequests and $42,000 in investment income ($6,000 of which relates to research grants). The entire amount was received in cash.

2. Research grants received in cash amounted to $458,000, including the $40,000 receivable at the beginning of the year. At the end of the year, notification of an additional $35,000 award was received (but not the cash).

3. The General Funds expended $432,000 for research and was reimbursed by the Specific Purpose Funds.

4. Additional investments costing $200,000 were purchased by the Specific Purpose Funds.

**Required:**
a. Prepare journal entries to record the transactions listed above.
b. Prepare, in good form, a Statement of Changes in Fund Balances for the Specific Purpose Funds for DeKalb Hospital for the Year Ended December 31, 19y1.
c. Prepare, in good form, a Balance Sheet for the Specific Purpose Funds for DeKalb Hospital as of December 31, 19y1.

12–9.  **Plant Replacement and Expansion Funds.** As of January 1, 19y1, the trial balance for the Plant Replacement and Expansion Funds for DeKalb Hospital was as follows:

| | | |
|---|---:|---:|
| Cash | $130,000 | |
| Investments | 535,000 | |
| Pledges receivable | 125,000 | |
| Estimated uncollectible pledges receivable | | $ 10,000 |
| Fund balances | | 780,000 |
| Totals | $790,000 | $790,000 |

During the fiscal year ended December 31, 19y1, the following transactions occurred:
1. Cash in the amount of $732,000 was received in funds restricted for building purposes, including the pledges receivable at the beginning of the year. An additional $80,000 in building fund pledges was received. The 1/1/x6 balance in Estimated Uncollectible Pledges Receivable is deemed adequate and not excessive.
2. Investment income, all received in cash, amounted to $47,000.
3. Fixed assets costing $590,000 were purchased for cash. (See Entry 11 of Exercise 12–7.)
4. Additional investments were purchased in the amount of $300,000.

**Required:**
a. Prepare journal entries to record the transactions listed above.
b. Prepare, in good form, a Statement of Changes in Fund Balances for the Plant Replacement and Expansion Funds for DeKalb Hospital for the Year Ended December 31, 19y1.
c. Prepare, in good form, a Balance Sheet for the Plant Replacement and Expansion Funds for DeKalb Hospital as of December 31, 19y1.

12–10.  **Endowment Funds.** As of January 1, 19y1, the trial balance for the Endowment funds for DeKalb Hospital was as follows:

| | | |
|---|---:|---:|
| Cash | $ 40,000 | |
| Investments | 5,500,000 | |
| Fund balance—permanent endowment | | $4,900,000 |
| Fund balance—term endowment | | 640,000 |
| Totals | $5,540,000 | $5,540,000 |

During the fiscal year ended December 31, 19y1, the following transactions occurred:

1. Additional permanent endowments of $100,000 and term endowments of $40,000 were received.
2. Investments costing $1,000,000 were sold for $1,115,000. $101,700 of the gain was allocated to the permanent endowment, and the remainder of the gain was allocated to the term endowment.
3. Additional investments costing $1,280,000 were purchased.

***Required:***
*a.* Prepare journal entries to record the transactions listed above.
*b.* Prepare, in good form, a Statement of Changes in Fund Balances for the Endowment Funds for DeKalb Hospital for the Year Ended December 31, 19y1.
*c.* Prepare, in good form, a Balance Sheet for the Endowment Funds for DeKalb Hospital as of December 31, 19y1.

# Chapter 13

# ACCOUNTING FOR VOLUNTARY HEALTH AND WELFARE ORGANIZATIONS

As is true for colleges and universities, and for hospitals, neither the FASB nor the GASB has issued a complete set of accounting and reporting principles for voluntary health and welfare organizations. Standards set forth in this chapter are those found in the AICPA *Audits of Voluntary Health and Welfare Organizations*. Under FASB *Statement 32*, the standards found in that audit guide are "preferable accounting principles" which should be followed pending issuance by the FASB of a Statement or Statements specifically applying to Voluntary Health and Welfare Organizations. In addition, accounting principles and more detailed guidance are found in *Standards of Accounting and Financial Reporting for Voluntary Health and Welfare Organizations* (revised 1988) issued by the National Health Council, the National Assembly of National Voluntary Health and Social Welfare Organizations, and the United Way of America.

### Summary—Voluntary Health and Welfare Organization Accounting

Voluntary health and welfare organizations are not-for-profit organizations that receive most of their support from voluntary contributions and are engaged in activities that promote the general health and well-being of the public. Typically, these organizations generate some revenues through user charges but receive most of their support from others who do not receive direct benefits. For example, a community mental health center may charge patients a fee, based on their ability to pay, and may receive allocations from a United Way drive and direct gifts, may have federal and state grants, and may receive donated services and materials. Other examples of Voluntary Health and Welfare Organizations include family planning agencies, charities such as the American Heart Association and the American Cancer Association, Meals on Wheels, senior citizen centers, Girl and Boy Scouts, and Big Brothers/Big Sisters.

A few summary comments may help guide the reader through the material in this chapter:

- Fund accounting is used when significant restrictions exist on the use of certain resources. Funds are classified as current—unrestricted; current—restricted; land, building, and equipment; and custodian and other. A governing board may designate certain resources, but those resources would be classified as unrestricted.
- Full accrual accounting is used. Revenues, and Expenses are recognized in **all** funds (except custodian), unlike colleges and universities and hospitals (where revenues and expenditures/expenses are reported only in the current/general funds.
- Funds can be restricted only by legally enforceable agreements with outside parties, as is true for all types of nonprofit organizations.
- The primary statements are the Balance Sheet, the Statement of Revenue and Expenses and Changes in Fund Balances, and the Statement of Functional Expenses. (See Illustrations 13–1, 13–2, and 13–3 which are shown later in this chapter.) Note that totals are shown and required for revenues and expenses in Illustration 13–2.
- Pledges receivable are recognized when obtained, subject to an allowance for uncollectibles. Support is recognized in the period intended by the donor, if known; otherwise, when the funds are available for use.
- Property, plant, and equipment are recorded in the land, building, and equipment fund. Depreciation expense is recorded in that fund. The Fund Balance is separated between that portion which is unexpended and that portion which is expended.
- Revenues are reported in three categories, when applicable. These categories are (1) public support, (2) revenue and grants from governmental agencies, and (3) other revenues. Public support includes *direct* donations of money, services, or materials, special events, or legacies and bequests, and *indirect* donations through United Way or other fund-raising organizations. Other revenues are earned by the organization and include fees for services, interest, realized and unrealized gains on investments, and membership dues.
- Expenses are categorized as *program services* expenses or *supporting services* expenses. Supporting services expenses include management and general fund-raising expenses. Program services expenses are reported for each program the organization provides.

## Public Support and Revenue

The distinction between public support and other revenues is for classification purposes on the Statement of Revenues and Expenses and Changes in Fund Balances; however, both are financial resource inflows recognized on the full accrual basis.

**Pledges and cash contributions**  These contributions are, typically, significant sources of public support. If donors do not restrict the category of use, the public support is recognized in the current fund—unrestricted. If donors specify the programs or activities the pledge or contribution is intended to support, the amount should be recorded as support in the current funds—restricted. If the pledge or contribution is for acquiring, replacing, or improving capital assets, the amounts should be recorded in the land, building, and equipment fund. Donors or grantors may restrict the year of use, as well as the category of use, of their support. If amounts received in one year are designated by donors or grantors as being for use in a subsequent year, such amounts are reported in the balance sheet as of the end of the year of receipt as "Support and Revenue Designated for Future Periods," a liability account. The amounts are recognized as support in the year in which the donors or grantors permit use.

**Donated services**  Health and welfare organizations typically rely on the efforts of volunteer workers to supplement the efforts of paid employees in the performance of program services, support services, and periodic fund-raising drives. The present position of the AICPA is that the value of donated services should be recorded as contributions and as expense only when all three of the following circumstances exist:

1. The services performed are a normal part of the program or supporting services and would otherwise be performed by salaried personnel.
2. The organization exercises control over the employment and duties of the donors of the services.
3. The organization has a clearly measurable basis for the amount.

The three criteria are intended to have the effect of limiting the recognition of the value of contributed services to those cases in which a volunteer is performing without pay work that would otherwise be performed by a paid person. The rate of pay normally commanded by a paid person performing a given function would serve as the "clearly measurable basis" specified in the third criterion.

**Donated land, buildings, property, equipment, and materials**  Donated land, buildings, and equipment should be recorded at fair market value at the time of receipt. Donated materials should be recorded at fair market value, if material and measurable. The use of the donated materials should be recorded as expenses, at their carrying value.

**Direct and indirect support**   Support may be received directly or indirectly. Proceeds of special events, and legacies and bequests are examples of direct support. Contributions may be received directly or indirectly from associated organizations. Allocations from federated fund-raising organizations, such as United Way organizations, represent an example of indirect support.

**Government grants and revenues**   Fees and grants from governmental agencies are usually reported as a separate item in the Revenue section of the operating statement because of the importance of the item. Membership dues, program service fees, sales of supplies and services, investment income, and gains (or losses) on investment transactions are typical "other" revenues of voluntary health and welfare organizations.

### Program Services and Supporting Services Expenses

Contributors to a voluntary health and welfare organization are assumed to be interested in how resources were acquired and how they were used by that organization. In order to disclose a breakdown of the resources used for each program conducted by the organization, and how the total used for programs compares with the amount used for management and general expenses and for fund-raising, current reporting standards require the Statement of Revenue and Expenses and Changes in Fund Balances (Illustration 13–2) to disclose, by fund, the expenses of each program conducted, and the supporting services expenses. Further disclosure is given in the Statement of Functional Expenses (Illustration 13–3). The latter statement presents, without regard to fund classifications, the allocation of salaries, fringe benefits, professional fees, supplies expense, depreciation on buildings and equipment, and all other object classifications.

If it can be demonstrated that a particular expense is for more than one purpose, that expense may be allocated to more than one function. For example, a mailing that describes the symptoms for a particular disease and suggests emergency treatment along with an appeal for funds might be partially allocated to the program function, "public health education," and partly to fund raising.

### Asset Valuation

Investments in securities are recorded at cost when purchased, or fair value, if received as a gift. After acquisition, standards allow investments to be reported at lower of cost or market or, alternatively, they may be reported at market, even if market is in **excess** of cost. If investments are carried at market, unrealized appreciation or depreciation should be reported in the Revenue section of the appropriate fund in the Statement of Revenue and Expenses and Changes in Fund Balances. Investments of all funds should be reported on the same basis, and that basis should be clearly disclosed in the financial statements, or notes thereto.

Fixed assets are recorded at cost (or at fair value, if received as a gift) in the land, building, and equipment fund. Depreciation expense is also recorded in that fund.

## Liabilities

Current liabilities to be paid from unrestricted current assets and current liabilities to be paid from restricted current assets are recorded in the current fund—unrestricted or in the current funds—restricted, as appropriate. Liabilities relating to the acquisition or improvement of plant assets are recorded in the land, buildings, and equipment fund. Similarly, liabilities related to endowments are accounted for by the endowment funds. All assets of custodian funds belong to persons or organizations other than the reporting organization, therefore the total assets of custodian funds are offset by liabilities in the same amount.

## Fund Balances

By definition, the entire Fund Balance of the current fund—unrestricted is unrestricted; however, the governing board of the voluntary health or welfare organization may designate that certain assets of that fund will be used for specified purposes. In such cases it is appropriate to segregate the Fund Balance account to disclose the effect of the designations upon net assets, and the amount of undesignated Fund Balance which is available for current operating purposes.

Similarly, the entire Fund Balance of current funds—restricted is restricted to comply with the requirements of donors or grantors. As illustrated in previous chapters, the Fund Balance is segregated to show the amount of net assets held for each major purpose specified by donors or grantors.

The Fund Balance of the land, building, and equipment fund is shown in two or more elements: the investment of the organization in land, buildings, and equipment is reported as **Fund Balance—Expended;** the total of cash, investments, and pledges receivable of this fund is reported as **Fund Balance—Unexpended.** If a portion of the current assets are held under donor or grantor restrictions, and a portion of the current assets are held by this fund at the discretion of the governing board, Fund Balance—Unexpended should be shown in two corresponding ele-

ments: Fund Balance—Unexpended—Restricted and Fund Balance—
Unexpended—Unrestricted.

Ordinarily, it is adequate disclosure to show only one Fund Balance
account for endowment funds, but that account may be shown in two or
more elements if the governing board deems it desirable. Custodian
funds, of course, have no Fund Balance since assets of those funds are
offset in total by liabilities.

## ILLUSTRATIVE TRANSACTIONS—VOLUNTARY HEALTH AND WELFARE ORGANIZATIONS

Although accounting and financial reporting **standards** for all voluntary health and welfare organizations are the same, there are many differences among organizations in this category in the kinds of program
services provided and in the sources of support and revenue utilized.
Accordingly, the transactions and accounting entries presented in this
section should be taken as illustrative of an organization which offers
programs in public health education, professional education and train-
ing, and community services, and which engages in a related research
program, but not necessarily illustrative of a voluntary health or welfare
organization which offers services of a considerably different nature.
The transactions illustrated are grouped by fund type. All transactions
and events, assumed to take place in fiscal year 19y1, relate to the Voluntary Health and Welfare Service.

### Current Fund—Unrestricted

Contributions amounting to $219,000 were received in 19y0, but were
specified by the donor for use in 19y1 at the discretion of the governing
board; therefore, in 19y0 they were recorded as a liability. At the beginning of 19y1 the contributions were transferred from the deferred support and revenue category to the current support category:

| | | | |
|---|---|---|---|
| 1. | Support and Revenue Designated For Future | | |
| | Periods . . . . . . . . . . . . . . . . . . . . . . | 219,000 | |
| | Contributions . . . . . . . . . . . . . . . . | | 219,000 |

Unrestricted pledges were received in 19y1 for use during that year
in the amount of $2,740,000; unrestricted cash contributions received in
19y1 amounted to $1,000,000:

| | | | |
|---|---|---|---|
| 2. | Cash . . . . . . . . . . . . . . . . . . . . . . . | 1,000,000 | |
| | Pledges Receivable . . . . . . . . . . . . . . | 2,740,000 | |
| | Contributions . . . . . . . . . . . . . . . . | | 3,740,000 |

Cash collections of pledges amounted to $2,433,000 during the year;
in addition, pledges of $182,000 were written off as uncollectible:

```
3.  Cash . . . . . . . . . . . . . . . . . . . . . . . . . .  2,433,000
       Allowance for Uncollectible Pledges . . . . . . .    182,000
           Pledges Receivable  . . . . . . . . . . .                   2,615,000
```

It is estimated that $195,000 of the current year's pledges will not be collected.

```
4.  Estimated Uncollectible Pledges . . . . . . . . .     195,000
       Allowance for Uncollectible Pledges . . . . .                    195,000
```

Special events held by the Voluntary Health and Welfare Service resulted in cash receipts of $285,000; costs related to the special events, all paid in cash, amounted to $181,000:

```
5a.  Cash . . . . . . . . . . . . . . . . . . . . . .     285,000
        Special Events . . . . . . . . . . . . . . .                   285,000
5b.  Cost of Special Events  . . . . . . . . . . . .     181,000
        Cash . . . . . . . . . . . . . . . . . . . .                   181,000
```

The 19y1 allocation from the United Way amounted to $313,000; related fund-raising expenses to be borne by the Voluntary Health and Welfare Service amounted to $38,000; the net allocation was received in cash:

```
6.  Cash . . . . . . . . . . . . . . . . . . . . .     275,000
       United Way Fund-Raising Expenses . . . . . . .      38,000
           Support Received from United Way . . . . .                   313,000
```

It should be noted that the cost of Special Events and the United Way Fund-Raising "Expenses" are reported not as expenses but as deductions from Support (see Illustration 13–2).

Cash collections of receivables accrued at the end of the prior year totaled $40,000. Cash was received from legacies and bequests, $92,000; and $17,000 in membership dues was collected.

```
7.  Cash . . . . . . . . . . . . . . . . . . . . . .     149,000
       Accrued Receivables . . . . . . . . . . . . .                    40,000
       Legacies and Bequests . . . . . . . . . . . .                    92,000
       Membership Dues . . . . . . . . . . . . . . .                    17,000
```

Investment income in the amount of $98,000 and miscellaneous revenues in the amount of $42,000 were accrued at the end of 19y1.

```
8.  Accrued Receivables . . . . . . . . . . . . . .     140,000
       Investment Income . . . . . . . . . . . . . .                    98,000
       Miscellaneous Revenues . . . . . . . . . . .                    42,000
```

Investments costing $950,000 were sold for $1,150,000; additional investments were purchased, as shown by Entry 9b:

```
9a.  Cash . . . . . . . . . . . . . . . . . . . . . .   1,150,000
        Investments—Marketable Securities . . . . .                   950,000
        Realized Gain on Investment Transactions  . .                   200,000
9b.  Investments—Long-Term . . . . . . . . . . . .      482,000
     Investments—Marketable Securities . . . . . . . .   1,075,000
        Cash . . . . . . . . . . . . . . . . . . . .                  1,557,000
```

Contributions of $245,000 were received in cash; the donors specified that these contributions were not to be used until 19y2.

```
10.  Cash . . . . . . . . . . . . . . . . . . . . .    245,000
         Support and Revenue Designated for Future
         Periods . . . . . . . . . . . . . . . . .                  245,000
```

Accounts payable at the end of 19y0 and research grants awarded by the Voluntary Health and Welfare Service in 19y0 were paid in 19y1:

```
11.  Accounts Payable . . . . . . . . . . . . .     139,000
     Research Grants Payable . . . . . . . . .      616,000
         Cash . . . . . . . . . . . . . . . . .                     755,000
```

Expenses for 19y1, recorded by object class, were as follows:

```
12.  Salaries . . . . . . . . . . . . . . . . . .    1,455,000
     Employee Benefits . . . . . . . . . . . . .        77,500
     Payroll Taxes . . . . . . . . . . . . . . .         75,500
     Professional Fees . . . . . . . . . . . . .         36,000
     Supplies . . . . . . . . . . . . . . . . .          56,000
     Telephone and Telegraph . . . . . . . . . .         74,000
     Postage and Shipping . . . . . . . . . . .          84,000
     Occupancy . . . . . . . . . . . . . . . . .        135,000
     Rental of Equipment . . . . . . . . . . . .         62,000
     Local Transportation . . . . . . . . . . .         120,000
     Conferences, Conventions, Meetings . . . . . .     169,000
     Printing and Publications . . . . . . . . . .      188,000
     Awards and Grants . . . . . . . . . . . . .      1,609,000
     Miscellaneous Expenses . . . . . . . . . . .        44,000
         Inventory . . . . . . . . . . . . . . . .                   55,000
         Accounts Payable . . . . . . . . . . . .                   148,000
         Research Grants Payable . . . . . . . . .                  596,000
         Cash . . . . . . . . . . . . . . . . . .                 3,386,000
```

Expenses are reported both by object class and by function. This may be done on one entry. However, the authoritative literature shows a second entry to allocate expenses to program services and supporting services:

```
13.  Research . . . . . . . . . . . . . . . . . .    1,257,000
     Public Health Education . . . . . . . . . . .      539,000
     Professional Education and Training . . . . . .     612,000
     Community Services . . . . . . . . . . . . .        568,000
     Management and General . . . . . . . . . .         567,000
     Fund Raising . . . . . . . . . . . . . . . .        642,000
         Salaries . . . . . . . . . . . . . . . .                 1,455,000
         Employee Benefits . . . . . . . . . . . .                   77,500
         Payroll Taxes . . . . . . . . . . . . .                     75,500
         Professional Fees . . . . . . . . . . . .                   36,000
         Supplies . . . . . . . . . . . . . . . .                    56,000
         Telephone and Telegraph . . . . . . . . .                   74,000
         Postage and Shipping . . . . . . . . . .                    84,000
         Occupancy . . . . . . . . . . . . . . . .                  135,000
         Rental of Equipment . . . . . . . . . . .                   62,000
         Local Transportation . . . . . . . . . . .                 120,000
         Conferences, Conventions, Meetings . . . . .               169,000
         Printing and Publications . . . . . . . . .                188,000
         Awards and Grants . . . . . . . . . . . .                1,609,000
         Miscellaneous Expenses . . . . . . . . .                    44,000
```

Additional inventory costing $64,000 was purchased for cash:

14.  Inventory . . . . . . . . . . . . . . . . . . . .        64,000
        Cash . . . . . . . . . . . . . . . . . . . . .                      64,000

Property and equipment costing $17,000 was purchased with unrestricted cash; the property and equipment are to be recorded as an asset in the land, building, and equipment fund (see Entry 29). Realized appreciation, totaling $100,000, on investments held by the endowment funds was transferred in cash to the current fund—unrestricted, as the terms of the endowment agreements provide that the funds are available for the general use of the Voluntary Health and Welfare Service (see Entry 34):

15a.  Transfer to Land, Building, and Equipment Fund—
        Property and Equipment Acquisitions  . . . . .        17,000
          Cash . . . . . . . . . . . . . . . . . . . .                      17,000

15b.  Cash . . . . . . . . . . . . . . . . . . . . . .      100,000
        Transfer from Endowment Funds—Realized
          Appreciation on Investments  . . . . . . .                    100,000

Nominal accounts of the current fund—unrestricted were closed as of the end of 19y1:

16.  Contributions . . . . . . . . . . . . . . . . . .    3,959,000
       Special Events . . . . . . . . . . . . . . . .      285,000
       Legacies and Bequests  . . . . . . . . . . .        92,000
       Support Received from United Way  . . . . . . .     313,000
       Membership Dues  . . . . . . . . . . . . . .        17,000
       Investment Income . . . . . . . . . . . . . .       98,000
       Realized Gain on Investment Transactions  . . . .   200,000
       Miscellaneous Revenues  . . . . . . . . . . .       42,000
       Transfer from Endowment Fund—Realized
         Appreciation on Investments  . . . . . . . .      100,000
           Estimated Uncollectible Pledges . . . . . . .                  195,000
           Cost of Special Events  . . . . . . . . . .                    181,000
           United Way Fund-Raising Expenses  . . . . .                     38,000
           Transfer to Land, Building, and Equipment
             Fund—Property and Equipment
             Acquisitions . . . . . . . . . . . . . . .                     17,000
           Research  . . . . . . . . . . . . . . . . .                  1,257,000
           Public Health Education  . . . . . . . . . .                    539,000
           Professional Education and Training  . . . . .                  612,000
           Community Services . . . . . . . . . . . .                      568,000
           Management and General  . . . . . . . . .                      567,000
           Fund-Raising  . . . . . . . . . . . . . . .                     642,000
           Fund Balance—Undesignated . . . . . . . .                      490,000

Also at the end of 19y1 adjustments were made to the Fund Balance accounts of the Current Fund—Unrestricted to reflect the designations by the board as of that date:

17.  Fund Balance—Undesignated . . . . . . . . .          4,000
       Fund Balance—Designated for Research Purposes .   596,000
         Fund Balance—Designated for Long-Term
           Investments . . . . . . . . . . . . . . .                      500,000
         Fund Balance—Designated for Purchases of
           New Equipment . . . . . . . . . . . . .                        100,000

## Current Funds—Restricted

During 19y1 grants receivable amounting to $46,000 were collected; also, investments of $72,000 were sold at book value:

| | | | |
|---|---|---|---|
| 18. | Cash . . . . . . . . . . . . . . . . . . . . . | 118,000 | |
| | Grants Receivable . . . . . . . . . . . . . | | 46,000 |
| | Investments . . . . . . . . . . . . . . . . | | 72,000 |

Grants restricted by grantors for the professional education programs amounted to $84,000; grants to be used only for the research program totaled $78,000. These grants are recognized immediately as Contributions when available for use. Cash received from these grants totaled $104,000 during 19y1. Income from investments restricted for use for the research program totaled $10,000; this amount was received in cash.

| | | | |
|---|---|---|---|
| 19a. | Grants Receivable . . . . . . . . . . . . . | 162,000 | |
| | Contributions—Restricted for Professional | | |
| | Education . . . . . . . . . . . . . . . | | 84,000 |
| | Contributions—Restricted for Research . . . . | | 78,000 |
| 19b. | Cash . . . . . . . . . . . . . . . . . . . | 104,000 | |
| | Grants Receivable . . . . . . . . . . . . | | 104,000 |
| 19c. | Cash . . . . . . . . . . . . . . . . . . . | 10,000 | |
| | Investment Income—Restricted for Research  . | | 10,000 |

Expenses, itemized below, amounted to $155,000, all paid in cash. In addition, $8,000 cash was returned to a grantor, as required by the conditions of the grant.

| | | | |
|---|---|---|---|
| 20. | Salaries . . . . . . . . . . . . . . . . . . | 100,000 | |
| | Employee Benefits . . . . . . . . . . . . . | 5,500 | |
| | Payroll Taxes . . . . . . . . . . . . . . . | 5,500 | |
| | Professional Fees  . . . . . . . . . . . . . | 20,000 | |
| | Supplies  . . . . . . . . . . . . . . . . . | 20,000 | |
| | Printing and Publications . . . . . . . . . . | 4,000 | |
| | Return of Research Grant to Donor  . . . . . . | 8,000 | |
| | Cash . . . . . . . . . . . . . . . . . . . | | 163,000 |

All expenses for the year related to the research program. The following entry shows the reclassification:

| | | | |
|---|---|---|---|
| 21. | Research . . . . . . . . . . . . . . . . . . | 155,000 | |
| | Salaries . . . . . . . . . . . . . . . . . | | 100,000 |
| | Employee Benefits . . . . . . . . . . . . . | | 5,500 |
| | Payroll Taxes . . . . . . . . . . . . . . . | | 5,500 |
| | Professional Fees  . . . : . . . . . . . . . | | 20,000 |
| | Supplies  . . . . . . . . . . . . . . . . . | | 20,000 |
| | Printing and Publications . . . . . . . . . . | | 4,000 |

Cash in the amount of $71,000 was invested.

| | | | |
|---|---|---|---|
| 22. | Investments . . . . . . . . . . . . . . . . | 71,000 | |
| | Cash . . . . . . . . . . . . . . . . . . . | | 71,000 |

Nominal accounts of Current Funds—Restricted were closed as of the end of 19y1:

23. Contributions—Restricted for Professional
    Education . . . . . . . . . . . . . . . . . . . . 84,000
    Contributions—Restricted for Research . . . . . . 78,000
    Investment Income—Restricted for Research . . . 10,000
    Fund Balance—Research Grants . . . . . . . . . 75,000
        Research . . . . . . . . . . . . . . . . . 155,000
        Return of Research Grant to Donor . . . . . 8,000
        Fund Balance—Professional Education . . . . 84,000

## Land, Building, and Equipment Fund

Pledges restricted for the acquisition or improvement of the land, buildings, and equipment of the Voluntary Health and Welfare Service during 19y0 were collected in cash in the amount of $20,000; also, pledges for that purpose in the amount of $4,000 were written off in 19y1.

24. Cash . . . . . . . . . . . . . . . . . . . . . . 20,000
    Allowance for Uncollectible Pledges . . . . . . . 4,000
        Pledges Receivable . . . . . . . . . . . . 24,000

Contributions to the building fund during 19y1 amounted to $78,500, of which $45,000 was received in cash. Estimated uncollectible pledges totaling $6,500 were recorded.

25a. Cash . . . . . . . . . . . . . . . . . . . . . 45,000
     Pledges Receivable . . . . . . . . . . . . . . 33,500
        Contributions to Building Fund . . . . . . 78,500

25b. Estimated Uncollectible Pledges . . . . . . . . 6,500
        Allowance for Uncollectible Pledges . . . . . 6,500

At year-end, cash was paid on the principal of the mortgage in the amount of $4,000. In addition, during the year, miscellaneous expenses of $8,000 were paid in cash.

26. Mortgage Payable . . . . . . . . . . . . . 4,000
    Miscellaneous Expenses . . . . . . . . . . . 8,000
        Cash . . . . . . . . . . . . . . . . . . . 12,000

Depreciation expense was charged in the amount of $34,000:

27. Depreciation Expense . . . . . . . . . . . . . 34,000
        Accumulated Depreciation . . . . . . . . . 34,000

The depreciation expense and miscellaneous expenses were allocated to functional categories, as shown in Entry 28:

28. Research . . . . . . . . . . . . . . . . . . 2,000
    Public Health Education . . . . . . . . . . . . 5,000
    Professional Education and Training . . . . . . 6,000
    Community Services . . . . . . . . . . . . . 10,000
    Management and General . . . . . . . . . . 9,880
    Fund Raising . . . . . . . . . . . . . . . . . 9,120
        Depreciation . . . . . . . . . . . . . . . 34,000
        Miscellaneous Expenses . . . . . . . . . . 8,000

Purchases of land, buildings, and equipment during the year amounted to $37,000. Of that amount, $17,000 was acquired by use of Current Fund—Unrestricted cash (see Entry 15a):

29.  Land, Buildings, and Equipment . . . . . . . . .    37,000
         Property and Equipment Acquisitions from
             Unrestricted Fund . . . . . . . . . . . .                17,000
         Cash . . . . . . . . . . . . . . . . . . .                   20,000

Additional investments were purchased in the amount of $32,000:

30.  Investments . . . . . . . . . . . . . . . . .       32,000
         Cash . . . . . . . . . . . . . . . . . .                    32,000

At the end of 19y1 the closing entry is made for the land, building, and equipment fund:

31.  Contributions to Building Fund . . . . . . . .      78,500
     Property and Equipment Acquisitions from
         Unrestricted Fund . . . . . . . . . . . .       17,000
             Estimated Uncollectible Pledges . . . . . . .            6,500
             Research . . . . . . . . . . . . . . .                   2,000
             Public Health Education . . . . . . . . .                5,000
             Professional Education and Training . . . . .            6,000
             Community Services . . . . . . . . . . .                 10,000
             Management and General . . . . . . . .                   9,880
             Fund Raising . . . . . . . . . . . .                     9,120
             Fund Balance—Expended . . . . . . . . .                  7,000
             Fund Balance—Unexpended . . . . . . . .                  40,000

Note that the Fund Balance—Expended increased by $7,000. This amount is the net result of increases of $37,000 for plant acquisitions and $4,000 for bond retirement, less $34,000 for depreciation expense. Note also that Fund Balance—Unexpended increased by $40,000. This resulted from increases of $72,000 in contributions and $17,000 in acquisitions financed by the current fund—unrestricted, less $37,000 expended for acquisition of equipment, $4,000 for mortgage repayment, and $8,000 for miscellaneous expenses. Remember that Fund Balance—Unexpended is offset by the cash, investments, and pledges receivable in the Balance Sheet whereas the Fund Balance—Expended is offset by the fixed assets less the debt associated with those assets (see Illustration 13–1).

## Endowment Funds

During 19y1 cash of the Endowment Funds of the Voluntary Health and Welfare Service increased in the amount of $6,000; $2,000 from contributions and $4,000 from legacies and bequests:

32.  Cash . . . . . . . . . . . . . . . . . .            6,000
         Contributions . . . . . . . . . . . . . .                   2,000
         Legacies and Bequests . . . . . . . . . . .                 4,000

Investments costing $100,000 were sold for $125,000 cash:

## ILLUSTRATION 13–1

## VOLUNTARY HEALTH AND WELFARE SERVICE
### Balance Sheets
### December 31, 19y1 and 19y0

### CURRENT FUNDS
#### Unrestricted

| Assets | 19y1 | 19y0 |
|---|---|---|
| Cash | $2,207,000 | $2,530,000 |
| Investments: | | |
| For long-term purposes | 2,727,000 | 2,245,000 |
| Other | 1,075,000 | 950,000 |
| Pledges receivable less allowance for uncollectibles of $105,000 and $92,000 | 475,000 | 363,000 |
| Inventories of educational materials, at cost | 70,000 | 61,000 |
| Accrued interest, other receivables and prepaid expenses | 286,000 | 186,000 |
| Total | $6,840,000 | $6,335,000 |

| Liabilities and Fund Balances | 19y1 | 19y0 |
|---|---|---|
| Accounts payable | $ 148,000 | $ 139,000 |
| Research grants payable | 596,000 | 616,000 |
| Contributions designated for future periods | 245,000 | 219,000 |
| Total Liabilities and Deferred Revenues | 989,000 | 974,000 |
| Fund balances: | | |
| Designated by the governing board for: | | |
| Long-term investments | 2,800,000 | 2,300,000 |
| Purchases of new equipment | 100,000 | — |
| Research purposes | 1,152,000 | 1,748,000 |
| Undesignated, available for general activities | 1,799,000 | 1,313,000 |
| Total Fund Balance | 5,851,000 | 5,361,000 |
| Total | $6,840,000 | $6,335,000 |

#### Restricted

| Assets | 19y1 | 19y0 |
|---|---|---|
| Cash | $ 3,000 | $ 5,000 |
| Investments | 71,000 | 72,000 |
| Grants receivable | 58,000 | 46,000 |
| Total | $ 132,000 | $ 123,000 |

| Liabilities and Fund Balances | 19y1 | 19y0 |
|---|---|---|
| Fund balances: | | |
| Professional education | $ 84,000 | $ — |
| Research grants | 48,000 | 123,000 |
| Total | $ 132,000 | $ 123,000 |

### LAND, BUILDING, AND EQUIPMENT FUND

| Assets | 19y1 | 19y0 |
|---|---|---|
| Cash | $ 3,000 | $ 2,000 |
| Investments | 177,000 | 145,000 |
| Pledges receivable less allowance for uncollectibles of $7,500 and $5,000 | 32,000 | 25,000 |
| Land, buildings, and equipment, at cost less accumulated depreciation of $296,000 and $262,000 | 516,000 | 513,000 |
| Total | $ 728,000 | $ 685,000 |

| Liabilities and Fund Balances | 19y1 | 19y0 |
|---|---|---|
| Mortgage payable, 8% due 19xx | $ 32,000 | $ 36,000 |
| Fund balances: | | |
| Expended | 484,000 | 477,000 |
| Unexpended—restricted | 212,000 | 172,000 |
| Total Fund Balance | 696,000 | 649,000 |
| Total | $ 728,000 | $ 685,000 |

### ENDOWMENT FUNDS

| Assets | 19y1 | 19y0 |
|---|---|---|
| Cash | $ 4,000 | $ 10,000 |
| Investments | 1,944,000 | 2,007,000 |
| Total | $1,948,000 | $2,017,000 |

| Liabilities and Fund Balances | 19y1 | 19y0 |
|---|---|---|
| Fund balances | $1,948,000 | $2,017,000 |
| Total | $1,948,000 | $2,017,000 |

Source: AICPA, Audits of Voluntary Health and Welfare Organizations, pp. 46–47. Copyright © 1988 by the American Institute of Certified Public Accountants, Inc.

# ILLUSTRATION 13–2

## VOLUNTARY HEALTH AND WELFARE SERVICE
### Statement of Revenue and Expenses
### and Changes in Fund Balances
### Year Ended December 31, 19y1
### (with comparative totals for 19y0)

| | 19y1 | | | | Total All Funds | |
| | Current Funds | | Land, Building, and Equipment Funds | Endowment Fund | | |
| | Unrestricted | Restricted | | | 19y1 | 19y0 |
|---|---|---|---|---|---|---|
| **Revenue:** | | | | | | |
| **Public support:** | | | | | | |
| Contributions (net of estimated uncollectible pledges of $195,000 in 19y1 and $150,000 in 19y0) | $3,764,000 | $162,000 | $ — | $ 2,000 | $3,928,000 | $3,976,000 |
| Contributions to building fund (net of estimated uncollectible pledges of $6,500) | — | — | 72,000 | — | 72,000 | 150,000 |
| Special events (net of direct costs of $181,000 in 19y1 and $163,000 in 19y0) | 104,000 | — | — | — | 104,000 | 92,000 |
| Legacies and bequests | 92,000 | — | — | 4,000 | 96,000 | 129,000 |
| Received from federated and nonfederated campaigns (which incurred related fund-raising expenses of $38,000 in 19y1 and $29,000 in 19y0) | 275,000 | — | — | — | 275,000 | 308,000 |
| Total Public Support | $4,235,000 | $162,000 | $ 72,000 | $ 6,000 | $4,475,000 | $4,655,000 |
| **Other Revenue:** | | | | | | |
| Membership dues | 17,000 | — | — | — | 17,000 | 12,000 |
| Investment income | 98,000 | 10,000 | — | — | 108,000 | 94,000 |
| Realized gain on investment transactions | 200,000 | — | — | 25,000 | 225,000 | 275,000 |
| Miscellaneous | 42,000 | — | — | — | 42,000 | 47,000 |
| Total Other Revenue | $ 357,000 | $ 10,000 | — | $ 25,000 | $ 392,000 | $ 428,000 |
| Total Revenue | $4,592,000 | $172,000 | $ 72,000 | $ 31,000 | $4,867,000 | $5,083,000 |

Expenses:

| | | | | | | |
|---|---:|---:|---:|---:|---:|---:|
| **Program services:** | | | | | | |
| Research | 1,257,000 | 155,000 | 2,000 | — | $1,414,000 | $1,365,000 |
| Public health education | 539,000 | — | 5,000 | — | 544,000 | 485,000 |
| Professional education and training | 612,000 | — | 6,000 | — | 618,000 | 516,000 |
| Community services | 568,000 | — | 10,000 | — | 578,000 | 486,000 |
|   Total Program Services | $2,976,000 | $155,000 | $ 23,000 | — | $3,154,000 | $2,852,000 |
| **Supporting services:** | | | | | | |
| Management and general | 567,000 | — | 9,880 | — | 576,880 | 638,000 |
| Fund raising | 642,000 | — | 9,120 | — | 651,120 | 546,000 |
|   Total Supporting Services | $1,209,000 | — | $ 19,000 | — | $1,228,000 | $1,184,000 |
|   Total Expenses | $4,185,000 | $155,000 | $ 42,000 | — | $4,382,000 | $4,036,000 |
| Excess (deficiency) of public support and revenue over expenses | 407,000 | 17,000 | 30,000 | 31,000 | | |
| **Other changes in fund balances:** | | | | | | |
| Property and equipment acquisitions from unrestricted funds | (17,000) | — | 17,000 | — | | |
| Transfer of realized endowment fund appreciation | 100,000 | — | — | (100,000) | | |
| Returned to donor | — | (8,000) | — | — | | |
| Fund Balances, beginning of year | 5,361,000 | 123,000 | 649,000 | 2,017,000 | | |
| Fund Balances, end of year | $5,851,000 | $132,000 | $696,000 | $1,948,000 | | |

Source: AICPA, *Audits of Voluntary Health and Welfare Organizations*, pp. 42–43. Copyright © 1988 by the American Institute of Certified Public Accountants, Inc., with modifications from National Health Council, et al.; *Standards of Accounting and Financial Reporting*. Copyright © 1988 by the National Health Council, Inc.; the National Assembly of National Voluntary Health and Social Welfare Organizations; and the United Way of America.

ILLUSTRATION 13–3

## VOLUNTARY HEALTH AND WELFARE SERVICE
### Statement of Functional Expenses
### Year Ended December 31, 19y1
#### (with comparative totals for 19y0)

| | 19y1 | | | | | | | | Total Expenses | |
| | Program Services | | | | | Supporting Services | | | | |
| | Research | Public Health Education | Professional Education and Training | Community Services | Total | Management and General | Fund Raising | Total | 19y1 | 19y0 |
|---|---|---|---|---|---|---|---|---|---|---|
| Salaries | $ 45,000 | $291,000 | $251,000 | $269,000 | $ 856,000 | $331,000 | $368,000 | $ 699,000 | $1,555,000 | $1,433,000 |
| Employee health and retirement benefits | 4,000 | 14,000 | 14,000 | 14,000 | 46,000 | 22,000 | 15,000 | 37,000 | 83,000 | 75,000 |
| Payroll taxes, etc. | 2,000 | 16,000 | 13,000 | 14,000 | 45,000 | 18,000 | 18,000 | 36,000 | 81,000 | 75,000 |
| Total Salaries and Related Expenses | $ 51,000 | $321,000 | $278,000 | $297,000 | $ 947,000 | $371,000 | $401,000 | $ 772,000 | $1,719,000 | $1,583,000 |
| Professional fees and contract service payments | 1,000 | 10,000 | 3,000 | 8,000 | 22,000 | 26,000 | 8,000 | 34,000 | 56,000 | 53,000 |
| Supplies | 2,000 | 13,000 | 13,000 | 13,000 | 41,000 | 18,000 | 17,000 | 35,000 | 76,000 | 71,000 |
| Telephone and telegraph | 2,000 | 13,000 | 10,000 | 11,000 | 36,000 | 15,000 | 23,000 | 38,000 | 74,000 | 68,000 |
| Postage and shipping | 2,000 | 17,000 | 13,000 | 9,000 | 41,000 | 13,000 | 30,000 | 43,000 | 84,000 | 80,000 |
| Occupancy | 5,000 | 26,000 | 22,000 | 25,000 | 78,000 | 30,000 | 27,000 | 57,000 | 135,000 | 126,000 |
| Rental of equipment | 1,000 | 24,000 | 14,000 | 4,000 | 43,000 | 3,000 | 16,000 | 19,000 | 62,000 | 58,000 |
| Local transportation | 3,000 | 22,000 | 20,000 | 22,000 | 67,000 | 23,000 | 30,000 | 53,000 | 120,000 | 113,000 |
| Conferences, conventions, meetings | 8,000 | 19,000 | 71,000 | 20,000 | 118,000 | 38,000 | 13,000 | 51,000 | 169,000 | 156,000 |
| Printing and publications | 4,000 | 56,000 | 43,000 | 11,000 | 114,000 | 14,000 | 64,000 | 78,000 | 192,000 | 184,000 |
| Awards and grants | 1,332,000 | 14,000 | 119,000 | 144,000 | 1,609,000 | — | — | — | 1,609,000 | 1,448,000 |
| Miscellaneous | 1,000 | 4,000 | 6,000 | 4,000 | 15,000 | 18,880 | 18,120 | 37,000 | 52,000 | 64,000 |
| Total Expenses Before Depreciation | $1,412,000 | $539,000 | $612,000 | $568,000 | $3,131,000 | $569,880 | $647,120 | $1,217,000 | $4,348,000 | $4,004,000 |
| Depreciation of buildings and equipment | 2,000 | 5,000 | 6,000 | 10,000 | 23,000 | 7,000 | 4,000 | 11,000 | 34,000 | 32,000 |
| Total Expenses | $1,414,000 | $544,000 | $618,000 | $578,000 | $3,154,000 | $576,880 | $651,120 | $1,228,000 | $4,382,000 | $4,036,000 |

Source: AICPA, *Audits of Voluntary Health and Welfare Organizations*, pp. 44–45. Copyright © 1988 by the American Institute of Certified Public Accountants, Inc.

| 33. | Cash . . . . . . . . . . . . . . . . . . . . . | 125,000 | |
| | Investments . . . . . . . . . . . . . . . . | | 100,000 |
| | Realized Gain on Investment Transactions . . | | 25,000 |

Cash in the amount of $100,000 was transferred to the Current Fund—Unrestricted. This amount had previously been generated through gains on investment transactions, and the terms of the endowment agreement provided that the funds were unrestricted (see Entry 15b):

| 34. | Transfer of Realized Endowment Fund Appreciation | | |
| | to Current Fund—Unrestricted . . . . . . . . | 100,000 | |
| | Cash . . . . . . . . . . . . . . . . . . . | | 100,000 |

Additional investments were purchased in the amount of $37,000:

| 35. | Investments . . . . . . . . . . . . . . . . . | 37,000 | |
| | Cash . . . . . . . . . . . . . . . . . . . | | 37,000 |

At the end of 19y1 nominal accounts of the endowment funds were closed:

| 36. | Contributions . . . . . . . . . . . . . . . . | 2,000 | |
| | Legacies and Bequests . . . . . . . . . . . . | 4,000 | |
| | Realized Gain on Investment Transactions . . . . | 25,000 | |
| | Fund Balance . . . . . . . . . . . . . . . . | 69,000 | |
| | Transfer of Realized Endowment Fund | | |
| | Appreciation to Current Fund—Unrestricted | | 100,000 |

## Financial Statements for Voluntary Health and Welfare Organizations

The AICPA audit guide, *Audits of Voluntary Health and Welfare Organizations,* illustrates three basic financial statements required for conformity with GAAP: Balance Sheet; Statement of Revenues and Expenses and Changes in Fund Balances; and Statement of Functional Expenses. A Statement of Changes in Financial Position is not presently considered to be required for conformity with GAAP.

Illustration 13–1 shows the Voluntary Health and Welfare Service Balance Sheet for all funds as of the end of fiscal year 19y1, and comparative figures for the end of the preceding fiscal year. Illustrations 13–2 and 13–3 present the Statement of Revenue and Expenses and Changes in Fund Balances, and the Statement of Functional Expenses, respectively, for the Voluntary Health and Welfare Service for the year ended December 31, 19y1, and comparative totals for the year ended December 31, 19y0.

## SELECTED REFERENCES

American Institute of Certified Public Accountants. *Audits of Voluntary Health and Welfare Organizations.* New York, 1988.

————. *Statement of Position 87–2: Accounting for Joint Costs of Informational*

*Materials and Activities of Not-for-Profit Organizations that Include a Fund-Raising Appeal.* New York, 1987.

National Health Council, National Assembly of National Voluntary Health and Social Welfare Organizations, and United Way of America. *Standards of Accounting and Financial Reporting for Voluntary Health and Welfare Organizations.* 3rd ed. New York, 1988.

## QUESTIONS AND EXERCISES

**13–1.**  Write the numbers 1 through 10 on a sheet of paper. Beside each number, write the letter corresponding to the best answer to each of the following questions:

1. A voluntary health and welfare organization received a pledge in 19y0 from a donor specifying that the amount pledged be used in 19y2. The donor paid the pledge in cash in 19y1. The pledge should be accounted for as:
   a. A Deferred Credit in the Balance Sheet at the end of 19y0, and as support in 19y1.
   b. A Deferred Credit in the Balance Sheet at the end of 19y0 and 19y1, and as support in 19y2.
   c. Support in 19y0.
   d. Support in 19y1, and no Deferred Credit in the Balance Sheet at the end of 19y0.

2. Which of the following funds of a voluntary health and welfare organization does not have a counterpart fund in governmental accounting?
   a. Current unrestricted.
   b. Land, building, and equipment.
   c. Custodian.
   d. Endowment.

   Questions 3 and 4 are based on the following data:

   Community Service Center is a voluntary health and welfare organization funded by contributions from the general public. During 19y0, unrestricted pledges of $900,000 were received, half of which were payable in 19y0, and were available for use that year. The other half were payable in 19y1 and were for use in 19y1. It was estimated that 10 percent of these pledges would be uncollectible. In addition, Selma Zorn, a social worker on Community's permanent staff, earning $20,000 annually for a normal workload of 2,000 hours, contributed an additional 800 hours of her time to Community, at no charge.

3. How much should Community report as net contribution revenue for 19y0 with respect to the pledges?
   a. $0.
   b. $405,000.
   c. $810,000.
   d. $900,000.

4. How much should Community record in 19y0 for donated service expense and as contributions?
   a. $8,000.
   b. $4,000.

     *c.* $800.

     *d.* $0.

5. Which basis of accounting should a voluntary health and welfare organization use?

     *a.* Cash basis for all funds.

     *b.* Modified accrual basis for all funds.

     *c.* Accrual basis for all funds.

     *d.* Accrual basis for some funds and modified accrual basis for other funds.

6. Aviary Haven, a voluntary welfare organization funded by contributions from the general public, received unrestricted pledges of $500,000 during 19y0. It was estimated that 12 percent of these pledges would be uncollectible. By the end of 19y0, $400,000 of the pledges had been collected, and it was expected that $40,000 more would be collected in 19y1, with the balance of $60,000 to be written off as uncollectible. Donors did not specify any periods during which the donations were to be used. What amount should Aviary include under public support in 19y0 for net contributions?

     *a.* $500,000.

     *b.* $452,000.

     *c.* $440,000.

     *d.* $400,000.

Items 7 and 8 are based upon the following information pertaining to the sale of equipment by Nous Foundation, a voluntary health and welfare organization:

| | |
|---|---|
| Sales price | $12,000 |
| Cost | 14,000 |
| Carrying amount | 10,000 |

Nous made the correct entry to record the $2,000 gain on sale.

7. The additional entry that Nous should record in connection with the sale is:

| | Debit | Credit |
|---|---|---|
| *a.* | Fund Balance—Expended | Fund Balance—Unexpended |
| *b.* | Fund Balance—Unexpended | Fund Balance—Expended |
| *c.* | Excess Revenues Control | Sale of Equipment |
| *d.* | Current Unrestricted Funds | Fund Balance—Undesignated |

8. The amount that should be debited and credited for the additional entry in connection with this sale is:

     *a.* $2,000.

     *b.* $10,000.

     *c.* $12,000.

     *d.* $14,000.

9. In a Statement of Revenue and Expenses and Changes in Fund Balances of a voluntary health and welfare organization, depreciation expense should:

     *a.* Not be included.

     *b.* Be included as an element of support.

     *c.* Be included as an element of other changes in fund balances.

     *d.* Be included as an element of expense.

10. The required financial statements for a voluntary health and welfare organization are:

   a. Balance sheet, activity statement, and statement of changes in financial position.

   b. Balance sheet, statement of revenue and expenses and changes in fund balances, and statement of changes in financial position.

   c. Balance sheet, statement of revenues, expenditures and transfers, and statement of changes in fund balances.

   d. Balance sheet, statement of revenue and expenses and changes in fund balances, and statement of functional expenses.

   (Items 1 through 9, AICPA, adapted)

**13–2.** Following are the adjusted current funds trial balances of Community Association for Handicapped Children, a voluntary health and welfare organization, at June 30, 19y1.

### COMMUNITY ASSOCIATION FOR HANDICAPPED CHILDREN
### Adjusted Current Funds Trial Balances
### June 30, 19y1

|  | Unrestricted | | Restricted | |
| --- | --- | --- | --- | --- |
|  | Debit | Credit | Debit | Credit |
| Cash | $ 40,000 |  | $ 9,000 |  |
| Bequest receivable |  |  | 5,000 |  |
| Pledges receivable | 12,000 |  |  |  |
| Accrued interest receivable | 1,000 |  |  |  |
| Investments (at cost, which approximates market) | 100,000 |  |  |  |
| Accounts payable and accrued expenses |  | $ 50,000 |  | $ 1,000 |
| Deferred revenue |  | 2,000 |  |  |
| Allowance for uncollectible pledges |  | 3,000 |  |  |
| Fund balances, July 1, 19y0: |  |  |  |  |
| Designated |  | 12,000 |  |  |
| Undesignated |  | 26,000 |  |  |
| Restricted |  |  |  | 3,000 |
| Contributions |  | 300,000 |  | 15,000 |
| Membership dues |  | 25,000 |  |  |
| Program service fees |  | 30,000 |  |  |
| Investment income |  | 30,000 |  |  |
| Deaf children's program | 120,000 |  |  |  |
| Blind children's program | 150,000 |  |  |  |
| Management and general services | 45,000 |  | 4,000 |  |
| Fund-raising services | 8,000 |  | 1,000 |  |
| Provision for uncollectible pledges | 2,000 |  |  |  |
|  | $478,000 | $478,000 | $19,000 | $19,000 |

*Required:*

   a. Prepare a statement of revenue and expenses and changes in fund balances, separately presenting each current fund, for the year ended June 30, 19y1.

   b. Prepare a balance sheet separately presenting each current fund as of June 30, 19y1.

   (AICPA, adapted)

**13–3.** The Anti-Illness Society, a voluntary health and welfare organization, was formed on July 1, 19y0 to promote preventive medicine through research, education, and counseling. The following transactions occurred during 19y0–19y1:

1. Contributions were received as follows: cash, $958,000; pledges, $108,000. Of the contributions, $35,000 was designated for future periods.
2. $63,000 in pledges were collected. Ten percent of the remaining balance of Pledges Receivable is expected to be uncollectible.
3. Special events held by the agency raised cash in the amount of $73,500. Costs related to the special events amounted to $58,000, all of which was paid in cash.
4. A grant from the United Way amounted to $100,000. Related fund-raising costs amounted to $12,500. The difference was received in cash.
5. Other support and revenue were: (1) legacies and bequests, $13,400; (2) membership dues, $25,000; and (3) miscellaneous revenues, $5,300. All but $10,200 was received in cash.
6. Inventories of materials and supplies were purchased in the amount of $135,000, of which $113,400 was paid in cash.
7. Inventories were used as follows: (a) research, $52,500; (b) education, $35,600; (c) counseling, $12,600; (d) management and general, $11,200; and (e) fund raising, $8,300.
8. Expenses, in addition to inventory usage (see transaction 7), were chargeable as follows: (a) research, $412,300; (b) education, $315,600; (c) counseling, $55,900; (d) management and general, $112,600; and (e) fund raising, $72,300. All but $33,200 was paid in cash.
9. A wealthy and public-spirited citizen allowed the organization to rent furnished space rent free. The rent normally would have cost $10,000 for the year and should be allocated as follows: (a) research, $2,500; (b) education, $2,500; (c) counseling, $3,000; (d) management and general, $1,000; and (e) fund raising, $1,000.
10. Closing entries were recorded.

### Required:
a. Record the above transactions on the books of the Anti-Illness Society. Assume all transactions are to be recorded in the Current Fund—Unrestricted. Record the functional expenses directly in this problem as indicated.
b. Prepare, in good form, a Statement of Revenue and Expenses and Changes in Fund Balances for the Anti-Illness Society as of June 30, 19y1.

13–4.  The Anti-Cruelty Society of Sycamore County had the following expenses (by object class) for the year ended December 31, 19y1:

| | |
|---|---:|
| Salaries and fringe benefits | $1,500,000 |
| Professional fees and contract services | 120,000 |
| Supplies | 220,000 |
| Telephone | 80,000 |
| Postage and shipping | 70,000 |
| Occupancy costs | 150,000 |
| Travel and meetings | 90,000 |
| Printing and publications | 310,000 |
| Depreciation of buildings and equipment | 190,000 |
| Total Expenses | $2,730,000 |

The programs offered by the Society during the year were: (1) counseling, (2) outreach, and (3) public education. Supporting services were (4) management and general, and (5) fund raising. The governing board wants to know the cost of each program service and each supporting service for the year. After discussion with persons engaged in offering each service, and perusal of records of the Society, you determine that the following distribution would be reasonably realistic:

| | Program Services | | | Supporting Services | |
| | | | | Manage- | |
| | | Out- | Public | ment and | Fund- |
| | Counseling | reach | Education | General | Raising |
|---|---|---|---|---|---|
| Salaries and fringes . . . . . | 23% | 16% | 19% | 22% | 20% |
| Professional fees, etc. . . . . | 30 | 10 | 20 | 10 | 30 |
| Supplies . . . . . . . . . . | 15 | 15 | 25 | 25 | 20 |
| Telephone . . . . . . . . . | 15 | 20 | 20 | 15 | 30 |
| Postage and shipping . . . . | 20 | 23 | 15 | 7 | 35 |
| Occupancy costs . . . . . . | 30 | 10 | 20 | 20 | 20 |
| Travel and meetings . . . . . | 40 | 10 | 15 | 25 | 10 |
| Printing and publication . . . | 17 | 5 | 33 | 20 | 25 |
| Depreciation . . . . . . . . | 38 | 15 | 15 | 20 | 12 |

*Required:*

Prepare a Statement of Functional Expenses for the Anti-Cruelty Society for the Year Ended December 31, 19y1.

**13–5.** Northland Humane Society, a voluntary health and welfare organization, and Northland County both had fiscal years ending December 31.

*a.* Assume the following transactions were transactions of Northland Humane Society. Prepare entries in general journal form to record each transaction in conformity with current accounting standards for voluntary health and welfare organizations. For each entry indicate the name of the fund, or funds, affected. You may ignore bond interest payments.

1. On January 1, 19y1, bonds were sold at par in the amount of $3,000,000 to finance the construction of a building.

2. On January 2, 19y1, a contract for the construction of the building was signed in the amount of $3,000,000.

3. On December 31, 19y1, the building was completed, and the contractor was paid the full amount.

4. On January 1, 19y2, a $500,000 research grant was received in cash from the federal government.

5. On December 31, 19y2, the grant work was completed at a cost of $500,000.

6. On December 31, 19y2, you note that the building constructed in transaction (3) is expected to last 30 years, with no salvage value. Unrestricted cash in the amount of $100,000 is designated by the governing board to be held for eventual replacement or expansion of the building.

*b.* If you did not solve Exercise 11–5, part (*b*), or 12–5, part (*b*), assume the above transactions were transactions of Northland County and prepare entries in general journal form to record each transaction in conformity with current accounting standards for state and local governments. For each entry indicate the name of the fund, or funds, affected. You may ignore bond interest payments. (If you did solve Exercise 11–5, part (*b*), review that solution before answering part (*c*), below).

       *c.* Comment on the differences between accounting for voluntary health and welfare organizations compared with accounting for state and local governments that are brought out by this problem.

**13–6.**    Listed below are four independent transactions or events that relate to a local government and to a voluntary health and welfare organization:

      1. $25,000 was disbursed from the general fund (or its equivalent) for the cash purchase of new equipment.

      2. An unrestricted cash gift of $100,000 was received from a donor.

      3. Listed common stocks with a total carrying value of $50,000, exclusive of any allowance, were sold by an endowment fund for $55,000, before any dividends were earned on these stocks. There are no restrictions on the gain, therefore cash in the amount of the gain is transferred to the general fund (or its equivalent).

      4. $1,000,000 face amount of tax-supported bonds payable were sold at par, with the proceeds required to be used solely for the construction of a new building. This building was completed at a total cost of $1,000,000, and the total amount of bond issue proceeds was disbursed in connection therewith. Disregard interest capitalization.

*Required:*

      *a.* For each of the above-listed transactions or events, prepare journal entries, without explanations, specifying the affected funds and account groups, and showing how these transactions or events should be recorded by a local government whose debt is serviced by general tax revenues.

      *b.* For each of the above-listed transactions or events, prepare journal entries, without explanations, specifying the affected funds, and showing how these transactions or events should be recorded by a voluntary health and welfare organization that maintains a separate plant fund.

    Problems 13–7 through 13–10 require entries in all of the fund groups used in voluntary health and welfare organization accounting with the exception of Custodian (Agency) Funds. Each problem can be done separately, or all of the problems may be assigned with combined, rather than individual fund group, statements assigned.

**13–7.**    **Current Fund—Unrestricted.** As of January 1, 19y1, the trial balance for the Current Fund—Unrestricted for the Westbrook Senior Citizens Society was as follows:

|  | Debit | Credit |
|---|---|---|
| Cash | $ 350,000 | |
| Investments—for long-term purposes | 2,500,000 | |
| Pledges receivable | 235,000 | |
| Allowance for uncollectible pledges | | $ 24,000 |
| Inventories, at cost | 168,000 | |
| Accrued interest receivable | 100,000 | |
| Prepaid expenses | 78,000 | |
| Other receivables | 35,000 | |
| Accounts payable | | 169,000 |
| Contributions designated for future periods | | 192,000 |
| Fund Balance—designated for long-term investments | | 2,500,000 |
| Fund Balance—undesignated | | 581,000 |
| Totals | $3,466,000 | $3,466,000 |

During the fiscal year ended December 31, 19y1, the following transactions occurred:

1. The $192,000 in contributions designated in 19y0 as being for future periods was recognized as an unrestricted contribution of 19y1.
2. Total contributions received for 19y1 amounted to $1,350,000 in cash and $1,235,000 in pledges.
3. Pledges collected during the year amounted to $1,250,000. In addition, pledges amounting to $23,000 were written off.
4. Contributions received in cash but designated for future years amounted to $175,000.
5. The 19y1 allocation from United Way amounted to $350,000; related fund-raising expenses to be borne by the Society amounted to $40,000; the net amount was received in cash.
6. Special events held by the Society resulted in cash receipts of $485,000. Costs related to the special events, all paid in cash, amounted to $225,000.
7. Cash received for interest on investments amounted to $200,000, including the $100,000 accrued at the beginning of the year. In addition, $100,000 interest was accrued at year-end.
8. Other support and revenue included: (a) legacies and bequests, $149,600; (b) membership dues, $25,000; and (c) miscellaneous revenues, $12,600. All but $12,300 was received in cash.
9. The $35,000 in "other receivables" at the beginning of the year was received in cash.
10. The accounts payable at the beginning of the year were paid.
11. Additional inventory was purchased amounting to $238,000. Additional insurance and other prepaid expense purchases amounted to $58,000. $180,000 in cash was paid for these items; the remainder was on open account at year-end.
12. Expenses for the year amounted to: (a) salaries, $2,145,000; (b) employee benefits, $195,100; (c) payroll taxes, $200,300; (d) professional fees, $51,000; (e) supplies, $125,400; (f) telephone and telegraph, $53,600; (g) postage and shipping, $72,700; (h) occupancy, $95,600; (i) awards and grants, $585,700; and (j) miscellaneous expenses, $72,200. Of the expenses, $50,000 represented a reduction of prepaid expenses, $259,600 represented a reduction of inventory, $39,100 was on open account, and the remainder was paid in cash.
13. Cash in the amount of $18,900 was transferred to the land, building, and equipment fund to purchase equipment. A transfer of $80,000 cash was received from the endowment funds.
14. It was estimated that 10 percent of the outstanding pledges will ultimately be uncollectible (round to nearest $1,000).
15. Expenses were allocated to program services and supporting services. The amounts were as follows: (a) transportation, $886,000; (b) educational programs, $1,125,000; (c) entertainment programs, $935,000; (d) management and general, $352,300; and (e) fund raising, $298,300.
16. Nominal accounts were closed.
17. The Board of Trustees of the Society decided to designate $200,000 of the Fund Balance for future plant renovation.

**Required:**

a. Prepare journal entries to record the transactions listed above.

b. Prepare, in good form, a Statement of Revenue and Expenses and Changes in Fund Balances for the Current Fund—Unrestricted for the Westbrook Senior Citizens Society for the Year Ended December 31, 19y1.

c. Prepare, in good form, a Balance Sheet for the Current Fund—Unrestricted for the Westbrook Senior Citizens Society for the Year Ended December 31, 19y1.

13–8.  **Current Funds—Restricted.** As of January 1, 19y1, the trial balance for the Current Funds—Restricted for the Westbrook Senior Citizens Society was as follows:

|  | Debit | Credit |
|---|---|---|
| Cash | $ 12,000 | |
| Investments | 78,000 | |
| Grants receivable | 25,000 | |
| Fund Balance—transportation | | $ 60,000 |
| Fund Balance—educational programs | | 55,000 |
| Totals | $115,000 | $115,000 |

During the fiscal year ended December 31, 19y1, the following transactions occurred:

1. The grants receivable at the beginning of the year were collected in cash. In addition, the investments, costing $78,000, were sold for $79,500.

2. Contributions for the year amounted to $198,000, of which $163,000 was received in cash. Investment income amounted to $19,600, all received in cash.

3. Expenses for the period were: (a) salaries, $55,000; (b) employee benefits, $5,300; (c) payroll taxes, $5,100; (d) professional fees, $45,700; (e) supplies, $10,600; (f) telephone and telegraph, $2,000; (g) postage and shipping, $2,100; (h) occupancy, $4,500; (i) awards and grants, $81,600; and (j) miscellaneous expenses, $2,100. All but $21,100 was paid in cash.

4. $13,000 cash was returned to a donor. In addition, investment purchases were made for cash in the amount of $80,000.

5. Expenses were closed to program functional categories. The amounts were as follows: (a) transportation, $116,000; (b) educational programs, $98,000.

6. Nominal accounts were closed. Fund Balance—Transportation increased by $3,000; Fund Balance—Education Programs decreased by $10,900.

**Required:**

a. Prepare journal entries to record the transactions listed above.

b. Prepare, in good form, a Statement of Revenue and Expenses and Changes in Fund Balances for the Current Funds—Restricted for the Westbrook Senior Citizens Society for the Year Ended December 31, 19y1.

c. Prepare, in good form, a Balance Sheet for the Current Funds—Restricted for the Westbrook Senior Citizens Society for the Year Ended December 31, 19y1.

13–9.  **Land, Building, and Equipment Fund.** As of January 1, 19y1, the trial balance for the Land, Building, and Equipment Fund for the Westbrook Senior Citizens Society was as follows:

|                                                      | Debit     | Credit    |
|------------------------------------------------------|-----------|-----------|
| Cash . . . . . . . . . . . . . . . . . . . . . . . . . . . . . . | $ 15,000  |           |
| Investments . . . . . . . . . . . . . . . . . . . . . . . .      | 250,000   |           |
| Pledges receivable . . . . . . . . . . . . . . . . . . . .       | 50,000    |           |
| Allowance for uncollectible pledges . . . . . . . . . . . .      |           | $  5,000  |
| Land . . . . . . . . . . . . . . . . . . . . . . . . . . . . .   | 50,000    |           |
| Buildings . . . . . . . . . . . . . . . . . . . . . . . . . .    | 200,000   |           |
| Accumulated depreciation—buildings . . . . . . . . . . . .       |           | 80,000    |
| Equipment . . . . . . . . . . . . . . . . . . . . . . . . . .    | 300,000   |           |
| Accumulated depreciation—equipment . . . . . . . . . . .         |           | 150,000   |
| Mortgage payable—10% . . . . . . . . . . . . . . . . . .         |           | 250,000   |
| Fund Balance—expended . . . . . . . . . . . . . . . . . .        |           | 70,000    |
| Fund Balance—unexpended . . . . . . . . . . . . . . . . .        |           | 310,000   |
| Totals . . . . . . . . . . . . . . . . . . . . . . . . . . .     | $865,000  | $865,000  |

During the fiscal year ended December 31, 19y1, the following transactions occurred:

1. Cash was collected in the amount of $46,000 on pledges existing at the beginning of the year. Pledges in the amount of $2,000 were written off.
2. During the year, cash contributions to the building program amounted to $129,600. In addition, pledges for the building program amounted to $73,200. An estimate of $6,000 in uncollectible pledges was made.
3. Cash was paid on the principal of the mortgage in the amount of $25,000. Interest was paid in the amount of $25,000 and charged to miscellaneous expenses. Additional miscellaneous expenses were paid in the amount of $13,000.
4. Depreciation was charged as follows: (a) buildings, $10,000; (b) equipment, $30,000.
5. The miscellaneous and depreciation expenses were allocated to program and supporting services as follows: (a) transportation, $26,000; (b) educational programs, $13,000; (c) entertainment programs, $13,000; (d) management and general $6,500; and (e) fund raising, $19,500.
6. Cash in the amount of $18,900 was received from the Current Fund—Unrestricted to be used for equipment purchases. This amount plus an additional $46,400 was used for the purchase of equipment.
7. Additional investments were purchased in the amount of $70,000.
8. Nominal accounts were closed. (Note: Remember that the Fund Balance—Expended should equal the cost of the plant less accumulated depreciation less the mortgage payable and that the Fund Balance—Unexpended should equal the remaining net assets.)

**Required:**

a. Prepare journal entries to record the transactions listed above.
b. Prepare, in good form, a Statement of Revenue and Expenses and Changes in Fund Balances for the Land, Building, and Equipment Fund for the Westbrook Senior Citizens Society for the Year Ended December 31, 19y1.
c. Prepare, in good form, a Balance Sheet for the Land, Building, and Equipment Fund for the Westbrook Senior Citizens Society for the Year Ended December 31, 19y1.

**13–10. Endowment Funds.** As of January 1, 19y1, the trial balance for the Endowment Funds for the Westbrook Senior Citizens Society was as follows:

|  | Debit | Credit |
|---|---|---|
| Cash . . . . . . . . . . . . . . . . . . . . . . . | $    28,000 | |
| Investments . . . . . . . . . . . . . . . . . . . | 1,100,000 | |
| Fund Balance . . . . . . . . . . . . . . . . . . . | | $1,128,000 |
| Totals . . . . . . . . . . . . . . . . . . . . . | $1,128,000 | $1,128,000 |

During the fiscal year ended December 31, 19y1, the following transactions occurred:

1. Cash was received in the amount of $125,000 for contributions and $55,000 for legacies and bequests. In addition, a pledge was received for a contribution in the amount of $162,000. The entire amount of the pledge is expected to be collectible.
2. Cash in the amount of $80,000 was transferred to the Current Fund—Unrestricted. This amount had previously been generated through gains on investments transactions, and the terms of the agreement provided that the funds were unrestricted.
3. Additional investments in the amount of $100,000 were purchased.
4. Nominal accounts were closed.

*Required:*
a. Prepare journal entries to record the transactions listed above.
b. Prepare, in good form, a Statement of Revenue and Expenses and Changes in Fund Balances for the Endowment Funds for the Westbrook Senior Citizens Society for the Year Ended December 31, 19y1.
c. Prepare, in good form, a Balance Sheet for the Endowment Funds for the Westbrook Senior Citizens Society for the Year Ended December 31, 19y1.
d. (Optional for those completing Exercises 13–7 through 13–10.) Prepare a Statement of Functional Expenses for the Westbrook Senior Citizens Society for the Year Ended December 31, 19y1. Object class expenses should be allocated to program services and supporting services in the following percentages or amounts.

|  | Program Services | | | Supporting Services | |
|---|---|---|---|---|---|
|  | Transportation | Educational Programs | Entertainment Programs | Management and General | Fund Raising |
| Salaries . . . . . . . . . | 32% | 30% | 20% | 10% | 8% |
| Employee benefits . . . . | 32 | 30 | 20 | 10 | 8 |
| Payroll taxes . . . . . . | 32 | 30 | 20 | 10 | 8 |
| Professional fees . . . . | — | 20 | 30 | 20 | 30 |
| Supplies . . . . . . . . | 40 | 20 | 20 | 10 | 10 |
| Telephone and telegraph . | 20 | 10 | 20 | 20 | 30 |
| Postage and shipping . . | 10 | 30 | 20 | 20 | 20 |
| Occupancy . . . . . . . | 20 | 40 | 30 | 5 | 5 |
| Awards and grants . . . . | 10 | 47 | 43 | — | — |
| Miscellaneous . . . . . . | $18,394 | $18,049 | $19,581 | $30,195 | $26,081 |
| Depreciation . . . . . . | 40% | 20% | 20% | 10% | 10% |

Chapter **14**

# ACCOUNTING FOR OTHER NONPROFIT ORGANIZATIONS

Until 1978, many nonprofit organizations did not have authoritative guidance for accounting and financial reporting principles. In that year, the AICPA issued *Statement of Position (SOP) 78–10,* which is now contained in *Audits of Certain Nonprofit Organizations (ACNO).*

A broad range of organizations are covered in *ACNO,* including cemetery associations, civic organizations, fraternal organizations, labor unions, libraries, museums, other cultural institutions, performing arts organizations, political parties, private schools, professional and trade associations, social and country clubs, research and scientific organizations, and religious organizations. Not-for-profit entities that operate essentially as commercial businesses for the direct economic benefit of members or stockholders (such as employee benefit and pension plans, mutual insurance companies, mutual banks, trusts, and farm cooperatives) are specifically excluded.

A few summary comments about accounting for other nonprofit organizations are:

- Fund accounting may or may not be used. If significant restrictions exist on assets, fund balances should be classified to disclose those restrictions.
- A variety of reporting formats are permitted. *Statement of Position 78–10* illustrates financial statements for 13 different types of organizations.

- The required financial statements are (1) Balance Sheet, (2) Activity Statement, and (3) Statement of Changes in Financial Position.[1] A separate Statement of Entity Capital and Statement of Functional Expenses may be prepared.
- Full accrual accounting is used. Fixed assets should be recorded at cost, and depreciation should be charged, except for those assets that normally increase in value, such as art collections, rare books, manuscripts, cathedrals, and similar items.
- All gifts and grants should be recorded at fair market value as of the date of the gift or grant.
- Revenues include membership dues and nonrefundable initiation and life membership fees. Membership dues should be recognized over the period to which the dues relate. If dues and other revenues are sufficient to cover costs, nonrefundable initiation and life membership fees should be recognized as revenue in the period in which they are receivable.
- Investments may be reported at the lower of cost or market, or market, even if market is higher than cost.
- Donated materials and donated services are recorded, when certain restrictions are met.
- Pledges receivable are recorded on the accrual basis, with a reasonable allowance for uncollectibles. Restricted gifts and grants are recorded as revenues when the restrictions are met, with restricted or other funds. Contributions restricted for use in future periods are recognized as revenues of the periods in which they are available for use.
- Accounting principles set forth in *SOP 78–10* are not "officially" GAAP in that no effective date was, or has been, set for adoption. However, these principles are the best available and are being followed by many organizations.

### Accounting and Financial Reporting Standards

Financial reports should be prepared on the full accrual basis of accounting. Some organizations may keep their books on a cash basis throughout a fiscal period and make adjustments at the end of the period to produce accrual basis statements; this practice is specifically allowed by ACNO.

Standards require the disclosure of resources restricted by donors or grantors as distinguished from *unrestricted* resources (those that are available at the direction of the governing board). Many nonprofit organizations achieve this disclosure by accounting for restricted assets in

---

[1]FASB's *Statement of Financial Accounting Standards No. 95,* which requires business organizations to present a Statement of Cash Flows instead of a Statement of Changes in Financial Position, specifically states that the requirement does not apply to not-for-profit organizations.

appropriately named restricted funds and accounting for unrestricted assets in a separate fund; it is common for plant assets to be segregated in a plant fund. Relatively small organizations may choose to account for all assets in a single fund; these organizations must disclose the existence of restricted assets by maintaining a Fund Balance—Restricted account as well as a Fund Balance—Unrestricted account.

Membership dues should be recognized in the period to which the dues relate. Initiation fees should be recognized in the period the fees are receivable as long as dues and other sources of income are reasonably expected to cover the costs of operations in future years.

The *Audit Guide (ACNO)* indicates that resources received for use in a future period should be reported as Deferred Revenue, a liability account. Likewise, resources restricted as to category of use should not be recognized as revenue until restrictions have been met. However, the restriction is considered to be met when "the organization incurs an expense for the function, program, project, object, or and in the manner specified in the donative instrument or grant award. . . . . . ,"[2] even if other funds (say, unrestricted funds) are used. Recognition of revenue in the current period from resources received for use in a future period is permitted by *ACNO* if unrestricted resources were used in the current period for the specified purposes in anticipation of receipt of the restricted resources.

Accounting for services donated to "other" not-for-profit organizations generally follows the guidelines for hospitals and for voluntary health and welfare organizations in that the donated services must be (1) a normal part of the efforts of the organization which otherwise would be performed by paid personnel, (2) under the control of the organization, and (3) have a clearly measurable basis for the amount to be recorded. In addition, it is required that:

> The services of the reporting organization are not principally intended for the benefit of its members. Accordingly, donated and contributed services would not normally be recorded by organizations such as religious communities, professional and trade associations, labor unions, political parties, fraternal organizations, and social and country clubs.[3]

Investments may be reported at the lower of cost or market, or at market (even when market is above cost). If an organization elects to carry marketable securities at market, unrealized increases or decreases in market value during the period should be recognized in the same

---

[2]American Institute of Certified Public Accountants, Inc., *Audits of Certain Nonprofit Organizations (ACNO)* (New York: AICPA, 1981), p. 75.

[3]Ibid., p. 78.

manner as realized gains or losses. In the absence of specific instructions in the endowment agreement, gains or losses on disposition of endowment fund investments would be added to or deducted from the principal balance. Endowment income is restricted only if specified in the agreement; otherwise it is available for unrestricted expenditures.

Depreciation is to be taken on most fixed assets. If a separate plant fund is maintained, depreciation should be recorded in that fund in the same manner as illustrated for voluntary health and welfare organizations. Museums, libraries, and similar nonprofit organizations are not required to recognize depreciation on works of art or historical treasures, if certain conditions set forth in FASB *Statement No. 93* are met.

If a reporting organization controls another organization having a compatible purpose, combined financial statements are usually necessary. However, this requirement does not apply when the organizations are loosely affiliated, for example when a national or international organization has local organizations which control their own program activities and are financially independent.

Entities that receive a significant amount of support from contributions are required to report expenses by function. The functional breakdown should, like voluntary health and welfare organizations, report program service expenses and supporting service expenses separately. The program service categories would depend upon the nature of the organization; for example, a performing arts organization may report regular performances, neighborhood performances, acting school, and so on. Supporting services expenses include general and administrative expenses and fund-raising expenses. General and administrative expenses finance related activities such as issuing the annual report. Fundraising expenses include those costs incurred for the purpose of generating contributions. When activities are for more than one purpose, whether program, management and general, or fund-raising, the cost may be prorated.

## ILLUSTRATIVE TRANSACTIONS—OTHER NONPROFIT ORGANIZATIONS

As mentioned earlier, some, but not all, of these organizations use fund accounting. The illustrative transactions in this chapter are for the Sample Performing Arts Organization, which is assumed to use fund accounting but which reports separate fund data only in the Equity section of the Balance Sheet and in the Statement of Entity Capital. The beginning balances are taken from Illustration 14–1, which appears later in this chapter:

|                                                              | Debit     | Credit     |
|--------------------------------------------------------------|-----------|------------|
| Cash                                                         | $169,466  |            |
| Marketable securities                                        | 50,967    |            |
| Accounts receivable                                          | 26,685    |            |
| Grants receivable                                            | 6,100     |            |
| Other current assets                                         | 13,441    |            |
| Investments and endowment funds cash                         | 256,648   |            |
| Property and equipment, at cost                              | 75,331    |            |
| Accumulated depreciation, property and equipment             |           | $ 35,105   |
| Rent and other deposits                                      | 9,130     |            |
| Accounts payable and accrued expenses                        |           | 166,351    |
| Deferred revenues—subscriptions                              |           | 193,042    |
| Deferred revenues—grants                                     |           | —          |
| Current portion of long-term debt                            |           | 50,000     |
| Long-term debt                                               |           | 69,740     |
| Entity capital:                                              |           |            |
| Plant fund                                                   |           | 38,594     |
| Endowment funds                                              |           | 256,648    |
| Unrestricted funds                                           | 201,712   |            |
| Totals                                                       | $809,480  | $809,480   |

## Unrestricted Funds

During the year, $1,986,652 in cash was received, and accounts receivable increased in the amount of $43,366 due to revenue generating activity of the Performing Arts Organization. Of that amount, $1,925,630 is recorded as current period revenues, and $104,388 represents increases in subscriptions received in advance, a liability account:

| 1. | Cash                                        | 1,986,652 |           |
|----|---------------------------------------------|-----------|-----------|
|    | Accounts Receivable                         | 43,366    |           |
|    | Admissions                                  |           | 1,557,567 |
|    | Dividends                                   |           | 5,000     |
|    | Interest                                    |           | 16,555    |
|    | Tuition                                     |           | 242,926   |
|    | Concessions and Other Support from          |           |           |
|    | Operations                                  |           | 103,582   |
|    | Deferred Revenues—Subscriptions             |           | 104,388   |

Due to a dramatic change in interest rates, $50,967 in marketable securities were sold for $105,667. That amount and an additional $160,663 was reinvested.

| 2a. | Cash                                      | 105,667 |        |
|-----|-------------------------------------------|---------|--------|
|     | Marketable Securities                     |         | 50,967 |
|     | Realized Gain on Sale of Marketable       |         |        |
|     | Securities                                |         | 54,700 |
| 2b. | Marketable Securities                     | 266,330 |        |
|     | Cash                                      |         | 266,330|

Unrestricted Cash in the amount of $901,409 was received as a result of fund-raising activity. Of that amount, $6,100 had previously been recorded as grant revenue and $42,562 represented a grant that is designated for a future period by the granting agency.

3.  Cash . . . . . . . . . . . .              901,409
        Grants Receivable . . . . . . . . . . . .              6,100
        Annual Giving  . . . . . . . . . . . .              150,379
        Grants . . . . . . . . . . . . . . .              702,368
        Deferred Revenues—Grants  . . . . . . .              42,562

Increases in other current assets (prepaids, etc.) for the year amounted to $25,937.

4.  Other Current Assets . . . . . . . . . . . .              25,937
        Cash . . . . . . . . . . . . . . . .              25,937

During the year, cash in the amount of $2,596,745 was paid for current expenses and expenses of a prior year. In addition, $5,291 in rent and other deposits was recognized as expense.

5.  Accounts Payable and Accrued Expenses  . . .              55,201
        Salaries, Payroll Taxes, and Employee Benefits .    1,654,616
        Professional Fees . . . . . . . . . . . . .              26,273
        Supplies  . . . . . . . . . . . . . . .              62,307
        Telephone  . . . . . . . . . . . . . .              11,936
        Postage and Shipping  . . . . . . . . .              18,255
        Occupancy . . . . . . . . . . . . . .              389,927
        Rental and Maintenance of Equipment . . . . .              66,435
        Printing and Publications . . . . . . . . .              10,381
        Travel  . . . . . . . . . . . . . . . .              5,824
        Conferences, Conventions, and Meetings  . . .              2,783
        Membership Dues . . . . . . . . . . . . .              756
        Scenery  . . . . . . . . . . . . . . . .              190,222
        Costumes . . . . . . . . . . . . . . .              107,120
            Rent and Other Deposits . . . . . . . . .              5,291
            Cash . . . . . . . . . . . . . . . . .              2,596,745

In order to properly report expenses by function, the expenses are reclassified. While, in practice, entries for expenses may record both object classes and functions, this method is illustrated in accord with authoritative literature:

6.  Production Costs  . . . . . . . . . . . . .              475,882
        Operating Expenses . . . . . . . . . . . .              796,494
        Ballet School . . . . . . . . . . . . .              473,058
        Neighborhood Productions . . . . . . . . .              378,154
        General and Administrative Expense  . . . . .              387,987
        Fund Raising . . . . . . . . . . . . . .              35,260
            Salaries, Payroll Taxes, and Employee
                Benefits  . . . . . . . . . . . . .              1,654,616
            Professional Fees . . . . . . . . . . . .              26,273
            Supplies . . . . . . . . . . . . . . .              62,307
            Telephone  . . . . . . . . . . . . . .              11,936
            Postage and Shipping  . . . . . . . . .              18,255
            Occupancy . . . . . . . . . . . . . .              389,927
            Rental and Maintenance of Equipment . . .              66,435
            Printing and Publications . . . . . . . .              10,381
            Travel  . . . . . . . . . . . . . . .              5,824
            Conferences, Conventions, and Meetings  .              2,783
            Membership Dues . . . . . . . . . . . .              756
            Scenery . . . . . . . . . . . . . . .              190,222
            Costumes . . . . . . . . . . . . . . .              107,120

The closing entry for the Unrestricted Funds would be as follows:

| | | | |
|---|---|---|---|
| 7. | Admissions . . . . . . . . . . . . . . . . | 1,557,567 | |
| | Dividends . . . . . . . . . . . . . . . . | 5,000 | |
| | Interest . . . . . . . . . . . . . . . . . | 16,555 | |
| | Tuition . . . . . . . . . . . . . . . . . . | 242,926 | |
| | Concessions and Other Support from Operations | 103,582 | |
| | Realized Gain on Sale of Marketable Securities . | 54,700 | |
| | Annual Giving . . . . . . . . . . . . . . | 150,379 | |
| | Grants . . . . . . . . . . . . . . . . . . | 702,368 | |
| | Production Costs . . . . . . . . . . . . | | 475,882 |
| | Operating Expenses . . . . . . . . . . . | | 796,494 |
| | Ballet School . . . . . . . . . . . . . | | 473,058 |
| | Neighborhood Productions . . . . . . . . | | 378,154 |
| | General and Administrative Expense . . . | | 387,987 |
| | Fund Raising . . . . . . . . . . . . . . | | 35,260 |
| | Entity Capital—Unrestricted Funds . . . . | | 286,242 |

## Endowment Funds

During the year, the Endowment Funds received a contribution in the amount of $11,221, which is to be invested and maintained in perpetuity:

| | | | |
|---|---|---|---|
| 8. | Cash—Endowment Funds . . . . . . . . . | 11,221 | |
| | Capital Additions . . . . . . . . . . . . | | 11,221 |
| 9. | Investments . . . . . . . . . . . . . . . | 11,221 | |
| | Cash—Endowment Funds . . . . . . . . | | 11,221 |

The account, "Capital Additions," is required to be classified separately in the Activity Statement after the "Excess from Current Endeavors" caption (see Illustration 14–2 later in this chapter). According to the *Audit Guide,* Capital Additions include "nonexpendable gifts, grants, and bequests restricted by donors to endowment, plant, or loan funds either permanently or for extended periods of time."[4] Capital additions also include legally restricted investment income and gains or losses on investments held in such funds that must be added to the principal.

The closing entry for the Endowment Funds would be:

| | | | |
|---|---|---|---|
| 10. | Capital Additions . . . . . . . . . . . . . . | 11,221 | |
| | Entity Capital—Endowment Funds . . . . . | | 11,221 |

## Plant Funds

During the year, the Performing Arts Society acquired equipment costing $20,368, paying $8,108 in cash and issuing long-term debt in the amount of $12,260:

| | | | |
|---|---|---|---|
| 11. | Property and Equipment . . . . . . . . . . . | 20,368 | |
| | Cash . . . . . . . . . . . . . . . . . . | | 8,108 |
| | Long-Term Debt . . . . . . . . . . . . . | | 12,260 |

---

4Ibid., p. 17.

In addition, $50,000 in long-term debt was repaid:

| 12. Long-Term Debt . . . . . . . . . . . . . . | 50,000 | |
|---|---|---|
| Cash . . . . . . . . . . . . . . . . . . | | 50,000 |

Depreciation was charged in the amount of $5,533. Depreciation is then spread to the appropriate functional expense categories, in a manner similar to Voluntary Health and Welfare Organizations:

| 13. Depreciation and Amortization . . . . . . . | 5,533 | |
|---|---|---|
| Accumulated Depreciation—Property and Equipment . . . . . . . . . . . . . | | 5,533 |
| 14. Production Costs . . . . . . . . . . . . . | 1,100 | |
| Operating Expenses . . . . . . . . . . . | 550 | |
| Ballet School . . . . . . . . . . . . . | 600 | |
| Neighborhood Productions . . . . . . . . . | 300 | |
| General and Administrative Expense . . . . . | 2,500 | |
| Fund Raising . . . . . . . . . . . . . . | 483 | |
| Depreciation and Amortization . . . . . . | | 5,533 |

The year-end closing entry was made:

| 15. Entity Capital—Plant Funds . . . . . . . . . | 5,533 | |
|---|---|---|
| Production Costs . . . . . . . . . . . . | | 1,100 |
| Operating Expenses . . . . . . . . . . . | | 550 |
| Ballet School . . . . . . . . . . . . | | 600 |
| Neighborhood Productions . . . . . . . . | | 300 |
| General and Administrative Expense . . . | | 2,500 |
| Fund Raising . . . . . . . . . . . . . | | 483 |

## Financial Statements

Because of the diverse nature of the organizations covered by *ACNO*, a great deal of flexibility is allowed in the preparation of statements. At a minimum, these organizations should prepare a Balance Sheet, a Statement of Activity, and a Statement of Changes in Financial Position.[5] In addition, organizations that receive significant support in the form of contributions from the general public may wish to prepare a Statement of Functional Expenses, in the form required for voluntary health and welfare organizations.

*Audits of Certain Nonprofit Organizations* presents illustrations of financial reports for 13 different types of organizations. Illustrations 14–1 through 14–3 reproduce the statements for the Sample Performing Arts Organization. Each of these statements is discussed in turn.

**Balance sheet** Note that this illustrative Balance Sheet (Illustration 14–1) is not organized by fund but discloses the Fund Balances of each fund type separately. Note that both assets and liabilities are separated into current and non-current categories. Note also the Deferred Revenues—Grants; this account is used to disclose restricted resources not

---

[5]See footnote 1 of this chapter.

**ILLUSTRATION 14–1**

**SAMPLE PERFORMING ARTS ORGANIZATION**
**Balance Sheet**
**June 30, 19x1, and 19x0**

|  | 19x1 | 19x0 |
|---|---:|---:|
| **Assets** | | |
| Current assets: | | |
| Cash . . . . . . . . . . . . . . . . . . . . . . . . . | $216,074 | $169,466 |
| Marketable securities . . . . . . . . . . . . . . . . . . | 266,330 | 50,967 |
| Accounts receivable, net of allowance for doubtful accounts . . . . . . | 70,051 | 26,685 |
| Grants receivable . . . . . . . . . . . . . . . . . . . . | — | 6,100 |
| Other . . . . . . . . . . . . . . . . . . . . . . . . . | 39,378 | 13,441 |
| Total Current Assets . . . . . . . . . . . . . . . . | 591,833 | 266,659 |
| Noncurrent assets: | | |
| Investments and endowment funds cash . . . . . . . . . . . . . . | 267,869 | 256,648 |
| Property and equipment at cost, net of accumulated depreciation . . . | 55,061 | 40,226 |
| Rent and other deposits . . . . . . . . . . . . . . . . . . | 3,839 | 9,130 |
|  | $918,602 | $572,663 |
| **Liabilities and Entity Capital** | | |
| Current liabilities: | | |
| Accounts payable and accrued expenses . . . . . . . . . . . . . | $111,150 | $166,351 |
| Deferred revenues—subscriptions . . . . . . . . . . . . . . . | 297,430 | 193,042 |
| Deferred revenues—grants . . . . . . . . . . . . . . . . . | 42,562 | — |
| Current portion of long-term debt . . . . . . . . . . . . . . . | 50,000 | 50,000 |
| Total Current Liabilities . . . . . . . . . . . . . . . | 501,142 | 409,393 |
| Long-term debt . . . . . . . . . . . . . . . . . . . . . | 32,000 | 69,740 |
| Contingencies | | |
| Entity capital: | | |
| Plant fund . . . . . . . . . . . . . . . . . . . . . . | 33,061 | 38,594 |
| Endowment funds . . . . . . . . . . . . . . . . . . . . | 267,869 | 256,648 |
| Unrestricted funds . . . . . . . . . . . . . . . . . . . . | 84,530 | (201,712) |
|  | $918,602 | $572,663 |

Source: AICPA, *Audits of Certain Nonprofit Organizations*, p. 132. Copyright © 1981 by the American Institute of Certified Public Accountants, Inc.

yet expended for authorized purposes, as well as resources restricted to use in a future period. The nature of the restrictions on fund balances and deferred revenues should be described in the Notes to the Financial Statements.

**Statement of activity** *ACNO* illustrates Statements of Activity for 13 different categories of nonprofit organizations. Some are captioned Statement of Support and Revenue, Expenses, Capital Additions, and Changes in Fund Balances. Others are captioned simply Statement of Revenue and Expenses. A variety of formats are presented, each considered to be an appropriate disclosure for a certain kind or size of nonprofit organization. For example, the statement for a library uses essentially the same format as voluntary health and welfare organizations and reports each fund in a separate column. The statement for a

**ILLUSTRATION 14–2**

### SAMPLE PERFORMING ARTS ORGANIZATION
#### Statement of Activity
#### Years Ended June 30, 19x1 and 19x0

|  | 19x1 | 19x0 |
|---|---|---|
| Revenue and support from operations: |  |  |
| Admissions . . . . . . . . . . . . . . . . . . . . . . . . . . . . . | $1,557,567 | $1,287,564 |
| Dividends and interest . . . . . . . . . . . . . . . . . . . . . | 21,555 | 2,430 |
| Net realized gains and losses . . . . . . . . . . . . . . . . . | 54,700 | 18,300 |
| Tuition . . . . . . . . . . . . . . . . . . . . . . . . . . . | 242,926 | 130,723 |
| Concessions and other support . . . . . . . . . . . . . . . | 103,582 | 68,754 |
|  | 1,980,330 | 1,507,771 |
| Production costs . . . . . . . . . . . . . . . . . . . . . | 476,982 | 427,754 |
| Operating expenses . . . . . . . . . . . . . . . . . . . . . | 797,044 | 685,522 |
| Ballet school . . . . . . . . . . . . . . . . . . . . . | 473,658 | 301,722 |
| Neighborhood productions . . . . . . . . . . . . . . . . . . . | 378,454 | 81,326 |
| General and administrative expense . . . . . . . . . . . . . . . | 390,487 | 469,891 |
|  | 2,516,625 | 1,966,215 |
| Deficiency from operations . . . . . . . . . . . . . . . . . | (536,295) | (458,444) |
| Donated services, materials, and facilities . . . . . . . . . . . | — | 8,000 |
| Annual giving . . . . . . . . . . . . . . . . . . . . . . . . . | 150,379 | 78,469 |
| Grants . . . . . . . . . . . . . . . . . . . . . . . . . . | 702,368 | 678,322 |
| Fund-raising costs . . . . . . . . . . . . . . . . . . . . . . | (35,743) | (50,454) |
|  | 817,004 | 714,337 |
| Excess from current endeavors . . . . . . . . . . . . . . . . | 280,709 | 255,893 |
| Capital additions . . . . . . . . . . . . . . . . . . . . . . | 11,211 | 18,250 |
| Total Increase in Entity Capital . . . . . . . . . . . . . . . | $ 291,930 | $ 274,143 |

Source: AICPA, *Audits of Certain Nonprofit Organizations*, p. 133. Copyright © 1981 by the American Institute of Certified Public Accountants, Inc.

country club simply lists first the revenues, then the expenses in a single-step format. Illustration 14–2, the Statement of Activity for a performing arts organization, is organized to show the gain or a loss from operations, followed by items referred to in the first section of this chapter as contributions and public support. Readers of this statement can readily see that the revenue and support from operations falls far short of the operating expenses incurred by the performing arts organization.

Whichever method is used, capital additions are shown as a separate item after the "Excess from Current Endeavors." Capital additions include gifts, grants, and bequests to endowment, plant, and loan funds restricted either permanently or for a period of time by parties outside the organization. Capital additions also include investment income that has been restricted by donors and gains or losses on investments that must be added to the principal of endowment, plant, and loan funds.

**Statement of Changes in Financial Position** A Statement of Changes in Financial Position (Illustration 14–3) is currently required by GASB

## ILLUSTRATION 14–3

**SAMPLE PERFORMING ARTS ORGANIZATION**
Statement of Changes in Financial Position
Years Ended June 30, 19x1, and 19x0

|  | 19x1 | 19x0 |
|---|---|---|
| **Funds provided by:** | | |
| Excess from current endeavors . . . . . . . . . . . . . . . . . . . | $280,709 | $255,893 |
| Add expenses not requiring outlay of working capital in current period: | | |
| Depreciation . . . . . . . . . . . . . . . . . . . . . . . . . . | 5,533 | 4,620 |
| Other deferred charges . . . . . . . . . . . . . . . . . . . | — | 7,500 |
| Funds provided from current endeavors . . . . . . . . . . . | 286,242 | 268,013 |
| Increase in long-term debt . . . . . . . . . . . . . . . . . . | 12,260 | — |
| Other . . . . . . . . . . . . . . . . . . . . . . . . . . . | 5,291 | — |
| Capital additions . . . . . . . . . . . . . . . . . . . . . | 11,221 | 18,250 |
| Total Funds Provided . . . . . . . . . . . . . . . . . . . | 315,014 | 286,263 |
| **Funds applied:** | | |
| Increase in noncurrent investments and cash . . . . . . . . . . . . . | 11,221 | — |
| Acquisition of property, plant, and equipment . . . . . . . . . . . | 20,368 | 4,362 |
| Reduction of long-term debt . . . . . . . . . . . . . . . . . . | 50,000 | 25,280 |
| Total Funds Applied . . . . . . . . . . . . . . . . . . . | 81,589 | 29,642 |
| Increase in Working Capital . . . . . . . . . . . . . . . . . | $233,425 | $256,621 |
| **Changes in the components of working capital:** | | |
| Increase (decrease) in current assets: | | |
| Cash . . . . . . . . . . . . . . . . . . . . . . . . . . . . . . | $46,608 | $220,342 |
| Marketable securities . . . . . . . . . . . . . . . . . . | 215,363 | 42,312 |
| Accounts receivable . . . . . . . . . . . . . . . . . . . . | 43,366 | 21,269 |
| Grants receivable . . . . . . . . . . . . . . . . . . . . | (6,100) | — |
| Other . . . . . . . . . . . . . . . . . . . . . . . . . . . | 25,937 | 15,413 |
| Increase in Current Assets . . . . . . . . . . . . . . . . . | 325,174 | 299,336 |
| (Increase) decrease in current liabilities: | | |
| Accounts payable and accrued expenses . . . . . . . . . . . . . . | 55,201 | 36,149 |
| Deferred revenues—subscriptions . . . . . . . . . . . . . . . . | (104,388) | (78,864) |
| Deferred revenues—grants . . . . . . . . . . . . . . . . . . | (42,562) | — |
| (Increase) in Current Liabilities . . . . . . . . . . . . . . | (91,749) | (42,715) |
| Increase in Working Capital . . . . . . . . . . . . . . . . . | $233,425 | $256,621 |

Source: AICPA, *Audits of Certain Nonprofit Organizations*, p. 135. Copyright © 1981 by the American Institute of Certified Public Accountants, Inc.

standards for proprietary funds, nonexpendable trust funds, and pension trust funds of state and local governmental units; and by AICPA audit guides for the general funds of a hospital, and for the types of nonprofit organizations covered in this section. This statement should summarize all changes in financial position, including capital additions, changes in deferred support and revenue, and financing and investing activities. It is probable that in the near future, standards for not-for-profit organizations will be revised to require a Statement of Cash Flows in place of the Statement of Changes in Financial Position.

## SELECTED REFERENCES

American Institute of Certified Public Accountants. *Audits of Certain Non-profit Organizations.* New York, 1981.

_____. *Statement of Position 78–10: Accounting Principles and Reporting Practices for Certain Nonprofit Organizations.* New York, 1978.

_____. *Statement of Position 87–2: Accounting for Joint Costs of Informational Materials and Activities of Not-for-Profit Organizations that Include a Fund-Raising Appeal.* New York, 1987.

Financial Accounting Standards Board. *Statement of Financial Accounting Standards No. 93: Recognition of Depreciation by Not-for-Profit Organizations.* Norwalk, Conn., 1987.

_____. *Statement of Financial Accounting Standards No. 99: Deferral of the Effective Date of Recognition of Depreciation by Not-for-Profit Organizations: An Amendment of FASB Statement No. 93.* Norwalk, Conn., 1988.

## QUESTIONS AND EXERCISES

**14–1.** Write the numbers 1 through 10 on a sheet of paper. Beside each number, write the letter corresponding to the best answer to each of the following questions:

1. In April, 19x7, Alice Reed donated $100,000 cash to her church, with the stipulation that the income generated from this gift is to be paid to Alice during her lifetime. The conditions of the donation are that, after Alice dies, the principal can be used by the church for any purpose voted on by the church elders. The church received interest of $8,000 on the $100,000 for the year ended March 31, 19x8, and the interest was remitted to Alice. In the March 31, 19x8 financial statements:

   *a.* $8,000 should be reported under support and revenue in the activity statement.

   *b.* $92,000 should be reported under support and revenue in the activity statement.

   *c.* $100,000 should be reported as deferred support in the balance sheet.

   *d.* The gift and its terms should be disclosed only in Notes to the Financial Statements.

2. The following expenditures were among those reported by a nonprofit botanical society during 19x7:

   | | |
   |---|---:|
   | Printing of annual report . . . . . . . . . . . . . . . . . . . . . . . . . | $10,000 |
   | Unsolicited merchandise sent to encourage contributions . . . . . . . | 20,000 |

   What amount should be classified as fund-raising costs in the society's activity statement?

   *a.* $0.

   *b.* $10,000.

   *c.* $20,000.

   *d.* $30,000.

3. Lane Foundation received a nonexpendable endowment of $500,000 in 19x6 from Gant Enterprises. The endowment assets were invested in publicly traded securities. Gant did not specify how gains and losses from dispositions of endowment assets were to be treated. No restrictions were placed on the use of dividends received and interest earned on fund resources. In 19x7, Lane realized gains of $50,000 on fund investments, and received total interest and dividends of $40,000 on fund securities. The amount of these capital gains, interest, and dividends available for expenditure by Lane's current unrestricted fund is:
   *a.* $0.
   *b.* $40,000.
   *c.* $50,000.
   *d.* $90,000.

4. In 19x7, the Board of Trustees of Burr Foundation designated $100,000 from its current funds for college scholarships. Also in 19x7, the foundation received a bequest of $200,000 from an estate of a benefactor who specified that the bequest was to be used for hiring teachers to tutor handicapped students. What amount should be accounted for as current restricted funds?
   *a.* $0.
   *b.* $100,000.
   *c.* $200,000.
   *d.* $300,000.

5. In 19x7, a nonprofit trade association enrolled five new member companies, each of which was obligated to pay nonrefundable initiation fees of $1,000. These fees were receivable by the association in 19x7. Three of the new members paid the initiation fees in 19x7, and the other two new members paid their initiation fees in 19x8. Annual dues (excluding initiation fees) received by the association from all of its members have always covered the organization's costs of services provided to its members. It can be reasonably expected that future dues will cover all costs of the organization's future services to members. Average membership duration is 10 years because of mergers, attrition, and economic factors. What amount of initiation fees from these five new members should the association recognize as revenue in 19x7?
   *a.* $5,000.
   *b.* $3,000.
   *c.* $500.
   *d.* $0.

6. On January 2, 19x7, a nonprofit botanical society received a gift of an exhaustible fixed asset with an estimated useful life of 10 years and no salvage value. The donor's cost of this asset was $20,000, and its fair market value at the date of the gift was $30,000. What amount of depreciation of this asset should the society recognize in its 19x7 financial statements?
   *a.* $3,000.
   *b.* $2,500.
   *c.* $2,000.
   *d.* $0.

7. Mr. Henry J. Moneybags gave $1,000,000 to the Science Museum with the stipulation that the moneys be invested permanently, with the income to be available for unrestricted use of the museum when it is earned. The $1,000,000 should be reported, in the year of the gift, as:
   a. Deferred support.
   b. Capital additions.
   c. Support.
   d. Revenue.

8. Capital Additions should be:
   a. Reported in the Activity Statement after the "Excess from Current Endeavors."
   b. Reported in the Activity Statement along with the other contributions.
   c. Reported in the Balance Sheet as Deferred Revenue until the asset is consumed.
   d. Reported only in the notes to the financial statements.

9. The required statements for "other nonprofit organizations" are:
   a. Balance Sheet, Activity Statement, and Statement of Changes in Financial Position.
   b. Balance Sheet, Activity Statement, and Statement of Functional Expenses.
   c. Balance Sheet, Statement of Revenues, Expenditures and Transfers, and Statement of Changes in Fund Balances.
   d. Balance Sheet, Statement of Revenues, Expenditures and Transfers, and Statement of Functional Expenses.

10. Which of the following organizations would not be covered by AICPA, *Audits of Certain Nonprofit Organizations?*
    a. Country clubs.
    b. Private schools.
    c. Farm cooperatives.
    d. Cemetery associations.

(Items 1 through 6, AICPA, adapted)

**14–2.** Accounting for fixed assets and depreciation differs among different organizations discussed in this book. Briefly outline the policies for fixed asset accounting and depreciation accounting for: *(a)* state and local governments, *(b)* colleges and universities, *(c)* hospitals, *(d)* voluntary health and welfare organizations, and *(e)* other nonprofit organizations.

**14–3.** What are the major differences between current accounting and financial reporting standards for voluntary health and welfare organizations and for the nonprofit organizations covered in *Audits of Certain Nonprofit Organizations?*

**14–4.** In 19x0 a group of civic-minded merchants in Albury City organized the "Committee of 100" for the purpose of establishing the Community Sports Club, a nonprofit sports organization for local youth. Each of the Committee's 100 members contributed $1,000 toward the Club's capital, and in turn received a participation certificate. In addition, each participant agreed to pay dues of $200 a year for the Club's operations. All dues have been collected in full by the end of each fiscal year ending March 31. Members who have discontinued their participation have been replaced by an equal number of new members through transfer of the participation certificates from the former members to the new ones. Following is the Club's trial balance at April 1, 19x7.

|  | Debit | Credit |
|---|---|---|
| Cash | $ 9,000 | |
| Investments (at market, equal to cost) | 58,000 | |
| Inventories | 5,000 | |
| Land | 10,000 | |
| Building | 164,000 | |
| Accumulated depreciation—building | | $130,000 |
| Furniture and equipment | 54,000 | |
| Accumulated depreciation—furniture and equipment | | 46,000 |
| Accounts payable | | 12,000 |
| Participation certificates (100 at $1,000 each) | | 100,000 |
| Cumulative excess of revenue over expenses | | 12,000 |
| | $300,000 | $300,000 |

Transactions for the year ended March 31, 19x8, were as follows:

1. Collections from participants for dues . . . . . . . . . . . . . $20,000
2. Snack bar and soda fountain sales . . . . . . . . . . . . . . . 28,000
3. Interest and dividends received . . . . . . . . . . . . . . . . 6,000
4. Additions to voucher register:
   House expenses . . . . . . . . . . . . . . . . . . . . . . . 17,000
   Snack bar and soda fountain . . . . . . . . . . . . . . . 26,000
   General and administrative . . . . . . . . . . . . . . . . 11,000
5. Vouchers paid . . . . . . . . . . . . . . . . . . . . . . . . 55,000
6. Assessments for capital improvements not yet incurred
   (assessed on March 20, 19x8; none collected by March 31, 19x8;
   deemed 100 percent collectible during year ending
   March 31, 19x9) . . . . . . . . . . . . . . . . . . . . . . 10,000
7. Unrestricted bequest received . . . . . . . . . . . . . . . . 5,000

**Adjustment data:**

1. Investments are valued at market, which amounted to $65,000 at March 31, 19x8. There were no investment transactions during the year.
2. Depreciation for the year:
   Building . . . . . . . . . . . . . . . . . . . . . . . . . . . . . $4,000
   Furniture and equipment . . . . . . . . . . . . . . . . . . . 8,000
3. Allocation of depreciation:
   House expenses . . . . . . . . . . . . . . . . . . . . . . . . 9,000
   Snack bar and soda fountain . . . . . . . . . . . . . . . . . 2,000
   General and administrative . . . . . . . . . . . . . . . . . . 1,000
4. Actual physical inventory at March 31, 19x8, was $1,000, and pertains to the snack bar and soda fountain.

**Required:**

a. Record the transactions and adjustments in journal entry form for the year ended March 31, 19x8.
b. Prepare the appropriate all-inclusive activity statement for the year ended March 31, 19x8.
c. Prepare a balance sheet as of March 31, 19x8.

(AICPA, adapted)

**14–5.** The Literary Museum is classified as an "other nonprofit organization," and has three funds: operating, endowment, and plant. Support and revenue come from admissions, gifts and grants, investment income, and the net proceeds from a museum store, which is operated by a private vendor. Program services include curatorial and conservation, exhibits, education, public information, and literary accessions. As of January 1, 19y1, the Literary Museum had the following account balances:

|  | Debit | Credit |
|---|---|---|
| Cash | $ 30,000 | |
| Investments (at market) | 150,000 | |
| Pledges receivable | 200,000 | |
| Grants receivable | 100,000 | |
| Endowment funds investments (at market) | 450,000 | |
| Property and equipment (excluding books, which are not capitalized) | 250,000 | |
| Accumulated depreciation—property and equipment | | $ 150,000 |
| Accounts payable | | 35,000 |
| Deferred revenues—gifts | | 120,000 |
| Current portion of long-term debt | | 40,000 |
| Long-term debt | | 40,000 |
| Fund balance—endowment | | 450,000 |
| Fund balance—plant | | 50,000 |
| Fund balance—operating | | 295,000 |
| Totals | $1,180,000 | $1,180,000 |

During the year ended December 31, 19y1, the following transactions took place:

**Operating Fund**

1. Admission fees were received in the amount of $250,000, all in cash.
2. Gifts and grants were received for operating purposes in the amount of $750,000, including all pledges and grants receivable at the beginning of the year. The deferred revenues—gifts balance at the beginning of the year was recognized in 19y1. In addition, pledges of gifts in the amount of $250,000 were received, all of which were designated for the donor to be used in 19y2. No additional grants receivable were recorded.
3. Investment income, all available for current purposes and received in cash, amounted to $50,000. Investments, valued at $50,000, were sold for that amount.
4. The net revenues from the museum store amounted to $75,000 cash.
5. Expenses for 19y1 included $350,000 for salaries and fringe benefits, $80,000 for utilities, $70,000 for professional fees, and $50,000 for supplies and miscellaneous. Cash was paid in the amount of $530,000; accounts payable increased by $20,000.
6. The expenses were reclassified. Salaries and fringe benefits were 20 percent for curatorial and conservation, 20 percent for exhibits, 20 percent for education, 10 percent for public information, 10 percent for literary accessions, 10 percent for general and administrative, and 10 percent for fund raising. Utilities were charged as follows: 5 percent for curatorial and conservation, 50 percent for exhibits, 5 percent for literary accessions, 20 percent for general and administrative, and 20 percent for fund

raising. Half of the professional fees were charged to curatorial and conservation and half to education. 20 percent of the supplies and miscellaneous were charged to curatorial and conservation, 10 percent to exhibits, 10 percent for literary accessions, 40 percent to general and administrative, and 20 percent to fund raising.

7. Books, costing $400,000, were purchased, using operating fund cash.
8. Closing entries were made.

**Endowment Funds**

9. Investments, carried at a balance of $100,000, were sold for $120,000. That amount was immediately reinvested.
10. The remaining investments, carried at $350,000 (the market value at the beginning of the year), had a market value of $375,000 at year-end.
11. A gift of cash in the amount of $200,000 was received. The terms of the gift indicated that the gift was to be invested and maintained forever, with the income available for general operating purposes of the museum. The $200,000 was invested.
12. Closing entries were made.

**Plant Funds**

13. New display equipment in the amount of $100,000 was purchased. Cash in the amount of $30,000 was paid; the balance was covered by a new issue of long-term debt.
14. Long-term debt in the amount of $40,000 was retired.
15. Depreciation charges for the year amounted to $25,000.
16. Depreciation expense was reallocated as follows: curatorial and conservation 10 percent, exhibits 40 percent, education 10 percent, public information 10 percent, general and administrative 20 percent, and fund raising 10 percent.
17. Long-term debt in the amount of $40,000 was reclassified as a current liability.
18. Closing entries were made.

*Required:*

a. Record the transactions listed above in journal entry form for the year ended December 31, 19y1.
b. Prepare an all-inclusive activity statement for the year ended December 31, 19y1.
c. Prepare a balance sheet as of December 31, 19y1.
d. Prepare a statement of changes in financial position for the year ended December 31, 19y1.

# INDEX

# INDEX

## A

Accounting entity, 5; *see also* Governmental reporting entity
Accounts, governmental
  balance sheet and operating, 21–23
  budgetary, 23, 27
Accrual basis of accounting, 7, 22
  accrual, 7, 8
  defined, 7
  modified accrual, 7, 22
Activity, defined, 37
Ad valorem taxes, 35–37
Advances, interfund, 201
Agency funds, 8, 171–75
AICPA; *see* American Institute of Certified Public Accountants
American Institute of Certified Public Accountants
  *Audits of Certain Nonprofit Organizations*, 3, 14, 324, 335
  *Audits of Colleges and Universities*, 3, 14, 235, 259
  *Audits of Providers of Health Care Services (Exposure Draft)*, 3, 14, 272, 286
  *Audits of State and Local Governmental Units*, 3, 14, 35, 64, 100, 117, 136, 159, 192, 222, 223, 226
  *Audits of Voluntary Health and Welfare Organizations*, 3, 14, 297, 313
  *Hospital Audit Guide*, 272, 286
  *SAS 63: Compliance Auditing Applicable to Governmental Entities and Other Recipients of Governmental Financial Assistance*, 222, 225, 226

Appropriations
  classified, 27, 37
  defined, 21
Appropriations, Expenditures, and Encumbrances Ledger, 33
Assets whose use is limited, 273–76
Audits of state and local governments, 221–26
  auditors' reports, 224–26
  compliance, 222, 225, 226
  economy and efficiency audits, 223
  financial audits, 222–23
  financial statement audits, 223
  generally accepted governmental auditing standards (GAGAS), 222, 224, 226
  performance audits, 223
  program audits, 223
  Single Audit Act, 222
Auxiliary enterprises, college; *see* College and university accounting
Available, defined, 7

## B

Balance sheets; *see* Financial reporting *and* references to financial statements for various nonprofit organizations
Basis of accounting, 7
Budgetary accounting, 9, 20–47
  accounts, 23, 27
  differences with GAAP
    entity, 23
    perspective, 23
    timing, 23

343

Budgets
  as legal documents, 21
  recording of, 27–29, 49
  revision, 55

# C

CAFR; *see* Financial reporting
Capital leases, 39, 83–84, 96–97, 130
Capital projects funds, 6, 75–93
  accounting for capital lease, 83–84
  bond anticipation notes payable, 77
  capitalization of interest, 79
  fund balance, meaning of, 80
  general nature of, 75–76
  illustrative entries, 76–83
  lease agreements, 83–84
  proceeds of long-term notes, 76
  re-establishment of encumbrances, 81
  retained percentages, 79–82
  special assessment debt, 84–85
  statements of
    balance sheet, 80–83
    revenues, expenditures, and changes in
      fund balance, 76, 81
Character, meaning of, 37
Comptroller General of the United States,
    *Governmental Auditing Standards,*
    222–24, 226
College and university accounting, 234–70
  accounting and financial reporting, 13,
    235–36
  agency funds, 240, 255, 258
  annuity and life income funds, 239, 247–48
  auxiliary enterprises, 236
  *College and University Business*
    *Administration,* 235
  current funds, 236–38, 240–45
    restricted, 237, 244–45
    unrestricted, 236–37, 240–43
  endowment and similar funds, 238–39,
    246–47
    endowment funds, 238, 246–47
    quasi-endowment funds, 239, 246–47
    term endowment funds, 238–39, 246–47
  fund types, 236–40
  illustrative transactions, 240–51, 255, 258
  jurisdiction over accounting principles,
    234–35
  loan funds, 238, 245–46
  mandatory transfers, 238, 242
  nonmandatory transfers, 248–42

College accounting—*Cont.*
  plant funds, 239, 248–51, 255
    funds for renewals and replacements,
      239, 250
    funds for retirement of indebtedness,
      239, 250–51
    investment in plant, 239, 251, 255
    unexpended plant funds, 239, 249
  statements of
    balance sheet, 252–53, 258
    changes in fund balances, 256–59
    current funds, revenues, expenditures,
      and other changes, 254, 258
Combining statements; *see* Financial
    reporting
Compensated absences, 130–31
Component unit, 12, 220
Comprehensive annual financial report; *see*
    Financial Reporting
Comptroller General of the United States,
    12
Construction expenditures, 78–80
Correction of errors, 54

# D

Debt
  general obligation, 126
  limited obligation, 126
  revenue, 126
  special assessment, 126
  tax increment, 126
Debt service funds, 8, 35, 109–25
  accrual basis, meaning for debt service,
    110
  additional uses, 110–11
  annuity, 111
  bank as fiscal agent, 111
  budgetary accounts, 111, 113
  capital lease payments, 110–11, 116
  Combining Balance Sheet, 117
  debt service accounting by general fund,
    111
  deferred serial bonds
    defined, 111
    procedures, 115
  interest on long-term debt, 110
  purpose of, 109
  regular serial bonds
    accounting procedures, 111–15
    defined, 111

Debt service funds—*Cont.*
  statements
    balance sheet, 114
    combining, 117
    statement of revenues, expenditures and
      changes in fund balance, 112, 115
    term bonds, 115–16
Deferred compensation funds; *see* Fiduciary
  funds
Discrete presentation, 220
Donated materials, 272, 299–300, 325
Donated services, 272, 299, 325, 326

**E**

Encumbrances
  accounting, 27, 30–33, 51, 76
  described, 30
  prior year's, 50
  re-establishment, 81
Endowment funds
  college and university, 238–39
  governmental; *see* Fiduciary funds
  hospitals and other healthcare providers,
    274, 281–82
  other nonprofit organizations, 330
  voluntary health and welfare
    organizations, 308–13
Enterprise funds, 8, 149–59
  accounting for nonutility enterprises,
    158–59
  accounting procedures, 150
  balance sheet items
    accrued utility revenues, 151
    allowance for funds used during
      construction, 153
    construction work in progress, 153
    customer deposits, 153–54
    utility plant acquisition adjustment,
      154–55
  customer advances for construction, 154
  illustrative case, 150–55
  original cost, 154
  purpose of, 149–50
  required segment information, 159
  statements
    balance sheet, 156
    changes in financial position, 158
    revenues, expenses and changes in
      retained earnings, 157
Entity; *see* Governmental reporting entity
Equity transfers, 39, 56, 203–4

Errors, correction; *see* Correction of errors
Estimated Equity Transfers, 49
Estimated Other Financing Sources, 27, 28,
  35
Estimated Other Financing Uses, 27
Estimated Revenues, 21, 27, 28, 34–35
Expendable funds, 6
Expendable trust funds, 8, 177–84
  illustrative case, 177, 181–83
  illustrative statements, 184
Expenditure
  accounting, 22, 30–33
  classifications, 37–38
  construction, 78–80
  defined, 22
  interest, 79
  prior-year, 50

**F**

FASB; *see* Financial Accounting Standards
  Board
Federal government agencies, 12
Fiduciary funds, 8, 171–99
  agency funds, 8, 171–75
    deferred compensation funds, 172–73
    reporting
      combined balance sheet, 175
      combining statement of changes in
        assets and liabilities, 176
    tax agency funds, 173–75
  expendable trust funds, 8, 171
  nonexpendable trust funds, 8, 171
  pension trust funds, 171, 183–92
  trust funds, 175, 177–92
Financial Accounting Standards Board, 1, 2,
  3, 10, 234
  objectives, 3, 14
Financial reporting
  auditor's report, 224–26
  Combined Balance Sheet, 11, 64, 210–13
  Combined Statement of Changes in
    Financial Position—All Proprietary
    Fund Types, 11, 218–19
  Combined Statement of Revenues,
    Expenditures, and Changes in Fund
    Balances—All Governmental Fund
    Types, 11, 23, 24–25, 64, 214–15
  Combined Statement of Revenues,
    Expenditures, and Changes in Fund
    Balances—Budget and Actual—

Financial reporting—*Cont.*
    General and Special Revenue Fund
        Types, 11, 216
    Combined Statement of Revenues,
        Expenses, and Changes in Retained
        Earnings (or Equity)—All
        Proprietary Fund Types, 11, 217
    combining statements, 64, 116–18, 220
    Component Unit Financial Report, 12
    Comprehensive Annual Financial Report
        (CAFR), 10, 207–21
    General Purpose Financial Statements
        (GPFS), 10–11, 209–20
    Financial Section, 10, 208–9
    individual fund and account group
        statements, 220–21
    interim financial reports, 208
    Introductory Section, 10, 208
    Notes to the Financial Statements, 11
    Required Supplementary Information, 11
    Statistical Section, 10, 208
Fiscal entity, 5
Function, reporting expenditures by, 37
Fund accounting, types of funds used by
        state and local governments
    agency, 8, 171–75
    capital projects, 6, 75–93
    debt service, 6, 35, 109–25
    enterprise, 8, 149–59
    expendable trust, 8, 177–84
    fiduciary, 8, 171–99
    general, 5, 20–73
    governmental, 5
    internal service, 8, 143–49
    nonexpendable trust funds, 8
    pension trust funds, 8, 183–92
    proprietary, 8, 142–70
    special revenue, 6, 20–73
    trust and agency, 8
Fund balance, 22, 27
Fund equity, 22
    reserve accounts, 22
Funds, number required, 8


## G

GAAP; *see* Generally accepted accounting
    principles
GAO; *see* U. S. General Accounting Office
GASB; *see* Governmental Accounting
    Standards Board

General Fixed Assets Account Group, 2, 21,
    75, 76, 94–108, 116
    accounting entity only, 6
    acquired by proprietary fund, 98–99
    acquisition, 39, 204
    buildings and improvements, 96
    construction work in progress, 96
    defined, 94
    depreciation, not recorded, 94–95
    disposition, 97, 99
    equipment, 96
    illustrative entries, 97–99
    investment in general fixed assets, 94
    land, 95–96
    leased assets, 96–97
    property accounts detailed, 99–100
    schedule of changes in general fixed
        assets, 100–102
    schedule of general fixed assets by
        function and activity, 100–101
    statement of general fixed assets by
        source, 95
General fund, 8–9, 20–73
    actual and estimated expenditures, 30–33
    closing entries, 58
    hospitals and other healthcare providers,
        271–96
    illustrative entries, 48–59
    inventories, procedures for recognition of,
        62–63
    statements
      balance sheet, 59
      revenues, expenditures, and changes in
        fund balance, 23, 60
      revenues, expenditures, and changes in
        fund balance—budget and actual, 61
General long-term debt account group, 6,
    21, 75, 76, 112, 126–41
    accounting procedure, 127
    capital lease obligations, 130
    claims, judgments, compensated absences,
        and other long-term debt not
        evidenced by bonds or notes,
        130–31
    debt limit, 131–33
    debt margin, 131–33
    direct and overlapping debt, 134–36
    illustrative case, 128–30
    principal and interest payable in future
        years, 134
    schedules
      of bonds and warrants payable, 132
      of direct and overlapping debt, 136

General long-term debt—*Cont.*
  statement of long-term debt, 129
  legal debt margin, 131–34
General obligation bonds, 126
General purpose financial statements; *see*
  Financial reporting
Generally accepted accounting principles, 1,
  9, 23
GLTDAG; *see* General long-term debt
  account group
Governmental Accounting Standards Board,
  1–4, 9, 10, 23, 33, 34, 60, 61, 76, 81,
  84, 234
  *Codification of Governmental Accounting
  and Financial Reporting Standards,*
  4, 10–14, 20, 39, 64, 85, 100, 117,
  136, 159, 192, 226
  *Concepts Statement No. 1: Objectives of
  Financial Reporting,* 4
Governmental auditing; *see* Audits of state
  and local governments
Governmental funds, 8, 22
Governmental financial reporting; *see*
  Financial reporting
Governmental reporting entity, 12, 206–7
  component unit, 206
  criteria, 206–7
  PERS, 190–92
GPFS; *see* General purpose financial
  statements
Grant accounting, 63–64

**H**

Healthcare Financial Management
  Association, 271
Hospitals and other healthcare providers,
  271–96
  accounting and financial reporting, 13,
  271–72
  assets whose use is limited, 273, 276
  explanation of fund structure, 272–73
  general funds, 273, 274–78
  illustrative transactions, 274–81
  restricted funds, 273–74, 279–81
    endowment, 274, 281–82
    plant replacement and expansion, 274,
    280
    specific purpose, 274, 279–80
  statements, 281–86
    balance sheet, 281–83
    changes in financial position, 285, 287

Hospitals and other healthcare
  providers—*Cont.*
  statements—*Cont.*
    changes in fund balances, 284, 286
    revenues and expenses, 284, 285
Human service organizations; *see* Voluntary
  health and welfare organizations

**I–L**

Interest and penalties receivable on property
  taxes
  accounting for, 57–58
  accrual, 57–58
Interest capitalization, 79
Interest expenditures, 79
Interfund transactions
  acquisition of general fixed assets, 39, 204
  creation or repayment of general long-term
    debt, 205
  entries, 55–56
  equity transfers, 39, 56, 203–4
  issuance of general long-term debt, 39, 205
  loans and advances, 201
  nature of, 200
  operating transfers, 38–39, 56, 203
  quasi-external, 38, 55, 201–2
  reimbursements, 38, 202–3
  summary, 200–205
Interim financial reports, 208
Internal service funds, 8, 143–49
  advances, 144
  contributions, 144
  establishment of and operation, 143
  illustrative case, 144–47
  statements, 147–49
Inventories, procedures for recognition of
  consumption method, 62
  governmental funds, 62–63
  purchases method, 62–63
Lease agreements
  capital leases, 83
  capital projects funds, 83–84
  debt service funds, 116
  general fixed asset account group, 96–97
  general long-term debt account group, 130
  operating leases, 116
Loans, interfund, 201

**M–N**

Mandatory transfers, colleges, 238, 242
Measurable, defined, 7

Measurement focus, 6
  flow of financial resources, 6
National Association of College and
         University Business Officers
         (NACUBO), 3, 235
  *College and University Business
         Administration,* 3, 14, 235, 259
National Council on Governmental
         Accounting, 4
National Health Council, et. al., *Standards
         of Accounting and Financial
         Reporting for Voluntary Health and
         Welfare Organizations,* 297, 314
Nonexpendable funds, 8
Nonexpendable trust funds, 8, 177–84
  endowment funds, 177
  illustrative case, 177–81
  illustrative statements, 181
Nonmandatory transfers, college, 238, 242
Not-for-profit organizations
  distinguishing characteristics, 2
  financial reporting objectives, 2–3
  jurisdiction over financial reporting, 1–3,
         13

## O

Object classification, 38
Objectives of financial reporting
  by governmental units, 2, 4
  by not-for-profit entities, 2, 3
Operating transfers, 22–23, 38–39, 56, 203
Other financing sources, 22–23
Other financing uses, 22–23
Other nonprofit organizations, 324–40
  accounting and financial reporting, 325–27
  illustrative transactions, 327–31
    endowment funds, 330
    plant funds, 330–31
    unrestricted funds, 328–30
  statements, 331–34
    activity, 332–33
    balance sheet, 331–32
    changes in financial position, 333–34
Oversight unit, 220

## P

Pension trust funds, 183–92
  balance sheet, 186, 190
  illustrative case, 187–90
  objectives, 185

Pension trust funds—*Cont.*
  required disclosures, 185–87
  summary of requirements, 190, 192
PERS; *see* Pension trust funds
Private schools, 13
Proceeds of debt issues, 39
Program classification, 37
Program services, 298–300
Property taxes
  accrual of interest and penalties, 57–58
  ad valorem, 35–37
  collections of
    current, 52
    delinquent, 52
  reclassification of current, 57
  recording levy, 51
  write off of uncollectibles, 56–57
Proprietary funds, 8, 142–70; *see also*
         Enterprise funds *and* Internal
         service funds
  accounting for capital grants, 143
  accounting for operating grants, 143
Public employee retirement systems; *see*
         Pension trust funds
Public schools, 12–13

## Q–R

Quasi-external transactions, 38, 55–56,
         201–2
Reimbursements, 38, 202–3
Reporting entity; *see* Governmental
         reporting entity
Reports, governmental; *see* Financial
         reporting
Reserve for encumbrances
  accounting, 30–32
  defined, 31
  prior-year, 50–51
Reserve for inventories, 62–63
Residual equity transfers; *see* Equity
         transfers
Retained percentages, 79–82
Retirement funds (PERS); *see* Pension trust
         funds
Revenue debt, 126
Revenues
  accounting, 22,29
  cash basis, 52
  classifications, 34–35
  ledger, illustration of, 30

# S

Single Audit Act, 222
Special assessments
  debt, 126
  debt service funds, use of, 109
  GASB standards, 84–85
  long-term debt, accounting for, 126
  as revenue source, 35
  special assessment fund type, elimination
    of, 84
Special revenue funds, 8, 63–64
Statements; *see* Financial reporting
Statistical tables; *see* Financial reporting
Subsidiary records
  appropriations, 27–33
  encumbrances, 27–33
  estimated revenues, 27–29
  expenditures, 27–33
  revenues, 27–30
Supplies fund; *see* Internal service funds
Supporting services, 298, 300

# T

Tax anticipation notes payable, 49, 52–53
Taxes, ad valorem, 35–37
  delinquent, 52
Transfers
  equity, 39
  mandatory, college, 238, 242
  nonmandatory, college, 238, 242
  operating, 38–39
Trust and agency funds, 8, 171–99

# U

U.S. Department of the Treasury, *Treasury
    Financial Manual,* 3
U.S. General Accounting Office
  *GAO Policy and Procedures Manual for
    Guidance of Federal Agencies,* 3, 14
U.S. Office of Management and Budget,
    *U.S. Government Standard General
    Ledger,* 3
University accounting; *see* College and
    university accounting
Utility funds; *see* Enterprise funds

# V-Z

Voluntary health and welfare organizations,
    297–323
  accounting and financial reporting, 13,
    297–302
  asset valuation, 300–301
    balance sheet, 309
    functional expenses, 312
    revenue and expenses, and changes in
      fund balances, 30, 310–11
  financial statements, 309–13
  fund balances, 301
  illustrative transactions
    current funds—restricted, 306–7
    current funds—unrestricted, 302–5
    endowment funds, 308–13
    land, building, and equipment fund,
      307–8
  liabilities, 301
  program services and supporting service
    expenses, 300
  public support and revenue, 299–300